EDITING.

The essential guide to better writing across today's media

BUCK RYAN &

MICHAEL O'DONNELL

cognella®
SAN DIEGO

WHAT PEOPLE ARE SAYING ABOUT THIS BOOK

" *Buck Ryan knows more about editing in journalism than anyone I know. He has earned the title of Maestro, a creative presence who knows how all the parts fit together.*"

—Roy Peter Clark, author of
"Writing Tools" and "Tell It Like It Is"

" *I wish I had this book to give the great PR people I hired over the years. For applicants it surely would have helped them pass our writing test. As the public relations director for a major corporation and the editor of my college student newspaper, I could have used it myself.*"

—Jack Guthrie, founder and CEO of
Guthrie/Mayes (now GMPR), one of the largest
independent public relations firms in the Southeast

" *This book is terrific! It's current, creative and comprehensive. It can support curriculum across a school! year or serve as a reference book. If you need a spark to get your students to see the importance of journalism, or their various media career options, or if you want them to understand ethical decision making, this book is for you. Most of all, it will help them improve their writing through editing.*"

—Tony Lococo, journalism adviser at
award-winning Trinity High School in
Louisville, Kentucky, retiring after 42 years

Active Learning

This book has interactive activities available to complement your reading.

Your instructor may have customized the selection of activities available for your unique course. Please check with your professor to verify whether your class will access this content through the Cognella Active Learning portal (http://active.cognella.com) or through your home learning management system.

BRIEF CONTENTS

DETAILED CONTENTS

FOREWORD

Adam Clayton Powell III

"Everyone needs an editor!"

That is a repeated saying in every newsroom where I have worked, invoked perhaps only slightly less frequently than "If your mother says she loves you, check it out."

You'll hear those expressions in this book, and there is so much more. What Buck Ryan and Michael O'Donnell have produced is an essential guide to better writing through editing. It's a comprehensive handbook with valuable advice and editing techniques that will serve us all well. Their advice rings true from my own experiences in the broadcasting and internet journalism worlds over the past six decades.

Especially valuable is their **Language Skills Survival Kit**. All good editors start at the beginning with spelling, grammar and other language fundamentals. Precision is essential. As the authors say, concise copy is ideal but more challenging. It is more difficult to "write tight" than to expand at length.

Ryan's Maestro Concept for storytelling leads writers with some basic questions, such as "Can you summarize your story in 30 words or fewer?" and "Why should I care?" When I am editing, I ask some other simple questions:

- How does it read? Will readers have difficulty understanding the story— or even a sentence?
- How does it sound? Is it appropriate? Writing about war is very different from writing about sports.
- How does it capture the richness, the cadence of language? Is it elegant?

Good copy editors go well beyond spell-check, looking for context and phrasing that can be misleading—or wrong. The authors warn against the limitations of artificial intelligence, which is plagued by what computer scientists label "hallucinations." That's when the software invents "facts" and "events" that never happened.

I have my own example to share.

Vint Cerf, co-inventor of the internet and now a vice president at Google, described to me what happened when he asked AI software to write his obituary. The software searched published obituaries for form and style and created what Vint said was a reasonably good obit. There was only one problem: The story included achievements that were not his and relatives that didn't exist.

In the book's Appendix you'll find a helpful guide on brevity and simplicity. This can be especially valuable when writing scripts for broadcast. Good editors are valued for spotting words and phrases that might be difficult to say aloud. When I was a young news writer, one anchor excoriated me for using the word "exacerbate" in his copy—after he had hit it cold on the air. Ah, if I had only written "worsen."

I was pleased to see the authors cite the wisdom of anchor Walter Cronkite, one of the very best editors I worked with when I was a writer for CBS News space coverage. Another CBS News colleague, Ed Fouhy, modeled for me how to be a good editor when I asked him to help me with a book I was writing, titled "Reinventing Local News: Connecting Communities Through New Technologies."

Ed kept asking, page after page, paragraph after paragraph, "How do you know that?" Time and again I had to return to my sources and research files to confirm, or reconfirm, assertions that were perhaps a bit ahead of conventional wisdom. Driven by Ed, line by line, my book became "bulletproof" to use his word.

This book's authors raise concerns about the use of anonymous sources. That reminded me of another role model, Brian Buchanan, who was my editor for a daily column I wrote on something new at the time: digital internet technology.

Brian refused to run stories with anonymous sources and pushed me to go back and interview them again on the record. Guess what: Almost all of them went on the record, including with their quotes.

One of the Core Principles of Editing in this book is about being loyal to truth. As an editor, you will be tested by writers, especially in competitive situations, who will push you to publish their "great story." Stand your ground and ask, "But is it true?"

The authors emphasize the importance of attribution. On major stories, it can be easy to be less than rigorous about attribution. But good editors keep asking: Who said that? How believable is that source?

One recent example occurred during the 2023 Middle East war between Israel and Hamas when an explosion took place in a hospital in the Gaza Strip, causing numerous deaths and injuries. The New York Times and other major news organizations initially reported that the hospital had been struck by an Israeli missile or bomb. But notice the attribution: *Hamas said* the hospital had been struck by Israel. Later the Times published an apology:

> *"[E]arly versions of the coverage—and the prominence it received in a headline, news alert and social media channels—relied too heavily on claims by Hamas, and did not make clear that those claims could not immediately be verified. The report left readers with an incorrect impression about what was known and how credible the account was."*

This book's authors talk about the importance of journalism to democracy, and nowhere are editors needed more than during war and elections when truth can be in short supply.

Every four years, in the month preceding a presidential election, it is not unusual to have an "October surprise," a charge that one candidate or another has hidden a misdeed in his or her background. I offer one story from my past that may help you in your future career as an editor dealing with candidate coverage.

In 1988, some of the best political reporters in Washington were telling editors like me that Dan Quayle, the Republican candidate for vice president, had committed a felony.

At National Public Radio, as vice president for news, I kept asking about their sources. As far as I could determine, it was a single source who was pretty shaky. Oh, and he wanted to be anonymous, of course. Not good enough, I said.

After hearing accounts of what had happened, Richard Salant, long-time president of CBS News, saw me at an event in Washington and took me aside.

"If they ever give out an award for keeping a story off the air," he said, "you deserve one."

As the authors point out, this decision-making process for editors is called news judgment. An essential trait for a good editor is restraint. Keep telling your reporters, don't write what we don't know.

If it's a huge story, you don't need to overwrite it. Take a lesson from **The Language Skills Survival Kit** and minimize adjectives and adverbs. If you think a story needs to be hyped, then maybe it's not ready to run.

Good editors have a feel for a story. It takes years of experience to develop the right touch. For you beginners, Buck Ryan and Michael O'Donnell have written a book that's a great place for you to get started.

Now, in honor of Core Principle No. 12, we'll return to where we started: "Everyone needs an editor!" And always remember to confirm your facts: "If your mother says she loves you, check it out."

About the Author

FIGURE 0.1
Adam Clayton
Powell III
(Photo Courtesy of USC)

Adam Clayton Powell III spent 16 years at CBS News and at CBS-owned television and radio stations in New York before he was named vice president for news and information programming at National Public Radio. Currently Powell is a senior fellow and director of Washington programs for the Annenberg Center on Communication Leadership and Policy at the University of Southern California. In that role he serves as executive director of USC's global initiative on election cybersecurity. He has written for publications including The New York Times and the Columbia Journalism Review. His column on digital internet technology won the 1999 World Technology Award for Media and Journalism sponsored by The Economist.

—Adam Clayton Powell III

REFERENCES

New York Times (2023, October 23). Editors' note: Gaza hospital coverage. https://www.nytimes.com/2023/10/23/pageoneplus/editors-note-gaza-hospital-coverage.html

Powell, A.C. III. (2006). *Reinventing local news: Connecting communities through new technologies*. Figueroa Press.

PREFACE

Editing is needed now more than ever. Don't believe us? Just check out these headlines, starting with a possible threat to national security:

Typo sends millions of US military emails to Russian ally Mali
(Debusmann, 2023)

The sensitive information was sent to Mali (.ml), not military (.mil). Johannes Zuurbier, a Dutch internet entrepreneur winding down his contract to manage Mali's email domain, identified the problem more than 10 years ago. Headed out the door, he flagged U.S. officials saying, "The risk is real and could be exploited by adversaries." According to the Financial Times newspaper, the errant emails included medical data, maps of U.S. military facilities, financial records, official trip plans and diplomatic messages. "Human error is by far the most significant security concern on a day-to-day basis," said Steven Stransky, a lawyer who had worked at the Department of Homeland Security. This is no secret: Little things are big things.

Please don't send your apology to "Ann" when her name is "Anne." Maybe it is "Alison," not "Allison," or "Aimee," not "Amy," or "Hilary," not "Hillary." Little letters in names are big deals. And don't confide in the boss something "just between 'you and I.'" She will think less of you because of the grammar mistake (should be "me"). And definitely don't be the student who starts an email with "Hey professor!" You may get an earful because the scholar objects not only to the informal "hey" but also to the missing comma for direct address (make it "Hello, professor!"). Tone matters. Commas matter.

Mistakes can be costly in many ways, but mostly to your credibility. Occasionally it's to your wallet, like the cost of having to toss a promotional flyer in the trash and pay for a reprint after somebody noticed a big mistake.

The key to good writing is editing. Learning to edit your own writing, however, is a special skill. It doesn't come naturally; you need a coach and a strategy. We're here to help.

If you are on a journey to take your writing to new heights, this book can be your sherpa. Do you ever start writing a sentence, then get stuck? When you don't know where to go next, we can be that little GPS voice giving you directions.

If you are looking for an editing job, our book can be your guide, as we explore an array of possibilities. You will hear professionals explain how they address challenges large (macro editing) and small (micro editing) across a diverse media spectrum:

- Newspapers and newsletters
- Broadcast news and podcasts
- Films and documentaries
- Social media
- Public relations and advertising
- News sites for nonprofit organizations

Do you ever wonder whether you have what it takes to work as a professional writer or editor? Our experience tells us, "You can do it!" We have seen thousands of uncertain students become confident pros. Our book is designed to help you as a writer improve your craft. We can sharpen your skills as an editor to the point you become the essential go-to person the boss asks, "Can you please take a look at this for me?" Another lesson from our past: Journalism students who went to law school discovered that judges appreciated their writing and editing skills. They were praised for delivering clear, concise briefs that got right to the point. While you can dress for success, sometimes you'll need to dress down your writing. Whether you end up in law or medicine, real estate or insurance sales, business or philanthropy, the skills we help you develop will be profitable.

That's because our book contains the secret sauce for your success—*confidence.*

Chapter by chapter you will build strength as a writer and an editor. You'll hear advice from professionals doing interesting and challenging work, and soon you will feel the confidence to join them. That's whether you're interested in working for a national publication or your hometown newspaper, or whether you want to produce a package for the "PBS NewsHour," or write a grant to fund your big idea for a documentary. We'll do our part to help you the best we can.

Beyond the value to you personally and professionally, we see a larger need for this book. It can help to restore equilibrium to a world getting turned upside down by the latest disruptive technology. Hold on tight for these headlines:

Fake ChatGPT Cases Cost Lawyers $5,000 Plus Embarrassment
(Strom, 2023)

You know what "AI" stands for, right? We think it means "awfully incomplete." Artificial intelligence might get you started, but you shouldn't finish—Don't press send!—without editing. Our approach to editing begins with eliminating "killer mistakes." Those can get you held in contempt of court by a judge. Or you might stumble in the court of public opinion. Unchecked reliance on AI has resulted in big mistakes, including misdiagnosis of COVID-19 patients; million-dollar losses for Zillow over bogus "Zestimates" of home values; and racist, misogynist and antisemitic tweets (Olavsrud, 2023). Problems do not end there.

Chatting and Cheating. Ensuring Academic Integrity in the Era of ChatGPT
(Cotton et al., 2023)

That's the title of an academic paper published in an education journal—written by the AI chatbot ChatGPT, not the professor who pretended to be the lead author. "We wanted to show that ChatGPT is writing at a very high level," Professor Debby Cotton, director of academic practice at Plymouth Marjon University in England, told The Guardian newspaper (Fazackerley, 2023). "This is an arms race," Cotton said. "The technology is improving very fast and it's going to be difficult for universities to outrun it." AI without editing and attribution generates YAIJ—your ass in a jam. That's a big problem for you, but nothing like the threat to democracy.

Our civil society demands that we the people put more good editors to work—fast. The Federal Election Commission is worried that deepfakes might create an AI-generated October surprise to swing an election (McKenzie, 2023). Editors are the guardians at the gate to protect society from these cyber-barbarians. Credibility concerns could not come at a worse time for journalism. Check out these headlines:

Americans' Trust in Media Remains Near Record Low
(Brenan, 2022)

Here's the gist from Gallup's survey results: *Just 7% of Americans have "a great deal" of trust and confidence in the media, and 27% have "a fair amount." Meanwhile, 28% of U.S. adults say they do not have very much confidence and 38% have none at all in newspapers, TV and radio.*

Trying to Tune Out the News These Days? New Study Shows You're Not Alone
(Folkenflik, 2023)

A few findings from the Reuters Institute for the Study of Journalism:

Some say it makes them feel angry and depressed. Others want a break from the never-ending flow of information. Some are more interested in celebrity updates on social media than old-fashioned newspaper or radio or TV news coverage.

You can't say we weren't warned. Neil Postman set off an alarm in 1985 with his book "Amusing Ourselves to Death: Public Discourse in the Age of Show Business."

At that time the debate about communication in society focused on who had it right: Aldous Huxley with "Brave New World" (1932, addiction to amusement) or George Orwell with "Nineteen Eighty-Four" (1949, oppression by state violence). Today you can buy a T-shirt, a baseball cap or even a tapestry emblazoned with "Make Orwell Fiction Again." So goes the people's trust in getting straight answers to their questions.

The best defense we can wage to retake the high ground is through editing. When writers are headed down a wrong path, editors are there to save them. Writing should be engaging—a turn-on, not a turn-off. When writing is not credible or is perceived as biased, the editor's job is to spot the weakness and help shore it up—or spike it. At the very least, if the writing is sloppy, the editor is there to revise it with precision.

For generations schoolteachers were committed to stamping out illiteracy. Today writing on social media looks more like litter than anything literary. An old-school rule of thumb for proofreading was to look only for OMGs. Today God only knows how many schoolteachers have cried to the heavens over errors in social media posts. We are inviting you to enlist as a soldier in a battle royale. Think of our book as "Grammar's Last Stand!" Strunk and White (1959) is still relevant. Illiteracy is not a virtue; it only makes your message look frivolous. Beware the people who care about grammar—they may be your bosses someday. You should write to be memorable, but for all the right reasons.

It's getting tricky out there. Sensitivity to the language has become so acute that when a suspect in a gay nightclub shooting insisted on "Mx." as a courtesy title, the internet broke over questions about whether the New York Times had changed its stylebook (no, it did not). Our book can be the training camp to help you deal with political footballs. Some of the pundits shouting the loudest about "misinformation" and "disinformation" today are just practicing their own forms of misinformation and disinformation—or playing journalists like cheap violins. Journalism's focus on "storytelling" can lead to writers sticking to a "narrative," then losing trust when readers can clearly see what's missing. Journalism carries great power in a double-edged sword: telling you something or not telling you something. This line of decision making is called news judgment, and it's a lack of judgment on the macro level that's costing journalists the attention of readers, listeners and viewers.

The challenge to understand effective and responsible news judgment begins for many students in high school. Our book can help them whether they are working on newspapers, yearbooks or literary magazines. The same goes for college journalism students, especially if they are semipros like those at Northwestern University, where a student newspaper led to the firing of a football coach, or at Stanford University, where a student reporter's coverage led to the president's resignation (Mastrangelo, 2023). Writers and editors across generations can find value in this book.

In **Section 1** we open with the Core Principles of Editing. Then we show you how they apply in the real world of community and metro newspapers, on the "PBS NewsHour," for an award-winning documentary, and across the websites of nonprofit advocacy organizations. We then profile what makes for The Good Editor and The Good Writer. In several chapters that follow, plus a five-part appendix, we create **The Language Skills Survival Kit** to help you grasp the intricacies of style, spelling, grammar, punctuation and standard English usage. We keep the instruction on the micro level simple and fun. Remember the infamous quote attributed to Texas Gov. Miriam Amanda "Ma" Ferguson: "If the King's English was good enough for Jesus Christ, it's good enough for the children of Texas!" Or so much for bilingual education. We're about the business of teaching English as a first language. Fear not, dream the dream; soon you will be shouting this across the office:

> *Don't you know you need a comma before a conjunction when joining two independent clauses that aren't closely related?*

See the heads turn in amazement. Ah, feel the power!

In **Section 2** we tackle editing news on deadline, from big-picture editing for lead stories to writing the smallest posts on X (formerly Twitter; Goswami, 2023). One problem that spans the generations is math anxiety, which can freeze the best of us. A White House reporter in July 2023 couldn't quite remember whether the latest aid to Ukraine amounted to millions or billions. Just like we put fun in the fundamentals of grammar, in **Section 2** you'll enjoy **Chapter 2.4: Stats, Graphs and Maps**, and gain more confidence to stop and check numbers. In a world where memes carry punch, the power of visuals is explored in **Chapter 2.3: The Indispensable Image**. **Section 2** will also help you understand how to deal with quotations, how to trim stories ("Less is more!"), and even how to keep yourself out of a lawsuit at a time when sports pages are filled with crime briefs.

Even though every writer needs a good editor, these days professionals are feeling more and more alone because of workplace cutbacks to time and talent. This book can fill that empty chair next to you and be that partner you miss. We'll walk you through the thicket to build your confidence as a writer and an editor. If you've read this far, we succeeded in hooking you in the first eight seconds, then gave you a reason to continue every few seconds afterward. Think about that: Average attention spans have dropped to eight seconds from 12 since the year 2000, according to a 2015 Microsoft study (McSpadden, 2015). Every edited word counts. Editing is needed now more than ever, so let's get started. You got this!

—The Authors

About the Authors

Buck Ryan created a new title in the world of editing—Maestro. He has conducted Maestro Concept storytelling workshops in a dozen countries, including Brazil, China, Russia, Spain, Sweden and Vietnam. He served as the eighth director of the University of Kentucky's century-old journalism school and has produced five documentaries for public television.

Michael O'Donnell created an award-winning student media outlet at the University of St. Thomas, where he taught editing for 23 years and oversaw high school journalism workshops. He worked with Ryan at the Chicago Tribune, and together they taught editing at Northwestern University's Medill School of Journalism. They have published four books on language skills and editing.

REFERENCES

Brenan, B. M. (2022, June 5). *Americans' trust in media remains near record low*. Gallup. https://news.gallup.com/poll/403166/americans-trust-media-remains-near-record-low.aspx

Cotton, D., Cotton, P., & Shipway, J. R. (2023). Chatting and cheating: Ensuring academic integrity in the era of ChatGPT. *Innovations in Education and Teaching International*, DOI: 10.35542/osf.io/mrz8h.

Debusmann, B. B., Jr. (2023, July 17). Typo sends millions of US military emails to Russian ally Mali. *BBC News*. https://www.bbc.com/news/world-us-canada-66226873#

Fazackerley, A. (2023, March 20). AI makes plagiarism harder to detect, argue academics—in paper written by chatbot. *The Guardian*. https://www.theguardian.com/technology/2023/mar/19/ai-makes-plagiarism-harder-to-detect-argue-academics-in-paper-written-by-chatbot

Folkenflik, D. (2023, August 4). Trying to tune out the news these days? New study shows you're not alone. NPR. https://www.npr.org/2023/08/04/1192246082/trying-to-tune-out-the-news-these-days-new-study-shows-youre-not-alone

Goswami, R. (2023, August 10). X CEO Linda Yaccarino explains reason for getting rid of Twitter name. CNBC. https://www.cnbc.com/2023/08/10/x-corp-ceo-linda-yaccarino-says-she-has-autonomy-under-elon-musk.html

Huxley, A. (2010). *Brave new world* (11th ed.). Vintage.

Mastrangelo, D. (2023, July 21). Stories at Northwestern, Stanford spotlight impact of student media. *The Hill*. https://thehill.com/homenews/media/4108697-scoops-at-northwestern-stanford-spotlight-impact-of-student-media/

McSpadden, K. (2015, May 14). You now have a shorter attention span than a goldfish. *Time*. https://time.com/3858309/attention-spans-goldfish/

McKenzie, B. (2023, August 24). Is that real? Deepfakes could pose danger to free elections. *UVA Today*. https://news.virginia.edu/content/real-deepfakes-could-pose-danger-free-elections#:~:text=University%20of%20Virginia%20political,the%20tide%20of%20an%20election

Olavsrud, T. (2023). 8 famous analytics and AI disasters. CIO. https://www.cio.com/article/190888/5-famous-analytics-and-ai-disasters.html

Orwell, G. (1949). *Nineteen eighty-four*. Secker & Warburg.

Postman, N. (1985). *Amusing ourselves to death: Public discourse in the age of show business (20th ed.)*. Viking Penguin.

Strom, R. (2023, June 22). Fake ChatGPT cases cost lawyers $5,000 plus embarrassment. *Bloomberg Law*. https://news.bloomberglaw.com/business-and-practice/fake-chatgpt-cases-costs-lawyers-5-000-plus-embarrassment

Strunk, W., Jr., & White, E. B. (1959). *The elements of style* (3rd ed.). Macmillan.

CALLING ALL EDITORS!

First, there was slow food (1980s), then slow travel (1990s), so you might suspect slow journalism (2000s) was not too far behind.

When Delayed Gratification (https://www.slow-journalism.com), "the world's first Slow Journalism magazine," debuted in 2011, it declared it was proud to be "Last to Breaking News." In its own way, Delayed Gratification, a quarterly publication, represented a plaintive cry over society's loss of an essential skill—editing.

Our whole world turned upside down once the prevailing news ethic switched from "Be First but Accurate" to "First Be Fast, Then We'll Clean It Up Later." Somewhere from the turn of the 20th century into the 21st, we entered the Era of Winging It.

Coinciding with this change came something radical for journalism schools across the country—they dropped the word "journalism" (Hare, 2014). As the focus shifted to multimedia, emerging media and cross-media, introductory courses opened their apertures to give students a broader picture of media content.

That's fine, but what we discovered was regardless of the content being delivered or discussed, the same old editing problems remained. What was really needed in the new curriculum was a cross-media *editing* class.

Do we have a book for you!

First, the big idea: Certain principles of editing transcend the media where writers and editors operate. We're here for you whether your work is headed for newspapers, television news, radio or podcasts, film and documentaries, emerging or creative media, advertising or public relations, or whether you're working as an editor for a nonprofit organization focused on advocacy or underserved communities.

Our book offers you two sections of editing instruction with 16 chapters, plus a five-part appendix. In a writing emergency, you can break the glass on **The Language Skills Survival Kit**. Each chapter opens with key points and ends with homework assignments to help you put your newfound knowledge to work. Then, if you wish to dig deeper, we'll offer a bibliography including links to other resources.

Welcome to Section 1

Chapter 1.1 outlines 12 Core Principles of Editing, then in **Chapter 1.2** we put those principles to the test, asking eight professionals how the principles apply to their work. Four of the professionals are in their 20s and the other four range in age from the early 50s to the mid-60s. Three work at newspapers, two are from television news, two work for nonprofits, and the last one we introduce to you in **Chapter 1.1** as "our resident award-winning filmmaker."

We then move to the top rope of the editing wrestling ring with a tag team and drop on you **Chapter 1.3: The Good Editor** and **Chapter 1.4: The Good Writer**. Editing someone else's writing, what we call "copy," can be a wrestling match sometimes. The chapter on how to be a good editor outlines an editing philosophy, suggests a rationale for changing copy, promotes an understanding of key concepts and, above all, offers a step-by-step editing strategy. In many ways **Chapter 1.3** picks up where **chapters 1.1 and 1.2** left off.

These days, more and more, you may find yourself out there all by yourself as a writer. **Chapter 1.4** starts with how to write an article in five easy steps, what we call "The What?! Approach to Writing," then we'll offer some rules for good writing. The final section, called "A Bugaboo Buzzer," lists writing mistakes that drive us nuts. In a bonus round, the chapter ends with Professor O'Donnell's mini-memoir entitled "The Five Writers You Don't Want to Meet in Heaven."

Chapter 1.5 on style offers a compare-and-contrast analysis of the Associated Press Stylebook (56th edition) and the Chicago Manual of Style (17th edition). Then we give you a healthy workout with lessons in spelling (**Chapter 1.6**), grammar (**Chapter 1.7**), punctuation (**Chapter 1.8**) and usage (**Chapter 1.9**). We supplement this instruction with **The Language Skills Survival Kit** in **Appendices A-E**.

Over the past four decades, as professors teaching editing at five universities, one of the most common questions we faced was "Can you recommend a good grammar book?" Now you have one—a book within a book.

There's much more here to help you build confidence as a writer and then, if you like, find a good-paying editing job and succeed in it. Slowly, very slowly, in **Section 1** we help you pick up speed with your writing and editing before we embark on the fast-paced world of a newsroom in **Section 2: Editing News on Deadline.**

Let's get started!

—The Authors

REFERENCES

Hare, K. (2014, February 28). What's in a name? Not "journalism" for some universities adapting to industry changes. Poynter. https://www.poynter.org/newsletters/2014/whats-in-a-name-not-journalism-for-some-universities-adapting-to-industry-changes/

THE CORE PRINCIPLES OF EDITING

KEY POINTS IN THIS CHAPTER

1. When you are engaged in storytelling, regardless of medium or profession, the 12 Core Principles of Editing can assist you, whether you're editing someone else's work or editing your own writing. They run from "The Basics" (Nos. 1–3), to "A How-to Guide" (Nos. 4–7), to "A Way to Add Punch" (Nos. 8–9), to "The Big Picture" (Nos. 10–12).

2. The nitty-gritty matters of editing deal with style, but this does not refer to a writer's style or voice. By style, we mean the rules of an organization's stylebook. Two prominent stylebooks in the publishing field are the Chicago Manual of Style and the Associated Press Stylebook.

3. When you're editing, you can't think big and small at the same time, or something inevitably will fall through the cracks. Try editing in sweeps, as time allows.

Attention! You've been called to duty to save writers from themselves. Step forward and identify yourself.

"I'm a copy editor for a print publication working on a cover story."

"I'm a video editor in a broadcast studio helping reporters tell their stories."

"I'm a film editor following the director's vision and using my skills to bring her vision to light."

"I'm an audio editor working hand in glove with a radio reporter/ podcaster to get the story just right."

"I'm a junior public relations associate working on a news release."

"I'm a writer on deadline who has only myself as an editor."

At ease, everyone. Help is on the way for you to do battle with words.

Now introducing ... the Dirty Dozen Core Principles of Editing! These rules can apply whatever your assignment.

Each core principle is punctuated with a quotable quote to help imprint the message like a sticky note on your forehead. Here goes:

I. The Basics

The first set of core principles, Nos. 1 to 3, focus on the basics.

Core Principle No. 1: Use the Writing + Editing Formula

> **"** *Formula for success: rise early, work hard, strike oil."*
>
> —John Paul Getty, once named the world's richest private citizen by the "Guinness Book of World Records"

Getty's formula is a shortcut to early retirement as an editor. If like us you are not yet there financially, then you can advance your editing career by employing our first Core Principle of Editing.

Let's begin with a brainteaser:

Writing + Editing = What?

Think about that hard, kick around a few ideas with friends and brainstorm with a classmate.

Here's the answer:

Writing + Editing = Writing!

At that glorious moment when you've finished writing, take a breath and realize that you've only just begun. Step away and take whatever time you need to clear your mind. Then dive back in and begin editing.

Cutbacks and layoffs across media companies have elevated the ability to edit your own writing to an essential skill (Pilkington, 2022). Even though every writer needs an editor, increasingly writers are on their own.

Here's where psychology works against you, so "Solw Dwon!" If you figured out that message is "slow down," you've got the idea. If you read your writing over and over again, your mind can "fix" mistakes that still exist. Some editors will read sentences backward to avoid that mental trap.

Flash to the image of a door opening to a magazine office in a Dutch publishing house. At the end of a long, narrow room, one man sits behind a Macintosh computer. He is the editor and sole full-time staff member for the magazine.

"I guess this means I must edit myself," he says, "so I will try my best."

Here's another quick quiz: Can you edit something without making a single change?

Cue the "Final Jeopardy!" music.

Answer: Yes!

FIGURE 1.1.1
White House photographer Pete Souza captured this over-the-shoulder image of Barack Obama's edits to his second inaugural speech in January 2013.

Pete Souza via Flickr

Editing is not changing things. It's assessing whatever is in front of you and deciding about every angle, word, transition, paragraph or piece of punctuation. If you're lucky, you're editing the work of a real pro who sweated every detail. Making a change then could be making a mistake.

Now that you have the formula straight, check out our next two core principles.

Core Principle No. 2: Know the Deadline

> **"** *I don't need time. What I need is a deadline."*
>
> —Duke Ellington, band leader and composer

Whatever you're assigned to edit, first ask, "What's my deadline?"

Time management is essential to good editing. A piece of writing can be endlessly improved. Each editing assignment comes with a value proposition, so always remember time is money.

Editing Economics Lesson No. 101: The law of diminishing returns states, "Profits or benefits will produce a proportionally smaller gain as more money or energy is invested in it."

Always keep your eye on the clock when editing. Do the best you can in the time allowed. As The New Yorker's legendary editor William Shawn, a perfectionist, once observed, "Falling short of perfection is a process that just never stops" (Pace, 1992).

And remember how a newspaper press foreman answered the question, "What do you do here?" He replied, "I start with reality and work backward."

Core Principle No. 3: Seek Help When in Doubt

> **"** *Life is not about you. It's about what you do for others. The faster you are able to get over yourself, the more you can do for the people who matter most."*
>
> —Tom Rath, author of "It's Not About You: A Brief Guide to a Meaningful Life"

That's a good rule for life and a core principle of editing. If it's a close call, let the author's words stand.

Resist the temptation to rewrite something the way you would say it. Remember, it's not your byline, it's theirs.

Writing is best when it's a collaboration between writers and editors. Every writer needs an editor, and every editor needs to have a good working relationship with the writer. The more distance between them, the more likely something can go horribly wrong.

The most common mistake editors make is to change something unclear to make it clearly wrong.

Seek help when in doubt. When working quickly, or especially on deadline, an editor can easily jump to a wrong conclusion about a writer's intended meaning. Don't jump, ask. A quick question by text will take less time than writing a correction and clarification, or an apology.

When you've finished editing a writer's handiwork, you are looking for a "Thank you!" If the writer uses a blunter word than "thank" before "you," then you no doubt violated the Core Principles of Editing. Which brings us to a note about profanity.

In 1972 comedian George Carlin made famous the "Seven Words You Can Never Say on Television" in a monologue (Ott, 2020). Today you can hear those curse words almost anywhere. Times change; rules for grammar and usage change.

When editing, flag any profanity and ask, "Can we say that?" If your boss responds, "$#%& no!" you'll be glad you asked. If the curse word is essential to a writer's meaning, then a middle ground is to replace a letter with a symbol or use hyphens after the initial letter.

Rather than get lost fixing small errors, good editors keep their heads up and ask important questions. Sometimes matters can be resolved easily; other times a story gets kicked back to a writer for a rewrite. Rarely, the fastest way to edit a story is to *spike it* or hit the trash can button.

II. A How-to Guide

The second set of core principles, Nos. 4 to 7, focus on providing a how-to guide.

Core Principle No. 4: Edit in Sweeps

> **"** *Start small, think big. Don't worry about too many things at once."*
>
> —Steve Jobs, who made his mark as co-founder, chairman and CEO of Apple

You can't think big and small at the same time. Rather than do that, you'll benefit from editing in sweeps. We suggest three, as time allows, fitting with three levels of errors: killer mistakes, embarrassing errors and tedious problems.

On your first sweep, look for the BIG MISTAKES.

Rufus Friday, former publisher of the Lexington Herald-Leader in Kentucky and the Tri-City Herald in Kennewick, Washington, was asked, "What's that one big mistake that has readers calling you to cancel their subscriptions?"

Without missing a beat, he replied, "There are two: a misspelled name in an obituary and the very hint of political bias in a news story." Therein lies the spectrum of BIG MISTAKES—ones easy to check and others that require you to check your own biases.

Every aspect of your life—age, gender, race, ethnicity, nationality, class, religion, sexual orientation, political affiliation, ability or disability—creates an opportunity for bias to blur your vision (Banaji & Greenwald, 2016). Those factors also weigh into stereotypes: positive, negative or harmful. Test your assumptions.

Always stop on names and their cousins, titles. Numbers can be tricky. When you're dealing with percentages of increase or decrease, you should include the numbers as well as the percentages. We could proclaim that we are giving our assistant a 100% raise! Then you would read we are now paying him $2 an hour up from $1.

Locations are stop signs, too. Check them out. Don't let up on quotations or sound bites—bear down. Quotes should advance the story. Paraphrase when necessary.

FIGURE 1.1.2   Rufus Friday served as publisher of the Lexington (Kentucky) Herald-Leader from 2011 to 2018.

Always assess the credibility of your sources. That will keep you from getting played or, worse, getting sued for libel.

Don't call a "burglary suspect" a "burglar." Be vigilant about adding attribution, like "police said," and using the word "alleged" as a qualifier. Be aware of words that assign blame, such as "for." Use neutral words like "on" or "in." So the suspect was not arrested "for burglary" but rather arrested "on a burglary charge" or "in connection with the break-in."

Repeat a checklist mantra in your mind—names, titles, numbers, locations, quotations, bias, libel—as you wrap up your first sweep. These are the time-consuming points to check. You'll need to speed up for your second and third sweeps.

FIGURE 1.1.3   Henry Fuhrmann was retired as the top copy editor from the Los Angeles Times when he started a one-man campaign to remove the hyphen when describing Asian Americans and African Americans.

On your second sweep, focus on embarrassing errors of grammar, punctuation and spelling. Embarrassing errors are the ones that elicit the "What an idiot!" reactions from touchy, judgmental readers.

Say "irregardless" rather than "regardless," and retired schoolteachers will become your pen pals from hell.

"Bussing immigrants" (kissing them) is not "busing immigrants" (transporting them). And don't confuse "its" with "it's" as autocorrect does. Always stop on the "s-sound" to check plurals and possessives.

Problems with transitions and parallel construction can be resolved on your second sweep. Notice how we are using "On your first sweep," then second sweep, to begin our transitions; that's parallel construction. Here we go one last time:

On your third sweep, clean up tedious matters, such as tightening, usage and style violations.

Heed the classic battle cry, "Omit needless words!" You can just say "few" rather than "few in number." That's the "B" in the ABCs of Editing: accuracy, brevity and clarity. A usage rule in the AP Stylebook (AP, 55) distinguishes between "compare to" (only similarities) and "compare with" (similarities and differences). So you can compare love "to" a rose, but you compare this year's budget "with" last year's. For more on style points, see our next core principle of editing.

A Note About Style

A "writer's style" refers to a unique tone of voice or a clever way with words. When editors use the word "style," however, they typically are referring to rules according to a stylebook.

If you've been assigned a term paper, you might have struggled with the difference between APA and MLA style, especially in the way you list citations. That's closer to what we mean by "style" in this book.

We're focused more on how to punctuate a quotation rather than how to cite works according to the American Psychological Association stylebook or the Modern Language Association stylebook. The two stylebooks used most in our world are the Chicago Manual of Style and the Associated Press Stylebook.

Take this sentence:

Albert Einstein once referred to this as 'insanity'.

Should you use single quotation marks or double? Does the period belong inside or outside? Those are style matters that pitted British publishers at Oxford University Press in the early 20th century against those at the University of Chicago Press.

"Just tell me what to do!"

We hear you. To ease the insanity, stylebooks will say "always" do this, "never" do that.

Let's hope you never have a boss like Britain's Business Secretary Jacob Rees-Mogg, who once demanded his staff double-space after each period.

There's value in hard-and-fast rules, but if you're looking for consistency in the English language, you'll go crazy.

Public relations writers, especially those in media relations, feel a kinship with newspaper journalists, as they both will adhere to AP style. Magazine and book writers, however, usually favor the Chicago Manual of Style.

Here's a taste of what we mean by the differences:

1. **Numbers** (spell out or use numerals):

   She is twenty-five years old. (CMS)

   She is 25 years old. (AP)

2. **Films and book titles** (italics or quote marks):

   He liked *My Dinner with Andre* but loved *Don Quixote*. (CMS)

   He liked "My Dinner With Andre" but loved "Don Quixote." (AP)

3. **Apostrophe "s"** (in some cases):

   Maria Davis's dog is the cutest thing. (CMS)

   Maria Davis' dog is the cutest thing. (AP)

The two stylebooks often agree, as in the placement of periods and commas inside end quotes. You asked what to do—here it is:

Albert Einstein once referred to this as "insanity."

Core Principle No. 5: Know Which Stylebook

" *Let's get down to the nitty-gritty."*

—Actor Jack Black starring as
Nacho, a man of the cloth who lives
the dream of becoming a Lucha Libre
wrestler in the film "Nacho Libre"

In this world, little things are big things. A top "word nerd" at the Los Angeles Times, Henry Fuhrmann, was celebrated for his fight against using the hyphen in "Asian American" and "African American" (Curwen, 2022).

He argued in a 2019 essay that "those hyphens serve to divide even as they are meant to connect," making second-class citizens out of "hyphenated Americans." That argument changed stylebooks.

Words matter, style matters. To get your bearings and to keep from creating problems, always begin an editing assignment with the nitty-gritty question, ""What stylebook are we using—and what edition?"

Let's say you write, "red, white and blue," and your editor, clutching the Chicago Manual of Style, says, "That's wrong! It should be 'red, white, and blue.'"

It's not grammatically right or wrong; you are just using a different stylebook.

That serial comma, or Oxford comma, or Harvard comma—the one before "and"—has brought writers and editors to the brink of nuclear war over the years (Kessler, 2022). In England, Health Secretary Thérèse Coffey banned employees from using Oxford commas, which she said she "can't bear."

She was channeling the Associated Press, whose stylebook is built for speed. A comma creates a pause. Keeping with the journalistic quick-quick-quick mentality, the Associated Press Stylebook deletes optional commas.

A rule that transcends all stylebooks, however, is to avoid possible confusion. Even the AP would have you write, "I'll have coffee, toast, and ham and eggs." It's not toast and ham you desire; just to be clear, you want the ham with your eggs.

Don't confuse "and" with an ampersand (&); they aren't interchangeable. It can get confusing, as Simon & Schuster (correct) is listed as "simonandschuster.com" for its website.

Correct spelling is defined by the stylebook, not any dictionary you can find online.

Here's the tricky part: Not all dictionaries are alike, and that means "preferred spellings" may differ. A dictionary's preferred spelling is listed first or is the version with a full definition.

Stylebooks simplify the task of identifying the preferred spelling of a word by listing it. An example that drives people nuts is AP's preference for "adviser" (er) over "advisor" (or). As "e" comes before "o" in the alphabet, the first spelling is the preferred one.

If you can't find how a word is spelled in your stylebook, it will refer you to its preferred dictionary. The AP Stylebook's 56th edition preferred Webster's New World Dictionary, but its 57th edition switched to Merriam-Webster.

The Chicago Manual of Style recommends three dictionaries: Webster's Third New International Dictionary and "the latest edition of its chief abridgment"; Merriam-Webster's Collegiate Dictionary, plus a nod toward the American Heritage Dictionary of the English Language. Be warned: Those dictionaries are created by people who do not always agree. As the Chicago Manual of Style advises, "At least for spelling, one source should be used consistently throughout a single work" (7.1, 418).

A final nitty-gritty note: Even though you can spend a career using only one stylebook, the rules can change on you. For example, the AP's 57th edition changed "Day One" to "Day 1" and dropped the hyphens in "G7" and "G20." In 2019, AP approved the percent sign with numerals after years of insisting on spelling out "percent." That's still the case in casual uses, such as "a zero percent chance of winning," and when spelling out a number to begin a sentence. Beware: Stylebook editions change every so often.

Core Principle No. 6: Find the Simple Solution

Simplicity is the ultimate sophistication."

—Leonardo da Vinci, who gave us Mona Lisa's simple smile

An essential editing guideline is derived from the great architect Ludwig Mies van der Rohe: "Less is more." When editing, make the **simplest fix possible**. Think of yourself as a surgeon, not a butcher.

Simplicity applies to word choice, too, especially if you're appealing to a mass audience. Choose the short word over the long word when no meaning is lost. The fewer the syllables the better.

Some examples: Fire, not conflagration. Concern, not consternation. Cut, not laceration. Bruise, not contusion.

Sentence length is related. Remember the old broadcast writer's saw: "one idea, one sentence." You'll know you're getting into trouble when you see more than two commas in a sentence.

Keep in mind the memo the crusty city editor sent to one of his more literary reporters:

....
....
....

The memo ended with a simple declarative sentence: "These are periods—use them."

Writing short is a lot tougher than writing long. Keeping a message short puts the focus not "on writing" but "on being read." The results can make for good business.

Axios media co-founder Jim VandeHei, also co-author of the book "Smart Brevity: The Power of Saying More With Less" (VandeHei, 2022), put it this way:

"Why it matters: *Too many people too often lard up ideas, processes, teams or companies with needless complexity. Simplicity, by contrast, greases velocity, productivity and profitability"* *(VandeHei, 2023).*

He expects Axios to grow "from 500 people to 1,000-plus in the coming years." We think his idea of having a "CSO (chief simplicity officer)" fits with our notion of an ideal editor.

You might have a psychological advantage in keeping your writing short and simple, but we live in a complex world. Therein lies the pain, whether you're a headline writer or a filmmaker.

"It's really a challenge when they ask you to summarize your film in 100 words, which may be just three sentences," our resident award-winning filmmaker says about completing a grant application.

"Then," he says, raising his eyebrows, "imagine what it's like when they ask you to do it in one sentence."

Core Principle No. 7: Think "Just One More Thing"

> **"** *Did you hear the creator of autocorrect died?"*
> *"Yes, I read the funnel is tomato."*
>
> —bad social media joke, as the inventor
> with the patent is still living

Speed kills.

I'm sure you know the pain of clicking "send" too quickly and revealing for all to see an embarrassing mistake, whether it's to one friend or to several strangers in a group chat.

Sure, you could be the victim of autocorrect, or maybe you just forgot to type the "l" in public. Mistakes happen.

When you think you are finished writing something, whether it be a text message or a chapter of your novel, hear the famous catchphrase: "Just one more thing."

That comes from the great detective Frank Columbo, played by actor Peter Falk. His parting comment led to a question that would corner a murderer or a criminal in the TV series "Columbo."

The same pause can save you from an embarrassing mistake, or something worse: an error that kills your credibility or lives in infamy.

In what's been dubbed "the best typographical error ever" in the Los Angeles Times, a copy editor in 2012 was disturbed by the placement of a design element in a profile of a retired Las Vegas sheriff who was voted out of office (Curwen, 2022).

In fixing the design, a slip of a key turned the conjunction "but" into the noun "butt." You guessed it; the story then read that "butt cracks" appeared in the sheriff's public persona.

We guarantee you that on further inspection you will find at least "one more thing" to fix, especially after you try to fix something.

III. A Way to Add Punch

The third set of core principles, Nos. 8 and 9, focus on how to add punch.

Core Principle No. 8: Twist a Cliche

> **"** *It is a cliche that most cliches are true, but then like most cliches, that cliche is untrue."*
>
> —Stephen Fry, an English actor and comedian
> who can write cliches in eight languages

If you have heard it before, don't say it again.

That's true of cliches, those worn-out expressions you've heard many times before.

You will naturally write or see cliches in a first draft: You're busy as a bee, there are plenty of fish in the sea, you're thinking outside the box.

But when you start editing, attack them with Dr. Evil's laser. One key to memorable writing is to twist a cliche.

So you're busy as a "B" student, there are plenty of phish in the sea of email, you're thinking outside the box office. You get the idea.

It's easier to make these changes in your own writing. When you see cliches in another writer's work that you're editing, point them out, then make suggestions, as in "How about we say this …"

Either way, try not to be a one-shot wonder. See if you can add value by playing off the twist later in the writing. Give yourself an "A" for a final grade, try not to get hooked yourself by the phish and punch your ticket to success.

The best way to steer clear of the Groan Zone is through originality. Coin a new word or phrase that other writers want to repeat.

Core Principle No. 9: Deliver a One-Two Punch: Picture + Words

> **"** *If a picture is worth a thousand words, photographers are worth a million."*
>
> —Tupac Shakur, considered one of the
> most influential rappers of all time

"No pictures, no story."

It's the golden rule for TV news reporters, and it applies across the media. That's true even for radio news writers who paint pictures in a listener's mind.

SAHAN JOURNAL   DONATE ≡

■ **DEMOCRACY & POLITICS**

Driver's License for All bill passes in the Minnesota House, clearing first hurdle to becoming law

The bill would allow undocumented immigrants to obtain driver's licenses. Advocates for the bill are hopeful it will finally pass this year with Democrats in control of the House, Senate, and Governor's office.

 By **HIBAH ANSARI**
JANUARY 30, 2023

Community members celebrate in the State Capitol after the Minnesota House passed the Driver's License for All bill on January 30, 2023. The bill would allow undocumented Minnesotans to obtain driver's licenses. Credit: Jaida Grey Eagle | Sahan Journal

FIGURE 1.1.4   A dramatic photo showing peak emotion adds punch to this story in the Sahan Journal of St. Paul, Minnesota.

Sahan Journal, used by permission

Then they use "nat" (natural) sound to make images come to life. The same goes for memorable podcasts.

The marriage of visuals and words creates the one-two punch that gets attention, whether it's the cover of a magazine or a photo with a headline to promote a radio news story on the station's website. Without that attention-grabber, everything is lost. First someone must stop and read, or listen or view, before any understanding happens.

There's something else beyond attention that a powerful visual-word marriage can produce: emotion. Editors control the levers of the emotion meter, making people laugh, cry, be outraged or choked up, be delighted or inspired, whatever change of emotion reflects the story's point.

First getting attention, then raising emotions are essential steps in teaching. Good writers and editors at their best are teachers.

A picture is worth a thousand tears. Which brings us to the Maestro Concept, where a photo is considered "the lede" of a story, and the headline or title is the second paragraph. The concept looks at editing from a reader's perspective (Ryan, 1993).

It also directs editors to lead with questions for writers rather than edicts, beginning with "Can you summarize your story in 30 words or fewer?" and then, "Why should I care?" The answers to those questions create the first draft of a headline, and that headline inspires a powerful visual to go with it.

Efficiency meets time management and visual communication. We can't speak highly enough about visuals, so on to our next core principle.

IV. The Big Picture

The fourth and last set of core principles, Nos. 10 to 12, focus on big-picture ideas to help writers and editors succeed.

Core Principle No. 10: Let People See Themselves

> **"** *Cinema is a mirror that can change the world."*
>
> —Diego Luna, Mexican actor, singer and director

People need to see themselves in whatever is written, produced or filmed. Creating that mirror image is the heart of engagement. But what people?

8th-grader Ryan Serem wins Chatham County Schools District Spelling Bee

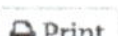

Ryan Serem, the winner of the Chatham County Schools Spelling Bee Monday night, poses with his family and school board members Jane Allen Wilson and Del Turner. Serem is a student at Margaret B. Pollard Middle School.

STAFF PHOTO BY PEYTON SICKLES

Posted Wednesday, February 1, 2023 10:07 am | Updated: Wednesday, February 1, 2023 12:47 pm

From Chatham County Schools

PITTSBORO — Among the more than three dozen spellers who qualified to compete in the district-wide Spelling Bee Monday, Margaret B. Pollard 8th-grader Ryan Serem emerged as the top speller.

FIGURE 1.1.5   A community news site such as the Chatham (North Carolina) News + Record knows the importance of posting pictures that reflect the members of its community.
(Chatham News + Record)

Editors need a firm grip on the target reader, listener or viewer. Being able to picture that person in the editor's mind, as well as deliver that image in the presentation, is the key to grabbing attention. It also focuses decision making on everything from story topics and word choice to design and soundtracks.

The concept of a general audience, as with the AP Stylebook, is what made people rich in the past. They were publishers of the "penny press" newspapers of the 1830s, Sam Walton with the 1962 opening of the first Walmart, or Jeff Bezos working out of his Bellevue, Washington, garage in 1994 to create Amazon. The bigger the audience, the more the revenue.

But even media outlets that are broadcast far and wide, such as National Public Radio, base their news judgment on a target listener among their 57 million listeners. Here's the demographic profile: 55% men; about half are between 25 and 54 years old; mostly white; median household income $103,000 a year; 75% identify as regular voters (Clark, 2023). Data on consumer buying habits can fill out a more complete target profile.

A lesson from the founding of USA Today in 1982 is instructive. Its mission was "to serve as a forum for better understanding and unity to help make the USA truly one nation" (Prichard, 1987). Page One editors paid special attention to using photos of women and Black newsmakers. Studies showed that the newspaper had high credibility with those two demographic groups. When people can see themselves in what you're doing, they're more likely to pay attention and appreciate your creative efforts.

Nothing succeeds like success. Take PinkNews, for example (Cohen, 2010). Founder Benjamin Cohen turned a side hustle into a multimillion-dollar global publication, offering lessons in how an LGBTQ+ brand can reach a Gen Z audience for those born between 1997 and 2012.

The latest watchword is "DEI" for diversity, equity and inclusion, but that can get complicated. The Maynard Institute for Journalism Education, with "45 years of driving diversity" in journalism, suggests that the goal isn't "inclusivity" but rather "belonging."

Maynard Institute's Fault Lines newsroom training helps journalists understand their unconscious bias in seeing the world as it is aligned across five fault lines: race, gender, class, generation and geography.

This core principle's larger point is this: Your job as an editor is to ensure that people are turned on to a story, not turned off. If they see themselves in what you're doing, they're more likely to be turned on. One misplaced word or phrase—or missing image—can turn them off.

Core Principle No. 11: Whatever You Do, Be Loyal to Truth

" *I write truth, you write fiction."*

—Author Salman Rushdie, speaking
to more than 1,000 editors and publishers
in an address to the American
Society of Newspaper Editors in 1996

Words matter. Truth matters.

Whether you are writing and editing fiction or nonfiction, whether it's a news story or a news release, whether you are using a typewriter or writing a novel on an iPhone, it pays to wield an essential tool. Ernest Hemingway put it best:

> *The most essential gift for a good writer is a built-in, shockproof, sh*t detector. This is the writer's radar and all great writers have had it.*

Hemingway, a journalist turned fiction writer, understood he had a higher calling than pursuing objectivity, and that was achieving credibility through truth-telling.

There's a difference between the truth, the whole truth and nothing but the truth (court of law, a journalist's goal) and a selective truth (public relations). It depends if your loyalty is to citizens and a public good or to a client and private gain. Either way, it's truth that lends credibility.

Hemingway started writing as a cub reporter for The Kansas City Star newspaper. But Salman Rushdie began work as a copywriter for the advertising agency Ogilvy & Mather. Both had a love for words and an intense desire to get to truth through fiction.

When Rushdie told journalists, "I write truth, you write fiction," he set the stage for what today is called "the Objectivity Wars." Journalists who wave a banner of objectivity, in fact, make a series of subjective decisions: Is this a story? How should we cover it? Who should be interviewed? How much play should we give the story?

In their book "The Elements of Journalism," authors Bill Kovach and Tom Rosenstiel argue that objectivity is best viewed as a method rather than a goal (Kovach & Rosenstiel, 2021). Journalists are advised to use a version of the scientific method to test assumptions on the way to finding truth. Critics of this framing consider journalistic practices anything but scientific and call objectivity more a style of writing.

Whatever the approach, words and truth are what unite us around the Core Principles of Editing.

So if you see a quotation in a news story that reads just a little too perfectly, question it. If the story itself reads just a little too neatly, question it. If you get lost in a "he said/they said" exchange and don't understand what's really going on, question it.

Fiction can be hiding in a cloak of nonfiction.

Walter Lippmann borrowed on a quotation in his book "Public Opinion" to make an important point in Chapter 1, "The World Outside and the Pictures in Our Heads" (Lippmann, 1922). The chapter is all about seeing the world, or truth, clearly. The quotation assigns editors an important task: "The murder of a beautiful theory by a gang of brutal facts."

Core Principle No. 12: Tie the Beginning and End Together

> *Genius knocks on the door and gets no answer but its own echo."*
>
> —Gutzon Borglum, the American sculptor who brought us Mount Rushmore

Do you remember this chapter's "nut graph"? A good nut graph, like a lede, summarizes the point of your story and creates an outline for the rest of your storytelling. Here's that nut graph again:

> *At ease, everyone. Help is on the way for you to do battle with words.*
>
> *Now introducing … the Dirty Dozen Core Principles of Editing! These rules can apply whatever your assignment.*

"The Dirty Dozen" screenplay was based on a 1965 bestseller by E.M. Nathanson, who was inspired by the World War II heroics of the "Filthy Thirteen" paratrooper group. So here's a filthy (read dope) last core principle of editing for you:

End with an echo of your beginning.

Think of your beginning and ending in the same light. When you ask yourself, "What's the best way to begin this story?" you also are creating the first draft of your ending.

Sometimes that great idea for an ending will inspire a rewrite of the beginning. So goes the challenge of drawing attention to the beginning and leaving a lasting impression of closure with the ending.

Speechwriters will recognize this core principle from their formula: "Tell 'em what you're going to tell them, tell 'em it, then tell 'em what you told 'em."

Whether it's a sermon, a feature article or a novel, the same core principle applies. You can test it by enjoying the beginning of a work, then quickly flipping to the end and listening for the echo.

It's only natural that writers will end their stories otherwise; they get tired and stop. That's why we have editors.

For filmmakers, the ending carries added value, as it can do more than echo the beginning: It also can illustrate the major theme.

"The end is what lingers with the audience," our resident filmmaker says. "It's what they think about on their way home from the theater or as they shut the TV off and go to bed. It needs to make them think about all that came before and carry an emotional punch."

In advertising, a key concept is known as "the takeaway." You spent a lot of time and money on a 30-second spot (up to $7 million for the Super Bowl). Now what's the takeaway, the message viewers remember most?

Unfortunately, many times you can hear someone talk about an awesome commercial, then not remember the product or brand.

The takeaway question is a valuable one for editors to assess a story's impact as they wind up a writing project, regardless of the medium.

In the film "Amadeus," Emperor Joseph II explained his concern to Mozart about a new composition: "There are simply too many notes." Editors exist so writers can strike the right chords and not send mixed or confusing messages.

The legendary editor Joseph Pulitzer said it best. His words relate not only to newspapers but to all the media where the Core Principles of Editing apply:

"What a newspaper needs in its news, in its headlines, and on its editorial page is terseness, humor, descriptive power, satire, originality, good literary style, clever condensation, and accuracy, accuracy, accuracy!"

At ease, all you editors! That's it for now. Review these principles again and again until they are top-of-mind. As you read on, you will see we will devote entire chapters to elaborating on many of these Core Principles of Editing.

HOMEWORK

Try these exercises at home to see if you grasp some of the Core Principles of Editing.

Assignment No. 1

Pick up a newspaper or a magazine or find an interesting article on your favorite website. Circle or highlight a name of a person or company in the article, then check it out. Did you find that name spelled more than one way online? What about the title that goes with the name? Is it stated correctly?

Assignment No. 2

Find a story on a controversial topic, whether it be about politics, transgender athletes, critical race theory, abortion or banning books in school. Look for the markers of potential bias: age, gender, race, ethnicity, nationality, class, religion, sexual orientation, political affiliation, ability or disability. Who is allowed to speak as a source? Which sources are missing? Then ask, "Is a stereotype used here?" If so, label it as positive, negative or harmful, and explain why.

Assignment No. 3

Find a sentence in an article with "and" in a series, such as "red, white, and blue" or "Rita Moreno sang, she danced and the Academy Award winner celebrated all night long." (Notice in the examples, the first has a comma before "and," but the second does not.) Whether it's words or simple sentences in a series, look to see if a comma is used before the "and" (Chicago Manual of Style) or not (Associated Press Stylebook). Then find a second example. Was the editor consistent with the punctuation?

Assignment No. 4

Did you notice the twist of a cliche in **Core Principle No. 9**? "A picture is worth a thousand words" became "A picture is worth a thousand tears." Go back to something you wrote that included a cliche, then see if you can twist it into a memorable line. Can you echo back to the twist in a later line? In our example here, the echo would be a line like: "The photo made me cry my eyes out."

Assignment No. 5

In his book "The Metaverse: And How It Will Revolutionize Everything," Matthew Ball launches his introduction with a reference to Vannevar Bush, the electrical engineer and presidential adviser. Beginning in the 1930s, Bush foresaw something like Google. In Ball's conclusion, 312 pages later, he opens with a line about how Bush "had an uncanny ability to predict the devices of the future." This is a great example of **Core Principle No. 12**.

Sometimes the echo comes in a word, phrase or anecdote, sometimes in a visual or in natural sound. How many other examples can you find in a:

a. Book
b. Film
c. Documentary
d. Newspaper feature story
e. Magazine article
f. Podcast
g. In-depth TV news package

REFERENCES

Associated Press. (2022). *The Associated Press stylebook: 2022–2024* (56th ed.). Basic Books.

Associated Press. (2024). *The Associated Press stylebook: 2024–2026* (57th ed.). Basic Books.

Banaji, M., & Greenwald, A. (2016). *Blindspot: Hidden biases of good people*. Bantam Books.

Clark, H. (2023). By the numbers: Who is actually listening to public radio? Market Enginuity. https://blog.marketenginuity.com/by-the-numbers-who-is-actually-listening-to-public-radio

Cohen, B. (2010, September 2). Meet Ben Cohen: The 27-year-old teenage millionaire. *Wired*. https://www.wired.co.uk/article/meet-ben-cohen-the-27-year-old-teenage-millionaire

Curwen, T., (2022, September 14). Henry Fuhrmann, *Times* editor and "word nerd" who fought for fairness in grammar, dies. *Los Angeles Times*. https://www.latimes.com/california/story/2022-09-14/henry-fuhrmann-times-editor-dies

Kessler, C. (2022, May 4). The great Oxford comma debate: Journalists, PR pros & the Associated Press weigh in. *Muck Rack*. https://muckrack.com/blog/2022/05/04/oxford-comma

Kovach, B., & Rosenstiel, T. (2021). *The elements of journalism: What newspeople should know and the public should expect* (4th ed.). Crown.

Lippmann, W. (1922). *Public opinion*. Simon & Schuster.

Merriam-Webster. (2020). *Merriam-Webster's collegiate dictionary* (11th ed.).

Ott, T. (2020, May 19). How George Carlin's "seven words" changed legal history. *Biography.* https://www.biography.com/news/george-carlin-seven-words-supreme-court

Pace, E. (1992, December 9). William Shawn, 85, is dead; *New Yorker*'s gentle despot. *The New York Times.* https://www.nytimes.com/1992/12/09/obituaries/william-shawn-85-is-dead-new-yorker-s-gentle-despot.html

Pilkington, E. (2022, December 15). *Washington Post* chief announces job cuts— and refuses to answer questions. *The Guardian.* https://www.theguardian.com/media/2022/dec/15/washington-post-layoffs-job-cuts-fred-ryan

Prichard, P. S. (1987). *The making of McPaper: The inside story of USA Today.* Andrews McMeel.

Ryan, B. (1993). The maestro concept: A new approach to writing and editing for the newspaper of the future (report and video). American Society of Newspaper Editors.

University of Chicago Press Editorial Staff. (2017). *The Chicago manual of style* (17th ed.). https://www.chicagomanualofstyle.org/home.html

VandeHei, J. (2023, Jan. 12). Axios finish line: The simplicity doctrine. Axios. https://www.axios.com/2023/01/13/simplicity-doctrine-business-startup-occams-razor

VandeHei, J., Allen, M., & Schwartz, R. (2022). *Smart brevity: The power of saying more with less.* Workman.

Webster's new world college dictionary (5th ed.). Houghton Mifflin Harcourt.

FURTHER READING

Best, J. (2012). *Damned lies and statistics: Untangling numbers from the media, politicians, and activists.* University of California Press.

Cohen, B. (n.d.). Founder and CEO, PinkNews. https://careers.thepinknews.com/people/1219800-benjamin-cohen-he-him

Dunlap, D. W. (2017, July 20). When the copy desk was the "heart of the newspaper." *New York Times.* https://www.nytimes.com/2017/07/20/insider/when-the-copy-desk-was-the-heart-of-the-newspaper.html

Goldberg, B., & Morrissey, E. (2014). *Bias: A CBS insider exposes how the media distort the news* (Revised). Regnery Publishing.

Lehrman, S. Diversity toolbox: How to cross your "faultlines." Society of Professional Journalists. https://www.spj.org/dtb2.asp

McKee, R. (1997). *Story: Substance, structure, style and the principles of screenwriting.* ReganBooks.

Tucher, A. (2022). *Not exactly lying: Fake news and fake journalism in American history.* Columbia University Press.

CREDITS

Fig. 1.1.1: Pete Souza, "Speech," https://www.flickr.com/photos/obamawhitehouse/4455914253, 2013.

Fig. 1.1.2: Rufus Friday, https://ci.uky.edu/about/directory/rufus-m-friday, Rufus M. Friday, 2021.

Fig. 1.1.3: Source: https://www.instagram.com/p/CbDU1o1JKrd/.

Fig. 1.1.4: Sahan Journal, "License," https://sahanjournal.com/democracy-politics/minnesota-house-drivers-licenses-for-all-bill-undocumented-immigrants/. Copyright © 2023 by Sahan Journal. Reprinted with permission.

Fig. 1.1.5: Chatham News + Record, "Spelling," https://chathamnewsrecord.com/stories/8th-grader-ryan-serem-wins-chatham-county-schools-district-spelling-bee,15439. Copyright © by Chatham News+Record. Reprinted with permission.

EDITING IN THE REAL WORLD AND YOU

KEY POINTS IN THIS CHAPTER

1. The meaning of "deadline" runs from one that's a hard 7 p.m. ET showtime for a production assistant working on the "PBS NewsHour" to the self-imposed ones by a filmmaker until "deliverables" are due. A newspaper copy desk chief at a metro daily has late-evening deadlines. For the publisher and editor of a weekly, Tuesday is crunch time. Nonetheless, the core principle applies: Know the deadline.

2. Words like "truth" and "objectivity" will have different meanings if you're working for a nonprofit organization as an editor, especially if your publications are involved in advocacy.

3. Editors can advance their careers, gaining more responsibility, by flagging errors on final proofs in line with the core principle: Think "Just One More Thing." They also can be recognized for their ability to twist a cliche and deliver a one-two punch with visuals and words.

4. To find work as an editor, start with internships and student media opportunities at your college, then network with those you meet and continue to grow by reading and watching quality media.

Yes, This Will Be on the Final Exam

OK, thanks to **Chapter 1.1**, you're now fully up to speed on the 12 Core Principles of Editing. So it's time for a quiz! Ready? Here goes:

What Is Editing, Really?

No, it's not a trick question. What do you think: Is it a calling? Maybe just a necessity. We know it's an art, and certainly it's a process. But most important for editors and their families, it's a paycheck, right?

In **Chapter 1.2** we're going to answer that question by putting the core principles to the test in the real world. We started our research project with this hypothesis:

When you are engaged in storytelling, regardless of medium or profession, the 12 Core Principles of Editing can assist you, whether you're editing someone else's work or your own writing.

Remember, the principles run from "The Basics" (Nos. 1–3), to "A How-to Guide" (Nos. 4–7), to "A Way to Add Punch" (Nos. 8–9), to "The Big Picture" (Nos. 10–12).

We engaged in Zoom interviews, email exchanges and in-person conversations with eight professionals. We asked them how they performed their various editing tasks and then we matched up what they said to the Core Principles of Editing.

Four of the pros are in their 20s and the other four range in age from the early 50s to the mid-60s. Three work at newspapers, two are from television news, two work for nonprofits and the last one we introduced to you in **Chapter 1.1** as "our resident award-winning filmmaker." He faced the challenge of making a pitch for grant money with just one sentence—and more than $250,000 on the line. That's as real as it gets.

We end the chapter with a little treat: We asked them for advice on how you, too, can get a good-paying editing position.

If you have your pencils and scorecards ready, we'll give you the lineup of our eight professionals:

NEWSPAPERS

Bill Horner III, a third-generation newspaper publisher, is now executive editor for CityView in Fayetteville, North Carolina. The publication has partnered with The Assembly to create a collaborative newsroom to cover several communities. For nearly five years he was publisher and editor of the Chatham News + Record, a weekly print newspaper also doing podcasts and publishing a magazine, a parenting newsletter and a Spanish-language spinoff publication. Horner called his innovative and award-winning paper a 145-year-old "startup," as it proclaimed itself "Chatham County's news source since 1878." He launched the newspaper's social media presence on Facebook, Instagram and Twitter (now X).

Amy Kuebelbeck is a copy desk chief for the Star Tribune, the largest newspaper in Minnesota, which has moved to a digital-first model in which most stories are first published online and later funneled to the print newspaper.

Elena Neuzil works as the letters editor for the Star Tribune and doubles as a copy editor for staff-written editorials. Her work involves not just editing and headline writing but also layout and design.

TELEVISION NEWS

Solveig Rennan is a public television production assistant for "PBS News Weekend" and "Washington Week" based in Washington, D.C. Solveig (pronounced SOUL-vay), a 2019 graduate of the University of St. Thomas in St. Paul, was born and raised in Duluth, Minnesota.

Simeon Lancaster is associate producer and editor for the Under-Told Stories Project, "a journalism project focused on consequences of poverty and the work of change agents addressing them." The project's reports appear routinely on the nightly "PBS NewsHour."

NONPROFIT ORGANIZATIONS

Samantha HoangLong is the audience growth manager for a nonprofit newsroom, Sahan Journal, serving Minnesota's immigrant and minority communities.

Bernadette Kinlaw is a copy editor on the digital team at the Southern Poverty Law Center, a nonprofit legal advocacy organization specializing in civil rights and public interest litigation. It was founded in Montgomery, Alabama, in 1971, and among its founders was civil rights leader Julian Bond.

FILM

Paul Lamont of Lockport, New York, is an award-winning documentary filmmaker and founder of Toward Castle Films. His film "The Songpoet" about singer-songwriter Eric Andersen appeared on your local public television station as it was distributed nationally by American Public Television. It was eight years in the making, taking Lamont to Canada, Europe and Western New York, where Lamont had first met Andersen in 1976 after a gig at "a rough and tumble blues joint" south of Buffalo. Andersen entered the vanguard of the folk music scene in the '60s and has picked up a devoted international following, according to Lamont.

FIGURE 1.2.1   Paul Lamont directs a segment for his documentary "The Songpoet" about singer-songwriter Eric Andersen. Lamont has worked with the same editor, Chris Bové, for more than 20 years.
(Photo courtesy of Paul Lamont)

For some of these professionals, their primary task is polishing the work of others and delivering them from error. For others, editing is inseparable from creating media that serves their audience and perhaps does some good. All stressed the importance of the core editing principles in their daily work. Here's what they had to say:

Core Principle No. 1: Writing + Editing = Writing

The Chatham News + Record in Siler City, North Carolina, has a small news staff to cover Chatham County, which is divided more ways than a roulette wheel: politically, racially, socioeconomically, even linguistically with a significant Spanish-speaking population.

Finding a target reader was a difficult challenge for Bill Horner III when he was at the helm as publisher and editor, overseeing the work of two news reporters, a sports editor and a photojournalist. He also served as the paper's lead columnist.

During his tenure, the News + Record won more awards from the North Carolina Press Association than any other newspaper in its division as a small weekly (3,800 paid circulation, about half from street sales). Like many small newspapers, the News + Record is a steppingstone to bigger things, so most of Horner's hires were straight out of journalism school. For him, being an editor starts with being a coach and mentor, and that starts upfront with planning to save time, reduce frustration and spare a nightmare for reporters—the painful rewrite.

"A reporter can spend hours working on a story," Horner said, "and you get it, and it's just like, 'This is not what I envisioned at all.' And then you've got to start over."

For filmmaker Paul Lamont, many hours working on a story can turn into months and even years in pursuit of that Maestro Concept story-planning notion of being able to summarize a story in 30 words or fewer. In filmmaking that summary is often the nut graph in a one-pager called "a treatment."

FIGURE 1.2.2   Bill Horner III wore many hats at the Chatham News + Record in North Carolina: publisher, editor-in-chief and lead columnist. He is now executive editor of CityView in Fayetteville, North Carolina.

(Photo courtesy of Bill Horner III)

"The thing about documentary is that it's a very fluid form of filmmaking," Lamont said, "because you really don't know what the story is before you start talking to people and learning the story from the inside out, and then trying to piece the puzzle together as you go along."

The "digital-first" approach to newspapering runs the risk of changing Writing + Editing into Publish Quick, then Edit, says Amy Kuebelbeck, a copy desk chief for the Star Tribune in Minneapolis. While acknowledging that breaking news sometimes doesn't allow time for a careful copy edit, she stresses the general need for stories to be copy edited first. "Online errors are embarrassing for the reporter, and they damage the credibility and reputation of the news organization," she said. "Sure, you can always go back and fix mistakes and republish, but readers aren't going to come back to re-read a story after it's been cleaned up. You get one chance at readers' eyeballs."

At the other end of the editing spectrum we find Solveig Rennan, a production assistant for public television in Washington, D.C. For a national news show, such as the "PBS NewsHour," editing is still "a pretty rigorous process," she said.

"The coordinating producer writes, the line producer edits, the executive producer edits, and then the anchor edits," she said, and all that is for a 30-second headline segment to begin the news program.

As audience growth manager for Sahan Journal, Samantha HoangLong works in a nonprofit digital newsroom so small, "we don't really have a line for a copy editor."

The journal, founded in 2019, sees its target reader as a person from an immigrant or minority community. The newsroom hires freelance editors to supplement work by an editorial director and a managing editor.

It's a whole new experience for HoangLong compared with her work on the digital team of a network-affiliated TV station in the Twin Cities.

"I didn't have an editor," she said. "What would happen is I would just write up the story and post it, or I would maybe have my co-worker look over it like briefly. But they wouldn't do a deep dive and look at it to see if it's a well-written story."

That's why, as you'll see particularly in **chapters 1.3 and 1.4**, we have written a book to help both writers and editors. Or as we say: "The world will revolve more smoothly … when The Good Writer assumes the role of The Good Editor, too."

Core Principle No. 2: Know Your Deadline

The word "deadline" conjures up a drop-dead time when a story or project must be finished. For Simeon Lancaster, associate producer and editor for the Under-Told Stories Project, most deadlines are not hard but soft.

"Like we say we're going to deliver this (to PBS) by the end of the month," Lancaster said. "And then, even once we do have it in, it's not unusual for a story to sit on the shelf for a week before it gets broadcast because it's not hard, hard news."

For Elena Neuzil, the letters editor for the Star Tribune in Minneapolis, the word "deadline" might also mean "deadlines," a series of waypoints on the road to a finished product.

Neuzil plans her day by the clock. The first half of her day involves sifting through her email inbox for candidates for the letters column.

"I edit them," she said. "I have to design them on the page, make sure it's the right length to fit, write little headlines for the letters."

Longer submissions went to Scott Gillespie, the editorial page editor and Neuzil's boss, since retired. By 2 or 3 in the afternoon, Neuzil is ready to do the second edit on staff-written editorials.

"There's a deadline—that between you and me is not often met—of the editorial being ready by 2 in the afternoon," she said.

Her last task is to lay out the editorial page using InDesign before signing off at 6 p.m. when the editorial page "goes live" on the internet. The first print deadline for the outstate edition: 9 p.m. for color pages that require more processing time and 9:45 p.m. for black-and-white pages. For the metro edition, the deadlines are 10:45 p.m. for color, 11 p.m. for black-and-white. Sports pages go to press a bit later. The deadlines are about 90 minutes earlier for the massive Sunday paper.

FIGURE 1.2.3. As letters editor for the Star Tribune of Minneapolis, Elena Neuzil faces a series of deadlines throughout her workday.
(Photo courtesy of Elena Neuzil)

For Kuebelbeck, those deadlines are her hard stops. Even before she begins the evening shift, stories will be posted online by reporters and their team leaders, whose deadline is ASAP.

For Horner at the weekly News + Record, deadlines were much different. Off-site presses started to roll at 6 p.m. each Tuesday, and papers were mailed to subscribers on Wednesday for Thursday delivery.

An email newsletter, the Chatham Brew, was sent Mondays, Wednesdays and Fridays, either previewing or promoting content, which could be digested along with a cup of the paper's special coffee blend, also named the Chatham Brew. On Saturday, The Chatham Scorecard newsletter got posted by the sports editor.

The copy deadline was technically 11 o'clock on Tuesday morning. "The last thing you want to do is have all your stories come in 11 o'clock on Tuesday," Horner said. So he tried to work on the production flow to get stories in and done so he had time to read them.

The two reporters and the sports editor wrote three or four stories a week, so sometimes Horner was dealing with 20 stories, ranging from short items to 1,500-word features.

"As an editor, if I've got 15 minutes to read a story on the day of publication versus getting it two or three days in advance, where I have a chance to really take some time with it," Horner said, "it really makes a difference in story presentation."

For Rennan at PBS, deadlines meet an unbreakable wall. When airtime rolls around, the show must go on. That would be 7 p.m. ET, earlier on weekends.

For filmmaker Lamont, it's a different story about deadlines.

"Deadlines are generally fairly fluid because I'm an independent producer," Lamont said, "and even though everything that I've done winds up on PBS, I'm going to PBS after my film is done. So I'm not under any strict deadlines."

However, deadlines are tied to "deliverables," such as a "tech check" to make sure the film is broadcast quality, as well as 10-, 20- and 30-second promos and closed captioning. If the film is going to DVD, extra features must be provided in advance. Advance deadlines can range from 8 to 16 weeks before release.

The core principle still holds—know your deadline—but it's not as simple as it sounds.

Core Principle No. 3: When in Doubt, Seek Help

Neuzil faces the unique challenge of editing the work of complete strangers. The further away an editor is from a writer, the more likely something bad can happen. Recall this line from **Chapter 1.1**:

> *The most common mistake editors make is to change something unclear to make it clearly wrong.*

"Being an editor, sometimes you can think that you understand something, and accidentally edit it in a way that makes it confusing or makes it not what they meant," Neuzil said. "It's only happened to me a couple of times, and then you have to deal with the person, and it's my fault."

She calls fact-checking a "delicate dance." One of her favorite letters came from a man living in Golden Valley, Minnesota, who had been involved in a racial profiling incident in the 1960s with the Golden Valley Police. Something wonderful happened, he wrote—the mayor came to his house and officially apologized for his treatment.

Quick quiz: What do you need to do as an editor?

Right, call the mayor's office to confirm that really happened. It did happen, so Neuzil happily published the letter.

Not all exchanges end happily, however. In her job Neuzil is walking a tightrope.

"I try to avoid people being angry because they are upset with how I edit their letter," Neuzil said. "That means that I've slightly failed, because I really try to contact people if I'm confused about something."

Horner used to enjoy sitting face-to-face with reporters when editing their stories. Now he often works Zoom-to-Zoom. Rather than just fixing things, he asks questions like: "Yeah, what were you thinking? Why did you use this word? Why did you put this here?"

"I like to ask some questions," Horner said, "to get them thinking about their process because I think that's part of the training that a reporter needs to get better."

Lamont has worked with the same editor, Chris Bové, for more than 20 years.

"Sometimes we hit perfectly," Lamont said. "Other times, we're kind of at loggerheads. He's saying, 'No, you've got to do it this way, because ...' and I really respect his opinion."

As we said in **Chapter 1.1**: Writing is best when it's a collaboration between writers and editors.

Core Principle No. 4: Edit in Sweeps

Every editor, especially those who grew up working fast on newspaper copy desks, develops a personal editing strategy.

Digital team copy editor Bernadette Kinlaw edits in sweeps. On the first sweep, she checks the little things like style and commas, then, "I'll double-check names, any proper nouns. I'll check online to make sure the spelling is correct. Then probably the third time or so, I'll just read it as a story and see what doesn't sound right, what questions pop up."

"I'm still in the newspaper habit of editing fast," Kinlaw said. "I have started working at places where you don't have to be that fast," such

FIGURE 1.2.4   Bernadette Kinlaw has had to break the newspaper habit of racing through copy to beat a deadline. "You know you're working for a good company when they give you the time to edit," she said.
(Photo courtesy of Bernadette Kinlaw)

as the Southern Poverty Law Center. "You know you're working for a good company when they give you the time to edit what you have to edit."

Freelance copy editing can be high-pressure work, she said.

"I have worked for a company—I got the job online—where they wanted me to read a 15-inch story in three minutes. And catch every mistake. And if you don't read it in three minutes and you don't catch every mistake, you get dinged for it."

At the Under-Told Stories Project, Simeon Lancaster takes the first crack at the script, then several layers of editing begin before any video is matched to the script.

"After we're back in from the field shooting something and ingest all the footage, we go over all the footage, do all the transcriptions, look for quotes that really jump out and key moments in the video," Lancaster said. "We take those things and weave a script around those."

Lancaster passes the script to correspondent Fred de Sam Lazaro. From there, the script is subject to several sweeps, but not all by the same person.

It goes next to a first editor at "PBS NewsHour," who is "more of a big-picture kind of editor, like is the concept working? Is the theme working? Am I following the story?" Lancaster said.

A second PBS editor focuses on the nitty-gritty. Once the script is approved, only then do Lancaster and de Sam Lazaro begin on the video treatment. Storytelling, and editing, is a team effort at PBS.

As we advised in **Chapter 1.1**, the reason to edit in sweeps is that you can't think big and small at the same time, or something will fall through the cracks.

Core Principle No. 5: Know Which Stylebook

In **Chapter 1.1** we reported on the duel between the Associated Press Stylebook and the Chicago Manual of Style over the Oxford comma.

In this corner, we have charter members of the AP fight club: Bill Horner III, Bernadette Kinlaw, Amy Kuebelbeck and Elena Neuzil. Notice: no comma before the *and* in a simple series. Both stylebooks have online versions for quick searches.

"I will never go back to the print AP stylebooks again," Kinlaw said. "I have the online account. I can just search for things, by word, and it's perfect."

Local style is an escape hatch from any stylebook's rules, and at the Southern Poverty Law Center, Kinlaw sees a lot of exceptions.

"We use AP, thankfully, because that's what I know," she said, "but we also do have a decent-sized local stylebook that has variations from the

A Story's Trip to Publication

Amy Kuebelbeck describes the copy flow at the Star Tribune newspaper:

- Reporters write using the online content management system (CMS).
- Team leaders edit in the CMS and publish online.
- A rim editor copy edits the story, writes headlines and cutlines, then republishes online.
- The story moves to the print side for layout, which is done using InDesign.
- A rim editor, typically the same person who already handled the story for online, does further copy editing and processing using InCopy: headlines, cutlines and trimming to fit the "news hole," or the available space on pages around advertising.
- The "slot" reads the story and its accompanying elements, especially headlines. The slot is the person on the copy desk who gives the story one last read before printing.
- Last comes proofreading the finished pages, formerly done on hard copy but now using PDFs via Slack.

After more than two years of working almost entirely remotely, some copy editors began returning to the office, Kuebelbeck said, at least occasionally. "Even if all of us returned to the newsroom, I think proofing PDFs in Slack is superior," she said. "Especially for A1, it allows multiple copy editors to read a page at the same time on deadline, and we often have quick conversations in the Slack thread about something that caught someone's eye. It's better for transparency, too."

AP Stylebook. Like we wouldn't use 'slave.' We'd use 'enslaved person' because we would want to humanize people.

"We don't use 'prisoner.' We say 'incarcerated person' to add humanity and not put people into a category like that. Same with disabled people."

AP style says, "Both 'people with disabilities' and 'disabled people' are acceptable terms" (AP 84–85).

Like many journalism school graduates, Simeon Lancaster had AP style pounded into his head. Now that he works as producer and editor for the Under-Told Stories Project for PBS, it's less of a priority.

"Of course we still follow the stylebook for titles and all these kinds of things," he said, "but it just doesn't seem like it comes up as much as I thought it would, issues of style.

"Why is that exactly? Mostly because we don't have text articles. Things are written more to voice and ear."

Core Principle No. 6: Find the Simple Solution

What's simple and what's complex has a lot do with your target reader. Sometimes an editor seeking simplicity can be made to feel like a simpleton. That was the challenge for Kinlaw when she worked as an online editor for Yes! magazine.

The "ezine" describes itself this way: "Our explanatory journalism analyzes societal problems in terms of their root causes and explores opportunities for systemic, structural change" (About YES! 2021, October 12).

The magazine's authors write at an almost academic level, as in this sentence: "Both individual and collective subjugation are important pieces of this concept: The colonization of land is interconnected to the hierarchies placed on our bodies to maintain capitalism" (Froio, 2022).

"The first few times, I would say, 'I don't understand what this means,'" Kinlaw said about raising questions with staff members. "And I would hear, 'Oh, everyone who reads this magazine knows what that means.'"

FIGURE 1.2.5   Simeon Lancaster spends much time in the field, but once the video is shot for the Under-Told Stories Project, the real work of editing begins.

(Photo courtesy of Simeon Lancaster)

When a documentary moves into complex territory, the editor needs to decide how best to deliver the information—through sound bites or narration.

"My belief was always that your interview subjects don't necessarily need to give you that technical information that can be put into a voice-over," Paul Lamont said.

For Simeon Lancaster, simplicity for PBS means appealing to a mass audience.

"Short sentences, fewer syllables, and let the video do more talking than you do," Lancaster said. "It almost makes my job easier, too. It's just like don't try to write too much. Don't try to say too much."

Core Principle No. 7: Think "Just One More Thing"

Times change and so does the meaning of "B.C." for old-time editors—Before COVID-19. That's when page proofs would be printed off in newspaper newsrooms so those on the copy desk could take one more pass at the stories.

"First off" copies would come up to the newsroom, and everyone would read as much as possible before working on the next edition.

At the Star Tribune, before remote work, each page was printed full-size and marked up by hand by a single editor, and final changes were made by a page designer in InDesign. With the advent of remote work, PDFs of each page are sent to a Slack channel, and copy editors go back into online and print stories to fix any stragglers.

Lancaster knows that after PBS approves a script, the work has just begun at the Under-Told Stories Project.

"Once the script is approved, we do the video treatment," Lancaster said. "Probably the first two edits, we review and revise internally before we send it to 'PBS NewsHour.' And that's where we catch so many things, because as good as a script is, until it's on video, we can't see how it looks and how the rhythm, the pacing are and everything."

Kinlaw says catching final-proof mistakes has boosted her career.

"My role has expanded because a lot of times the project is about to come out, and I'll give it one final read, even though I wasn't asked to," Kinlaw said. "I'll find numerous mistakes."

Core Principle No. 8: Twist a Cliche

Avoiding cliches takes discipline, all the more so for the headline writer. The clever turn of a phrase in a headline is highly prized in newsrooms.

Star Tribune letters start with a label headline, then a subhead. Here are a couple of Elena Neuzil's gems:

VIRUS IN THE NAVY

His voyage closed and done

For a letter about USS Theodore Roosevelt Capt. Brett Crozier being relieved of his command for taking measures to stop the spread of COVID-19.

STATES

Desperate times, disparate measures

For a letter protesting the practice of states bidding against each other for vital resources to treat COVID-19.

"I try not to be overly clever on letters headlines unless I know I've really got a good one," Neuzil said. "My priority is to distill the letter writer's argument into one short phrase that accurately describes what they're saying, and sometimes, getting too clever can wander away from the writer's meaning."

She says the real trick is trying to express someone else's opinion and not blur it with her own views.

"You really have to step into the letter writer's shoes, and think, What would I want my headline to be if this was my opinion?"

And just like in design, where colors look different next to other colors, she says it's important to take a step back and see a larger picture.

"I also consider the headline in the context of the entire package: Are there too many question or label-style headlines? If so, I'll adjust."

Core Principle No. 9: Deliver a One-Two Punch: Picture + Words

Solveig Rennan has one main responsibility in her job with PBS: Find compelling video and photos to go with the news of the day.

"The bulk of my job is finding and ingesting and organizing videos from AP and Reuters and elsewhere for stories," Rennan said. "A producer will write a script, and then I'll have to cover it with video."

FIGURE 1.2.6   In choosing video for "PBS NewsHour Weekend," Solveig Rennan seeks a balance between compelling images and those that seem exploitive.

(Photo courtesy of Solveig Rennan)

She looks for images and sound bites that pack emotion.

"But in some cases, especially when we're doing stories about like a school shooting or something like that, a video that's a camera shoved into a crying person's face can seem kind of invasive," she said. "So there's a balance between finding something that's compelling but not exploitive."

The all-important opening shot calls for "the best footage we have," Simeon Lancaster said of his PBS segments for the Under-Told Stories Project, whose executive director is Fred de Sam Lazaro.

"Fred's saying things like don't write what you're seeing," Lancaster said. "Let the pictures stand for themselves and write something complementary to them."

That opening frame also must advance the story. Lancaster remembered a story about supplying water to families on the Navajo reservation stretching across parts of Arizona, New Mexico and Utah ("How off-grid residents are getting running water," 2018, June 21).

"We were torn between beautiful vistas or this woman with a water hose pouring into empty pickle jars at these poor houses," he said. "We ended up going with one shot of her truck with a beautiful vista, and then straight into the very compelling tight shot of water hose blasting out and kids trying to catch water from it."

FIGURE 1.2.7   Samantha HoangLong faces the challenge of engaging a diverse audience at Sahan Journal.

(Sam Luloff, photo courtesy of Samantha HoangLong)

Bernadette Kinlaw said she had to be made aware of just how important it is to have an image with a social media post.

"It makes such a difference for how many people will look at it, how many people will really click on it, whatever," Kinlaw said. "It's really, really important to have an image."

The Southern Poverty Law Center has a creative department in charge of providing photos and videos. The department makes sure an image is appropriate in line with its mission as "a catalyst for racial justice in the South and beyond."

As Kinlaw said about SPLC: "Like we never ever will post on anything with the Confederate flag."

Core Principle No. 10: Let People See Themselves

A good publication, video or film acts like a mirror so the people can see themselves. A lot of editing decisions for a media outlet become easier when there's a clear target reader, listener or viewer. That's not always so easy.

For HoangLong, the challenge of finding a target reader is complicated by the reality that the people served by Sahan Journal come from immigrant communities that speak many languages, primarily Hmong, Somali and Spanish.

Adding to the challenge were results from focus group "listening sessions" revealing that Somali and Hmong mainly, but also Spanish-speaking people, prefer to receive news through video or audio.

"And so now we're looking into expanding how we can get them their news in those multimedia ways over reading news," HoangLong said.

As a way to segment the audience and tailor more news and information, the journal responded by launching native-language newsletters for Somalis (Sahan Journal, 2022, December 22) and Afghani (Sahan Journal, 2023, January 6).

The newsletters deal with many "very basic topics," HoangLong said. "But they are resources that people need. So what is Halloween? And why are people dressing up? Something simple like that."

Bill Horner III is still trying to solve the mystery of which story will really resonate with his North Carolina readers.

"There are stories that we do that we just pour our heart and soul into, and it's like, 'This is really going to score well with readers.' And it doesn't. And then there are stories, where we say, 'Okay, yeah, we'll put this on the inside page,' and then it resonates."

Paul Lamont sees victory when one of his documentaries can spur curiosity and stimulate conversation.

"You want them to go out and say, 'I want to find out more about this,'" Lamont said. "And I've always said if a film can create discussion, I can ask for no more."

Elena Neuzil tries to reflect the Star Tribune's readership in how she selects letters.

"On some other issue, say, if there's like an 80–20 split, I'm not going to just pick one letter on each side. It's not exact, but I might pick two anti and one pro or something, just to try to imply that it's not an even split on a given issue."

Core Principle No. 11: Whatever You Do, Be Loyal to Truth

Objectivity, Paul Lamont said, is "sometimes difficult to maintain because, as a filmmaker, you have a certain feeling about a film. That's why you're doing it."

His documentary "Lake of Betrayal" (2017) tells the story of the Kinzua Dam, built in 1965 on the Allegheny River in Pennsylvania. The 27-mile reservoir behind the dam flooded large areas of the Seneca Indians' ancestral lands. The Seneca were forced to leave in violation of a treaty that dated to 1794.

"I feel that the Seneca were wronged," Lamont said. "But I have to bring all sides into this conversation. We had to talk to the Army Corps of Engineers, find out what their point of view was on this. Also you're looking at something that took place 50 years ago. So there is that historical context that goes with it as opposed to today."

Lamont says his longtime editor, Chris Bové, takes a different approach: "He doesn't want to know anything about the subject prior to him getting the footage and getting the script. … He wants to have that, call it *tabula rasa,* if you will. You know, that blank slate that he can look at it very objectively, then not be overly invested in the story. He can look at it objectively as an editor."

The concepts of truth and objectivity take on different meanings for advocacy organizations like the Southern Poverty Law Center. "We do have a very distinct separation of stories," Kinlaw said.

She explained that "C3" stories focus on advocacy, "but it's more about telling people what's going on," and "C4" stories are a call to action from something that operates more like a political action committee, or PAC.

"If you're going to have any sort of promotion, like endorsement of candidates and things like that, you would never put that in C3. That's always C4," Kinlaw said. "So we always have to keep those separate; otherwise, you get in huge trouble."

Core Principle No. 12: Tie the Beginning and End Together

Paul Lamont's documentary "The Songpoet" (2021) runs 1 hour, 53 minutes.

HOW IT STARTS

A friend of singer-songwriter Eric Andersen, looking at some of Andersen's old photos and home movies, talks about Andersen as a person. Then as one of Andersen's songs plays, the opening credits appear over film of rails rolling behind a train, processed with a slightly sepia tone.

HOW IT ENDS

In the last minute of the film as Andersen's music again plays under narration, we see him sitting on a train, followed by another shot of rails receding in the frame done in

FIGURE 1.2.8   Paul Lamont's film "The Songpoet" begins with credits appearing over sepia-toned railroad tracks (top). To echo the beginning, Lamont uses a picture of Eric Andersen on a train (middle) at the end, then cuts to rail tracks in the same sepia tone (bottom).

(Top and bottom courtesy of Getty Images, the Prelinger Collection. Middle courtesy of Toward Castle Films)

the same color tone as the opening. The final shot is of Andersen completing his song and saying, "Finis."

We can't illustrate this last core principle any better than that.

Job-Hunting Advice: Now It's About You!

We hope you now have a newfound interest in editing and will possibly consider it as a career choice. The world needs more good editors. Some of our professionals took a moment to reflect on the start of their careers and offered some advice for you. Let's get started on your job hunt!

TIP NO. 1: GET AN INTERNSHIP OR JOIN COLLEGE STUDENT MEDIA

The younger editors in this chapter—Samantha HoangLong, Simeon Lancaster, Elena Neuzil and Solveig Rennan—all worked at TommieMedia.com, the online student news organization at the University of St. Thomas.

As an online-only news outlet, TommieMedia.com allows students to practice editing in a variety of media: text, photo, video and audio.

"One thing I'm really grateful for is that St. Thomas gave me a bunch of multimedia skills," HoangLong said, "so I can jump in and do a video or edit a video for a story. Those can be really nice assets, exploring different ways of presenting the story. Different ways of engaging with stories is really important."

HoangLong, Lancaster and Rennan all were interns for a semester for Fred de Sam Lazaro at the Under-Told Stories Project. Neuzil interned at the Star Tribune before she was hired full time. Those internships gave them valuable connections for future jobs.

TIP NO. 2: YOU'RE BETTER THAN YOU MIGHT THINK

It's only natural that beginners will feel insecure about their skills. But by getting internships they can find themselves in professional settings and come to the same conclusion as Lancaster: "I'm like, hey? I'm not so bad."

One of the core principles of cinematography that Lancaster learned in school was about "the nose axis," an invisible line between two subjects connecting their noses, also known as the axis of action or the 180-degree rule.

Cinematographers know that crossing this line breaks the continuity of a scene, but it happens sometimes when shooting interviews.

"Half the time it's because they want to get the reverse shot, but oh, gosh! That window is so bright! And then they're just like, Oh, I'll just move over here, and that bright window makes them forget about the axis."

Yes, professionals do make mistakes, just like students. By being on the job in the real world, you can make a difference.

"If I'm there," Lancaster said, "I'll say, shift the chairs slightly, or something like that."

TIP NO. 3: READ GOOD WRITING

Almost everyone Bill Horner III hired at the News + Record was a brand-new graduate of the Hussman School of Journalism and Media at the University of North Carolina-Chapel Hill.

"I've been very, very fortunate," Horner said, because they were good reporters and strong writers. But one thing was missing: They didn't read enough good writing.

He knows they read Twitter (now X) and TikTok, just not the New York Times or the Wall Street Journal. Horner has subscribed to The New Yorker magazine for 40 years.

"If you're not reading," Horner said, "if you're not spending time reading a lot of really good writing, how are you going to learn?"

TIP NO. 4: NETWORKING IS VITAL

Bernadette Kinlaw has one bit of advice for those seeking to work as editors:

"You will find a job through word of mouth," she said. "Those are the best jobs. Word of mouth is so important to finding a job."

After graduating from Northwestern University's Medill School of Journalism in 1988, she took the traditional path of joining the copy desk at The Virginian-Pilot newspaper in Norfolk, Virginia, where she worked for 25 years. When the newspaper went into economic decline along with many others, Kinlaw took a buyout in part to care for her husband, who was ill.

A person she worked with at The Virginian-Pilot had moved on to WABE, the NPR station in Atlanta.

"When I was a freelancer, they had just lost an editor," Kinlaw said. "I said do you want me to fill in for a few weeks? I ended up working quite a while for them. And then the woman who was our boss there ended up working at SPLC. And that's how I got this job. It's like a circuitous route."

May you have the same luck on your job hunt! Stay tuned as our next two chapters tell the story of what it takes to be The Good Editor and The Good Writer.

HOMEWORK

Assignment No. 1

Let's read. Go to the web page announcing the 2024 winners of the American Society of Magazine Editors awards (American Society of Magazine Editors, n.d.). Home in on the journalistic stories and save the fiction and the personal memoirs for later. Read a piece carefully. What core principles do you see in the story? Does anything surprise you? Look for errors. Do you see any? Copy and paste examples into a new document for future discussion.

Assignment No. 2

Let's watch. Go to the Under-Told Stories Project webpage (www.undertold-stories.org) and watch a segment. Or visit the "PBS NewsHour" online (https://www.pbs.org/newshour) and dive into one of the longer pieces. Again, look for examples of the core principles, surprises, errors. Jot down those examples for discussion.

Assignment No. 3

Let's hunt. Go to indeed.com. In the "Job title" box, type in "editor." Then indicate the name of your state. You should see a substantial list of job offerings. What types of companies are hiring editors? Make a list of four or five that surprise you. Do you see any news organizations? Jot down those, too. How would you rate the availability of editing jobs? Explain.

REFERENCES

About YES! (2021, October 12). *YES! magazine.* https://www.yesmagazine.org/about

American Society of Magazine Editors. (n.d.). ASME announces winners of 2024 national magazine awards. https://asme.memberclicks.net/american-society-of-magazine-editors-announces-national-magazine-awards-2024-winners

Froio, N. (2022, November 21). Transforming ourselves to transform the world. *YES! magazine.* https://www.yesmagazine.org/issue/bodies/2022/11/21/transforming-ourselves-to-transform-the-world

FURTHER READING

American Psychological Association (2019). *Publication manual of the American Psychological Association, 7th edition.* (APA).

Associated Press. (2022). *The Associated Press stylebook: 2022–2024* (56th ed.). Basic Books.

Jacques, A. (2017). House of style: Q-and-A with the *AP stylebook*'s editor. Public Relations Society of America. https://www.prsa.org/article/q-and-a-with-the-ap-stylebook-s-editor

Ryan, B. (2021, March 22). The good, the bad and the ugly as a N.C. weekly seeks sustainability: Kentucky professor Buck Ryan describes his "participatory case study" with the *Chatham News + Record*. Medill Local News Initiative. https://localnewsinitiative.northwestern.edu/posts/2021/03/22/buck-ryan/

Sahan Journal. (2022, December 22). *Tani Waa Su'aashayda.* https://sahanjournal.com/somali-newsletter-minnesota-tani-waa-suaashayda/

Sahan Journal. (2023, January 6). *New Home newsletter, No. 10.* https://sahanjournal.com/wp-content/uploads/2023/01/January-6-newsletter-.pdf

Star Tribune (2020, April 4). Readers write: Library closures, virus in the Navy, hazardous-duty pay, weddings, state strategies. https://www.startribune.com/readers-write-library-closures-virus-in-the-navy-hazardous-duty-pay-weddings-state-strategies/569365752/

Star Tribune (2022, December 27). Readers write: Nicollet Mall, Trump's taxes, congressional capabilities, apologies, tree planting, climate legislation, storm prep. https://www.startribune.com/readers-write-nicollet-mall-trump-taxes-congress-apologies-trees-climate-legislation-storm-prep/600238813/

University of Chicago Press Editorial Staff. (2017). *The Chicago Manual of Style,* 17th edition. University of Chicago Press. https://www.chicagomanualofstyle.org/home.html

Films, Segments, Stories, Resources
BY PAUL LAMONT

Lake of betrayal (2017). Vision Maker Media. visionmakermedia.org/lake-of-betrayal

The songpoet. (2021). PBS. www.pbs.org/video/the-songpoet-nlfpwh/

Toward Castle Films. www.towardcastlefilms.com/

BY THE UNDER-TOLD STORIES PROJECT

How off-grid residents are getting running water. (2018, June 21). www.undertoldstories.org/2018/06/21/how-off-grid-navajo-residents-are-getting-running-water/

The legal revolution. (2022, December 13). www.undertoldstories.org/2022/12/14/the-legal-revolution/

PHOTOS: The water supply struggle. (2020, February 14). www.undertoldstories.org/2020/02/14/photos-the-water-supply-struggle/

The pipe organ monastery. (2022, November 15). www.undertoldstories.org/2022/11/16/
the-pipe-organ-monastery/

Project ECHO expands health care (2022, November 23). www.undertoldstories.
org/2022/11/28/project-echo-expands-health-care/

THE GOOD EDITOR

KEY POINTS IN THIS CHAPTER

1. The trick to editing is knowing when to speed up and when to slow down. Trust your gut. If you feel something needs your attention, don't talk yourself out of it.

2. Deadlines are for real, but you'll always have enough time to slow down for the killer mistakes. Remember, not all errors carry the same weight.

3. Read enough of an article to get the gist, then step back and ask yourself, "What's it about?" If you have trouble summarizing the point, your reader, listener or viewer will struggle to understand it, too.

4. Never assume.

Profile of the Good Editor

In **Chapter 1.3** we're going to flesh out and dress up some of the Core Principles of Editing that we introduced in **Chapter 1.1**. So if some points sound familiar, that's because we want you to get them down cold.

In **Chapter 1.4** we'll flip the script and look at editing from a writer's perspective. Then in **chapters 1.5 to 1.9**, we'll open the editor's toolbox and help you sharpen your language skills: style, spelling, grammar, punctuation and usage. We'll add some finishing touches in the Appendix, beginning with The Fixtionary, a quick guide to fixing mistakes large and small.

What often surprises us is how unsure many professional writers and editors are about what they're doing. These professionals tend to be governed by a list of do's and don'ts built up through years of experience. If you asked them why they wrote a certain way or made a particular editing change, a common response would be something like, "I was told to do it that way."

The answer to "Who told you?" might range from a high school English teacher to a college professor or some boss. Our favorite response was "My former editor at the Klaxon-Star told me to do it that way, and he's a journalism legend." Unfortunately, what that legendary editor told them was either wrong or incomplete.

In **Chapter 1.1**, when we advised you to edit in sweeps, we classified language mistakes as embarrassing errors. Yes, they are, but misspellings, ungrammatical language and misused words cause deeper problems. They undermine the confidence in a media outlet, just as shoddy workmanship drives away a carpenter's customers.

Studies suggest grammar mistakes can cost you money (Birkett, 2020). In an article with the catchy title "Your Typo Is Costing You 12% Extra on Your Google Ads Spend," writer Shira Stieglitz (2021) outlines two major research findings: Ads with typos can lead to a 70% decrease in clicks, and the "bounce rate" for a website landing page with typos was 85% higher than the clean version. A bounce rate was defined as "the percentage of visitors who leave your website after only looking at a single webpage."

This is nothing new, of course. A study commissioned by the American Society of Newspaper Editors 25 years ago stated that a newspaper's credibility often is undermined by language mistakes. More than one-third of respondents said they see spelling or grammatical mistakes in their newspapers more than once a week, and 21% said they see them nearly every day. With editing staffs being cut to the bone, those errors have only increased.

As companions to our language skills chapters, we'll offer Active Learning workouts to help you build your confidence. We'll ask you to solve problems, then compare your work with how we would do it. Step by step, we aspire to turn you into a good editor. Good editors have a philosophy, a rationale, an understanding of key concepts and, above all, an editing strategy.

A Philosophy: Get Me Hippocrates on the Horn!

It's not that editors take an oath like some physicians, but they should have a guiding philosophy. In **Chapter 1.1** we advised you to edit like a surgeon, not a butcher. Put another way, "*Primum non nocere,*" the Latin translation for "First, do no harm" from the original Greek, à la Hippocrates in his classic work "Of the Epidemics" (Greek medicine, n.d.).

There is a line from one translation of the Hippocratic Oath, however, that's a good "nut graph" for an editor's philosophy. Just replace "patients" with "readers":

> *"I will follow that system of regimen which, according to my ability and judgment, I consider for the benefit of my patients, and abstain from whatever is deleterious and mischievous."*

Good editors keep in mind three ideals:

- **Make the simplest fix possible.** Some editors see a one-word mistake and use it as an excuse to rewrite a sentence. Don't be like that.
- **For close calls, let the writer's words stand.** The editor might not like the sound of what is written, but the writer prevails in matters of taste and word choice.
- **When in doubt, seek help by asking questions.** Yes, you can look up certain details, but the best source is the writer. It's better to ask questions than jump to wrong conclusions.

A Rationale: Reasons to Change Copy

A writer asks, "Why did you change that?" Good editors have a valid reason for every change they make in a story, or what we call "copy." Editing is an art, not a science. Nonetheless, it's always nice to be able to cite research for reasons to change copy.

Many of today's rules for the way journalists write for print and broadcast date to research done by Rudolf Flesch in the 1940s and adopted by the Associated Press. A "Flesch test" involved a readability formula to assess a score for "reading ease" and "human interest" that Flesch included and updated in several books, including "The Art of Readable Writing" (Flesch, 1949).

The formula's steps include figuring average sentence length (ideally 20 words or so), calculating the number of syllables per 100 words (fewer the better) and counting the number of "personal words" (pronouns, identifiers like "father" and "sister" and words like "people" and "folks").

These ideas endure, even with some results duplicated in later studies by the American Press Institute and others (Siteimprove, 2022). You'll see their influence in what we believe are good reasons to change copy. Some believe the ABCs of Editing are focusing on accuracy, brevity and clarity. For sure, but we'll add three more for good measure. Here goes:

Accuracy. This is the No. 1 reason for changing copy. It starts with correcting "killer mistakes," usually errors of fact and misspelled names. Accuracy extends to spelling and grammar. Writers appreciate changes that save them from embarrassment.

Brevity. Long, complex sentences are difficult to read and understand. Yes, an optimum average sentence length for readability may be 20 words, but good writers use a pleasing mix of long and short sentences to arrive at that average.

Clarity. If the editor doesn't understand something, the reader won't either. Problems of clarity often require editors to ask reporters what they mean. Never assume—ask. As the crusty city editor once wrote to the cub reporter: "Never 'assume,' or you'll make an 'ass' out of 'u' and 'me.'" When editors assume, they tend to "fix" something that is unclear to make it clearly wrong.

Coherence. For a story to hang together, it must have smooth transitions. They may be as simple as finding the right conjunction or phrase ("however," "but," "on the other hand") or using quotes or sound bites logically. In extreme cases, shifting the order of paragraphs or video segments might be needed. "A bad cut will take your audience out of the experience faster than just about anything," filmmaker Noam Kroll says (Kroll, n.d.).

Consistency. If a writer talks about five people and names only four, there's a consistency problem. Figures must add up. Consistency also has to do with style. There are many stylebook rules, including those about using figures, capitalization, punctuation and abbreviations. But even stylebooks like the Chicago Manual of Style or the Associated Press Stylebook can't cover everything. Local style sheets address homegrown matters unique to a publication, website or broadcast station. Follow those style guides to achieve consistency.

Simplicity. Multisyllabic words are difficult to read and understand. Military, government and academic experts are fond of using them, but police may be most notorious. Beware the police report about a chokehold described as an assault "impeding breath circulation." Here's our rule: Use the short word over the long word when no meaning is lost. Consider "start" rather than "initiate," "try" rather than "endeavor" and "trouble" rather than "inconvenience." How about "cuts" rather than "lacerations," "bruises" rather than "contusions" and "scrapes" rather than "abrasions"?

The simpler, the better.

An Understanding of Key Concepts

1. REWRITING VS. EDITING

As soon as editors abandon the ideal of making the simple fix and begin to rewrite a story, they risk changing the original meaning and introducing errors.

Writers care about what they do and take pride in their writing. Respect them and they'll respect you as an editor. Ask before you rewrite.

This is especially true for rewriting a story's first line, what journalists call "the lede," or the "nut graph" that follows an anecdotal opening. A nut graph, like a lede, serves two purposes: It summarizes a story's point and sets up the organization for the rest of the writing.

Typically editors will want to "punch up" the lede or nut graph. That's done best in consultation with the writer in a question-driven way described next.

2. QUESTIONS DRIVE THE PROCESS

Enter the editing process with an active mind. After you've gotten the gist of an article, test yourself by trying to answer three questions: 1. What's the story about? 2. Why should I care? 3. What's the most interesting part of the story? The notion that questions drive the design of a story is central to a story planning process called the Maestro Concept (Ryan, 1993).

If you have trouble answering the first question, your reader, listener or viewer will struggle to understand the point, too. Don't skip this step and, if necessary, put the question gingerly to the writer: "How would you summarize your story in 30 words or so?" You can explain you're working on the headline and want to hit the right notes.

In assembling the answer, adopt Al Tompkins' fill-in-the-blank approach by identifying WHO-DID-WHAT. Consider the difference between starting the sentence with "A baby formula shortage" and "A mother with infant triplets." The first phrase is the WHAT and the second one is the WHO.

A variation of the second question can be, "Now I think somebody would really care to read this story because (insert your thought). Does that sound right to you?"

The answer to "Why should I care?" depends on the target reader, listener or viewer. It ranges from "I'm a mother in the same sinking boat" to "Gee, I'm so sorry. I would like to help that mother who's short on baby formula."

People will not stop on a story unless they care about it. A good writer makes them care, and if the reason is not clear, then the editor helps to sharpen the message.

As you are clarifying the answers to the first two questions, you are focusing the lede or nut graph and creating the first draft of the headline, title or promo.

The answer to the third question inspires a visual to package with the headline to create a one-two punch. Identifying "the most interesting part" is a way to hook readers with a visual that gets them to stop and look. If they don't do that, they'll never read and understand.

3. INTERPERSONAL EDITING SKILLS

It's easier to "edit in the air" than to edit words in print. That's because once a writer has invested a lot of time, energy and ego into a piece, editing changes become more painful.

Ideally an assignment editor will spend time talking with a writer up front about a story's focus. That's not always the case, and sometimes more than one editor gets involved.

After writers file their copy and you get the chance to talk directly with them, take the following steps:

a.   **Start with a compliment**

Surely the story has something you like. Start with mentioning that.

Then ask, "How are you feeling about the piece?"

It's better for the writer to suggest shortcomings than for you to weigh in first. Listen to the writer's areas of concern, then address them one by one. Maybe you can put the writer's mind at ease by saying something like, "No, I think you're good there."

b.   **Begin big**

When the writer asks for your suggestions, begin with something big and obvious. Don't let the conversation get lost over something small and questionable.

c.   **Frame advice with questions, sometimes leading ones**

Ask, "What would you think if we say this...?" or "Let's break out the list of possible solutions to the baby formula shortage in a sidebar graphic, OK?"

d.   **Never offer a feeling without a suggestion**

The fastest way to frustrate a writer is to say something like, "I don't feel good about this part," then not offer a suggested change. Those half-thoughts just waste time and add anxiety.

An Editing Strategy for Beginners

Time is short, but you'll always have enough time to catch the BIG MISTAKES. The idea that errors don't carry the same weight zips us back to **Chapter 1.1: Core Principle No. 4: Edit in Sweeps.** Remember, you can't think big and small at the same time, or mistakes will fall through the cracks. You need an editing strategy, something that begins with editing in sweeps, as time allows.

Our three-sweep approach is the basis for an editing strategy that feels more like training wheels for professionals on deadline. "Three sweeps?" they say, "I'm lucky if I get one." More on that later in **Section 2**.

For now, here's a refresher on points we made about the three sweeps and more details about the warning signs and the different levels of mistakes: killer, embarrassing and tedious.

First Sweep

We give the BIG MISTAKES a nickname—"killer errors"—because they can kill your publication's credibility or your reputation as a writer or editor. Let us introduce you to the **Seven Flashing Lights** to heed on your first sweep.

1. NAMES AND THEIR FIRST COUSINS, TITLES

Long ago in Western New York, a young man won a college scholarship. The first two words of the "local boy makes good" newspaper story were "Ryan Leland," as if no one could believe the kid's name was Leland Ryan. That hurt. Feel the pain.

Every time a name passes your eyes in print, or you're handling a script where a name is to be pronounced, slow down. Sweat every letter and every syllable.

Script writers add help with pronunciation. China's leader is Xi (she, not zee). That's easier than the challenge of pronouncing the name of France's president, Emmanuel Macron. You'll hear ma-COH (very French) or ma-CROH-n (acceptable for Americans). It gets trickier when the French call their palace and gardens Versailles (ver-SIGH) while Kentuckians call their city Versailles (ver-SAILS). Misspell or mispronounce a name and you'll lose credibility.

The pace of editing is knowing when to slow down and when you need to speed up. You can't slow down for everything, but you must for names and titles.

Search online for the capitalized name of a person, place or thing and see if it's spelled multiple ways. That's particularly true if the name came from a different alphabet, such as Arabic, Chinese or Hebrew, and the English version is phonetic.

You have to keep on your toes. The AP Stylebook now spells the prophet's name Muhammad, like the boxing legend Muhammad Ali, after years of preferring Mohammed.

Titles can be equally tricky. Titles change, but old stories on the internet remain the same. You can't always trust what you read online, so a newsroom tradition is for writers to "cq" a name or title, meaning "checked."

An old trick in Journalism 101 is for the professor to hold a press conference with "Mayor John Smith," then open up for questions. The professor waits patiently for a bright student to ask, "How do you spell your name?"

Answer:

J-O-N S-M-Y-T-H

Every name and title present their own flashing light. The sign reads, "Your credibility is at stake."

2. NUMBERS ARE STOP SIGNS, TOO

There's an epidemic of math anxiety among journalists and artists. Their eyes tend to glaze over when they see numbers, or they tend to give the numbers too much credibility. If you're an editor, then you need to do the opposite. Question the numbers and check them out. If it's a phone number, call it. If it's a percentage, do the math to verify it. If a sports story includes statistics, double-check them. To help you gain confidence dealing with numbers, we wrote an entire chapter. In case of emergency, break glass on **Chapter 2.4: Stats, Graphs and Maps**.

3. LOCATIONS, LOCATIONS, LOCATIONS

If a story contains an address that appears unreasonable or if it mentions a neighborhood that doesn't sound right, check it out. It helps an editor to know the community and how it's laid out. Find the locations on a map, whether it's a city or a country.

As Mark Twain once observed, "God made war to teach Americans geography." Know that China is roughly the same size as the United States but with only one time zone compared with our four. Russia, three-fourths larger than the U.S., has 11 time zones. Iran doesn't border Saudi Arabia. British Columbia is in Canada, not anywhere near Colombia in South America.

Closer to home, double-check addresses in a story. Watch those directionals: NEWS. Know that 435 N. Michigan Ave. (old Chicago Tribune Tower) is not 435 S. Michigan Ave. In a Washington address, NW and SW, or NE and SE, can put the same number and street address in different parts of town. Double-check locations.

4. QUOTATIONS—AND YOU CAN QUOTE ME ON THAT

Treat them like numbers: Don't let up, bear down. Feel free to delete stupid ones or paraphrase weirdly wordy ones unless the goal is to characterize the speaker.

Always attend to the attribution, being clear who is saying what after the first break, like so: "I often quote myself," Irish playwright George Bernard Shaw said. "It adds spice to my conversation."

Whether you're editing a newspaper or a magazine article, or a television or radio news script, or a film or documentary, the tendency is to let up when you come upon a quotation, soundbite or close-up interview. It's like somehow those voices speak for themselves—well, not exactly.

Enter quotation editing guideline, Part I: frame it!

How you set up the words of a subject and how you move on are just as important as the words themselves. Legendary TV news anchor Walter Cronkite explained the problem isn't just the misquote, it's the malquote—the exact words but without the proper context.

Now, Part II: Always make sure that the quotation, sound bite or close-up comment advances the story. Watch out for needless repetition.

5. BIAS AND ITS COUSINS, STEREOTYPES

Bias—and the turnoffs it produces—comes in many shapes and forms, so many that the 56th edition of the AP Stylebook added a new chapter on **inclusive storytelling**.

"Inclusive storytelling seeks to truly represent all people around the globe," the stylebook editors say, "giving voice and visibility to those who have been missing or misrepresented in traditional narratives of both history and daily journalism" (AP, 349). They focus on unconscious biases, sensitivity to words and phrases, sources and story ideas, among other points of editing.

Sadly, we saw a rise in anti-Asian bias and rhetoric coincide with the start of the COVID-19 pandemic. Words matter. Rarely a day goes by without a news item about gender and sexual orientation. The AP Stylebook responded in its 56th edition by adding more than 25 new or revised entries, including references to LGBTQ, transgender, nonbinary, gender fluid and gender dysphoria. The AP later added a plus to LGBTQ, but no LGBTQIA+ entry.

What's not so new is political bias and how it can turn off readers, listeners and viewers. In his book "Bias: A CBS Insider Exposes How the Media Distort the News," Bernard Goldberg tells the story of the New Yorker film critic who declared at a cocktail party: "No one I know voted for Nixon." She was referring to 1972 when President Richard Nixon was re-elected, having won 49 of 50 states (Goldberg, 2002).

Goldberg's book about liberal bias observes that not only do journalists lean left but also the news leans to the Northeast, where only 17% of the U.S. population lives.

From an NFL perspective, if you're a fan of the Buffalo Bills, the Cincinnati Bengals or the Seattle Seahawks, you know only two kinds of sports news get major coverage: either the New York Jets, or the New York Giants, are really good or really bad.

As your mother once advised, "Be careful who your friends are," as you may be living in an echo chamber. As Edward R. Murrow once observed, journalism begins when you are quoting someone you totally disagree with.

6. GETTING PLAYED: ALWAYS QUESTION YOUR SOURCES

Scrub the sources and ask, "Who's telling you what for what reason?" Whether the source is selling soap or a political candidate, or is being used to support or debunk something, don't let yourself be used to advance a product or a cause.

That goes for police reports or "intelligence officials" too. The world is littered with "official" reports that don't jibe with what we later discover. Attribution is one thing, truth is another—and it takes a lot of hard work and sharp questioning to get there.

Think of truth as being at least three-dimensional: There's what people are saying (quotable quotes), what's really going on (maybe something very different behind the scenes) and a historical perspective (crime in New York City has never been higher; well, actually it has been).

Good editors are death on anonymous sources, as the chances of getting played and doing harm zoom exponentially. Withholding the identity of a gang crime witness is one thing, as identification would put the person in danger. But allowing someone to make a scurrilous allegation anonymously is just asking for a lawsuit.

And so we wind down BIG MISTAKES with legal matters.

7. GETTING SUED: TRUST BUT VERIFY, AND GET IT IN WRITING

An online multimedia editor for NBC's "Today" show put it this way: "Half my job is getting permissions."

Here's the golden rule: You are responsible for getting written permission to use any material created by a third party. We are living in a rip-off culture, so be careful out there. Protect your own copyrights and be respectful of others' rights, too.

When it comes to libel and slander, there's another golden rule: Any time your story turns negative, stop and double-check your facts and phrasings, and be sure that you have the proper attribution.

Anytime you're dealing with criminal charges, civil cases, accusations or negative comments, you must be accurate and fair to all sides. This can get complicated, so we've written an entire chapter on editing crime stories in **Chapter 2.6.**

Second Sweep

Focus on transitions and embarrassing errors with your second sweep. Transitions are the guideposts that keep a reader, listener or viewer on track, especially in long pieces.

Transitions. They may be words ("likewise" or "however"), phrases ("Meanwhile, back at the ranch"), or subheads ("Second Sweep"). Parallel construction is a handy device, meaning transitions in the same form ("first," then "second," not "secondly").

Oh, that's embarrassing. Dodge those embarrassing errors—grammar, punctuation, spelling—that make retired schoolteachers go bananas.

For us, there are two kinds of people: those who say, "Hi, Buck!" or "Happy Birthday, Mike!" and those who drop the commas in direct address. Careful writers battle autocorrect so they don't confuse "it's" (it is or it has) with "its" and they always watch their pronouns.

If you are a grammar nerd—a good thing!—that can strengthen your editing and tightening, but be careful you don't get sucked down into rewriting. Then you'll get distracted and miss something big.

Speaking of distraction, if you are laying down music under video and layering in "lower thirds," or typography to identify subjects or topics, mute the sound when double-checking that writing. Something about music can make you miss mistakes, even in the credits roll at the end of a production.

Third Sweep

Clean up little things, including matters of style, usage and tightening, on your third sweep. We call these "tedious mistakes." Some of these mistakes will go unnoticed by many readers. It's your supervisor who matters most. Here are some tedious errors:

Style mistake. Unless it's a glaring inconsistency or oddity, many readers won't be bothered by style. But whether you use "%" or spell out "percent" (one word or two), write "10" or "ten," abbreviate "Dept." or not, style mistakes are a big deal to a boss who's memorized your stylebook. A good way to impress that boss is to show your attention to detail, having mastered the stylebook, too.

Usage mistake. Readers aren't always aware of the niceties of standard English usage. Many of these points will go over their heads. For example, say, "The 2024 budget dropped 18% compared with (not "to") last year's budget, though salaries remained the same." Stylebooks not only will cover spelling and grammar points but also will weigh in on usage matters. Take your guidance on them from your stylebook.

Lack of tightening. "Omit needless words!" Although readers can feel uneasy about all those words passing under their eyes, they will read loose writing if the content is interesting enough. The good editor takes pride in omitting needless words, phrases or clauses. For motivation, think of each word as being worth $5. Delete words and save money for your retirement! This concept is consistent with the idiom "Time is money." Readers, listeners and viewers are time-starved and short on attention. Fewer words have more impact.

A Few Closing Thoughts

Don't lose track of the basics. One old hand at editing had a simple rule when scanning a finished page proof: Every sentence must begin with a capital letter and end with punctuation. Sometimes you can get so wrapped up in the editing process that you overlook simple things like that.

Trust your gut. We can't count the times an issue came up early in a project, got ignored for a while, then in the final hours emerged again—it just wouldn't go away. Trust your gut. If something bothers you at a glance, pay attention. It's better to deal with it sooner than later.

The worst mistake. The worst mistake you can make when editing is a mistake you introduce. Your job is to improve copy. If you do a great job of cleaning up a story but introduce a typo, all that hard work goes for naught.

Editing takes a lot of skill, knowledge and concentration. And the good editor possesses at least one more thing—fingertips. Keep reading, thinking and working along with us. Soon you too will get that professional feel.

HOMEWORK

Try these exercises on for size to see how well you grasp some of the key points regarding The Good Editor.

Assignment No. 1

Review the **Rewriting vs. Editing** segment that explains WHO-DID-WHAT. Then find a news article with a strong "lede," an opening that summarizes the story's overall point and sets up the organization for the rest of the story. Do the first few words describe a WHO or a WHAT? If it's a WHAT, can you rewrite the lede to give it a more human touch by beginning with a WHO?

Assignment No. 2

Repeat Assignment No. 1, but this time find an article with an anecdotal opening that ends a few paragraphs later with a "nut graph." The nut graph serves the same purpose as the lede, summarizing the story's overall point and setting up the organization for the rest of the story. Do the first few words of the nut graph describe a WHO or a WHAT? If it's a WHAT, can you rewrite the nut graph to give it a more human touch by beginning with a WHO?

Assignment No. 3

Review the **Interpersonal Editing Skills** segment and team up with a fellow writer. Share with each other something you've written. Choose a short piece, not something long and involved. The goal here is just to feel the rhythm of the exchange. Remember, start with a compliment, let your friend go first with any criticism, then make one big suggestion—something bound to get a thankful reaction. Frame the rest of your coaching with questions like, "What would you say if we change it to this?" Then turn the tables and feel what it's like to be edited in a professional way.

Assignment No. 4

Review **An Editing Strategy for Beginners** and break out the pens or three different colored highlighters. Go hunting in an article for six gems, two items each in the categories of first sweep, second sweep and third sweep. Box a name with your pen, or color it blue. Underline a difficult spelling word or paint it yellow. Circle a style point or color it pink. Then repeat to find other potential killer, embarrassing or tedious errors.

REFERENCES

Birkett, A. (2020). Are grammar mistakes costing you money? CXL. https://cxl.com/blog/grammar-mistakes-costing-money/

Flesch, R. (1949). *The art of readable writing.* Harper & Row. https://dc135.files.wordpress.com/2012/11/flesch-the-art-of-readable-writing.pdf

Goldberg, B. (2002). *Bias: A CBS insider exposes how the media distort the news.* Regnery Publishing.

Greek medicine. (n.d.) National Library of Medicine. https://www.nlm.nih.gov/hmd/greek/greek_oath.html

Kroll, N. (n.d.). *The psychology of film editing & its impact on your audience.* Noam Kroll. https://noamkroll.com/the-psychology-of-film-editing-the-impact-on-your-audience/

Ryan, B. (1993). *The maestro concept: A new approach to writing and editing for the newspaper of the future* (report and video). American Society of Newspaper Editors.

Siteimprove (2022). Readability: Why are sentences over 20 words? https://help.siteimprove.com/support/solutions/articles/80000447968-readability-why-are-long-sentences-over-20-words. Refers to "Readers' Degree of Understanding," American Press Institute. The research, based on studies of 410 newspapers, correlated the average number of words in a sentence with reader comprehension.

Stieglitz, S. (2021, March 8). Your typo is costing you 12% extra on your Google ads spend. Website Planet. https://www.websiteplanet.com/blog/grammar-report/

FURTHER READING, RESOURCES

Associated Press. (2022). *The Associated Press stylebook: 2022–2024* (56th ed.). Basic Books.

Flesch, R. (1979) *How to write plain English.* HarperCollins. Chapter 2: Let's start with the formula. https://pages.stern.nyu.edu/~wstarbuc/Writing/Flesch.htm

Merriam-Webster. (n.d.). *Merriam-Webster's collegiate dictionary.* (11th ed.).

Twain, M. (1999). *The wit and wisdom of Mark Twain: A book of quotations.* (New ed.). Dover Publications.

University of Chicago Press Editorial Staff. (2017). *The Chicago manual of style.* (17th ed.). https://www.chicagomanualofstyle.org/home.html

Webster's new world college dictionary. (5th ed.). Houghton Mifflin Harcourt.

THE GOOD WRITER

KEY POINTS IN THIS CHAPTER

1. Don't try to write and edit at the same time. It's a two-step process. Remember **Core Principle No. 1: Writing + Editing = Writing.**

2. Building a sentence is like writing a story: Both have a beginning, middle and end. Bury what's least interesting, but still important, in the middle.

3. "Kill your darlings": Delete that one brilliant writing flourish that's more suited for another article. Do that before an editor has to do it for you.

4. Clean copy gives editors confidence that you have attention to detail. Fixing embarrassing and tedious mistakes yourself before you submit your work reduces the chances of a rewrite train wreck.

Profile of the Good Writer

In **Chapter 1.3** we talked about what makes for The Good Editor. It certainly helps if The Good Editor is working with a good writer. In **Chapter 1.4** we'll take a four-part approach to defining what it means to be The Good Writer. First we'll look at the big picture focusing on a writing strategy, then we'll offer tips to add flair and rules for good writing. Finally we'll introduce the bugaboo buzzer as a way to zap the kinds of second sweep and third sweep mistakes we outlined in **chapters 1.1 and 1.3**.

Remember, the first sweep addresses the BIG MISTAKES, or the killer variety; the second sweep embarrassing mistakes; and the third sweep tedious errors. The more mistakes you can catch yourself as a writer, the cleaner your copy will be and the less likely you'll suffer the train wreck of having an editor totally rewrite your copy and introduce errors.

Everyone needs an editor, but sometimes you'll find yourself out there all alone. You can be your own best friend when you are your own best editor. Good writers possess a writing strategy, a memorable flair, an understanding of key concepts and a bugaboo buzzer. Let's start with a chat about the writing process.

I. A Writing Strategy: The What?! Approach

Remember Rudolf Flesch, author of "The Art of Readable Writing"? If so, then it may come as no surprise that a couple of years later, he published another book, "The Art of Clear Thinking" (Flesch, 1951). That's because clear writing goes hand in hand with clear thinking.

Good writers think fast and write fast. If you aspire to that kind of efficiency, then we'll offer you a five-part way to organize your thoughts and focus your writing energy. This is not meant to apply to every story assignment, but it can take you far when dealing with feature stories or personal columns.

Paint by Five Numbers

Here goes the five parts with examples just to help you grasp what we call "The What?! Approach to Writing."

1. START WITH A CLEVER OPENING LINE

Make the readers or listeners say, "What?!" Now you got their attention. The first line you write is 10,000 times more important than the second line. You have some people who won't even get to the second line. How about this:

Ben Franklin was a Founding Mother.

2. PROVIDE A CLARIFIER, A KIND OF DECOMPRESSION CHAMBER

What you say next has two jobs: first, to relieve the anxiety and, second, to set up the nut graph, which carries the point of the story. The clarifier acts like a decompression chamber, bringing your readers and listeners gently down so they're in position to receive the point. Something like this:

Yes, he helped to write the Declaration of Independence with the young Thomas Jefferson as a Founding Father, but Franklin was 70 years old in 1776 and he was already famous because he was the mother of invention.

3. HIT THE NUT GRAPH

The nut graph likewise serves a dual purpose: It summarizes the point of the story and sets up the rest of the writing. Keywords and phrases in the nut graph, usually in order, create an outline (a, b, c) for what follows. Something like this:

Franklin was many things to many people: a scientist, a diplomat, a revolutionary, a seducer of French women, a father of an estranged son who was born out of wedlock. But what made him an international icon were his inventions. And for his many successes, Franklin had an ancient partner—China.

Let's pause here: Do you see the a, b, c? This is really important because our next part depends on it. Here goes: a) many things, b) international icon, c) China partner.

4. WORK THE ACCORDION

We call the next part—the body of the story—an accordion because it can be stretched long or short depending on how much time and space you have to tell the story. The key to a successful accordion is clear **transitions** that pick up on keywords or phrases from the nut graph.

The accordion for the Franklin story provides elaboration like so:

- **Many things**: Illustration of ways Franklin was a scientist, a diplomat, a revolutionary, a seducer of French women, a father of an estranged son who was born out of wedlock. You may not know this, but Franklin's diplomatic work in France helped fund the Revolutionary War, which created a permanent breach between him and his son.
- **International icon**: Explanation of how Franklin's many inventions made him famous around the globe.
- **China partner**: Revelation of how Franklin parlayed inventions made in China to achieve many of his accomplishments: the kite to conduct his lightning experiment, the movable type and printing press to build his young career, the compass used on his eight treks across the Atlantic, the paper on which to write the Declaration of Independence and the gunpowder to fight his revolution.

5. END BY ECHOING A WORD OR PHRASE FROM YOUR OPENING LINE

You begin to wind down your story by setting up a clincher for your ending. We talked about the importance of your first line, but you want people reading right up to the end.

A Hollywood script doctor said at a writing workshop that when he's called to rescue an overbudget film in production, the first thing he writes is the ending. His lecture point went something like this: "How do you want people to feel? Should they laugh or cry or feel peace or outrage? The ending of a film is the last thing people will remember, so it's the most important part."

Well, one thing's for sure, the ending should echo the beginning. So for the Franklin story, our last line might be something like:

If necessity is the mother of invention, then Franklin really needed all those Chinese ancestors for him to go down in history as a Founding Father of America.

As you can imagine, there are many variations of the five-part What?! Approach: a nut graph with two or five key points; an opening that's more than one line; a clarifier that runs several paragraphs.

But the real advantage is the way it creates a paint-by-numbers approach. Writers can hold off on "the 1"; tag their notes for material that goes into "the 4"; maybe start with writing surefire sentences to create "the 5." If your challenge is to write short, then you can deliver just a 1–3–5.

Now for a few more bits of strategic advice:

DON'T FREEZE—DO SOMETHING!

When you're staring at a blank page, just write something. It can be a list or a few incomplete sentences, but the point is you need to clear your head about what you want or need to write about.

If you're a reporter with a packed notebook, put those notes aside and just write from memory. You can always go back to fill in details. Start with what was most interesting or surprising about your story topic. Don't let those ideas get lost in the writing grinder.

Try writing short first. Give yourself 10 or 12 words and draft a headline. Take the fill-in-the-blank approach of answering WHO-DID-WHAT. Slowly you're gaining focus. Focus leads to clarity and clarity makes for good writing.

THINK IN THREE-PART HARMONY

For time immemorial, even before Rudolf Flesch, the best stories are told in threes. So begin to develop your story by asking yourself, "What are the top three most interesting or important points I want to make?"

Out of that list comes what we call a "lede" or a "nut graph." These are valuable because they summarize the point of your story and set up the organization for the rest of the storytelling. Often they will take the form of WHO-DID a) WHAT, b) WHAT and c) WHAT. That little outline offers coherence and allows you the chance to begin crafting transitions from one key point to the next one.

Start with three, but be flexible. Sometimes you may end up with just two key points or maybe four or more. Back up and circle the nut graph sentence for this chapter. That's the one that summarizes the point of the chapter and sets up the rest of the writing. See it? Here goes:

Good writers possess a writing strategy, a memorable flair, an understanding of key concepts and a bugaboo buzzer.

There's the WHO (good writers), plus an action verb for DID (possess), then a four-part WHAT: a) strategy, b) flair, c) concepts and d) buzzer.

Now scan the chapter and note the boldfaced headings that signal transitions. See how the nut graph creates the structure for the rest of the writing? Each of the four headings has several subpoints that grew out of a list from brainstorming on a blank page.

It's not magic. The point is, the harder your thinking, the easier the writing. And when you present your work to an editor, the response will be, "Oh,

I see. I get it." Any work from there will be a little fine-tuning rather than a kickback to you for a complete rewrite.

MANAGE YOUR TIME

A writing strategy would not be complete without a word about time management. As you embark on a first draft, push all the way through. As you search for an ending, go back to your beginning and see what word or phrase you can echo. Take a break, then begin the serious work of editing and, when necessary, rewriting. The more time you can spring for that, the better.

If you have the right strategy, writing can be fun—which brings us to the Zinger Factory.

II. A Memorable Flair—The Zinger Factory

We all want to be memorable, and good writers live forever with memorable lines. Some of them we can call zingers. You know you've written a zinger when it's the one line that gets repeated, either in a headline, in a tweet or in casual conversation with your readers or listeners.

The Zinger Factory is where you can create "the 1" (clever opening line) and match it with "the 5" (echo), or add to "the 4" (accordion) to keep readers' attention pulling them through your story. It's not something for "the 2" (clarifier) or "the 3" (nut graph), as the goal with those two is to be straight and clear.

You'll recognize that the Zinger Factory employs "figures of speech," each with their own kick or punch. Here goes, starting with six tools.

1. Simile

Tell me what it's "like." Good writing, like good teaching, works best by making associations. You compare something new with something familiar to readers or listeners. A simile is a comparison of two things using "as" or "like." For example:

> *She was as strong as Gorilla Glue.*

> *Learning grammar was like getting a root canal.*

2. Metaphor

Metaphors serve the same role as similes only without using "as" or "like." For example:

Grammar is a sore tooth.

He was the Mount Everest of men.

3. Personification

Attributing human qualities to inanimate objects is another way to create a memorable line. Something like this:

On Halloween the professor's chalk talked to us with a creepy screech.

The siren slapped us across the face.

4. Twist a Cliche

Remember from **Chapter 1.1**, "If you have heard it before, don't say it again" (**Core Principle No. 8: Twist a Cliche**). Try this one:

This morning I got out of the wrong side of my head.

Bob Dole, the late great U.S. senator from Kansas and former presidential candidate, delivered this zinger at the 98th Annual Dinner at The Gridiron Club in Washington, D.C. (Dole, 1983):

History buffs probably noted the reunion at a Washington party a few weeks ago of three ex-presidents: Carter, Ford and Nixon. See no evil, hear no evil … and evil.

5. Play on a Name

This one is tricky because you have to start with a famous name. Malcolm X nailed this zinger in a 1964 speech:

Our forefathers weren't the Pilgrims. We didn't land on Plymouth Rock; the rock was landed on us (Malcolm X, 1964).

Or you can make a joke like the "Car Talk" brothers, Tom and Ray Magliozzi, of National Public Radio fame. They listed in their credits:

Chief Legal Counsel, Hugh Louis Dewey of Dewey, Cheetham & Howe (Car Talk, n.d.).

(Apologies to all attorneys, but particularly the one married to your co-author. Sadly, Tom Magliozzi has died.)

6. Coin a Word or Phrase

This is the grand-prize zinger, something that can change dictionaries. There are two ways to do it: either create a new word ("Snowmageddon," "Snowpocalypse," "Snowzilla") or take an old word or phrase and give it new meaning ("nasty," "ridiculous," "break his ankles"—as good athletic moves).

You may like strawberry-rhubarb pie, but rhubarb is also now defined in the dictionary as a fight. How did that happen? We credit Karen Hill for this remarkable etymology:

> *Legendary Brooklyn Dodgers broadcaster Red Barber first used rhubarb on-air to describe a baseball altercation in 1943. He said he heard it from reporter Garry Schumacher, who picked it up from another reporter, Tom Meany, who learned it from an unnamed Brooklyn bartender. The anonymous bartender used it to describe an incident in his establishment when a Brooklyn fan shot a Giants fan.*
>
> *And that's how rhubarb became baseball slang for a fight or argument. (Hill, 2022)*

Now onto some key concepts—and a friendly warning.

III. An Understanding of Key Concepts —Rules for Good Writing

Ever write a sentence and feel like you're slowly losing control? That's why we're here, to put you back in charge. But just like air traffic controllers trying to talk you down to a safe landing, we'll have to speak in some technical terms.

CAUTION: Grammarian at work!

To explain some of these rules for good writing, we'll need to use a foreign language—grammar. Long gone are the days, if they ever existed, when an editor could clearly shout: "Don't you know you use a comma before a conjunction when joining two independent clauses that aren't closely related!"

Yeah, right.

Nonetheless, to have confidence as a writer, you'll benefit from spending a little time with us to grasp some unfamiliar terms. We'll start slowly, don't worry.

1. Use Sentence Structure to Emphasize What's Important

Good writers know what they want to emphasize and how to express it. Think of a sentence as having three parts: a beginning, a middle and an end. The least emphatic part is the middle. The beginning and the end are the more emphatic, but the greatest emphasis falls on what you say last. Take this sentence:

In the heat of the night, he left the house.

Now compare the emphasis with this version:

He left the house in the heat of the night.

The first sentence emphasizes "the house," the second one "the night." Although all the words are the same, the sentences are different.

Now let's apply this notion to news writing. What do you think of this sentence?

Firefighters battled an inferno that raged out of control for hours, engulfing and destroying the historic Empire State Building Thursday night.

Well, the two most emphatic parts—the beginning and the end—are occupied by two of the least important facts. What happened? A historic building was destroyed. Why? An inferno. Compare the original lede with this one:

The Empire State Building was destroyed Thursday night as firefighters battled flames that raged out of control for hours and engulfed the historic structure in an inferno.

In the middle you find the two least important facts—the time element (Thursday night) and the firefighters (doing their job fighting fires).

2. Use Passive Voice Only When Necessary

So what's passive voice? A verb, like "to drive," can be written in the past tense either in active voice ("She **drove** the car") or in passive voice ("The car **was driven** by her").

With active voice, the subject ("She") does the action. With passive voice, the subject ("The car") is acted upon.

There are three tipoffs to passive voice: 1) a form of the verb "to be" ("**was**"), 2) a past participle ("**driven**") and 3) the word "**by**," either expressed or implied. Got it? Let's see. Take another look at this sentence:

The Empire State Building was destroyed Thursday night as firefighters battled flames that raged out of control for hours and engulfed the historic structure in an inferno.

Is it in passive voice?

Yes. With passive voice the subject ("**the Empire State Building**") is acted upon by the verb ("**was destroyed**"). Check-check-check for the three tipoffs: There's a form of the verb "to be" ("**was**"), a past participle ("**destroyed**") and the word "by" is implied ("**by an inferno**").

So what's the rap against passive voice? Active verbs carry more punch, but that's not always better. Let's flip the sentence into active voice:

An inferno that raged out of control for hours as firefighters battled the flames Thursday night engulfed and destroyed the historic Empire State Building.

This is active voice because the subject ("**inferno**") does the action of the verbs ("**engulfed**" and "**destroyed**").

So which lede is better? We think the passive voice one.

News writing is another way of saying get to the point. In this case the point is the Empire State Building was destroyed. With good ledes, the first few words summarize the heart of a story.

If you can picture a screaming headline, it might go like this:

Empire State Building destroyed in inferno

Yep, both the lede and the headline are written in passive voice.

Active voice works great, but sometimes the action's doer doesn't need to be mentioned ("The kidnap suspect **was arrested**") or is just not known ("The mysterious fire **was set** in the office").

A variation of passive voice comes in the present tense for the verb "to be" ("am," "is," "are") with a present participle ("being") before a past participle. So these sentences are in passive voice, too:

I am being attacked by an awful person.

The neighborhood is being destroyed every moment of the day by neglect.

All the exam scores are being adjusted by the professor on an unfair curve.

Can those sentences be flipped into active voice? Yes, easily, but should they? Remember the larger point: **Use sentence structure to emphasize what's important.** The writer of those present-tense, passive-voice sentences wanted to pound the words **"awful person," "neglect"** and **"unfair curve."**

You probably have heard some English teacher shout, "Never use passive voice!" Well, we say never say never. Sometimes passive voice is the best way to go.

3. Watch Out for False Passives

Now that you understand passive voice, it will be easier to avoid false passives. That's a given!

Take this sentence: The **student was given** the answers by the teacher.

See the problem? The student was not "given"; the answers were. To keep the sentence in passive voice, make it: "The **answers were given** to the student by the teacher."

Or better yet, here's where active voice is preferred: "The teacher gave the answers to the student."

False passives show up in headlines, too, like this one:

Teen neighbor given award for bravery

Make it:

Teen neighbor gets award for bravery

4. Keep Subjects and Verbs Close Together

The subject of an action verb is the doer of the action. You should keep the subject and verb close together. Take another look at this sentence:

An inferno that raged out of control for hours as firefighters battled the flames Thursday night engulfed and destroyed the historic Empire State Building.

Can you see the subject-verb connection? Here's the problem: the subject ("inferno") is too far away from its verbs ("engulfed" and "destroyed"). Think of what this would look like as two sentences:

An inferno engulfed and destroyed the historic Empire State Building. Firefighters battled the flames Thursday night as they raged out of control for hours.

Can you count the number of subject-verb connections, or what we call "clauses"? Three, right? 1) Inferno engulfed and destroyed, 2) firefighters battled, and 3) they ("the flames") raged. Three clauses in two sentences, which brings us to another rule for good writing.

5. Try to Keep One Idea to One Sentence

This is a battle cry for broadcast writers, as they are writing for the ear rather than the eye. Long, complex sentences for a broadcast or podcast are more difficult to understand, especially when the listener is multitasking.

The battle cry is also something that fits with the Flesch test for readable writing as you're more likely to end up with an average sentence length of 20 words or so. Remember that's an average, so you can write one sentence—a provocative question—that's 39 words long, then the next sentence can deliver a one-word answer: "No!"

One trick for tightening is to zero in on words like "who," "which" and "that." They often introduce sentences within sentences, or what we call clauses. Packing more than one idea into a sentence is inevitable. The least you can do is omit words by turning clauses into phrases. Take these three examples:

1. *Alvin Jones, who is leader of the fan club, arrived on time.*

    Better: ***Fan club leader Alvin Jones arrived on time.***

2. *The president achieved his main goal, which was reduced spending.*

    Better: ***The president achieved his main goal of reduced spending.***

3. *Council members attacked the plan that was being considered by the special committee, which was set up by the mayor.*

    Better: ***Council members attacked the plan being considered by the special committee set up by the mayor.***

6. Stop on "It" and "There"

Good sentences have strong subjects like the Empire State Building. That's why you should stop when you see sentences begin with "It" or "There." First, the quick fixes, then the grammar.

It is cold in Chicago

… becomes **Chicago is cold**.

There were four rules broken

… becomes ***Four rules were broken.***

The word "it" is fine when it is a pronoun taking the place of a noun, as in "I love Chicago. It is a great city."

I love Chicago (noun). It (pronoun) is a great city. We say the pronoun has a clear antecedent, a word that gives it meaning.

In the sentence "It is cold in Chicago," "**it**" doesn't really stand for anything. You'd have to guess. Do you mean "the weather," or "the air," or "the lake," or "the very heart of a Bears fan," or what?

When "it" has no clear antecedent, we call it an "expletive." Good writers, like all decent people, delete expletives.

"There," as in "There were four rules broken," is another expletive. It's a hollow word and not a great start. You can typically drop it, find a strong subject (like "Four rules") nearby and flip the sentence.

Just like "it" can be a good and useful pronoun, the word "there" can be used as a modifier telling where. That's called an adverb. So compare these sentences:

There are the racehorses. See, they're over there.

There are two racehorses in the field.

The difference is you can write the word "there" out of the second example ("Two racehorses are in the field"), but not the first example because "there" is being used as an adverb, not an expletive.

That's a good rule of thumb for both words: If you can drop them, do. If you can't, you need them.

7. Watch Tenses and Time Elements

We subscribe to the long-held notion that the most important part of speech is the verb. So, the more you know about verbs the better. Writers use the present tense ("is," "says," "carry," "confirm") for a sense of immediacy. The same is true for headline and caption writers, though that version is called the "historical present tense" because the present tense is used to refer to something that happened in the past.

The past tense ("was," "said," "carried," "confirmed") is used naturally with time elements, such as yesterday, the day of the week, last month or last year.

So a headline reads in the present tense ("says," "is"):

FBI says it is investigating foreign espionage at the university

And a caption reads in the present tense ("carry"):

FBI agents carry out boxes marked "Top Secret" from a foreign language professor's office.

But the lede reads in the past tense ("confirmed") with time elements ("Tuesday," "last week"):

The FBI's regional office confirmed Tuesday that agents conducted a raid last week on the university office of a foreign language professor, seizing several boxes marked "Top Secret" in an espionage case.

Books and documents speak in the present tense (the book "says," the document "states"). People speak in the past tense in news stories (he "said," she "said"), but in feature stories they may speak in the present tense (the quiltmaker "says").

Keeping tenses consistent can be tricky. You may weave in and out of present tense as need be. Go with what sounds the most natural.

8. Play the Verbs, Bench the Nouns and Adjectives

Good writers preserve the power of action verbs by freeing them from getting buried in nouns or adjectives. By nouns we mean words ending in "-tion," "-ance" or "-ing." By adjectives, we mean words ending in "-ful."

Beware of words like "gave," "make," "conduct" and "hold" as they may mask stronger verbs kidnapped into nouns.

Some examples:

1. *The doctor gave the patients **examinations**.*

    Shun the -tion words and rewrite the sentence to read: *The doctor examined the patients.*

2. *The city will make an **inspection** of the sewers.*

    Better: *The city will **inspect** the sewers.*

3. *The university will conduct an **investigation** of the fraternities.*

    Getting easy now, right? Better: *The university will **investigate** the fraternities.*

4. *Council members will hold a **meeting** to address the crime issue.*

Ah, yes: *Council members will* **meet** *to address the crime issue.*

5. *The aid workers gave* **assistance** *to the injured tornado victims by applying tourniquets.*

Rescue the verb "assist": *The aid workers* **assisted** *the injured tornado victims by applying tourniquets.*

Long ago writers turned the noun "contact" (to make contact) into a handy verb meaning to call, write, email, direct message, text, whatever. When "contact" is followed by only one option, use the specific verb. So don't say, "For more information, contact the office at (phone number)." Make it: "For more information, call …"

Make the same shift back to verbs with adjectives ending in "-ful." Some examples:

1. *She is* **hopeful** *she will win the race.*

    Better: *She* **hopes** *she will win the race.*

2. *We are* **watchful** *of the weather situation.*

    Better: *We are* **watching** *the weather.*

3. *Money is* **helpful** *to our cause.*

    Better: *Money* **helps** *our cause.*

Favoring strong verbs over nouns and adjectives adds punch to your writing. But not too much punch. Sometimes a writer will take a noun and twist it into a verb, as in:

The man was **shotgunned** *to death.*

Sticking with a regular verb and preserving the noun for clarity sounds more natural:

The man was shot to death with a **shotgun***.*

Sometimes editors should add words, not just delete them.

Sportswriters have a way with words but not always the best way. Sometimes you'll see an adjective like "best" twisted into a verb, as in:

The Yankees **bested** *the Red Sox 11–1.*

Better to go with "defeated" or maybe even "trounced." English offers thousands of verb options, so there's no need to bring in more out of left field.

9. "Kill Your Darlings"

If you are editing your own work, sometimes you need to muster the strength to do the impossible: "kill your darlings," as the saying goes. That means deleting that one special writing flourish you are so proud of. You'll gulp when you finally realize it's more of a distraction and best saved for another tale.

10. Prepare for the Haircut

Our last key concept deals with ego and story length, which editors often estimate at the assignment stage but can be subject to change. As a good writer, you can keep control by marking "optional trims."

Determining the right length for a story can get tricky. Broadcasters time it out: a reader, 15 to 20 seconds; a story, 30 seconds; or a "long" package, 90 seconds or "a minute 30."

At the other end of the spectrum are magazine writers. Seasoned ones get a feel for when they are writing too long and will mark certain paragraphs as optional trims.

New Yorker writer Seymour Hersh once apologized to his legendary editor, William Shawn, for turning in a 12,000-word article. "Oh, Mr. Hersh," Shawn, said, "stories are never too long or too short. They're too interesting or too boring" (Hersh, 2018).

A related view came from the Future of Newspapers Committee for the former American Society of Newspaper Editors: "The problem is not the long story that's long. The problem is the short story that's long."

Sometimes trimming a story becomes a wrestling match. A longtime Chicago Tribune sportswriter, asked to trim 4 inches from his epic article, asked, "Can't you just make the type smaller."

When trimming a story becomes necessary, think of paragraphs as either making a point, providing support for the point or adding elaboration. Start your trimming with the elaboration in "the 4," or the accordion. Tipoffs come in phrases like "For example" or "In another case." Sometimes elaboration takes the form of a superfluous quotation.

As we have advised often, when in doubt, ask. If you have any questions about what should be trimmed or not, seek advice from your editor. We'll offer more in-depth advice in an upcoming chapter on trimming.

IV. A Bugaboo Buzzer

The more writers get to know their editors, the more they understand what bugaboos—sometimes eccentricities—set them off.

Once your co-author was industriously working away on the rim of a Chicago Tribune copy desk when his boss, known as "the slot" for his position inside the desk, shouted, "'Mid-air'! There is no such thing as the middle of the air. This was an 'in-air' collision."

Your co-author had to pause to remember that he handled a plane crash story a while ago, then understand that the comment was addressed to him. Such is the quality of newsroom communication. He said nothing out loud, only to himself: "That's ridiculous. Of course, there's no such thing as the middle of the air. But mid-air (or, as the AP Stylebook prefers, 'midair') is a common term."

Nonetheless, every time he worked with that slot he avoided the use of "mid-air." With other slot people, not so much. This is what we mean by a bugaboo. What follows is a short list of our bugaboos.

1. Contractions

Contractions lend a light air to writing in a conversational tone. They work well in feature stories, but you'll also find them in business stories, as writers try to lighten up what can be dense information. For the same reason, you'll see them sprinkled across textbooks like this one.

Be careful, though, when stories demand a formal tone. For example, you would not want to say, "The jury couldn't decide on the death penalty." Here you need "could not."

You'll see plenty of contractions in quotations echoing the point about a conversational tone. In quotes you might also see odd contractions, such as "she'd" for "she would" and "it'll" for "it will." Those are fine if they characterize the speaker.

2. Misplaced Modifiers

Adjectives, which can be words or phrases, modify nouns and pronouns. Here's where the language can get a little tricky. What's wrong with this sentence?

> *Though currently incurable, researchers are hard at work trying to find a cure for this devastating genetic disease.*

Right, the phrase "Though currently incurable" is an adjective in search of the right word to modify. The "disease" is incurable, not the "researchers." So here's the rewrite:

Though currently incurable, this devastating genetic disease has researchers hard at work trying to find a cure.

Here's another train wreck to unwind. What's wrong and how do you fix it?

Having attended multiple universities and wasted a lot of money, I wanted to help the poor student who was in search of the right major.

Yes, the "Having attended" phrase modifies the pronoun "I" but really refers to the "poor student." So a rewrite can go like so:

I wanted to help the poor student who was in search of the right major, having attended multiple universities and wasted a lot of money.

Just as you want to keep subjects close to their verbs, you want to keep adjectives close to the words they modify.

3. Parallel Construction

Good writers are orderly, so they express similar thoughts in the same way, or as we say, keep them "parallel."

What's wrong with this sentence?

He wants to attend college, to graduate and get a job.

You have a choice to make it parallel, either with to-to-to, as in:

He wants to attend college, to graduate and to get a job.

Or just three verbs in a row, as in:

He wants to attend college, graduate and get a job.

Notice how the "-ings" keep this sentence parallel:

He specializes in running good pass patterns, catching the ball and scoring touchdowns.

If you have a list of names with titles, keep them parallel, too. As in:

The speakers were Eric Adams, mayor of New York City; Condoleezza Rice, former U.S. secretary of state; and Joan Gabel, president of the University of Minnesota.

Keep an eye on words in a bulleted list. Here, the four articles make the list parallel:

The struggling couple faced four options:

- *a divorce*

- *a separation*

- *an annulment*

- *a session with a marriage counselor*

Now you be the judge. What's wrong with this list?

The president promised lower taxes, an improved leadership condition and higher household incomes.

Right, make the second item "better leadership."

Some phrases require parallel construction, such as "both/and," "either/or," "neither/nor" and "not only/but also." What follows the first word should be in the same form as what follows the second one. Here goes:

*Both a professional wrestler and **an** opera singer, he could impress a crowd in more ways than one.*

*Either **you** give us a raise or **you** give us more benefits.*

*We want neither **to** go nor **to** stay.*

*She asked for not only **a** little fairness but also **a** lot of truth.*

Starting a sentence with "Not only" gets a little tricky, but don't sweat it. Just go with what sounds the most natural. This is just fine:

Not only will I watch out for all these bugaboos, but also I will do my best to follow the rules for good writing.

Does the following sentence bother you?

He served as a priest, a vice president and a third baseman on the company's softball team.

We're glad it does! Although the sentence is parallel, the verb "served" works for only two of the three positions. You could replace "served as" with "was," or write something like:

He served as a priest and a vice president and played third base for the company's softball team.

4. Prepositions

Saving words is saving time. Zoom in on prepositions, which are words that show relationships. Among 150 or so prepositions are "in," "on," "by," "from," "over," "under" and "between." See if you can delete them and flip the phrase. For example, make it:

presidential candidates
… not candidates FOR president;
lake cottages
… not cottages ON the lake;
British literature
… not books BY British authors.

5. Split Infinitives

An infinitive is the "to" form of a verb ("to run," "to jump," "to hide"). A split occurs when a modifier called an adverb comes between the "to" and the verb: "to quickly run," "to almost jump," "to nearly hide."

You may have heard, "Never split infinitives!" But our rule of thumb is **split them only when necessary** or if you want **"to really emphasize"** something.

If you tune into infinitives, you can quickly undo awkward phrasing, such as:

You have the chance to swiftly and conveniently deactivate the system.

Rather make it:

*You have the chance **to deactivate** the system swiftly and conveniently.*

If you try to undo a split infinitive and it just doesn't work, don't worry about it. Here's an example:

*The president sought **to sharply reduce** taxes hindering business investment.*

The word "not" becomes a bugaboo. Don't write:

*He asked me **to not help** her.*

Make it:

*He asked me **not to help** her.*

6. Words With "-ize"

Some writers are hooked on "-ize" words and think nothing of writing something like:

The family members utilized the software to finalize plans for their dream home, allowing everyone to visualize what it would look like.

We say the fewer the better. Try this:

The family members used the software to finish plans for their dream home, allowing everyone to see what it would look like.

Some writers will crank up the "-ize" machine on proper nouns, such as:

Hopes are fading that soft power can Americanize China.

It's a handy shorthand, but what "Americanize" means exactly may not be clear. No need to revolutionize the language if you can find a simpler word or phrase. Sometimes the answer is to use a few more words, as in:

Hopes are fading that soft power can change China into a country with American values and democratic practices.

7. Basis and Manner

These two bugaboos are tipoffs that you can tighten your writing by making phrases into words. Like so:

The matters will be handled on a one-to-one basis.

Make it:

The matters will be handled individually.

And for this one:

She always deals with me in a polite manner.

You can say:

She always deals with me politely.

8. Only

Watch this one, as it can make you sound insensitive, and it often becomes a misplaced modifier.

Here is some troublesome phrasing:

The gunman opened fire at the shopping mall, but only two people were killed.

If those two were your mother and father, there's nothing "only" about that. Better to say, "The gunmen opened fire at the shopping mall and two people were killed."

Now watch how the meaning of this sentence changes as "only" gets moved along:

Only I hit him in the eye. (me, not my brother)

I only hit him in the eye. (I didn't stab him)

I hit him only in the eye. (not the ear)

Just make sure "only" lands next to the word you want it to modify. So do not write: "He only had one problem." Instead: "He had only one problem."

9. Failed, Ignore and Finally

Just as "only" can send the wrong impression, use care with words like "failed," "ignore" and "finally." They are very judgy-judgy and may put you into awkward situations. Take this sentence:

*The grand jury **failed** to indict the Teamsters leader.*

You're implying that the jury should have, and that's a big mistake. In your own way, you're indicting the criminal justice system. Out of fairness, you need to strike a neutral tone, such as:

*The grand jury **did not** indict the Teamsters leader.*

"Ignored" is another loaded word. It implies deliberately disregarding something when someone might have just forgotten something or chosen to reply long after careful consideration. "Failed" and "ignore" get you into people's heads in search of motivation. Good writers don't belong there.

"Finally" is a little different as it can imply exasperation. World leaders sometimes spend a long time on their death beds. Every day, maybe for weeks or months, there's the news that the person is "near death."

You grow weary of the news coverage, then the poor soul dies, and you're inclined to write something like the person "finally died." Don't. Just be specific about how long the person was in hospice care, or whatever, and just say "died" without the "finally."

If you're in the news business, save your opinions for the editorial page. But you'll struggle to top the obit on the legendary and controversial Generalissimo Francisco Franco, who ruled Spain from 1939 until his death in 1975. Much had already been published about his past because Franco hung in there for many news cycles before he died. That's when Richard Aregood, who won the 1995 Pulitzer Prize for Editorial Writing at The Philadelphia Daily News, penned one of the shortest editorials ever:

> *They say only the good die young. Generalissimo Francisco Franco was 82.*

Actually the complete text, which carried the headline "Adios, Dictator," read: "They say only the good die young. Generalissimo Francisco Franco was 82. Seems about right."

In retrospect, Aregood regretted the last sentence as being superfluous. You can't get enough of those **Core Principles of Editing**. As you'll recall from **Chapter 1.1**, "less is more."

10. Windy City

Some writers get nervous when they must repeat words. The Good Writer will say "Chicago" several times rather than substitute "Windy City" or, with all due respect to Carl Sandburg, "City of the Big Shoulders" or "Hog Butcher for the World." These are called "elegant variations."

Sometimes repeating a word falls flat, as in: "We need to help the poor and help the disadvantaged." No problem making it read: "We need to help the poor and aid the disadvantaged."

If you have to say "in England" more than once, don't feel the need to toss in an "across the pond" to break up the monotony. No need to get nervous about repeating words. Just use them to your best advantage.

Good writers use repetition for emphasis, as Martin Luther King Jr. did in his "I Have a Dream" speech: "Free at last. Free at last. Thank God almighty, we are free at last." Or President Abraham Lincoln did with this line from the

The Five Writers You Don't Want to Meet in Heaven

By Michael O'Donnell

Editing the work of others is as much a study of human nature as it is a study of the language. Otherwise rational people can turn into petulant children, jealous parents or raging idiots at the change of a word.

I've had writers refer to their work as their "babies." The archetypes that follow don't cover all the difficult people you'll meet in your editing life, and sometimes these will manifest themselves in combination, such as the legendary advocate or the tape-recorder slob.

Remember that your job is to make their work better, but be forewarned.

1. The Legend

Every newspaper, radio station or TV channel has its legendary reporters. They might be columnists who have earned the privilege of writing to suit themselves, or broadcast "personalities" whose ratings justify a degree of arrogance.

Sometimes through long tenure, such people can become bigger than the organizations that pay their salaries. You learn to tread carefully when assigned to edit their work.

Editing such writers is no fun, especially when you find a major error, because in their own minds, they are never wrong. The rule is you don't change anything without consulting them, a dreaded task.

Mike Royko was one such legend as columnist for the Chicago Tribune. Years ago, I was reading an early edition of the Tribune and noticed that Royko had mixed up former pro football player and actor Ed Marinaro with Miami Dolphins quarterback Dan Marino. When I pointed out the error to the city editor, his face went white.

"Can you call him?" he said. I demurred. As it turned out, Royko was gruff but gracious when he received the call. The best of these legends put their egos aside and remember **Core Principle No. 1: Use the Writing + Editing Formula.**

2. The Literati

Not every assignment can result in the greatest story ever told, unless you are the literary giant working in the features department at a backwater newspaper. At the Quad-City Times in Davenport, Iowa, such a person warned me as I began to edit her story: "Every word was written with precision. I'm a graduate of the Iowa Writers' Workshop."

One sportswriter I edited regularly insisted on using the Oxford English Dictionary as a higher authority than the Webster's New World College Dictionary we commoners used. This meant editing out all the Briticisms ("color" for "colour"), a waste of precious time.

I was once ordered to reduce one of this writer's stories from 32 column inches to 28. It took careful condensing and pruning to save as much of the story as possible, and the sports editor told me that I did a good job.

But the next day, the writer sent a department-wide email likening the editing to being emasculated. Apparently the complex sentences, full of commas and clauses, were more important than the story itself.

For the literati, no story is too long, and every adjective or adverb is a brushstroke in a work of art. Remember **Core Principle No. 6: Find the Simple Solution**.

3. The Advocate

Advocacy is the public support of a particular policy, and there's nothing wrong with engaging in it when it's part of the job.

Public relations executives know that they are hired to advocate for their clients. Likewise, opinion writing is all about advocacy for a certain cause or point of view.

However, a hint of advocacy can sow doubt as to the truthfulness of a piece. One word or phrase can set off a battle in today's culture wars.

One spring at the St. Paul Pioneer Press, a reporter circulated an email to copy editors complaining bitterly. In his story about increasing numbers of potholes on city streets, a copy editor changed the phrase "global warming" to "our warmer winters."

The email debate raged, with the writer saying that global warming was a scientific fact and the copy-desk chief replying that "global warming" was a loaded term politically.

All agreed that the writer should have been consulted before such a change was made.

That was in the early 2000s. Global warming is even more of a cultural third rail today. In the 56th edition of the Associated Press Stylebook, the entry for **climate change** (page 49) treads carefully around the subject and advises that "stories about individual events should make it clear that they occur in a larger context."

Recall **Core Principle No. 11: Whatever You Do, Be Loyal to Truth.** To the editor, this writer was slipping into advocacy when he cited "global warming" as a cause for potholes.

4. The Tape Recorder

A voice recorder can be a valuable tool for any writer. The problem arises when the story is basically a transcription of what's "on tape."

I've dealt with this problem often when a story had a tight deadline. The writer took the easy way out by just typing up the quotes. The result was page after page of quotations to the point where they became tiresome.

The answer was to paraphrase some paragraphs into transitions and "lead-ins," the paragraphs that introduce a speaker and offer context for the following quote.

A similar but different problem is the writer who types in a quote without some critical thinking. One writer who covered professional football regularly submitted stories with quotes that didn't make much sense or were non sequiturs, coming out of nowhere. When a quote didn't make sense, I would call the writer. His response usually was, "Well, that's what he said."

(continued)

In the broadcast world, where time is a golden commodity, the problem might be the opposite: a short sound bite that offers no context or, worse, mischaracterizes what the person said.

Editing begins with the writer, who must be willing to cast a critical eye on what is to be published. Likewise, when the deadline is tight, the writer should be forming the story as events unfold and use every minute available to polish the piece. Always keep in mind **Core Principle No. 2: Know the Deadline.**

5. The Slob

Every editor has had to deal with writers who dash off a story expecting the copy desk to clean it up. I believe these writers always have had someone to pick up after them, beginning with moms scooping up their dirty clothes and making their beds.

If the slob is a good reporter, an editor won't have much trouble with the major errors. Spelling, grammar and punctuation are another matter.

These writers won't take the time to look up a word. One pro football writer kept turning in stories about "parody" in the NFL. What he meant was "parity," the league's efforts to even the talent among its 32 teams. The mistake got into print at least once. By no mistake, The New York Times ran with the headline: "The NFL Season So Far Is a Parody of Parity."

Sometimes The Slob and The Tape Recorder team up. The writer hears a word on the recorder, doesn't know fully what it means but gives it a shot anyway.

Remember **Core Principle No. 7: Think "Just One More Thing":** Lack of attention to detail can earn you the reputation of being a slob.

As you do the important work of editing the writing of others, keep all the core principles in mind, have your stylebook at the ready and don't forget one of the biggest challenges you face is human nature.

Gettysburg Address: "But, in a larger sense, we cannot dedicate, we cannot consecrate—we cannot hallow—this ground."

Writers admire The Good Editor, who is clearly "an essential worker." The world will revolve more smoothly, however, when The Good Writer assumes the role of The Good Editor, too.

HOMEWORK

Assignment No. 1

Review the segment titled **Think in Three-Part Harmony** on how to identify the point of a story, then reread the **Prepare for the Haircut** segment on how to trim a story. Take another look at an article you recently enjoyed and mark it up to identify points, support and elaboration. Maybe you can use three different highlighters to identify the points (blue), separate from the support for them (yellow) and then adding the elaboration (pink). If you're using blue for a lede or nut graph, you have the right idea. If a lot of the quotations are in pink, you're on the right track.

Assignment No. 2

Review the segments titled **Use Sentence Structure to Emphasize What's Important** and **Use Passive Voice Only When Necessary.** Now call up the last paper you wrote or an interesting article you just read and hunt for passive voice. How many examples can you find? How many passive voice sentences do you think would be improved in active voice? Remember, with active voice the subject is doing the action of the verb. With passive voice you're able to identify a form of the verb "to be" ("is," "are," "was," "were"), possibly a present participle ("being") but always a past participle ("driven," "destroyed," "attacked") and the word "by," either expressed or implied.

Assignment No. 3

Review the segment titled **Stop on "It" and "There,"** then go on a hunt for sentences that begin with those words. Can you tell when the word "It" is a pronoun properly used? If so, then identify its antecedent or the word that gives it meaning. Can you tell when the word "There" is an adverb? If so, it's doing some good. But when both "It" and "There" are expletives, then you can drop them, flip the sentences and save some words. How many words can you save? Celebrate making those sentences shorter and more direct.

Assignment No. 4

Share your thoughts about the **10 bugaboos** with a friend or classmate. Individually choose the top three that really set off your buzzer. Then compare notes. Does your partner see where you're coming from or just not understand what the big fuss is about? Have fun with this exchange, but don't get lost in any "mid-air" or "in-air" disputes!

REFERENCES

Car Talk (n.d.) *The conclusive, definitive, official Dewey, Cheetham & Howe staff list.* https://www.cartalk.com/content/staff-credits

Dole, B. (1983, March 26). *Remarks of Senator Bob Dole; 98th Annual Dinner, the Gridiron Club*. Dole Archives, University of Kansas. https://dolearchivecollections.ku.edu/collections/speeches/030/c019_030_010_all.pdf

Flesch, R. (1951). *The art of clear thinking*. Harper & Row.

Hersh, S. M. (2018). *Reporter: A memoir*. Knopf Publishing Group.

Hill, K. (2022, March 3). Where did the term "rhubarb" for a baseball fight come from and what does the word mean? Zippy Facts. https://zippyfacts.com/where-did-the-term-rhubarb-for-a-baseball-fight-come-from-and-what-does-the-word-mean/

Malcolm X (1964, March 29). *Malcolm X warns, "it shall be the ballot or the bullet," Washington Heights, NY, March 29, 1964.* AMDOCS: Documents for the Study of American History. http://www.vlib.us/amdocs/texts/malcolmx0364.html

FURTHER READING, RESOURCES

Associated Press. (2022). *The Associated Press stylebook: 2022–2024* (56th ed.). The Associated Press.

Day, N. (2015, March 11). Editorials: Pungent, profound and path breaking. Nieman Reports. https://niemanreports.org/articles/editorials-pungent-profound-and-path-breaking/

McIntosh, B. (2016, February 22). The value of harsh editing: "Killing your children." Princeton Correspondents on Undergraduate Research. https://pcur.princeton.edu/2016/02/the-value-of-harsh-editing-killing-your-children/

Mehta, V. (1998). *Remembering Mr. Shawn's* New Yorker: *The invisible art of editing*. Overlook Press.

Public Relations Society of America. (n.d.). PRSA code of ethics. https://www.prsa.org/docs/default-source/about/ethics/prsa_code_of_ethics.pdf

The 74. (n.d.). Code of ethics. https://www.the74million.org/code-of-ethics/

The 74. (n.d.). About us. https://www.the74million.org/about/

Terry, D. (1997, April 30). Mike Royko, the voice of the working class, dies at 64. *The New York Times*. https://www.nytimes.com/1997/04/30/us/mike-royko-the-voice-of-the-working-class-dies-at-64.html

The University of Chicago Press Editorial Staff. (2017). *The Chicago manual of style*, 17th edition. University of Chicago Press. https://www.chicagomanualofstyle.org/home.html

Wang, S. (n.d.). Can Campbell Brown's education news site walk the advocacy–journalism tightrope? Nieman Lab. https://www.niemanlab.org/2015/07/can-campbell-browns-education-news-site-walk-the-advocacy-journalism-tightrope/

STYLE

KEY POINTS IN THIS CHAPTER

1. Stylebooks reflect changes in our culture. As focal points develop or shift, new entries emerge or current entries change. These entries involve having knowledge and making value judgments by people a lot like you, so don't be intimidated.

2. Stylebooks aren't sacred. If a stylebook point looks ridiculous, you have an escape hatch. It's called a local style sheet, which your organization can create and which can overrule the official stylebook.

3. Stylebooks can keep you out of trouble in a variety of ways. They can be like almanacs with world information, even guides on publishing technicalities, reporting and media law.

4. The rule above all style rules is to avoid possible confusion. You want your readers, listeners and viewers to skate along on smooth ice and not get tripped up by anything disturbing.

This Might Hurt a Little, but … (Take 1)

Welcome to the Anal-Retentive Cafe!

(Please note the hyphen.)

We'll be your chef—with a nod to a 2013 "Saturday Night Live" sketch, if you missed the reference. On the menu today we're serving up hot discussions about stylebooks, dictionaries and spelling.

Take a seat anywhere you like. Please let me apologize in advance if any of our servings give you a headache. What we have to say might hurt a little, but it's good for you.

In **Chapter 1.1** we began to distinguish between "a writer's style" (fun) and "style rules" (not so much). Here's the big picture: Writers of all stripes, regardless of the medium, benefit from looking professional, and carrying a stylebook around is a good look.

It's only human nature, however, that carrying a stylebook is different from reading it, studying all the rules and applying them consistently. That's why God made copy editors. They're the ones who worry about whether their chosen profession is spelled as two words, or "copyeditor," or perhaps "copy-editor."

Stylebooks aren't sacred. They are created by people and people are not perfect, and sometimes they even harbor ulterior motives. The Chicago Tribune's fearless leader for many years was Col. Robert McCormick. He became president of the Tribune in 1911 and served as its publisher and editor-in-chief from 1925 to 1955. One detractor called him "the greatest mind of the 14th century."

Old-timers on the Tribune copy desk told the story that when the colonel was lobbying to have McCormick Place built, they were instructed to change the style for referring to the International Amphitheatre, the main competition at the time, to "Amphitheatre in the Stockyards." Who in their right mind would prefer to hold an exhibition in that bloody place?

If you come across a style point that looks insane, you don't have to follow it. There's an escape hatch called "local style." Local style sheets, agreed upon by the powers-that-be at your publication, override the official stylebook, whether it's the Associated Press Stylebook, the Chicago Manual of Style, The New York Times Manual of Style and Usage, the style guides for the Modern Language Association or the American Psychological Association, or maybe even The Economist Style Guide or the Wall Street Journal Guide to Business Style and Usage.

Some style rules when carried out uniformly produce copy that looks slightly silly. Charles Manson orchestrated one of the most horrific crimes of the 20th century in August 1969, when he ordered his followers to murder seven people, including the actor Sharon Tate.

But as evil as Manson might seem, when he died in 2017, articles in The New York Times called him "Mr. Manson" on second reference (Stack, 2017).

The stylebook entry at play dealt with "courtesy titles," or as we say "honorifics": Mr., Mrs., Miss, Ms., Rev., Dr. (Ph.D.), Dr. (medical). As you'll see, this gets tricky. When Dr. Ben Carson, a neurosurgeon, was running for president, The Wall Street Journal got called out for identifying him as Mr. Carson.

The Journal's stylebook at the time advised: "For those in politics, avoid using Dr. (as well as Rev. and Gen.) when the honorific has little or nothing to do with the political roles of the individuals involved."

That changed as of May 17, 2023, when The Wall Street Journal announced that it would drop courtesy titles and go with last names only. Editor-in-Chief Emma Tucker in a memo to her staff wrote that "dropping courtesy titles is more in line with the way people communicate their identities. It puts everyone on a more-equal footing" (The Wall Street Journal, 2023).

If you read The New York Times, you'll notice articles will say Mr. Trump or Mr. Biden on second reference whereas you'll see just Trump or Biden in an AP story.

That's because the AP Stylebook rule says, "In general, do not use courtesy titles except in direct quotations" (AP, 65). Even that gets tricky as someone will say "Governor," not "Gov." ("guv"). Nonetheless, the AP insists on using the abbreviation before a name in a quotation.

The Dallas Morning News elevated the issue of courtesy titles to its ethics code, explaining:

> *"Appropriate titles are used in all news sections except in cases involving historical figures (e.g., Lincoln, Churchill, Hitler) or in sports. Mrs., Miss or Ms. is used according to individual preference, if known. If not known, Ms. is the default title. Mr. is the usual courtesy title for males" (News Leaders Association, n.d.).*

Although "Mr. Manson" is tough to beat, one of your co-authors had a brush with absurdity in his early days on the copy desk of the old Buffalo (New York) Evening News in the 1970s.

Back to "Mr." The rule on the Evening News copy desk was to use "Mr." on second reference for someone unless he had been convicted of a crime. Then he loses his "Mr."

Along comes David Berkowitz, the "Son of Sam Killer," so called because he claimed a dog owned by a neighbor named Sam ordered him to commit random killings on the streets of New York City.

While he was on trial in 1978, our stories read "Mr. Berkowitz" until the top brass couldn't take it anymore. A ruling came down to the copy desk: Berkowitz is losing his "Mr." prematurely—before conviction.

This is all by way of saying the more rules a stylebook has, the more trouble they can create.

The 56th edition of the AP Stylebook (2022-2024) we're citing is 10 times the length of AP's original 1953 edition (60 pages versus 612, plus 14 supplemental pages). Not to be outdone, the Chicago Manual of Style (17th edition) weighs in at 1,103 pages (1,144 with index). The AP's 57th edition added chapters on Artificial Intelligence, Criminal Justice and Technology and sections on digital journalism and self-editing. It dropped the media law and digital security chapters. New total pages: 502.

We're here to help you sort out style matters the best we can. There will be no substitute, however, for picking up your own stylebook—again and again. We'll begin our stylebook analysis with reverence to the Associated Press, which calls its guide "the journalist's bible." To show how stylebooks change, we'll cite entries and page numbers from the 56th edition, then update points from the 57th as need be.

Signs of the Times

Stylebooks evolve, both by changing rulings on style points and by adding entries and sections to reflect a changing culture. Nowhere is that clearer than in the 57th edition of the AP Stylebook, which can cost you in the range of $34.95 (retail, no discount) to $104,000 (online access for 10,000 named users).

The stylebook is not free, nor is it values-free. Take the abortion entry, which reads in part: "Use the modifiers 'anti-abortion' or 'abortion rights'; don't use 'pro-life,' 'pro-choice' or 'pro-abortion' unless they are in quotes or proper names" (AP, 2).

Don't say "pro-life"? That might sound right to some editor in New York City, where the Associated Press is based, but not everywhere in the country. In trying to reach neutral ground, the AP can't help but crash on the rocky road of an emotionally charged issue.

As we continue to navigate entries, keep two things in mind:

1. That Bernard Goldberg in his book "Bias" (2014) writes that an East Coast liberal bias exists in major news organizations that operate out of New York.

2. That we mentioned as an escape hatch, a "local style sheet" can overrule your stylebook if you think another approach appeals to your audience.

Under a "What's new" section, spanning three full pages, the 56th edition of the AP Stylebook includes these items:

> ***Pronouns****: As much as possible, AP now uses they/them/their as a way of accurately describing and representing a person who uses those pronouns for themself. This is an expansion on our more limited 2017 guidance. (AP, vi)*

In 2017 the AP took a half step in this direction, updating its stylebook to add the use of "they/them" pronouns for nonbinary individuals under "limited" circumstances. Still the stylebook won't endorse the use of neo-pronouns, even though in March 2019 the Oxford English Dictionary added "hir" and "zir," corresponding to the subject pronoun "ze," as gender-neutral third-person pronouns.

> ***Race-related coverage****: Revised guidance to not use Black(s) or white(s) as either a singular or plural noun; previously we had said the plural use was accepted in limited uses. (AP, vi)*

Let's put this in the analysis translator: First, if we were on Oprah's old show, you would win a car for noting the split infinitive ("to not use" rather than "not to use"). The test for a "noun" is to put the articles "a" or "the" in front of the word. So don't say "the Blacks," for example.

The AP made news on June 19, 2020, when a blog post by John Daniszewski, AP's vice president of standards, reported:

> *AP's style is now to capitalize Black in a racial, ethnic or cultural sense, conveying an essential and shared sense of history, identity and community among people who identify as Black, including those in the African diaspora and within Africa. The lowercase black is a color, not a person. (Daniszewski, 2020)*

Why the timing? As you may recall, protests began in Minneapolis on May 26, 2020, the day after George Floyd was killed; then on June 6, hundreds of thousands of people joined protests in more than 500 sites across the country. Millions joined Black Lives Matter protests that summer.

So did those waves put pressure on the AP to capitalize the "B" in "Black"?

Daniszewski, suggesting no, wrote, "Our revisions come after more than two years of in-depth research and discussion with colleagues and respected thinkers from a diversity of backgrounds, both within and from outside the cooperative" (Daniszewski, 2020).

The rules change to Black coincided with an AP decision to capitalize "Indigenous"—about 400 years after the so-called sale of Manhattan involving Indigenous New Yorkers (Connolly, 2018).

According to the blog post: "The AP said it expects to make a decision within a month on whether to capitalize the term white" (Connolly, 2020). Final decision, as you saw above: Keep "white" lowercase.

Sorry, if predicted, this chapter gives you a headache. One thing that's consistent about the English language is there's no consistency.

Remember the point we made in **Core Principle No. 10** about how words should be turn-ons, not turn-offs? That was echoed in the AP's "What's new" segment for 2021 updates made online. The item fell under race-related coverage with an admonition: Do not write in a way that assumes "white" is the default.

We think this bit of wisdom can be applied in other circumstances as well: "Be aware that some words and phrases that seem innocuous to one group can carry negative connotations, even be seen as slurs, to another" (AP, 245).

> *Gender, sex and sexual orientation: A renamed umbrella entry, including more than 25 new or revised entries. … We now use LGBTQ instead of LGBT. (AP, vii)*

The AP added a "+" to LGBTQ+ in a 2023 online update, then added it to the 57th print edition.

The expanding AP Stylebook mirrors changes in society and topics in the news. As you can see in the AP page numbers in parentheses, these are the times that try copy editors' souls:

The **gender, sex and sexual orientation** entry (119–123), plus gender-neutral language (124–125), cover 6½ pages but not more than **immigration, migration** spread across 8¼ pages (145–153). The entry on **race-related coverage** (245–253) tops them both with nine pages.

Various entries about the **military** plus **weapons** cover six pages (190–193, 307–310). The two-page entry **mental illness** (185–186) ends with reference to 10 related entries and a note: "See the **Health and Science** chapter." The entry **weather terms** (310–316) covers six pages. The entry **disabilities** (84–86) refers you to 36 related entries.

The stylebook's wheels move slowly. Just think it took the 57th edition to add an entry on **obesity, obese, overweight**. If it took the AP two years to get to Black, there's no telling what explains the timing to add an NFT entry as part of this expanded section:

> ***Cryptocurrency, blockchain, bitcoin, NFT, Web3***: *Renamed entry combines formerly separate entries, adds **NFT** and **Web3** and updates throughout. We now use lowercase bitcoin on all references. (AP, vii)*

A brief history of NFTs (non-fungible tokens) begins with the minting of "Quantum" by Kevin McCoy on the Namecoin blockchain on May 3, 2014, three years before the term NFT was coined in 2017 (Exmundo, 2023).

The AP Stylebook entry cites a $70 million sale in March 2021 as "kicking off an NFT boom" (AP, 69). In January 2022 the AP announced it was launching an NFT marketplace to showcase its historic and contemporary photos (AP, 12). So in this case it took AP five years to recognize NFT with an entry just as the news agency formally joined the trend.

Decisions on when to post and how to phrase stylebook entries are made by people like you, not some Higher Council of Humanity that hands down rulings from the gods. Read stylebooks critically and feel free to file your own challenges or suggestions anytime.

The rule above all other rules is to avoid possible confusion. You want your readers, listeners or viewers to skate along on smooth ice, not get tripped up by something weird or erroneous.

A Grammar and Usage Guide, Too

The AP Stylebook meshes the latest terms in society with grammatical ones that date back hundreds of years. Rather than deal with conjunctions ("that") or pronouns ("that," "which," "who," "whom") individually, with related punctuation issues, these two back-to-back entries in the AP Stylebook cover a lot of grammatical ground:

- **essential clauses, nonessential clauses** (101)
- **essential phrases, nonessential phrases** (101–102)

A seasoned grammarian might recoil, as the terms "restrictive," rather than essential, and "nonrestrictive," rather than nonessestial, are used traditionally. Clauses have subjects, like "people," and verbs, like "know" and "ask," whereas phrases do not. Let's take one sentence as an example:

People who don't know grammar should ask for help.

Which people? All people? No, just the ones who don't know grammar. In other words, the clause "who don't know grammar" restricts the meaning of "people." What an old-school grammarian would call a restrictive clause, the AP calls an essential clause. Notice the difference in meaning with the sentence punctuated like so:

People, who don't know grammar, should ask for help.

The meaning here is "all people" do not know grammar, but that's not true. Nonrestrictive, or nonessential, clauses come with commas. For example:

People, who are only human, need help.

The meaning here is "all people" need help.

Standard English usage plays a large role in the AP Stylebook. We offer a lot more discussion in an upcoming chapter, but here's an appetizer of entries with our own shorthand in parentheses:

- **affect, effect** (different meanings as nouns and verbs)
- **allude, refer** (whether you mention something or not)
- **among** (three or more), **between** (two)
- **amount** (can't count), **number** (can count)
- **another** (not a synonym for "additional")
- **anticipate, expect** ("anticipate" requires action)
- **assure** (give confidence), **ensure** (guarantee), **insure** (for a premium)
- **average, mean** (same as average), **median** (right in between), **norm** (the standard)
- **mishap** (can't kill you, but an accident can)

The Places We Will Go

The AP Stylebook takes a big leap assuming people's knowledge of geography in its **datelines** entry. It implies that a city's name is so obvious, you don't need to add the country or state. How about a test! We'll give you the location, then you give us the country. OK? Here goes, just four to make a point or two:

1. Brussels
2. Djibouti
3. Macao
4. San Marino

(Look for the answers at the end of the chapter.)

Here's the first point: Under **international datelines**, AP lists 49 cities, out of 4 million in the world, whose countries are so obvious they don't need to be mentioned. That's called "editorial judgment"; a curmudgeon might say it's winging it. Again, none of this is sacred, and you can come to your own conclusions.

Here's another point: The AP Stylebook under **domestic datelines** lists 30 U.S. cities out of more than 100,000 that don't need to add states. CHICAGO—No need for Illinois. Got it. For obvious reasons, the list doesn't include SPRING-FIELD, a city in 34 states, or LEXINGTON, a city in only 25 states (AP, 73).

That means an AP story will refer to Springfield, Illinois, or Lexington, Kentucky, so those cities are not confused with Springfield, Kentucky, or Lexington, Illinois. Except for one thing, and here's where local style comes into play: If your publication is in Springfield, Illinois, or Lexington, Kentucky, there's no confusion for your audience, so listing the state becomes superfluous.

An Almanac and Reporting Guide

One of your co-authors will never forget the day at 25 years old that he was assigned to The Chicago Tribune's foreign desk with copy editors who had worked at the newspaper longer than he had been alive. On break, one of his colleagues got out a scrapbook of the days he edited stories about Al Capone. Such a valuable grasp of history is known as "institutional memory."

In our early days of teaching editing at Northwestern University's Medill School of Journalism, we required not only the AP Stylebook but also an almanac filled with facts and history that extended beyond our students' lived experiences.

Occasionally you'll come upon an entry in the 56th edition of the AP Stylebook that reads like an almanac entry to keep editors from making another kind of mistake—a fact error. We'll list some entries here to give you a feel:

- **Academy Awards** Presented annually by the Academy of Motion Picture Arts and Sciences. Also known as the Oscars. (Both "Academy Awards" and "Oscars" are trademarks.) (AP, 3)

- **act, amendment, bill, law, measure, ordinance, resolution, rule, statute** (AP, 4–5).
- **Affordable Care Act** (AP, 7).
- **"alt-right"** (AP, 12–13) with sub items (sorry, "subitems" looks too weird) on racism, white nationalism, white separatism, white supremacy, neo-Nazism, antifa and, last, **"alt-left."** (See race-related coverage.)
- **Alzheimer's disease** (AP, 13).

To put a top hat on what we said in **chapters 1.1** and **1.3** about "getting played," you can feel the AP Stylebook take a turn as a reporting guide with its entry **anonymous sources** (AP, 17–18).

Just as we prefer skim milk with our latte at the Anal-Retentive Cafe, we have just begun to skim the surface of the AP Stylebook. But we hope we have enough so far to encourage you to buy your own "bible" and carry it around for a good look. Then dive in when you get that uneasy feeling about something in your editing stage of writing.

Sweet Home Chicago

The Chicago Manual of Style, whose first edition dates to 1906, is published by the University of Chicago Press, so it has an entirely different ("academic") feel, just like Chicago would never be confused with New York City. Yes, there are page numbers to guide you in the CMS (also known as CMOS or simply Chicago style), but the stylebook adds precision with a numbering system that begins with the chapter number, then a dot followed by the entry number. So, for example, the CMS begins with **Overview, Scholarly publishing** (1.1) on page 4.

Whereas the AP Stylebook opens with **a, an** on Page 1, the CMS takes you to Chapter 5 before offering its **a; an.** entry (5.250) on page 306. It's the first one under **Word Usage**, "Glossary of Problematic Words and Phrases" (306–358), ending with **your; you're**. The AP Stylebook ends its opening chapter with **zip line** (AP, 322).

Speaking of headaches, we figure if the ring-bound, paperback AP Stylebook were dropped on your head, it would leave a lump. If the same happened with our hardcover CMS, we fear a concussion for our money ($55.02, down from $70 with a discount). We refer you to the AP entry **brain trauma, traumatic brain injury, brain damage, brain-damaged** (AP, 35).

You can avoid injury by signing up for a free 30-day trial of the Chicago Manual of Style Online so you can get a feel for the manual's features and access to a users forum.

The editors of both stylebooks appear to have the same temperament, as the CMS follows its **your; you're** entry with a new section, **Bias-Free Language** (358). The opening paragraph hits the rationale nail on the head: **Maintaining credibility** (5.251).

You then can read about:

- Gender bias, other biases, bias and the editor's responsibility
- Techniques for achieving gender neutrality
- Gender-neutral singular pronouns
- Problematic gender-specific suffixes
- Necessary gender-specific language
- Sex-specific labels as adjectives
- Avoiding other biased language (5.251–5.260, ending on page 362)

A comma before the "and" in any list pays tribute to **Series and the Serial Comma** (6.19, 371). As we mentioned in **Chapter 1.1**, the battle over the AP style rule for punctuating "red, white and blue" (no comma before the "and") and the CMS rule requiring a serial comma, as in "red, white, and blue," has left copy editors black and blue. You can even buy a T-shirt proclaiming your membership in the Oxford Comma Preservation Society.

Or as CMS says, "Chicago strongly recommends this widely practiced usage, blessed by Fowler and other authorities (see bibliog. 1.2), since it prevents ambiguity."

Blessed? You see, this is a religious war. We won't take sides here. Our view is simple: Do what your boss wants, and if you're the boss, do what you think is right.

To be clear we're talking about the rule for commas in a simple series. Both the AP and the CMS advise a second comma in a complex series, as in "She ordered coffee, orange juice, and ham and eggs." Remember, the rule above all rules is to avoid possible confusion. You want your readers to skate along, then slow down with a comma, so they don't trip on thinking about "juice and ham."

In the AP Stylebook, an entire chapter is devoted to **Punctuation** (AP, 323–336), opening with an overview, citing "The Elements of Style" by William Strunk Jr. and E.B. White, and ending with an entry on slash (/). Likewise, the CMS devotes Chapter 6 to **Punctuation** (363–416), from the **Overview** (6.1), past the **Slashes** entries (6.105–6.113), to **Vertical lists with multiple levels (outlines)** (6.132).

The CMS begins its publishing rules at the other extreme from the AP's focus on daily, hourly, even minute-by-minute news coverage. **Part I, The Publishing Process**, covers these main topics: **Books and Journals** (3–58), **Manuscript Preparation, Manuscript Editing, and Proofreading** (59–124),

Illustrations and Tables (125–170) and **Rights, Permissions, and Copyright Administration** (171–222).

What constitutes the AP Stylebook mostly fits in Chicago style's **Part II, Style and Usage** (223–740) like the meat in a CMS sandwich. **Part III, Source Citations and Indexes**, covers **Notes and Bibliography** (741–890), **Author-Date References** (891–922) and **Indexes** (923–974). What follows is a **Glossary** (975–990) with entries like **em dash, halftone screen, measure (line length in picas), prepress proof, URL** and **widow (short line at top of page)**. Then comes a **Bibliography** (991–1013) and lastly a most valuable **Index** (1015–1144).

Just as the AP Stylebook is easy to navigate when its chapter entries are listed alphabetically, the best way to swim through the CMS is to find the editing issue you want to address alphabetically in the Index. The AP Stylebook has its own **Bibliography** (AP, 512–514) and **Index** (AP, 516–612).

The AP's index is particularly valuable because the stylebook shifts from topic to topic so many times. To be honest, none of the AP or CMS book searches is easy until you bounce around for a while—or give up and pay for the online search options. For example, with the AP, you may wonder whether "home run" is one word or two and go to the **Stylebook** chapter only to see entries jump from **homepage** to **hometown** (AP, 140).

Then you remember there's a separate **Sports** chapter (AP, 424–452), but don't look under "h" and get stuck seeing entries for **home field (n.), home-field (adj.)** (AP, 441). You need to look under "b" for **baseball** (AP, 426) and scan past italicized terms like "fair ball" and "fastball" until you see, yes indeed, "home run" is two words.

Alas, the AP's index fails you, moving from **homepage** to **home schooling** (AP, 558). Sadly, the CMS index is silent, too, jumping from **home pages (two words)** to **homonyms** (1062).

On its Contents page, the AP Stylebook lists other titles, such as:

- **Business**
- **Inclusive storytelling**
- **Data journalism**
- **Polls and surveys**
- **Health and science**
- **AP social media guidelines**
- **Digital security for journalists** (57th edition adds **Digital Journalism** section)
- **Religion**
- **Briefing on media law** (moved to online only)
- **AP statement of news values and principles**

Two of those AP chapters lend themselves to alphabetical entries, such as under **Religion** from **abaya** (robe, AP, 390) to **Zoroastrianism** (3,800-year-old religion, AP, 422) and under **Sports** from **abbreviations** (NFL, PGA, MLB and the like; AP, 424) to the spelling words **zone, zone defense** (AP, 452). The other chapters provide narratives with boldfaced headings. As a sign of the times, the AP's 57th edition adds an **Artificial Intelligence** chapter with 11 key terms. A new **Technology** chapter combines individual tech-related and social media entries. A **Criminal Justice** chapter combines entries and offers guidance on using the term **child sexual abuse images** (not child porn).

We hope you enjoyed this trek through styleland—and your head doesn't hurt too much.

International Datelines Quiz

Before you go on to read our chapters on spelling, grammar, punctuation and usage, check your score for our little quiz:
And the answers are in order:

1. Brussels, **Belgium**
2. Djibouti, **Republic of Djibouti**
3. Macao, **China** (AP used to spell the autonomous region as Macau)
4. San Marino, **Republic of San Marino**

HOMEWORK

Assignment No. 1

Write a one-page compare-and-contrast analysis of the AP Stylebook, 56th edition, and the Chicago Manual of Style, 17th edition. How are they both in tune with changing American culture? How do they both use alphabetical entries for easy access to style points? How do they differ in tone and format? How would you define the target reader and user for each stylebook?

Assignment No. 2

What's your position on the "comma-and/no comma" debate over punctuation for listing words or phrases in a simple series? Do you favor the serial comma (Oxford comma)? If so, why? How would explain the AP's rationale for the "optional comma, no comma" rule in its stylebook? Alas, why do you think editors defend their positions so fiercely?

Assignment No. 3

Show that you understand the difference between the punctuation of a simple series in AP style and a complex series. Write three sentences with a simple series of words or phrases (no comma before the "and"). Then write three sentences with a complex series where you need the comma before the "and" to avoid possible confusion.

Assignment No. 4

Congratulations! You've just been appointed editor-in-chief of a magazine focusing on your favorite hobby. If you had the choice between the AP Stylebook or the Chicago Manual of Style as your primary guide, which one would you choose, and why? Now think of the top three items you would list on your "local style sheet" reflecting how your writers and editors would disagree with a particular style point and create their own rule.

REFERENCES

Associated Press. (2022). *The Associated Press stylebook: 2022–2024* (56th ed.). Basic Books.

Associated Press. (2024). *The Associated Press stylebook: 2024–2026* (57th ed.). Basic Books.

Connolly, C. (2018, October 5). The true native New Yorkers can never truly reclaim their homeland. *Smithsonian.* https://www.smithsonianmag.com/history/true-native-new-yorkers-can-never-truly-reclaim-their-homeland-180970472/

Daniszewski, J. (2020, June 19). The decision to capitalize Black. Associated Press. https://blog.ap.org/announcements/the-decision-to-capitalize-black

Exmundo, J. (2023, March 21). Quantum: The story behind the world's first NFT. NFT Now. https://nftnow.com/art/quantum-the-first-piece-of-nft-art-ever-created/

Goldberg, B. (2014). *Bias: A CBS insider exposes how the media distort the news.* Regnery Publishing.

News Leaders Association. (n.d.). *The Dallas Morning News*: Ethics code. https://members.newsleaders.org/resources-ethics-dallas

Stack, L. (2017, November 20). Charles Manson, unhinged pop culture figure. *The New York Times.* https://www.nytimes.com/2017/11/20/arts/charles-manson-pop-culture.html?searchResultPosition=4

University of Chicago Press Editorial Staff. (2017). *The Chicago manual of style* (17th ed.). https://www.chicagomanualofstyle.org/home.html

The Wall Street Journal. (2023, May 16). Vol. 36, No. 5: Honorifics. https://www.wsj.com/articles/vol-36-no-5-honorifics-ba2543d8

FURTHER READING, RESOURCES

Try the Chicago Manual of Style Online for 30 days free. Your trial includes the full features of the manual, including access to its users forum. No credit card is required to sign up. Visit bitly.com/cmostrial to get started.

LaRoque, P. (2002, February 6). Courtesy titles are about more than respect. *Quill.* https://www.quillmag.com/2002/02/06/courtesy-titles-are-about-more-than-respect/

Pappas, C. B. (2022, May 2). The *AP stylebook* should update its entry on pronouns | opinion. *Newsweek.* https://www.newsweek.com/ap-stylebook-should-update-its-entry-pronouns-opinion-1702285

Payack, P. J. J. (2022, January 3). Global Language Monitor (GLM) names the numerals the top words of the year 2021 for global English. EIN Presswire. https://www.einpresswire.com/article/559667614/global-language-monitor-glm-names-the-numerals-the-top-words-of-the-year-2021-for-global-english

Tumin, R. (2018, March 22). The elements of the stylebook. *The New York Times.* https://www.nytimes.com/2018/03/22/insider/new-york-times-stylebook.html

Woods, B. (2017, November 20). Charles Manson was not a product of the counterculture. *The New York Times.* https://www.nytimes.com/2017/11/20/opinion/charles-manson-counterculture.html

SPELLING

KEY POINTS IN THIS CHAPTER

1. When it comes to spelling, check the stylebook first, not the dictionary. Not all stylebooks agree on how to spell a word, nor do all dictionaries. Go with your organization's stylebook and the dictionary it recommends.

2. You'll see multiple spellings of names, places and words translated to English phonetically from foreign-language alphabets. Be careful because not only phonetics but also politics can be involved. Check your stylebook for the preferred spelling.

3. Stylebooks tend to agree on commonly misspelled words, either just listing the words or offering a few words of clarification about what or what not to do.

4. Playwright George Bernard Shaw's quote that England and America are "two countries separated by a common language" is true when it comes to spelling. We consider all those "u's" in proper British spellings, such as "colour," "favour" and "labour," to be superfluous.

This Might Hurt a Little, but … (Take 2)

"Hey, Mom!" you shout to your poor mother as you work on your term paper for an elective high school class on cooking. "What's that word? Is it spelled chicken Kiev or Kyiv?"

"Look it up in the dictionary!" she responds.

And so you unwittingly unleashed a geopolitical battle. Ah, for the simple life, when you thought "that word" had one and only one spelling (and pronunciation), and the answer lay in "the dictionary."

Now that you've read **Chapter 1.1** and started to live a professional's life, you realize your loving mother gave you bad advice. She should have responded, "Look in your stylebook!" as the stylebook overrules the dictionary when it comes to spelling.

And if it's not one thing, it's your mother—again. "Which dictionary?" was your proper response. Zoom back to **Core Principle No. 5:** For starters, there's Webster's New World College Dictionary, 5th edition; Webster's Third New International Dictionary; Merriam-Webster's Collegiate Dictionary; and the American Heritage Dictionary of the English Language.

And to make matters worse, there's another question: "Which stylebook?" Remember that the Associated Press Stylebook and the Chicago Manual of Style don't always agree. When it comes to spelling, you might even get stumped on whether to make "stylebook" one word or two.

If a word is not listed in the stylebook, the default position is to have you check a particular dictionary. Alas, different dictionaries do not always agree.

The AP Stylebook's 56th edition cited Webster's New World College Dictionary before AP switched to Merriam-Webster while the Chicago Manual of Style put the other three to use. Or to be more specific about two of them, the CMS says, "If, as occasionally happens, the Collegiate disagrees with the Third International, the Collegiate (or its online counterpart) should be followed, since it represents newer lexical research" (7.1, 418).

This "lexical research" is not done in a vacuum. One constant challenge over the years is spelling and word choice debated for political reasons. In 1982, when England engaged in a 10-week undeclared war with Argentina in the South Atlantic over the Falkland Islands, editors in the Western news media chose not to refer to what Argentina called those islands, Las Islas Malvinas.

When war in Ukraine broke out on Feb. 24, 2022, writers and broadcasters were confronted with the decision to call the capital either "Kiev (kee-EV)," a bow to Russia, or "Kyiv (KEEV)," a nod toward an independent Ukraine. Even calling the country "the Ukraine," rather than just "Ukraine," became an issue. "The" is a Russian throwback.

The dish "chicken Kiev" got cooked up in St. Petersburg, Russia, in 1912, when the last czar, Nicholas II, still reigned as emperor of Russia. Using "Kiev" for that dish is generally accepted, politics aside.

Foreign Words Meet Politics

World politics and foreign names can cause style-book editors to do backflips. When Vladimir Lenin died in 1924, St. Petersburg was renamed Leningrad. Once the Soviet Union fell, the city returned in 1991 to be known as St. Petersburg. Of course, as the Chicago Manual of Style points out, "Lenin's real name was Vladimir Ilyich Ulyanov (given name, patronymic, family name)" under a subsection **Russian names** (8.12, 465) in "Non-English Names in an English Context."

One of the more prominent names in the news these days is "Zelensky." Wait, isn't it "Zelenskyy" with two "y's"? The official website of the president of Ukraine spells his name "Volodymyr Zelenskyy." And so that's the way you'll see the name spelled for the AP, The Guardian, Al Jazeera, "The PBS NewsHour," NBC News and CNBC.

FIGURE 1.6.1   The official website of Ukrainian President Volodymyr Zelenskyy provides the definitive spelling of his name—definitive for some news organizations, at least.

Meanwhile, The New York Times, The Washington Post, The Wall Street Journal, Newsweek, CNN, The Hill, C-SPAN, BBC News and Britannica say one "y" is enough and write "Zelensky." So what's the deal?

You may recall that in **Chapter 1.3** we talked about the challenge of dealing with words that are phonetic spellings from languages using a different alphabet, such as the artistic images of Arabic or the painted symbols of Mandarin Chinese. The same is true for the Russian alphabet with its Cyrillic script. Russian was the language of Zelenskyy's youth.

The "single-y" decision is strange. The AP Stylebook under **names** (AP, 199) says, "Generally use the name a person prefers." That remains the gold standard for spelling people's names—ask them how they want their names spelled.

In its entry on **Russian names** (AP, 261), the Associated Press recommends changing "Aleksandr" to "Alexander," for example, and for last names it says use "the English spelling that most closely approximates the pronunciation in Russian." Well, some media outlets overruled Volodymyr on how he thinks his last name sounds in English. Weird.

The AP Stylebook also addresses this point with entries on **Arabic names** (AP, 20–21) and **Chinese names** (AP, 45–46), but as you might guess not to everyone's satisfaction because simplicity is the enemy of nuance. Then, of course, AP editors will change their minds. For years the correct spelling for the Muslim holy book was "Koran." In the 56th edition, the entry **Koran** (AP, 168) says use **Quran** in all references except when preferred by an organization or in a specific title or name.

We know some of you are too young to remember the terrorist attacks on Sept. 11, 2001, but soon thereafter the AP needed to make calls on how to spell "**Osama bin Laden**" and his base of support, "**al-Qaida**" (translates to "the base").

The 9/11 Commission Report, the U.S. government's official document, uses the shorthand of UBL to refer to "**Usama Bin Ladin**," indicating his first name sounded more like an "ooh" than an "oh," and the last name ending with an "in" sound. Meanwhile, other news organizations like the BBC referred to "**al-Qaeda**" ("e," not "i") and its leader, **Osama Bin Laden** (capital "O" and "B" with "en" at the end). You get the idea—that's why writers welcome stylebooks. AP makes it clear with its entry **bin Laden, Osama** (AP, 31).

Under **Chinese names** AP's advice is to "use the new spelling for 'Mao Zedong,'" new for someone who died in 1976. The "old" first name, as you might see on marxists.org, was written "Tsetung" or "Tse Tung."

Mao was his last name. It's also a common noun. When pronounced across Mandarin's four tones *mao* can mean *mother, linen, horse* or *scold*. The AP could transmit the accent marks to show the different pronunciations, but as it says in its **accent marks** entry (AP, 3), its clients might not have the technology to receive them.

You'll also see AP entries for **Korean names** (AP, 168) and **Spanish names** (AP, 274). So let's just say the world is complicated, and that's why we can enjoy stylebooks making decisions for us.

Preferred Spelling Comes First

The way a word is listed in a stylebook defines the "preferred spelling." It is derived from a particular dictionary that provides a full definition of the word. If you find a word in the dictionary and it doesn't have a full definition, keep looking. That's not the preferred spelling. For instance, "usable," the preferred spelling, is also listed in Webster's New World College Dictionary as "useable" but with no definition. Merriam-Webster calls the extra "e" a variant.

Beware of the word "or." The dictionary might list more than one spelling for a word. For example, for "cancel," you may see the past tense listed as "-celed" or "-celled." Go with the first spelling, as it is preferred. If you can't find a word in the stylebook and you turn to a dictionary, be sure that you're using the same edition, including online varieties, as your colleagues.

What if a word is listed two ways with different definitions? For instance, "voluntarism" and "volunteerism." Some news organizations just punt and recommend "volunteerism" for all usages.

In the dictionary you might see other spellings for a word with abbreviations such as "also," "var.," "alt." or "Brit." Go with the preferred version, or the first one listed, not the "variant" or the "alternate" spelling or the "British" spelling.

As playwright George Bernard Shaw put it, America and Britain are "two countries separated by a common language." When it comes to our American stylebooks, we show economy by dropping all those extra "u's" in British spellings ("colour," "honour," "odour," "favour"). And we'll use a "z," thank you, rather than an "s," as in "analyze," not "analyse." As the Chicago Manual of Style notes (7.3, 418), "In quoted material, however, spelling is left unchanged."

For British spellings, you can consult New Hart's Rules: The Oxford Style Guide or The New Oxford Dictionary for Writers and Editors. They are favored in the United Kingdom, Canada and Australia. Under spelling you can read about "US usage."

We hope by now you're getting the same feeling as us when you hear a writer try to justify spelling a word one way by saying, "Well, it's in the dictionary!" That's not the preferred—or professional—way of thinking.

Crazy as a …

Stylebooks offer online editions and blogs to provide updates, so learning to spell is a moving target. As the language changes, new words get added at a brisk pace. We know what you're thinking: thanks a million. On June 13, 2009, the Global Language Monitor announced that the 1,000,000th word in the English language was coined that week (GLM, n.d.). The GLM estimates that a new word is created every 98 minutes.

Crazy, right? Read on.

As we noted in **Chapter 1.5**, stylebooks can get a little crazy. There's no better example than the first Chicago Tribune stylebook we encountered as young editors in the early 1980s. It included its own dictionary for spelling simple words, like cigaret (not cigarette), employe (not employee) and frater (not freighter).

The old Buffalo (New York) Evening News, like other family-owned newspapers back in the day, also had a stylebook filled with idiosyncrasies. When "The Happy Hooker" film debuted in 1975, the publisher insisted on airbrushing the movie ads to read "The Happy Hoofer," as the word "hooker" was not appropriate for use anywhere in the paper.

This view is known as "the family newspaper concept," and it still guides some editors to this day, even though kids may know and use more dirty words than their parents ever did. Not to be outdone by Gen Z, Joe Biden of the Silent Generation came through on hot mics during the first half of his presidency with both the f-word and the b-word, sending editors to their stylebooks for advice on how to report those words, if at all—and how to spell them.

"No one f**ks with a Biden," he told Fort Myers Beach's mayor on Oct. 5, 2022, as he was surveying damage caused by Hurricane Ian in Florida. On Jan. 24, 2022, Biden directed a line under his breath at Fox News White House reporter Peter Doocy, saying, "What a stupid son of a b**ch," when Doocy shouted out a question about whether inflation was a political liability for him. As vice president in 2010, at a March 23 White House press conference celebrating the passage of the Affordable Care Act, nicknamed Obamacare, Biden whispered to President Obama: "This is a big f**king deal" (Cirilli, 2012).

We'll talk more about all this in **Chapter 2.5, Get Me a Quote!,** but know for now that the AP Stylebook addresses curse words and what to spell out—or not spell out. Under **obscenities, profanities, vulgarities** (AP, 212), the stylebook advises using only the first letter, then hyphens (f ---, b----, s ---). Other times, it says, you might just replace the curse word with a generic word in parentheses, like (obscenity).

We Beg to Disagree

Something else can drive you crazy: when the AP Stylebook and the CMS differ.

The Chicago Manual of Style says spell out centuries whereas the AP says use numbers after nine. For example:

- the eighteenth and early nineteenth centuries (CMS, 9.32, 556)
- the first century but the 18th and early 19th centuries (AP, 43)

And the CMS has its own rules about abbreviating the United States, the United Nations and the United Kingdom:

- US, not U.S. (reserve for adjective, like US dollars; prefer to spell out United States as a noun, though "the US" is acceptable). (10.32, 585–86)
- UN, not U.N., as in the UN General Assembly (8.62, 487)
- UK, not U.K., for United Kingdom (14.297, 886)

According to the AP, some abbreviations come with periods—U.S., U.N., U.K.—and some not—GI, ID, EU and don't forget AP (AP, 2).

The stylebooks also disagree on whether to abbreviate months with dates: "Mar." and "Apr." for CMS (10.39, 588) while the AP says "March" and "April" (AP, 196).

When it comes to contractions, the AP and the CMS aren't always on the same page. So, for example:

- dos and don'ts (CMS)
- do's and don'ts (AP)

On using OK or okay, the AP offers this entry: **OK, OK'd, OK'ing, OKs** Do not use "okay." (AP, 214). The CMS has no comparable entry.

Common Mistakes, AP-Style

Let's dip into the AP Stylebook for a deeper look. The quickest way to check a spelling is to find the word listed alphabetically. An entry may involve just listing a word without explanation. The 57th edition deletes most of these words to save space:

- **accommodate**
- **acknowledgment**
- **admissible**

- **ad nauseam**
- **airfare**
- **indispensable**
- **jack-o'-lantern**
- **judgment**
- **liaison**
- **minuscule**
- **permissible**
- **reconnaissance**

Some listings will do battle with your autocorrect, such as:

- **airstrike**
- **AmeriCorps**
- **drugmaker**
- **email**
- **likable**
- **onetime, one-time, one time**
- **Ph.D., Ph.D.s**
- **p.m., a.m.**
- **politicking**
- **supersede**
- **voicemail**
- **zero, zeros**

Occasionally you'll see an entry, followed by a quick "Not" or "No," as in:

- **adviser** Not advisor.
- **afterward** Not afterwards.
- **amid** Not amidst.
- **Johns Hopkins University** No apostrophes.
- **teen, teenager** (n.), **teenage** (adj.) Do not use teen-aged.
- **till** or until. But not 'til.
- **toward** Not towards. (See **-ward, -wards**)

Prefixes and Suffixes

Although the quickest way to check a spelling is to find the word listed alphabetically, a slew of words will be listed in an entry that begins with a prefix or a suffix in the 56th edition. For example:

- **anti-**
- **co-**

- ex-
- full-
- half-
- in- and -in
- -like and like-
- off- and -off
- -out and out-
- -over and over-
- post-
- pre-
- super-
- un-
- under-
- -up and up-
- -wide and wide-
- -wise

The 57th edition groups these items under new entries **prefixes** and **suffixes**.

Spelling Rules

An AP Stylebook entry titled **spelling** (AP, 275) offers this rule of thumb: If the emphasis is on the first syllable (CAN-cel), then no double letter ("canceled"). If the emphasis is on the second syllable (in-CUR), then use a double letter ("incurred").

Alphabetically, you'll see entries like these, listing a verb's past tense (also past participle) and present participle (the -ing version), and occasionally a noun form:

- **dispel, dispelled, dispelling**
- **emcee, emceed, emceeing**
- **kidnap, kidnapped, kidnapping, kidnapper**
- **parallel, paralleled, paralleling**
- **picnic, picnicked, picnicking, picnicker**
- **recur, recurred, recurring**
- **travel, traveled, traveling, traveler**

When it comes to **abbreviations and acronyms** (AP, 2), the stylebook offers guidance on rules to abbreviate titles for **before a name** (Rep., Sen., the Rev., see five other entries), **after a name** (Jr., Sr., see **company names** and

academic degrees), with dates or numerals (A.D., B.C., No., see **months**), **in numbered addresses** (1600 Pennsylvania Ave.) and for situations where you want to **avoid awkward constructions.** That means don't follow an organization's full name with an abbreviation or acronym in parentheses. If such an abbreviation is not recognizable, don't use it.

The AP says these abbreviations are acceptable on first reference, spelled as you would pronounce them (AP, 2; AP, 424):

- CIA
- FBI
- LPGA
- NCAA
- NFL

Some plural versions with multiple letters (AP, 227):

- ABCs
- IOUs
- VIPs

However, for single letters (AP, 227):

- Mind your p's and q's.
- Learn the three R's so you can get A's and B's on your report card.

Capitalization

When it comes to **capitalization** (AP, 40), the stylebook offers guidance on **proper nouns, proper names** with reference to 26 entries, **popular names, family names, informal names, derivatives, sentences, compositions** (see three other entries), **titles** and **abbreviations.**

Capitalization can make all the difference, such as whether you're referring to China (the country) or china (the porcelain dinnerware). But the latest trend, which your boss might find annoying, is TO CAPITALIZE EVERYTHING to make a point.

Under **proper names,** the Associated Press says lowercase the common noun in plurals, as in:

- Democratic and Republican parties
- Main and State streets
- lakes Erie and Ontario

But for formal titles with full names, keep the caps:

- Presidents Jimmy Carter and Gerald Ford

Some corporate names, like "eBay," get tricky. The AP says make it "EBay" if it begins a sentence (AP, 95).

In separate entries for proper nouns, you'll find these items with special notes:

- **Clinton, Hillary Rodham** (AP, 50). She prefers to use her full name, Hillary Rodham Clinton. On second reference: Clinton. Elsewhere, you can read that if a story refers to both Bill and Hillary Clinton, and using just "Clinton" on second reference might cause confusion, then you can repeat the first and last name. So "Hillary Clinton" rather than "Mrs. Clinton."
- **Kriss Kringle** (AP, 169). Not "Kris." ... See **Santa Claus, Santa**.
- **Stalin, Josef** (AP, 276). Not Joseph.

Remember personal preference? When it comes to **capitalization** you can add **e.e. cummings,** the American poet, painter, essayist and playwright, and **k.d. lang,** the Canadian pop and country singer-songwriter, to the list of those going their own way.

Wait, Is That a Grammar Rule, Too?

We'll offer entire chapters on grammar, punctuation and usage, but while we're sizing up the AP Stylebook for spelling, a few notes are in order. The names of holidays carry an implied grammar rule. Compare these two sets:

- Father's Day (AP, 107) and Mother's Day (AP, 196)
- Veterans Day (AP, 303) and Presidents Day (AP, 234)

So why the apostrophe (possessive) for the first ones and not the others (descriptive)? When the implied preposition is "of," then it's possessive. So a day "of" a father or a mother is "Father's" Day or "Mother's" Day.

If the implied preposition is "for," then no apostrophe to note a day "for veterans" or "for presidents." The same rule applies for the implied preposition "by." That's why we would write about a "teachers strike" (a strike by teachers).

The "for" rule applies to a **teachers college** (AP, 285), and the "of" rule applies to **states' rights** (AP, 278), **Valentine's Day** (his day, a possessive, derived from the saint, AP, 302) and **April Fools' Day** (you own it if you get tricked, AP, 20).

This leads us to entries addressing **colloquialisms** (AP, 52) and **dialect** (AP, 81), such as "ain't," "gonna" and "wanna." The AP takes it a hilarious step further by saying there may be a compelling reason to write something like this:

"Din't ya yoosta live at Toidy-Toid Street and Sekun' Amya? Across from da moom pitchers?" (AP, 81)

Chicago Food for Thought

Truth be told, there's a lot of agreement between AP and Chicago styles, though the tone of voice is distinctly different, one journalistic and the other scholarly, even eccentric. The CMS goes to places that don't appear to be obvious concerns, such as the spelling of "shh." When it comes to telling someone to be quiet, how many "h's" are possible? The CMS says it's "plausible" to write three: "Shhh!"

There's nothing quiet about **rock 'n' roll,** and both stylebooks agree on that spelling for the music genre. The AP notes, however, that the official name for the Cleveland tourist site is spelled like so: **Rock & Roll Hall of Fame** (AP, 260).

In a segment on **How to Proofread and What to Look For,** the CMS notes these common spelling errors (2.111, 108) with our added comments in parentheses:

- "breath" for "breathe"
- "it's" (contraction for "it is" or "it has") for "its" (possessive)
- "lead" (pronounced both LED and LEED) for "led"
- "out" for "our"

The CMS offers this good advice under **Keeping an editorial style sheet** (2.55, 82): "To ensure consistency, for each manuscript the editor must keep an alphabetical list of words or terms to be capitalized, italicized, hyphenated, spelled, or otherwise treated in any way unique to the manuscript."

A word about possessives: The AP and the CMS agree on how to spell singular common nouns ending in "s," even when the word that follows begins with "s":

- a bass's stripes (CMS, 7.16, 422)
- the virus's spread (AP, 230)

Both stylebooks advise on tricky spellings for plurals:

- fathers-in-law, coups d'etat, courts-martial (CMS, 7.7, 419)
- the Jones family, pl. the Joneses (CMS, 7.9, 420)
- passerby, passersby (AP, 221)
- weeklong, weekslong (AP, 316)
- yearlong, yearslong (AP, 321)

In 2014 the AP made a big turn in the direction of the Chicago Manual of Style under **state names** (AP, 277) when it ruled: "The names of the 50 states should be spelled out when used in the body of story, whether standing alone or in conjunction with a city, town, village or military base." The CMS used the example: "Lake Bluff, Illinois, was incorporated in 1895" (10.27, 583).

Tools to Help With Spelling

We'll wrap up this chapter with a few final words to the wise. Spelling presents two basic challenges, the first concerning names of people and places and the second involving common words. The same rule applies: When in doubt about a word, look it up. These days you'll hear, "Google it!" But regardless of your search engine, be aware of the limitations of your online discoveries and websites, as they may be operating under their own stylebooks, not yours.

If writers and editors had to rely only on memory, spelling would be worse than it is. In today's world, they have more tools than ever to fight the spelling battle. Most writing and editing tasks are done on iPads, tablets, laptops or desktop computers using off-the-shelf software, most often Microsoft Word.

Writers can run their stories through computer spell-checkers, and editing programs come with built-in dictionaries. For names and places, the internet gives editors a path right to the source to check spelling. Let's take a deeper look at these electronic resources.

Spell-checking programs. The spell-checker can speed the editing process if the editor understands how it works. The spell-checker must use the news organization's dictionary of choice. One advantage is that the spell-checker dictionary can be customized to reflect local style. Spell-checkers don't catch misused words, such as "their" instead of "there." They can be unreliable with names. But used right, the spell-checker gives the editor an undeniable advantage on deadline. Many copy desks require that every story be run through spell-check.

Online clipping services. Most large newspapers and many smaller ones have electronic "morgues," or libraries. These online clipping files can go back decades. An editor or writer can access the electronic morgue through the internet. In addition, some news organizations may be a part of a collective electronic clipping service. These services allow the writer or editor to search clipping files from many newspapers and magazines using keywords. Just one warning is in order: Checking facts from a past article will work only if the article was correct in the first place. Sometimes checking a spelling against a clipping only perpetuates a mistake.

Internet search engines. Finding a specific organization's name or a company's official website usually takes little time. So, is the company spelled "Wal-Mart" or "Walmart"? An internet search engine quickly turns up the answer: "Walmart." A company website would also be considered an authoritative source for spelling company officers' names.

Nobody likes misspelled words. Spelling something wrong in an article makes you look bad. Spell it wrong in a headline, and you look like an incompetent fool subject to ridicule. It's easy to say spelling matters, but as you've learned in this chapter, there's really nothing easy about spelling.

Please, we beg of you, don't be like the student who praised us in a teaching evaluation for our instruction on "grammer"—misspelled!

HOMEWORK

Assignment No. 1

If you were in charge of a news organization, what would be your style ruling for spelling the last name of the president of Ukraine: **Zelenskyy** or **Zelensky?** Imagine that you had to write a memo to your staff about your ruling. How would you explain your decision? How would you explain why other news organizations do the opposite?

Assignment No. 2

For years the Associated Press preferred the spelling of **Koran** and **Mohammed.** Now the AP says use **Quran** and **Muhammad** instead. The holy book is also spelled "Qur'an," meaning "a reading or reciting," and the prophet's name has also been spelled "Mohammad," "Muhammed," "Mohamed," "Mohamad," "Muhamad," "Muhamed," "Mohamud," "Mohummad," "Mohummed," "Mouhamed," "Mohammod" and "Mouhamad." If you were handed the challenge of deciding how to spell the name of the holy book and the prophet, where would you seek your guidance and what would be your final decisions? Why do you think the editors of the AP Stylebook changed their minds?

Assignment No. 3

What do you think of the **"family newspaper concept"** that provided guidance on the use and spelling of profanity? There was a time, long ago, when a newspaper was delivered to a home and several members of a family of various ages would read sections of it. The concept held that the entire newspaper should be family friendly. If you were in charge of a publication, would you adopt the same concept? How would you spell out your guidance to your staff on dealing with sensitive issues?

Assignment No. 4

The two stories below are ones the Associated Press would like to forget from March 2004. The first suffers from rapid and sloppy use of **spell-check.** The second was a correction sent shortly after the first. How many errors can you find in the original based on your reading of the corrected version?

ORIGINAL

GENEVA (AP)—Sir Peter Ustinov, a brilliant wit and mimic who won two Oscars for an acting career that ranged from the evil Near in "Quo Vida's" to the quirky detective Hercules Point, has died. He was 82.

He died of heart failure Wednesday at a clinic near his home at Burins overlooking Lake Geneva, close friend Leon Advice ... said.

In a career lasting some 60 years, Ustinov played a wide range of roles and won Academy Awards for supporting actor in the films "Spartans" and "Topkapi" in the 1960s.

CORRECTED

GENEVA (AP)—Sir Peter Ustinov, a brilliant wit and mimic who won two Oscars for an acting career that ranged from the evil Emperor Nero in "Quo Vadis" to the quirky detective Hercule Poirot, has died. He was 82.

He died of heart failure Sunday night at a clinic near his home at Burins overlooking Lake Geneva, said close friend Leon Davico. ...

In a career lasting more than 60 years, Ustinov played a wide range of roles and won Academy Awards for supporting actor in the films "Spartacus" and "Topkapi" in the 1960s.

REFERENCES

Associated Press. (2022). *The Associated Press stylebook: 2022-2024* (56th ed.). Basic Books.

Associated Press. (2024). *The Associated Press stylebook: 2024–2026* (57th ed.). Basic Books.

Cirilli, K. (2012, September 11). The 5 curses of Joe Biden. Politico. https://www.politico.com/story/2012/09/the-5-curses-of-joe-biden-081074

Global Language Monitor. (n.d.). "Millionth English word" declared. https://language-monitor.com/number-of-words-in-english/no-of-words/

The University of Press Editorial Staff. (2017). *The Chicago manual of style,* 17th edition. University of Chicago Press. https://www.chicagomanualofstyle.org/home.html

FURTHER READING, RESOURCES

Dickinson, P. (2019, June 9). Zelensky, Zelenskiy, Zelenskyy: Spelling confusion doesn't help Ukraine. Atlantic Council. https://www.atlanticcouncil.org/blogs/ukrainealert/zelensky-zelenskiy-zelenskyy-spelling-confusion-doesn-t-help-ukraine/

National Commission on Terrorist Attacks upon the United States. (n.d.). https://www.9–11commission.gov/

New Oxford dictionary for writers and editors. (2014). Oxford University Press.

Waddingham, A. (2014). *New Hart's rules: The Oxford style guide* (2nd ed.). Oxford University Press.

CREDIT

Fig. 1.6.1: Copyright © by President.gov.ua (CC BY 4.0) at https://en.wikipedia.org/wiki/File:Volodymyr_Zelensky_Official_portrait.jpg.

GRAMMAR

KEY POINTS IN THIS CHAPTER

1. Learning grammar is like studying a foreign language. In fact, many students discover English grammar rules by studying the way other languages are constructed. In either case you can't escape the importance of building a vocabulary to help you understand how the language works, starting with the parts of speech.

2. You don't need to know everything about grammar, just several core principles. Once understood, those principles can give you more confidence as a writer and an editor.

3. You should start with mastering the basics, such as knowing what's singular or plural, ensuring subject-verb agreement in different clauses, finding the right verb tenses and moods, and sorting out pronoun cases: nominative, objective and possessive.

This Might Hurt a Little, but ... (Take 3)

Teaching grammar is like teaching auto mechanics. Sure, you can turn a key or push a button to start your car and drive it smoothly for a while, but at some point—just like with writing—the thing breaks down.

That's when you need to open the hood, figure out what went wrong and fix it. To do that, you need to know the system and structure of the engine, just like we'll explain the way syntax builds strong sentences. Don't worry, fellow travelers, we're here for you—moving slowly and trying to explain terms as we go.

Typically grammar lessons begin with the parts of speech, and knowing those is important to understanding rules. You may want to turn now to our sidebar, "The First Step," for a quick tutorial. We will provide full grammar explanations in **Appendix B** as part of **The Language Skills Survival Kit**. Our approach to grammar here in **Chapter 1.7** is to focus on problem-solving sentences to keep you out of trouble.

While working through those sentences, we will refer to parts of speech—including noun, pronoun, verb, adjective, adverb, preposition, conjunction—but in a context that will help you grasp their meanings. "Thank goodness!" (interjection) you say.

We know from personal experience, spanning 40 years in the classroom, that many students welcome grammar lessons they can understand to improve their writing. We've been eyewitness to the grammar/writing challenge for only a relatively short period of time. Get this: "More than half of first-year students at Harvard failed an entrance exam in writing—in 1874" (Goldstein, 2017).

This *Forbes* magazine report intrigued us: "We Get National Reading Test Results Every 2 Years. Writing? Try 20" (Wexler, 2022). We had a feeling that grammar knowledge and writing proficiency had hit the skids, but getting the data was difficult. Then we stumbled on a 2016 blog post line from a former president of the National Council of Teachers of English:

> *"It is important for educators to know that, among recent research studies, not one justifies teaching grammar to help students write better." (Yatvin, 2016)*

We can say with full confidence, "That's baloney!" It's even scary like the baloney you left in the back of your refrigerator for a year. The statement is blind to **Core Principle No. 1: Writing + Editing = Writing**. To teach students to be better writers, they need to become better editors of their own work.

The process of becoming better editors includes paying attention to spelling (**Chapter 1.6**) and grammar (you are here!). That's because if you make a spelling mistake or a grammar error, you'll have some readers think you're an idiot. Forget the rest of your writing if you lose that kind of credibility.

Don't get us wrong, we love teachers—we're teachers ourselves—and we know teaching English, especially grammar, is a real challenge. One thing we know for sure: Teachers play to their strengths. A teacher can have nightmares about the kid who asks a tough grammar question in class, in front of everyone, and the teacher has no answer.

That has happened to us. So we begin with humility but also with the fervent belief that your confidence will grow as you begin to grasp more and more grammar concepts. The more confidence you have in your writing, the better your writing will be.

Just a quick stylebook note: The Associated Press Stylebook has a separate **Punctuation** section, but not one for grammar. Instead, you'll see grammar points weaved into various entries. The Chicago Manual of Style, however, has a **Grammar** section (beginning 5.1, 225), which includes this disturbing passage:

> *Somewhat surprisingly, modern grammarians cannot agree on precisely how many parts of speech there are in English. At least one grammarian says there are as few as three. Another insists that there are "about fifteen," noting "the precise number is still being debated."*

Aren't you glad we're sparing you from that madness? On with the show!

The First Step

The first step to understanding grammar is knowing the parts of speech, the job each one does and then (here's the tricky part) the function a word plays in a sentence. The same word can mean different things as it changes its role in a sentence. Let's start with a quick sketch of the parts of speech:

Noun—it's the name of a person, place or thing.

Pronoun—it takes the place of a noun.

Verb—it can be an action verb ("run," "jump," "write") or a linking verb ("to be," "to feel").

Adjective—it modifies a noun ("good guy") or pronoun ("she is nice").

Adverb—it modifies a verb ("run quickly"), adjective ("really nice") or other adverb ("very slowly").

(continued)

Preposition—it shows relationship ("up," "down," "over," "between").
Conjunction—it joins ideas ("and," "but," "or").
Interjection—it shouts ("holy cow!").
Article—it sets up a noun ("a," "an," "the").

If you're counting, that's nine. Some grammarians lump articles in with adjectives because they are modifiers and say we have eight parts of speech. Whatever.

Here's the tricky part: A little word like "down" can be a chameleon. See what we mean:

It was she who fell down. (**adverb** telling where)
I feel down, a little depressed (**adjective** meaning sad)
They walked down the street. (**preposition**)
"Hurry, 'down' the missile!" (**verb**)
My mother gave her the down comforter. (**adjective** meaning feathery)
The quarterback made a first down. (**noun**)
The boxer wobbles. Down! (**interjection**)

You get the idea. If you can't identify parts of speech, then you're not sure if you're using words properly. And that means you're not in total control of your writing.

There's more to this, of course. And that means functions in a sentence. So let's work on a little more vocabulary. Parts of speech are one way to parse a sentence; labeling functions is another way. Here goes:

Subject—the doer. In the seven "down" sentences, there are **eight subjects**, in order:

* **It**, a pronoun.
* **who**, a pronoun.
* **I**, a pronoun.
* **They**, a pronoun.
* **you**, a pronoun, understood as the subject of the verb "down."
* **mother**, a noun.
* **quarterback**, a noun.
* **boxer**, a noun.

Predicate—it's the verb, only with a new name, that connects with the subject. Every subject has a predicate. In the seven "down" sentences, **eight predicates** were matched with subjects. That means eight "clauses." They are in order:

* **was** ("It was")
* **fell** ("who fell")
* **feel** ("I feel")
* **walked** ("they walked")
* **down**, ("you down")
* **gave** ("mother gave")

- **made** ("quarterback made")
- **wobbles** ("boxer wobbles")

Direct object—what the action verb delivers.
Indirect object—the receiver of the direct object.
Quick quiz: Do you see two objects in this sentence?

My mother gave her the down comforter.

Right, "comforter" is the direct object and "her" is the indirect object.

Object of the preposition—the noun or pronoun that follows a preposition.
Quick quiz: So what's the object of the preposition in this sentence?

They walked down the street.

Right, "street."
Predicate adjective—it follows a linking verb and modifies the subject.
Quick quiz: So what's the predicate adjective in this sentence?

I feel down, a little depressed.

Right, "down" for sure, but you also can say "depressed." Both are predicate adjectives following the linking verb "feel" and modifying the subject "I."

Predicate nominative—it's a noun or pronoun that follows a linking verb and modifies the subject.
Quick quiz: So what's the predicate nominative in this sentence?

It was she who fell down.

Right, "she."

OK, take a breath. Get a glass of water. Then dive into the core principles. If you would like to tune up further on parsing, then turn to **Appendix B**.

Core Principles of Grammar

Grammar rules help you decide the order of words and the proper form of them to use. We'll need to rely on some basic terms, but as usual we'll try not to assume too much and wherever possible start explanations from scratch. We won't bombard you with a million grammar rules; we'll just begin by talking you through **a dozen core principles.**

1. Beware the -ing Ding and the -ed Dud

Let's say you, quite embarrassed, tell a friend:

Climbing the fence, my pants ripped.

There's more here to your embarrassment than just the ripped pants showing your underwear. Grammatically, we call this a dangling or misplaced modifier. Our term is "the -ing ding."

Be careful starting a sentence with an "-ing" word. Here's where those parts of speech and vocabulary come in. If you say …

Climbing is fun!

… there's no problem because here "climbing" is a **noun (gerund)** and it serves as the subject of the verb "is."

But an "-ing" word in a phrase followed by a comma acts as an **adjective**, modifying the first word after the comma. Do you see it now? Your pants were climbing the fence, not you! Here's the fix:

Climbing the fence, I ripped my pants.

Adjectives modify nouns ("fun climbing") and pronouns ("Climbing … I").

Writing can get twisted when writers hear in the back of their heads some former authority shouting, "Don't use I!" We understand that admonition, but when it comes to writing, our view is "Never say never."

For the record, climbing can be a third part of speech—a **verb**. Like in this sentence:

I was climbing the fence when I ripped my pants.

One more test before we go. How do you assess this sentence?

Baking in the oven all day, Grandma grew weary.

Right, poor Grandma—she's toast! Grandma wasn't in the oven; all her bakery goods were. That's another misplaced modifier. What you meant to say:

Grandma grew weary from baking all day.

A variation of this embarrassing mistake is "the -ed dud." That's when you start a sentence with a past participle (many end with "-ed") rather than a present participle (ending "-ing"). Both act as **adjectives**, so be careful of misplaced modifiers. For example:

Racked with pain, the trainer helped the player off the field.

No, make it:

Racked with pain, the player was helped off the field by the trainer.

or

The trainer helped the player, racked with pain, off the field.

Another example of a misplaced modifier:

Loved to the end, the obituary said the pope was surrounded by his family on his deathbed.

Nope again. Make it:

Loved to the end, the pope was surrounded by his family on his deathbed, the obituary said.

Here, try this one: What's wrong?

Based on a large data set, the researcher introduced an exciting new theory on why dogs bark.

You got this one! Right:

The researcher studying why dogs bark introduced an exciting new theory based on a large data set.

In **Appendix B**, we'll help you build your grammar muscles by parsing sentences. For now we'll stick with explaining more core principles as we ease you into the vocabulary of grammar.

2. Just Between You and I …

A reverse problem with the use of "I" is that somehow it sounds more formal and correct, but in all the wrong places. Use "I" for subjects and "me" for objects.

One of your co-authors, invited to his university president's house for a holiday party, stood in a greeting line behind a faculty colleague who began his small talk with the president by saying:

"Just between you and I …"

Your trusty co-author couldn't resist thinking to himself, "How embarrassing!" So what's the problem? You need to use the right word for the object of the preposition. The faculty member should have said:

*"Just between you and **me** ..."*

Another preposition that will give you an object is "among." If someone else jumped into the conversation, then the discussion would have been "among" the three of them.

Sometimes it looks like three, but only two parties are involved. So you would say:

*The negotiations **between** the NFL owners and the players and their union representatives continued into the night.*

If Congress got involved, then you would say the discussions continued "among" the three parties. If you were one of those players, you could say, "The negotiations were **among** the owners, Congress and me."

Listen to any podcast very long or scan social media and you'll find an **I** when it should be a **me**. That's why you should study your prepositions. A former college football coach tweeted a nice family photo of a grandson standing "with Karen and I." No, **with** is a preposition, so it should be "Karen and **me**."

3. Who or Whom Is Being Annoying?

Just as some speakers or writers will get their hands crossed using "I" because it sounds more proper, they'll also try to impress someone by tossing a "whom" into a conversation. Like so:

Whom shall I say is calling?

I don't know whom is going to the party.

Both of these should be "who" and for the same reason: They are subjects linked to verbs. The trick to understanding whether to use "who" or "whom" is starting with verbs and matching up their subjects.

First, know that you can have more than one subject-verb combination in a sentence. Those are called "clauses."

Take the first example and sort out the two clauses. What's the first verb? "shall say." What's its subject? "I shall say." What's the second verb? "is calling." What's its subject? "who is calling." See? You need the subject "who" not the object "whom."

You can sort out the second example in the same way: "I don't know" and "who is going to the party."

See it now? Good!

If you're going to use "whom"—and we're not saying you have to—then it has to be an object, like "me." Ben Franklin observed, "Three can keep a secret if two of them are dead." So, in an astonished tone of voice, you might say to a friend:

You want to keep that secret just between Sally and whom?

More on this in a bit, don't worry.

4. Who or That, and Which Comes With Commas

See anything wrong in this sentence?

The cardinal that became pope saw a cardinal that flew into his yard at the Vatican.

You should use "who" for people or pets and "which" or "that" for things. So make it:

The cardinal who became pope …

Saying "that" for the bird ("cardinal that") is fine.

Think of "which" as **comma-which-comma.**" So you would say:

The cardinal, which flew into the yard, landed at the Vatican.

Note the comma before "which" and one after "yard." Commas come in pairs.

The pronoun "which" is the subject of the verb "flew." The clause is called nonessential.

An essential clause uses the word "that." Compare the phrasing with these clauses:

The cardinal that flew into the yard was luckier than the cardinal that flew into the wall.

These clauses using "that" are called essential because they distinguish one cardinal from the other. Note there are no commas with "that" clauses.

Also note that those cardinals don't have names like pets. For pets, you use "who." You would say:

My pet bird, Charlie, who flew across the room, scared me.

Beyond "who," "that" and "which," another troublesome pronoun is "whose." See anything wrong with the following sentences?

Whose there? I want to know who's been sleeping in whose bed.

Just one fix: "Who's there?" You need the contraction for "who is."

Now "who's" can also be the contraction for "who has," so "who's been" sleeping is fine.

"Whose" is the possessive form of the pronoun "who," so "whose bed" is fine, too.

These pronouns can be tricky. Slow down for them.

5. 'Tis I or It's All About Me

The phone rings, a prospective employer asks for you, and you say, "'Tis I."

Do you get the job?

Yes, maybe from the Pilgrim Moving Co.!

Sometimes being grammatically correct will make you sound like a Pilgrim. That's why over time, proper English gets violated so often that the grammatical error becomes "acceptable."

Let's back up a step. "'Tis I"—a contraction for "This is I"—is grammatically correct, just as you would say, "This is he" or "This is she."

That's because the verb "to be," also known as a linking verb, is a weak verb. It acts like an equal sign, so what's on one side of it should be in the same form as what's on the other side.

The pronoun "this" (a subject) is in the same form as the pronoun on the other side, one that you would use as a subject ("I," "he" or "she").

Now take a look at this sentence:

This hit him.

Now we say "him" because the nature of the verb changed, from a weak verb to an action verb like "hit." You'll hear a grammatical rule for good writing that encourages the straight talk of delivering "subject-verb-object." That's what we did here:

This (subject)

hit (verb)

him (object).

Back to the phone exchange: Do you see grammatically why we would say, "This is he," and not "This is him"? Likewise, why we wouldn't say "'Tis me" or "This is her"?

Except for one thing: People say "This is him" and "This is her" all the time. So the grammatical mistake has become acceptable. You can say both versions are OK, but now you know what's grammatically correct.

Here's a reason that knowledge can come in handy. You'll never shout something like this:

Whom do you think I am!

So embarrassing! It should be "Who." Remember, for "who" or "whom" questions, start with the verbs and line up their subjects. Here you have two clauses:

you do think

and

I am who

Feel the power of learning grammar! It's really about embarrassment prevention. Now for a few lessons about what many grammarians consider the most important part of speech—the verb.

6. Can You Please Tell Me What Time It Is?

In grammar, the word "tense" means time. Verbs have different tenses to indicate different points in time.

Some languages, such as Mandarin Chinese, have just one tense: "I go today," "I go yesterday," "I go tomorrow." It's like driving a one-gear Koenigsegg Regera.

In English, verbs have six tenses:

present

past

future

present perfect (has or have + participle)

past perfect (had + participle)

future perfect (will have + participle)

So writing English is like driving a Porsche 911 with its six-speed gearbox. Do you see a difference in these two sentences?

He said he was a superstar.

He said he had been a superstar.

The difference lies in the tenses. In the first sentence, "said" and "was" are both in the past tense. In the second sentence, "had been" puts us in the past-past, or the "past perfect" tense.

Why is it important? Sequence of tenses can provide clarity and avoid confusion. See here:

He says he is a superstar. (He spoke today.)

He said he was a superstar. (He spoke yesterday.)

He said he had been a superstar. (He spoke yesterday about a time in the distant past.)

7. Verbs Can Get Moody, Very Moody

What do you think of someone who says:

I be a superstar!

Now think again as the person explains:

My parents demand that I be a superstar.

Wait, what happened there? The grammatical term is the verb's mood. Verbs have three moods:

Indicative mood: telling it straight.

I am a superstar.

Imperative mood: delivering a command.

Be a superstar!

Subjunctive mood: making a demand.

My ballet instructor insisted that I be a superstar.

Subjunctive mood also kicks in with making a **wish**. In the indicative mood, you would say, "I **was** a superstar." But when the verb switches to subjunctive, it changes to "I **were**," as in:

I wish I were a superstar.

Likewise, with statements contrary to fact, such as:

If I were a superstar (I'm not), I would be rich.

The subjunctive mood is also used when expressing a **doubt, prayer, necessity, resolution** or **recommendation**, as in *The board recommended that the motion be passed*. More about this in **Appendix B**.

Subjunctive mood is different from a conditional verb form used to express a hypothetical or an unlikely situation. So compare this sentence:

I would be a superstar if I got my big break.

Conditional verbs can be in the present, past or future tense. Tipoffs will be the use of the helping verbs "will or would," "can or could," "may or might." Typically, the sentences are in an "If-comma-then" construction, like so:

If I can go to the party, then you will be the first to know.

8. Agree to Be Agreeable

Another way writers can get their hands crossed is loading up on their subjects and losing track of their verbs. Take a look at this sentence:

The devastation of the bombing causing lost days of work for thousands of weavers at the factory paint a grim picture for the town's future.

Do you see the problem? Grammatically it's called subject-verb agreement.

Agreement just means singular subjects ("it," "he," "she," "everyone") take singular verbs ("is," "was," "dances," "sings"), and plural subjects ("they," "you," "players," "choirs") take plural verbs ("are," "were," "dance," "sing").

So what's the subject of our sentence? "Devastation," right. That's singular like "it," so the verb needs to be singular, too—"paints," not "paint."

9. Now for the Tricky Ones

Some subjects have really got your number. Take "couple," for example. Would you say, "The couple is …" (singular) or "The couple are …" (plural)?

"Couple" is one of those words that are singular or plural depending on their meaning. So you would say:

The couple is required to pay a $5 cover charge.
(Two people treated as one customer.)

The couple are divorced.
(Two people going their separate ways.)

The word "media" is the plural of the singular noun "medium," right? Now take a look at this sentence:

The media is biased!

Is that correct? Yep.

Sometimes "media" refers to one "monolithic group," the AP Stylebook says (**media** AP, 184), so it can take a singular verb like "is." The Chicago Manual of Style, under **Plural form with singular sense** (5.14, 229), states that the word has "gradually acquired a mass-noun sense."

But "media" can be plural, too. Both stylebooks give examples using "are" as the proper verb:

Media are lining up for and against the proposal. (AP)

The media are largely misrepresenting the event. (CMS)

Whether it's "couple" or "media," the key to finding the right verb is to ask yourself, "Does the word mean 'it' or 'they'?"

Now take the "data" challenge. Do these sound right?

The data looks sound.

The data do not add up.

Both are correct. The data set (it/one thing) is sound while the data (they/bits and pieces) are out of whack.

Some words look singular but take plural verbs (the police are) while others end in "s" and look plural but take singular verbs (politics is, economics was, American Airlines has, General Motors gives).

As phrasing changes for some words, so do the verbs. For example, you would say "the scissors are sharp," but "a pair of scissors is on sale."

The AP Stylebook sees a difference whether the subject is "**the** average" or "**an** average" (AP, 26):

*The average **is** 74. (singular)*

*An average of 100 new jobs **are** created daily. (plural)*

The grammatical term for whether a word is singular or plural is its "number." Now you can enjoy the opening line again—we've got your number!

10. Take One of Those Advanced Classes

Take another look at this sentence:

"Couple" is one of those words that are singular or plural depending on their meaning.

Should it be "that are" or "that is"? Well, how many subject-verb combinations do you see? Two, right. Here's the first one:

"Couple" is

The subject is the word "couple" (it), so it takes the verb "is."
The second one is not so obvious:

that are

"That" is a pronoun, so you need to look to the word that gives it meaning, or its antecedent. Don't look far—it's right next to it: "words." Because "words" is plural, then "that" is plural, so the verb "are" is correct.

Whoa, got that? Pronouns are like chameleons—they take on the characteristics of what's right next to them.

Let's give this grammar rule another spin, but this time with the pronoun "who." Does this sentence look right?

Johnny is one of those guys who always gets upset at football games.

Nope. The second verb should be "get," not "gets," as in "guys who get."
Let's try it again, but we'll kick up the challenge a notch. Let's say you write this sentence:

Sally is one of those people who is always correcting writers' grammar, which is very annoying.

What needs to be fixed? Two out of the three clauses, right.

First clause: "Sally is"—no problem.

Second clause: "who is"—you mean "who are." Just like you would say "people are."

Third clause: "which is very annoying"—wait, what is very annoying?

It's not grammar; it's Sally's habit. To avoid possible confusion, consider this rewrite:

> *Sally is one of those people **who are** always correcting writers'
> grammar. That **habit is** very annoying.*

One more take on pronouns and their antecedents. Please look at this sentence and tell me who's happy:

> *After a long search, the father found the boy and **he was happy**.*

Now, was the father happy he found the boy or was the boy happy to be reunited with this father?

Good writing does not present Rorschach tests. Make sure your pronouns have a clear path back to their antecedents, or the words that give them meaning. These sentences are clearer:

> *After a long search, the father found the **boy, who was happy**.*

> *After a long search, **the father was happy** to have found the boy.*

Anytime you see "they" in a sentence, ask, "Who's they?" It should have a clear antecedent. Too often writers or speakers just wing it, attributing some idea or opinion to a nebulous "they." Or "they" may be the preferred pronoun of one person, so make that clear, too.

11. But What Did You Come Here For?

Starting a sentence with a conjunction and ending one with a preposition aren't grammar errors. They may just be the most natural way to express a thought.

If starting a sentence with a conjunction is good enough for our Founding Fathers, then it's good enough for us. Check out this line from the Declaration of Independence, where "one idea/one sentence" did not rule:

> ***But** when a long train of abuses and usurpations, pursuing
> invariably the same Object evinces a design to reduce them under
> absolute Despotism, it is their right, it is their duty, to throw off such
> Government, and to provide new Guards for their future security.*

The Oxford Dictionary of Quotations offers other examples (Stack Exchange, n.d.), such as:

***And** therefore death is no such terrible enemy, when a man hath so many attendants about him that can win the combat of him.*

—Francis Bacon in his essay "Of Death"

***Yet** my great-grandfather was but a water-man, looking one way, and rowing another: and I got most of my estate by the same occupation.*

—John Bunyan in "The Pilgrim's Progress"

And for a final blessing of this writing approach:

***But** of the tree of the knowledge of good and evil, thou shalt not eat of it: for in the day that thou eatest thereof thou shalt surely die.*

—The Bible (King James version)

Ending a sentence with a preposition is something you can put up with. It's fine, but not as witty as the line, attributed to Winston Churchill, objecting to any rule against doing so:

This is the type of arrant pedantry up with which I will not put.

Take any foreign language class, and you'll learn to say these sentences in a different tongue:

*Where are you **from**?*

*What are you hungry **for**?*

*What is the film **about**?*

So relax. As long as you're clear, you're fine grammatically.

12. Be "Better Than" and "Different From" —Follow Through on Your Comparisons

We've loved a saying from St. Jerome since kindergarten, but a question still haunts us till this day. Perhaps you know this gem:

Good, better, best,

Never let it rest,

'Til your good is better

And your better best.

The question is, better than what?

The saying was an early lesson in what grammatically is called "declining" an adjective. That means moving from the positive ("good") to the comparative ("better") to the superlative ("best"). Let's try a few more:

- *quick, quicker, quickest*

- *smart, smarter, smartest*

- *different, more different, most different*

Now zoom in on the comparative. It takes a "than," as in:

- *quicker than a cat*

- *smarter than a fourth grader*

- *more different than anyone else on earth*

See, when you start a comparison, you need to finish it. Tune into writing, often advertising, that proclaims a product will make something better, smoother, softer or healthier. Feel free to ask, "Than what?"

A parting note about "different": one thing is "different from" another, not different "than." Reserve "than" for the comparative form ("more different than").

Congratulations! You've run the course. That rounds out what we hoped to accomplish in this grammar chapter.

We know this must feel like a big, thick grammar book to you. But there's plenty more if you feel the need for a deeper dive into grammar in **Appendix B**. We'll see you on the other side for some core principles of punctuation.

HOMEWORK

Assignment No. 1

Take another look at an article you enjoyed recently and zoom into words ending in "-ing." Can you tell which are nouns or verbs or adjectives? Do the adjectives modify the nouns or pronouns properly, or are you hearing "the -ing ding"?

Assignment No. 2

Using the same article in Assignment No. 1, or another one of your choice, go hunting for prepositions. As we mentioned, grammarians have identified 150 or so possibilities for you. An EnglishClub article runs down an impressive list (EnglishClub, n.d.).

Then tune into the objects of the prepositions. They may be nouns or pronouns, hopefully (just between you and me) in the objective case. Then take one more step with three examples: see how many prepositional phrases are acting as adverbs telling where (in the house, by the phone, over the fence).

Assignment No. 3

One of the common grammar errors we discussed was the use of "that" or "which" when the pronoun really should be "who." How many examples can you find when "who" should be used for people or pets, but a "that" or a "which" is used instead?

REFERENCES

Associated Press. (2022). *The Associated Press stylebook: 2022–2024* (56th ed.). Basic Books.

EnglishClub. (n.d.). Preposition list. https://www.englishclub.com/grammar/prepositions-list.php

Goldstein, D. (2017, August 2). Why kids can't write. *The New York Times*. https://www.nytimes.com/2017/08/02/education/edlife/writing-education-grammar-students-children.html

Stack Exchange. (n.d.) What great writers have used coordinating conjunctions at the start of sentences? English Language & Usage. https://english.stackexchange.com/questions/192294/what-great-writers-have-used-coordinating-conjunctions-at-the-start-of-sentences/192320#192320

University of Chicago Press Editorial Staff. (2017). *The Chicago manual of style,* 17th edition. University of Chicago Press. https://www.chicagomanualofstyle.org/home.htm

Wexler, N. (2022, January 26). We get national reading test results every 2 years. Writing? Try 20. *Forbes.* https://www.forbes.com/sites/nataliewexler/2022/01/26/we-get-national-reading-test-results-every-2-years-writing-try-20

Yatvin, J. (2016, Oct. 3). Is teaching grammar necessary? National Council of Teachers of English. https://ncte.org/blog/2016/10/teaching-grammar-necessary/

FURTHER READING, RESOURCES

Grammar Books Recommended by the Chicago Manual of Style

Allen, R.L. (1972). *English grammars and English grammar*. Scribner.

Burchfield, R. (1991). *Unlocking the English language*. Hill and Wang.

Gray, E.W. (1967). *A brief grammar of modern written English*. World Pub. Co.

Trask, R.L. (1995). *Language: The basics*. Taylor & Francis.

References and Writing Guides Recommended by the AP Stylebook

Butterfield, J. (Ed.). (2016). *Fowler's concise dictionary of modern English usage* (3rd ed.). Oxford University Press.

Garner, B.A. (2016). *Garner's modern English usage* (4th ed.). Oxford University Press.

Other References

Authorama. (n.d.). *Essays of Francis Bacon*. http://www.authorama.com/essays-of-francis-bacon-3.html

National Archives. (1776). *Declaration of Independence: A transcription*. https://www.archives.gov/founding-docs/declaration-transcript

PUNCTUATION

KEY POINTS IN THIS CHAPTER

1. Just as musicians score music to indicate pauses, so do writers use punctuation to slow down readers in a proper rhythm. Pause the least with commas and the most with periods.

2. The Associated Press Stylebook and the Chicago Manual of Style disagree on the Oxford comma for a simple series but agree on the use of a semicolon before the "and" in a complicated sentence.

3. Use a colon or a dash to set off an idea, but one acts quietly (the colon) while the other (the dash) comes with a shout, maybe even an exclamation point. Notice the parentheses? Use them to whisper a thought.

4. A comma can stand alone by replacing the word "and," but most often commas come in pairs.

This Might Hurt a Little, but ... (Take 4)

A brief history of how we got here begins with this excerpt from the General Prologue of "The Canterbury Tales" (1392) by Geoffrey Chaucer:

A FRIAR there was, a wanton one and merry,

Who begged within a certain limit. None

In all four orders was a better one

At idle talk, or speaking with a flair.

Writing was meant to be spoken out loud, so punctuation served to slow the speaker down to find the right rhythm. It's still true today. Many writers will speak their lines for editing purposes.

Somewhere between "The Canterbury Tales" and this next story came typing class, where the instructor insisted on two spaces after a period. No more!

A more recent epiphany for one of your co-authors—let's say 600 years or so after "The Canterbury Tales"—came as he walked into a Teaching Newspaper newsroom to meet one of his Medill School of Journalism advisees at midterm.

"Don't use semicolons!" the city editor shouted in the direction of his student. "People don't speak in semicolons."

Later, in a quiet moment away from the newspaper, your co-author told his student: "That's ridiculous. People don't speak in capital letters, either. We're just trying to approximate what people say and how they say it. We need all the punctuation we can get."

For some reason, the semicolon gets a bad rap. Its most prominent detractor might be Kurt Vonnegut, who wrote this in his book "A Man Without a Country" (Vonnegut, 2005):

Here is a lesson in creative writing. The first rule: do not use semicolons. They are transvestite hermaphrodites representing absolutely nothing. All they do is show you've been to college.

Ouch. Nonetheless, probably the most used and abused piece of punctuation is the comma. The most overused might be the dash, just outpacing the ellipses for some writers. An overdose of dashes or ellipses can be annoying, but what's worse is the confusion and embarrassment that can come from the lack of an apostrophe ("womens volleyball") or an unnecessary one, as in "five dollar's off" (omg).

For us, adding to the challenge are the stylebooks, which send mixed signals as you've already seen in the Oxford comma debate. But as evidence that punctuation really matters, the index in the Chicago Manual of Style (1110–1111) lists 56 reference points under punctuation, ending with a list of punctuation marks that include braces, guillemets (double arrows) and suspension points (something's missing).

In a separate **Punctuation** section (AP, 323–336), the AP Stylebook lists 15 punctuation marks with rules attached: apostrophe, brackets, colon, comma, dash, ellipses, em dash/en dash, exclamation point, hyphen, parentheses, periods, question mark, quotation marks, semicolon and slash.

So there are plenty of rules for you to read and enjoy. But as you know by now, that's not our style. We wish to remain your language-skills strength coach, talking you through sentences to focus on concepts we think are most valuable.

Just like with grammar, we come to you with punctuation pointers out of humility. Truth be told, we were winging it right up to graduate school. As the grad school faculty adviser told one of your co-authors, based at the offices of The Sunday Times of London newspaper in England, "You're sprinkling commas around like they're currants on pudding."

Oh, how we wish we'd had a book like this! Now you do.

BTW, that's about all the exclamation points we would like to see. The fewer the better, unless you're playing around!!! Let's get serious now chatting about **a dozen core principles.**

Core Principles of Punctuation

At its best, punctuation provides clarity, nuance and efficiency. Let's begin with some core principles, then as you like, you can take a deeper dive into **The Language Skills Survival Kit, Appendix C,** for more punctuation rules, terms and guidance. Here go our do's and don'ts:

1. Pause for Effect

In music, composers use rests to provide pauses that give a song its phrasing, emphasis and rhythm. Long rests signal the end of one phrase and the beginning of the next. Short rests add texture and meaning to the music.

So it is with punctuation marks: a period equals a whole rest, a semicolon equals a half rest, a colon or a dash equals a quarter rest, and a comma equals an eighth rest.

Got it? Let's see. Please rise and step behind the lectern for a dramatic reading of the following sentences:

He came, he saw, he conquered.

He came; he saw; he conquered.

He came. He saw. He conquered.

Thank you so much for your performance! Now for a critique: You moved beautifully from the least pause with the commas to the most pause with the periods. The amount of pause with the semicolons fell somewhere in between. Bravo!

As we'll see, dashes or parentheses can add a certain dynamic to writing, like crescendo-decrescendo marks. What a writer places between dashes is emphasized and is to be read in a loud voice. Writing enclosed in parentheses is read with a low voice, maybe even a whisper.

For members of your audience, let the writing be music to their ears.

2. Know the Long and Short of Commas

Generally speaking, if you start a sentence with an introductory phrase, the longer it is, the more you need a comma. Wow, count those commas! Unfortunately, this does get a little tricky. First, compare these two sentences:

In 2020 I felt lost. (no comma)

In 2023 after a long spring break, I returned to campus full of energy. (yes comma)

A short introductory phrase is a couple of words; a long one can be three or more. Here's why we didn't say one word:

However, I did not give up.

Fast, you need to go fast.

Holy smokes, that was awesome.

Billy, I would like to see you in my office.

If you are going to join sentences with words like "however," "therefore" or "for instance," you'll need a semicolon-comma combo, like so:

In 2020 I felt lost; however, in 2023 after a long spring break, I returned to campus full of energy.

A few final words, including two with built-in commas ("yes" and "no"):

Yes, this punctuation rule can be difficult.

No, you'll master it soon enough.

3. Add "Slow Down" Signs in Long Lists

For short lists, commas can work just fine. But remember the difference between AP style and Chicago style for a simple series:

*We went to the game, the crowd was **loud and** victory was ours. (AP)*

*We went to the game, the crowd was **loud, and** victory was ours. (CMS)*

When the sequence gets more complicated, then a combination of commas and semicolons is best to slow down the reader to aid comprehension. Both the AP and the CMS agree on the use of a semicolon before the "and" in a sentence like this:

We went to the game, a titanic struggle between two first-place teams; the crowd was loud, all 103,000 voices filling the air; and victory was ours, as the Good Lord intended.

The AP entry **semicolon [;]** addresses this point **to clarify a series** (AP, 335). For the CMS entry, see **Semicolons in a complex series** (6.60, 391).

4. Don't Go to the "Mens Room"

Ah, the missing apostrophe—it's a signage epidemic. The possessive form of plural nouns can get tricky, but some things are painfully obvious: "Men" is the plural of "man," so the possessive form takes an **'s.** So make it:

- *men's room*
- *men's clothing*

For women's sports we'll also see missing apostrophes. So make it:

- *women's volleyball*
- *women's swimming and diving*

Any time you see an "s" or an "'s," **hear the hissing sound "ssss"** and STOP! Ask, is this a plural word or a possessive? Remember the difference between an implied "of" (possessive) and a "by" or "for" (not possessive). See the differences here:

*My teacher's pet peeve (the pet peeve **of** my teacher)*

*A teachers union (a union **for** teachers)*

*A teachers strike (a strike **by** teachers)*

*It's the women's bathroom (possessive), but the ladies room (bathroom **for** women)*

Maybe that **"s" sound** is a contraction. See the difference between:

There's a problem (there is).

The problem is theirs (possessive form of "they").

The "s" sound is always worth slowing down for, especially with possessive pronouns. We talked about how the contraction "it's" ("it is," "it has") often gets confused with "its" (blame it on autocorrect!). But the rule to make nouns possessive with an **'s** spills over to possessive pronouns in the wrong way. Be sure to make them:

- *hers, not her's*

- *ours, not our's*

- *yours, not your's*

If you tune your ear to the "s" sound, you inevitably will find a punctuation error.

5. Don't Let Hyphens Keep You in Suspense

The hyphen joins words into what are called compound modifiers. That means two or three words add up to one idea.

So you can say the boy was 10 years old, or you can call him a 10-year-old boy.

Back to the "s" sound: If there's an "s" in years, then no hyphen. If you use the word "year," then you need hyphens.

Good so far, right? Well, something that can be downright baffling is called **suspended hyphenation**. That's when you see something like this:

The 4- and 5-year-old performers went last.

Their recitals came at 1- to 2-minute intervals.

These are correct. Note the spaces after 4- and 1-.
You might see something like this in a simple series:

The 16-, 17- and 18-year-olds went first. (AP style)

*The sixteen-, seventeen-, and eighteen-year-olds went first.
(Chicago style)*

6. Set Off Ideas in Style—With a Dash or Parentheses

Occasionally writers will want to deliver a jolt with a dash. What follows a dash should be short and loud, like so:

That guy's shopping list included one of the essentials—bourbon.

You'll know the dash is the punctuation of choice when the sentence ends with an exclamation point. Let's say you attend a Beethoven piano recital and get this surprise:

The last girl who performed was exceptional—she was 4 years old!

Sometimes writers will want to pack one sentence inside another one using dashes. Something like this:

*As I walked along the picturesque lake—the one that the great
American artist John Frederick Kensett brought to life with his
1869 oil painting—I felt all the beauty and history that Lake
George evokes.*

As an editor, you can yield to the writer if the move is rare, but beware the dasher. If it gets too much, then break the construction into two sentences. An aside is best short. See how this aside works with parentheses:

*John Frederick Kensett's brilliant oil painting ("Lake George," 1869)
wrapped me in beauty and transported me through history.*

Rather than shout with a dash, the parentheses introduce a whisper.
The AP Stylebook under **dash [—]** (AP, 328–329) offers these as acceptable uses of the dash:

*Through her long reign, the queen and her family have adapted—
usually skillfully—to the changing taste of the time.*

He listed the qualities—intelligence, humor, conservatism, independence—that he liked in an executive.

Beware the dasher. A good rule for punctuation, and writing overall, is whatever the technique, don't overdo it.

7. Here Are Rules for Commas With But, And, Because

A decision to use commas before conjunctions, such as "and," "but" or "because," can cause headaches. Here are a few pointers to keep in mind:

BUT …

When you're joining two complete sentences, or clauses, with the conjunction "but," think "comma-but." Compare these two sentences:

*I offered her an **apple, but** she really wanted a doughnut.*

For two separate sentences with subjects and verbs ("I offered," "she wanted"), you need a comma before the conjunction "but."

*I finished **all but one** of the doughnuts.*

Just one subject and verb ("I finished"), no second subject or verb, so no comma. "But" is a preposition meaning "except," not a conjunction.

SEMICOLONS INSTEAD …

A semicolon can efficiently replace a "comma-but" to join two closely related ideas. So you could say:

*We went to the **store, but** it was closed.*

or

*We went to the **store; it** was closed.*

Beware of something called the comma splice. That's when you use a comma instead of a semicolon, so the sentence above would be **mistakenly written** as:

We went to the store, it was closed. (nope)

The same semicolon switch works for other comma-conjunction combos, as with "for," "or," "nor," "yet" and "so." The word "for," like "but" sometimes, is used as a conjunction. Here's the difference compared with a preposition:

*I donated the **watch for him**. (preposition)*

*I donated the **watch, for it** was the right thing to do. (conjunction)*

*I donated the **watch; it** was the right thing to do. (semicolon switch)*

HOWEVER, … BUT NOT BUT,

Occasionally a sentence begins with the word "But." In that case there's **no comma** after the word. If the sentence starts with "However," then, yes, you use a comma. For "but" it's either "comma-but" or no comma.

***But** we could not stand the pain of watching the Vikings lose. (no comma after "but")*

***However,** the team rallied to beat the Packers. (comma after "however")*

AND …

Whether you use a comma before "and" as a conjunction to join two complete clauses depends on if the ideas are closely related. See these examples:

*We are visiting **Washington and we can't wait** to see the White House.*

No "comma-and" because the clauses are closely related. The same is true if you drop the second subject:

We are visiting Washington and can't wait to see the White House.

Now compare this sentence:

*We are visiting **Washington, and our senator** called to say she is out of town.*

Different subjects ("We," "senator") and shift in content: Add the comma.

BECAUSE …

Don't use a comma before "because" or you'll slow down the cause-and-effect. So you would write:

*He dropped **the comma because** it was the right thing to do.*

If you see a comma before "because," it's likely closing the door on a previous clause or phrase. So for example:

*He dropped the **comma,** a pesky piece of **punctuation, because** that's the rule.*

*We went to the **store,** which was right down the **block, because** we were starving.*

We hope these pointers can keep you from a comma-coma.

8. First Learn What's an Adverb, Then Don't Hyphenate the "-ly" Variety

Quick quiz: Do you need a hyphen between "deadly" and "dull" in this sentence?

She ducked out of the deadly dull lecture.

Answer: Yes. Make it "deadly-dull lecture." But wait, the AP Stylebook says, "Do not use a hyphen between adverbs ending in **-ly** and adjectives they modify" (AP, 179).

Right, but "deadly" is an adjective, not an adverb, and so is "dull." Remember, adjectives modify nouns and pronouns. So we would say:

- *deadly weapon (adjective modifying noun)*

- *I am dull (predicate adjective modifying pronoun I)*

"Deadly-dull" is a compound modifier, meaning you have two adjectives doing one job, describing how bad the lecture was. The key to hyphens is they avert possible confusion. A man eating shark is not a man-eating shark.

Remember adverbs by definition modify adjectives, so no hyphen is needed. Here are AP examples:

- *an **easily remembered** rule (adverb "easily" modifies adjective "remembered")*

- *a **badly damaged** island (adverb "badly" modifies adjective "damaged")*

- *a **fully informed** voter (adverb "fully" modifies adjective "informed")*

No possible confusion: These "-ly" adverbs don't need the extra help that a hyphen provides to make connections.

One exception to the rule that adverbs don't need to be hyphenated when modifying adjectives is the adverb "well." It's a tricky word because **"well"** can be both an **adjective** meaning "not sick" and an **adverb** meaning "skillfully." So a hyphen can help to avoid possible confusion. Hyphenate these modifiers then:

She is well-known.

He is a well-known musician.

The patient is well-cared for.

The case is well-documented.

9. Use a Colon, the Quiet Separator

Another quieter way to set off an idea or a list is with a colon. We've used a lot of colons in these book chapters, as they neatly introduce points. Some writers will confuse the colon with the semicolon, so beware of mistakes like this:

*These were the items on her grocery **list;** chocolate, wine, biscotti. (nope)*

Make it:

*These were the items on her grocery **list:** chocolate, wine, biscotti.*

The AP Stylebook and the Chicago Manual of Style agree that if what follows a colon is a single word, a phrase or a list, then the first word is lowercase. So, for example:

*The general was missing a key **attribute: courage**.*

*She was in search of something **rare: an** honest man.*

*He was limited in his choice of **colors: black**, white or orange.*

When a full sentence follows, the CMS used to view the colon something more like a semicolon. Here's an example from the 17th edition (6.61, 391):

*They even relied on a chronological **analogy: just** as the Year II had overshadowed 1789, so the October Revolution had eclipsed that of February.*

The 18th edition, however, aligns the rule with the AP Stylebook under **colon [:]** (326), so the "Just" would be capitalized. As the stylebook states: "Capitalize the first word after a colon only if it is a proper noun or the start of a complete sentence." Here's the AP example:

*He promised **this: The** company will make good on all the losses.*

10. Place Commas and Periods Inside End Quotes

One way the two stylebooks agree is regarding the use of punctuation with quotations.

The AP says it straight up under **placement with other punctuation** in the **quotation marks [" "]** entry (AP, 335): "The period and comma always go within the quotation marks."

The CMS adds to the rule under **Periods and commas in relation to closing quotation marks** (6.9, 367): "Periods and commas precede closing quotation marks, whether double or single."

"So no more of this, please". (Ha!) Save this punctuation for your friends in Canada or the United Kingdom, where the rules are different.

The CMS examples:

*He described what he heard as a "short, sharp **shock.**"*

*"Thus conscience does make cowards of us **all,**" she replied.*

In Table 6.1 (367) the CMS explains that other punctuation marks, such as colons and semicolons, go outside the end quotes, either double or single. Here are our examples:

*Don't forget this wisdom from **"Hamlet":** "To thine own self be true."*

*She didn't watch **"Amadeus"; instead** she went to see "Rent."*

When it's part of a quotation, an exclamation point or question mark goes inside; if not, then outside (6.10, 368). Again our examples:

*Can you believe she said her favorite Shakespeare play was **"As You Like It"**?*

*When I asked her whether she liked **"Hamlet,"** she said, **"No!"***

*I said, **"Are you kidding?"***

*Who was the Shakespeare character who said, **"All the world's a stage"**?*

Headline writers will use single quote marks just to save space. If you're wrapping a quote within a quote, and end with a single quote mark, then it will look like this:

*"He said he got stabbed in the back by his **'best friend.'"***

The AP offers this doozy to explain quotes within quotes:

She said, "I quote from his letter, 'I agree with Kipling that "the female of the species is more deadly than the male," but the phenomenon is not an unchangeable law of nature,' a remark he did not explain."

Please don't do that. This example falls into the category of stylebook-correct but not advisable.

11. Know the Difference Between a Single Comma and a Door Opener

Sometimes a comma can replace "and." And sometimes it is opening a door that needs to be closed. Compare these two sentences:

The tall, thin man entered the room.

The man, who was tall and thin entered the room.

What do you think?

In the first sentence, the comma is just fine, as it replaces the word "and." In the second sentence, the comma opens a door that needs to be closed, like so:

*The **man, who was tall and thin,** entered the room.*

Very often commas come in pairs, so you don't want to use one and forget the other.

The words "tall, thin" are **coordinate adjectives**, meaning the modifiers carry the same weight. The test is whether you can switch them or add the word "and," like so:

*The **thin, tall** man*

*The **tall and thin** man*

If you can't do that, then no comma. For example:

*The **tall log** cabin*

The "log, tall cabin" makes no sense, nor does the "tall and log cabin." That means "log" carries more weight as a modifier for "cabin."

Remember, commas come in pairs when you're writing dates. Open the door and close it, as in:

*Don't miss the **May 27, 2025,** ceremony to celebrate our company's anniversary.*

As a general rule, if you're using more than two commas in a sentence, stop and consider a period rather than more punctuation.

Yes, it's possible to pack a lot of ideas into a sentence, and, yes, writing benefits from a combination of long and short sentences, but we'll defer to cognitive load theory on the limits of the working memory and say enough is enough—keep one idea to one sentence.

(See what we did there? Ha, tricked ya!)

The world has a long and complicated history, so sometimes long, complicated sentences are needed to make a point. Keeping one idea to one sentence—a broadcast writing mantra—is easier said than done.

But it's a good idea that keeps the reader or listener in mind. If writers don't make points easy to understand, then that's why we have editors to assist them.

12. Wait Now, How Many Dots?

The AP Stylebook has an interesting take on the use of an ellipsis, the dot-dot-dot. Its entry **ellipsis [...]** (AP, 329) opens like this:

In general treat an ellipsis as a three-letter word, constructed with three periods and two spaces, as shown here. …

Ellipses are best used "to signal the omission of a word, phrase, line, paragraph or more from a quoted passage" (CMS, 13.50, 728). The AP Stylebook adds: "An ellipsis also may be used to indicate a thought that the speaker or writer does not complete" (AP, 329).

Some writers will use ellipses to show hesitation or a change of mood. Be careful, though, because they just might get under your reader's skin.

The three periods become four, but with a space, when a complete sentence precedes the ellipsis indicating something is missing. See what happens with these two examples:

ORIGINAL

The concert came to an end. Thousands of people headed to the exits in the wintry evening. It was so cold. But the fun had only begun.

*The concert came to an **end.** ... But the fun had only begun.*

The same spacing and use of three dots works with other punctuation, too, as in:

*Now tell me again, what time is **it?** ... Your loyal fans are waiting.*

The Chicago Manual of Style offers this example under **Ellipses with other punctuation** (13.54, 729–730):

*It does not **build,** ... nor cherish the arts, nor foster religion.*

Under **quotations,** the AP Stylebook says not to use ellipses at the beginning or end of quotations, so don't do this:

"... it has become evident to me that I no longer have a strong enough political base ...," Nixon said.

Rather make it:

"It has become evident to me that I no longer have a strong enough political base," Nixon said.

The CMS says something similar in its entry **When not to use an ellipsis** (13.52, 729). Both stylebooks caution that removing content should never distort meaning.

Ta-da, that concludes our dozen core principles! For more, you can enjoy a deeper dive into **Appendix C.** We'll see you on the other side for our core principles of usage.

HOMEWORK

Assignment No. 1

Take one of your favorite articles and zoom in on all the commas. Can you find commas for words, phrases or short sentences in a simple series? If so, is there an Oxford comma before the "and" in keeping with the Chicago Manual of Style, or does it look like your article abides by the AP Stylebook?

Assignment No. 2

In the same article, or perhaps another one of your choice, look for conjunctions: "and," "but," "for," "or," "nor," "yet," "so." Now look to see if a comma comes before them, joining a complete clause with a subject and verb. Can you find examples of "but" and "for" used as prepositions, not conjunctions? See if replacing the comma-conjunction combo with a semicolon can work.

Assignment No. 3

Turn to the latest brilliant article you've written and see if you can find a sentence with three or more commas. Stop and see if you can insert a period and break the sentence into two. Can you really keep one idea to one sentence, or do you think that leads to an unpleasant staccato rhythm?

Assignment No. 4

Read through your article and listen for **the "s" sound**. How many of those words are plurals and how many are possessives? Maybe you found a plural possessive, but is the apostrophe in the right place? Is there an "it's" that should be an "its"?

REFERENCES

Associated Press. (2022). *The Associated Press stylebook: 2022–2024* (56th ed.). Basic Books.

University of Chicago Press Editorial Staff. (2017). *The Chicago manual of style* (17th ed.).

University of Chicago Press Editorial Staff. (2024). *The Chicago manual of style* (18th ed.).

Vonnegut, K. (2005). *A man without a country*. Random House.

FURTHER READING, RESOURCES

Casagrande, J. (2014). *The best punctuation book, period: A comprehensive guide for every writer, editor, student, and businessperson*. Ten Speed Press.

Strunk, W., & White, E.B. (2000). *The elements of style* (4th ed.). Macmillan Publishing.

Grammar Books Recommended by the Chicago Manual of Style

Allen, R.L. (1972). *English grammars and English grammar*. Scribner.

Burchfield, R. (1991). *Unlocking the English language*. Hill and Wang.

Gray, E.W. (1967). *A brief grammar of modern written English*. World Pub. Co.

Trask, R.L. (1995). *Language: The basics*. Taylor & Francis.

References and Writing Guides Recommended by the AP Stylebook

Butterfield, J. (Ed.). (2016). *Fowler's concise dictionary of modern English usage* (3rd ed.). Oxford University Press.

Cappon, R.J. (1989). *The word: An Associated Press guide to good news writing* (6th ed.). Associated Press.

Garner, B.A. (2016). *Garner's modern English usage* (4th ed.). Oxford University Press.

USAGE

KEY POINTS IN THIS CHAPTER

1. Usage means precision in your word choice. It's short for standard English usage, which rises above grammar and punctuation to the "self-actualization" of a writer or editor.

2. The AP Stylebook and the Chicago Manual of Style offer a similar list of usage rules, though as usual there are some disagreements. The CMS' 17th edition packs hundreds of alphabetical usage entries into a 53-page section titled "Glossary of Problematic Words and Phrases." The AP instead sprinkles usage entries throughout its 322-page Stylebook section, the first of 13 chapters or sections, in the 56th edition.

3. The source of many usage rules is etymology, the study of word origins from their Latin and Greek roots and how the meanings have changed over time. Good writers and editors try to keep words to their original meanings but must be aware of their current usage to avoid distraction or confusion.

4. Usage mistakes tend to start with the ear as many words sound the same but have different meanings and spellings. These usage errors fly under the radar of spelling checkers, giving editors job security.

This Might Hurt a Little, but ... (Take 5)

Welcome to class!

So nice of you to make it. Today's topic is standard English usage. Now, what is the highest standard for writing?

"That it can be understood easily," a brave student volunteers.

OK, how about this: "Me Tarzan. You Jane." You can understand that easily, right?

"Yes, sir."

Class, has anyone ever heard of Maslow's hierarchy of needs?

"I have, professor."

Yes?

"There are five levels in his pyramid, ranging from basic needs to self-actualization."

Brilliant! My young scholar, you have just defined the Ryan-O'Donnell Hierarchy of Editing.

*We started with a basic understanding of style (**Chapter 1.5**), then moved to safety from spelling errors (**Chapter 1.6**), then the love and belonging that comes from joining with fellow grammarians (**Chapter 1.7**), and then the esteem that accrues from a perfectly punctuated sentence (**Chapter 1.8**).*

"And now?"

*And now we've arrived at the top tier of language skills—standard English usage (**Chapter 1.9**)—also known as the self-actualization of a writer or editor.*

Ah, if only your lectures in college were that short. Unfortunately, if you pick up the Associated Press Stylebook or the Chicago Manual of Style, you will be confronted with a long list of usage entries.

The CMS' 17th edition offers hundreds of entries over 53 pages in a "Glossary of Problematic Words and Phrases" (5.249–5.250, 306–358) from **a; an** to **your; you're**. The AP Stylebook, which doesn't always see the same problems, instead sprinkles usage entries throughout its 322-page Stylebook chapter, the first of 13 chapters or sections in its 56th edition.

Fortunately, we've covered some of this ground already, and as you know, our approach is to look for connections that can be wrapped into core principles. But first, to give you some street cred with your bosses, we'll discuss a brief history of how we were introduced to the fine art of usage.

That's standard English usage. In France, the official custodian of the language, the Académie Française, dates to 1635 in an effort to counter foreign influences. For English we don't have an official authority on the language, only self-appointed guardians.

Our Usage Experts

The Godfather of Usage didn't reign as far back as Chaucer and the "The Canterbury Tales," only a couple of centuries later, or 1564–1616 to be precise. That, of course, is William Shakespeare, who is credited with coining or introducing more than 1,700 words still in use today, according to the Shakespeare Birthplace Trust (n.d.).

A scholar estimates that all of Shakespeare's known writings account for 884,647 words (Spevack, 1974). But what makes Shakespeare an icon for usage lovers is that he used 14,376 words only once (Kottke, 2010). Think of how precise your word choice must be to achieve a literary accomplishment like that!

A few centuries later, but also in England, Henry Watson Fowler published his Dictionary of Modern English Usage in 1926. It remains quite the curiosity as it provides not only a style guide to British English usage but also rules for pronunciation and writing.

Part of the curiosity to us is that the dictionary is billed as providing "in-depth coverage of both British and American English usage issues, with reference also to the English of Australia, Canada, India, New Zealand, and South Africa" (Butterfield, 2016). Knowing full well how English is taught in China, we assure you that the British way of speaking and writing is practiced there, too.

"Fowler's Dictionary" was always a good place for us to start to answer editing questions back in the day. Other usage experts also heavily influenced our professional careers and our bosses' thinking as well. Any old-school editors worth their salt can cite from "The Careful Writer" by Theodore Bernstein. The 1965 handbook was subtitled "A Modern Guide to English Usage."

At the time, Bernstein was a senior editor at The New York Times and the guardian of the newspaper's language. He would publish six books on standard English usage. When he died in 1979 at the age of 74, his obituary made front-page news for the Times.

Bernstein was brilliant and funny, humorous and a little kooky. For example, in an entry for **exit** he argued that "entrance" signs should be replaced with **"adit"** signs, just to keep the Latin origins of the words parallel. To understand the Bernstein mind, you'll need to take a course in etymology, which is the study of word origins with their Latin and Greek roots and how meanings change over time.

A brief etymology lesson: Take the word "irregardless." The prefix "ir" is transformed from "in-," meaning "not." The suffix "-less" means "without." So "not without regard" means "with regard." But you mean the opposite, "regardless," so just say that.

Bernstein's humor glimmered in an in-house newsletter, "Winners & Sinners," that "went viral," as we say in today's parlance, reaching journalism schools and other newsrooms with its critiques of the language. For the headline "Elm Beetle Infestation Ravishing Thousands of Trees in Greenwich," Bernstein titled his critique "Insex" and opined: "Keep your mind on your work, buster. The word you want is 'ravaging.'"

"The Careful Writer" followed "Watch Your Language: A Lively, Informal Guide to Better Writing Emanating From the News Room of the New York Times" (Bernstein, 1958) and "More Language That Needs Watching" (Bernstein, 1962).

You can buy paperback versions of his books dirt cheap, and we highly recommend that you do so if you're interested in a professional career as an editor.

For us Bernstein was succeeded by Edwin Newman, a CBS News radio and NBC News TV legend. As a nationally recognized keeper of the usage flame, Newman was more judgy-judgy. The subtitle of Newman's "Strictly Speaking" book, one of many, was "Will America Be the Death of English?"

Catchy but crazy, that subtitle misses a key point: Changes in the English language by its many users come like unstoppable waves that can be logged but never logjammed.

These days we would hand the baton to Roy Peter Clark of the Poynter Institute for Media Studies, a school for journalists. You might enjoy his charming book, "The Glamour of Grammar: A Guide to the Magic and Mystery of Practical English" (Clark, 2010). Here's an excerpt:

> *"Was there ever in the popular imagination a word less glamorous than grammar? But what if I were to tell you that at one time in the history of our language, grammar and glamour were the same word? Need proof? Let's consult the Oxford English Dictionary."*

To Clark the commonality lies in the power to charm. Once you've warmed up with that book, you can read the 10th anniversary edition of "Writing Tools: 55 Essential Strategies for Every Writer" (Clark, 2016) and "Tell It Like It Is" (Clark, 2023).

Now It's Your Turn

You're getting the idea. In every generation, there comes along someone with a love, even passion, for the language who wishes to carry the standards banner. We hope we can inspire you to be the next one for your generation.

Hurry forth, quickly now! Onto—or is it "on to"?—**a dozen core principles** of usage.

The Core Principles of Usage

Usage, or word choice, is one of those puzzles that tend to get solved best when the items are listed in alphabetical order, as in the AP Stylebook or the Chicago Manual of Style. It looks easier that way at times, but like everything else with language skills, nothing is easy.

We're taking a different tack by summarizing core principles. Nonetheless, we offer you advice at a glance alphabetically in The Fixtionary (**Appendix A**) and a pretty neat Index at the end of the book.

For the moment, let's say you're wondering whether to use "onto," which the CMS says implies motion and "has an adverbial flavor even though it is a preposition" (5.250, page 344).

If you look in the AP Stylebook, you get only as far as the entry **on** (AP, 214), which is no help. In fact, the AP advises you not to use the word "on" (*The meeting will be held Monday, not on Monday*) unless you need to (*John met Mary on Monday*).

So back to the CMS, which offers these examples:

The gymnast jumped onto the bars. (preposition)

The gymnast held on to the bars. (verb phrase held on, preposition to)

So we should say, "Jump onto **a dozen core principles!**" Here goes:

1. Listen for the Right Choice, but Don't Be Fooled by What You Hear

Take the articles "a" and "an"—easy enough, right? You might have learned a rule like, "Use 'a' with words that start with a consonant; use 'an' when they start with a vowel." What's missing is the word "sound."

Focus on how the next word is pronounced and not just the first letter (consonant). Say or write:

- a history student (hiss)
- an honorable woman (on)
- an 1898 Spanish-American War battle (ay)

Don't be fooled by words that sound alike but are spelled differently, such as:

- peak (top)
- peek (look)
- pique (stimulate or irritate)

Repeat after us: *The peak piqued my interest so I peeked.*

Some words like "peek" are easy to remember if you see those two "e's" in the middle like eyes looking at you. So "peek" means to look quickly.

It's the same way we remember how to spell "liaison," as we think of the "i" in the middle acting as a liaison between "Lia" and her "son." We hope these memory tricks "pique" your interest.

Although pronounced the same, we like to think of "pique" as meaning to stimulate your curiosity, not irritate you, though the word can mean that, too.

We hope your energy will not "peak" as we plow through these usage points. We know it must feel like we are climbing to the "peak," or top, of a mountain. OK, enough of that!

Here are some other examples in a flashcard format:

- aid (help), aide (person)
- accept (receive), except (exclude)
- cannon (gun), canon (rule or book)
- capital (city), Capitol (building)
- cite (mention), site (place), sight (vision), sights (for tourists; set your sights on)
- complement (complete), compliment (praise)
- core (center), corps (Marine Corps)
- council (board), counsel (attorney)
- discreet (shh), discrete (separate)
- foreword (introduction), forward (direction)
- gibe (insult), jibe (fit neatly)
- hangar (airplanes), hanger (clothes)
- here (arrived), hear (ear)
- its (its possession), it's (it is or it has)

- lets (to rent out an apartment), let's (go!)
- medal (award), meddle (interfere)
- pedal (by foot), peddle (by selling)
- principle (belief), principal (school leader or primary concern)
- rain (water), rein (in), reign (over)
- rack (your brain), wrack (ruin)
- rites (like last ones for a funeral), rights (fight for them!)
- should of (kidding, right?), should have (right)
- there (locale), their (owners), they're (they are)
- to (somewhere), too (also or too much), two (number)
- weather (climate), whether (or not)
- your (not my or mine), you're (you are)

Problems with sound-alike words can arise with autocorrect, so be careful. Don't glance over them; stop and spell them out in your mind.

2. Watch for the Pesky Look-Alikes

Then there are words that look alike and can give you trouble if you're not careful about their pronunciation. For example:

- adverse (bad), averse (opposed)
- advice (tips), advise (consult)
- beside (next to), besides (also)
- breath (mouth), breathe (lungs)
- comprise (embrace all), compose (make up)
- confidant (companion), confident (certain)
- conscious (awake), conscience (voice in your head)
- continuous (no interruptions), continual (brief interruptions)
- desert (sand), dessert (yum!)
- dispersed (smoke cleared), disbursed (a loan)
- gantlet (ordeal), gauntlet (glove, thrown down as a challenge)
- hanged (executed), hung (your clothes)
- imply (speak), infer (hear)
- lose (sorry!), loose (not tight)
- metal (steel), mettle (your character)
- pour (a drink), pore (over material)
- proved (shown to be successful), proven (a proven success)
- quite (just so), quiet (shh)
- raise (elevate), raze (destroy)
- refute (prove wrong), dispute (question or challenge)
- staunch (firm), stanch (stop)
- then (time), than (compare)
- were (past), we're (we are), where (location)

Problems with look-alike words can arise with autocorrect, too, so be careful. When you say them out loud, slow down for proper diction.

3. Run From This Problem

Let's ponder one more pesky look-alike: "run" and "ran." Sadly, even people with advanced degrees can sound not so smart. Take this Facebook post from a university vice president:

The Detroit Aquarium is one of the oldest aquariums in the country.

It is now completely ran by volunteers.

See the problem? The word should be "run" for the past participle. In **Appendix B**, we'll have you conjugate verbs, like so:

- *run (present tense)*
- *ran (past tense)*
- *run (past participle)*

So, we say: I run today, I ran yesterday and I will run tomorrow. The past participle is also used with other helping verbs, as in "is run," "was run," "were run," "will be run."

Remember "the -ed dud" from **Chapter 1.7, Grammar**? Well, "run" is a past participle not formed with "-ed." We call these irregular verbs, and they can make copy editors feel irregular.

So for our Detroit example, we could say:

Now completely run by volunteers, the aquarium is one of the oldest in the country.

As we can't help ourselves, we would suggest a final version:

Now completely run by volunteers, the Belle Isle Aquarium in Detroit, which opened in 1904, is one of the oldest public aquariums in the continental United States.

Now run along to our next core principle.

4. Feel the Effect of Affect

Some troublesome words—like "affect" and "effect"—are easily solved by assigning meanings once you determine whether they are nouns or verbs. Then substitute the meanings to make sure you're using them properly.

For a **noun**, just put "the" in front of the word, like so:

- the effect—result
- the affect—emotion

When they are used as **verbs**, the meanings change, as in:

- effect—to bring about
- affect—to influence

To feel confident using those words, create sentences like these to get your bearings:

The effect (result) of the mayor's attempt to effect (bring about) change was remarkable.

The affect (emotion) associated with a piece of chalk, something I choked on as a kid, affected (influenced) me every time I went to the blackboard.

5. Be Politically Correct for Civility's Sake, but Watch the Quicksand

A scholar at the Wharton School of the University of Pennsylvania focused his research on the CEMs of CEOs. Those are the **Career-Ending Moves** by business executives under pressure. In today's media environment it pays to have usage fingertips to ensure your job security.

News over the 2022 holidays broke that North Carolina State radio broadcaster Gary Hahn was suspended indefinitely after referring to "illegal aliens in El Paso" during a Duke's Mayo Bowl football game. We get it.

For the record, he was giving an update on an early score in the first half of the Sun Bowl on Dec. 30, 2022, when he said: "Down among all the illegal aliens in El Paso, it's UCLA 14 and Pittsburgh 6."

The AP Stylebook has an **illegal** entry (AP, 145) that begins: "Except in sports and game contexts, use 'illegal' only to mean a violation of the law." On the next page, with the subtitle **illegal immigration**, the AP says, "Except in direct quotes essential to the story, use illegal only to refer to an action, not a person: 'illegal immigration,' but not 'illegal immigrant.'" Three graphs later it says do not use the term "alien."

The lengthy glossary in the Chicago Manual of Style has no entry for "alien" or "illegal alien," only the **immigrate; emigrate** entry that says one word means enter ("immigrate into") and the other means leave ("emigrate from"). In the section that follows, **Bias-Free Language** (5.251–5.260, 358–362), you might infer that using "illegal alien" is a bad idea, but there's no specific example.

Sometimes stylebook entries read like no-brainers to avoid sexist language: use "firefighter," not "fireman"; use "police officer," not "policeman"; use "weathercaster" or "meteorologist," not "weatherman," and so on. But other times they read more like pet peeves than usage rules.

The AP Stylebook, for example, devotes an entry to **mistress** (AP, 195), which it calls an "archaic and sexist term." But its alternatives fall short, like "lover" (maybe love is not involved), "companion" (a lot of companions are not lovers) and "friend" (that's an understatement). The CMS makes no such objection to "mistress." This is the kind of quicksand that usage experts can create when they attempt to be politically correct. The solution lies in a **Chapter 1.1** core principle to keep in mind your target reader, listener or viewer as you weigh your words; let them decide what's a turn-off.

On the use of the pronoun "they" for a singular person, the AP Stylebook strikes the right note in its **pronouns** entry (AP, 238): "Try to honor both your readers and your story subjects. As in all news writing, clarity is paramount."

6. Don't Forget to Use the Urban Dictionary

You'll remember that we listed several dictionaries associated with the AP Stylebook and the Chicago Manual of Style, but one missing on their lists is the Urban Dictionary. It rates a link to the Library of Congress, which explains:[1]

About this item:

Title

Urban Dictionary: Define Your World

Summary

Urban Dictionary is a crowdsourced online dictionary of slang words and phrases that was founded in 1999 as a parody of Dictionary. com and Vocabulary.com by then-college freshman Aaron Peckham. Some of the definitions on the website can be found as early as 1999, but most early definitions are from 2003. At the start of 2014, the dictionary featured over seven million definitions, while 2,000 new daily entries were being added.

We know this may surprise you, but we have been in faculty meetings when a male colleague says about a student: "I need to *hook up* with her."

Library of Congress, "Urban Dictionary: Define Your World," Library of Congress, Library of Congress.

When exactly "hook up" changed from meaning "connect" to "have sex with" we're not sure, but such is the mystery and challenge of usage. As you might expect, the CMS is silent on this point, and the closest the AP gets is the spelling-word entry **hooky** (AP, 141), as in "to play hooky," or to skip class.

Enter the Urban Dictionary to the rescue (spelling errors and all):

1.) **hookup** *(v)*

other spellings/forms:

hook-up, hook up, hooked up, hooking up

To have any form of intamicy [sic] with a member of the prefered [sic] sex that you don't consider a significant other. Usually, when said by modern youth it means to make out, and when said by people between the ages of 20 and 35 it generally means to have sex, and if a very old person says it, it probably means to simply spend time with somebody.

And, in case you're wondering, here's the entry on **Old person**:

Person over 30 years old.

-How long since you got your prostate checked?

-Man, I'm barely 32. …

-Then you are a few years late; you are an old person already.

For more examples of coined words or changes in word usage, you can always turn to sports radio. Standard dictionaries may still be stuck on old definitions for words like these:

> That play was "**sick**"!
> Oh, what a "**nasty**" move!
> How many "**tuddies**" does your quarterback have?
> Really? He's "**ridiculous**."

Of course, musicians have been at this game for a long time, even longer than when Michael Jackson turned "bad" into something "good" with his 1987 song and album by the same name.

As college professors for a combined near-century, we have had the advantage of consistently starting a school year with 18-year-olds as we turned a

Source: https://www.urbandictionary.com/define.php?term=hookup.
Source: https://www.urbandictionary.com/define.php?term=Old%20person.

year older. To be a good editor or writer, it pays to spend time talking with young people—and searching the Urban Dictionary.

7. Let Me Count the Ways

Usage purists will draw distinctions between words that are either concrete or abstract, measurable or not measurable. Often a good gauge is to ask, "Can I count them?" For example:

- *further (more), farther (distance in miles)*
- *amount (of courage), number (of people or things)*

The AP's **amount**, **number** entry (AP, 15–16) offers rules and exceptions. So here's an example following the rule:

- *less (energy), fewer (dollars)*

And then here's an acceptable exception:

- *Write the jingle in 25 words or less.*

Count the number of times you hear someone with a live report talk about the "amount" of people at a concert or protest, and don't be like that.

For years the AP Stylebook advised to use "over" only for spacial relationships. So this was the rule:

- *over (the moon), more than (10%)*

As can happen with the language, the guardians get mugged by a crowd of violators long enough that they give in. A usage rule moves from preferred to acceptable.

Here's what the entry **over** says in the 56th edition: "Acceptable in all uses to indicate greater numerical value" (AP, 218). As for the Chicago Manual of Style, its **over** entry (5.250, 345) gives you a free pass, too: "As an equivalent of *more than*, this word is perfectly good idiomatic English."

8. Say What You Mean, but Watch for Cheap Plugs

Another set of problems arise when you don't say what you mean clearly. Sometimes a writer will call something "ironic" when, in fact, it's just a "coincidence."

Fans will say they ate "during halftime" (from whistle to whistle?) when they mean "at halftime." A reporter announces that the mayor will "unveil" her three-point environmental plan like she's going to remove a veil from a piece of paper, or something. Or you'll read that a "trio of robbers" knocked over a bank, then be disappointed to learn they were not musicians.

Slow down, think about what you're saying or writing, and watch out for words that can be confusing or confused. Let's start with *and/or* (I'm sorry, what?). It pays to spend a few more words to be clear. So you might say, "I'll buy this shirt or that tie, or both."

Here are some other watch words to keep straight:

- anxious (anxiety), eager (hurry up)
- billion (a thousand million), trillion (a thousand billion)
- can (ability), may (permission)
- center around (nope, say "center on" or "revolve around")
- connote (oblique mention), denote (direct mention)
- currently (now), presently (soon)
- disinterested (impartial), uninterested (bored)
- empathy (I understand), sympathy (compassion)
- et al. (and others), etc. (same list as before)
- good (nice!), well (not sick), well (skillfully)
- include (only with an incomplete list)
- lie (recline, fib), lay (reclined, place)
- literally (actually), figuratively (not actually)
- parity (same), parody (joke)
- persuaded (to do something), convinced (that or of something)
- reveal (was hidden), present (introduce)
- since (time), because (cause and effect)
- unique (one of a kind), very unique (AP lifted ban to mean rare)

Sometimes you'll say what you mean by using a brand name. Media outlets are on guard, however, for cheap plugs, or as we say in the advertising game, "earned media." That means you get to promote your brand, product or company without paying for it. So you may have bosses who prefer that you go generic, as in:

- artificial grass for AstroTurf
- gelatin for Jell-O
- photocopy for Xerox
- plastic foam cup for Styrofoam
- soft drink for Coke

The AP Stylebook addresses this issue in its **trademark** entry (AP, 293).

9. Shall We Make That One Word or Two?

Meaning changes depending on whether it's one word or two. For example:

- allot (give out), a lot (much)
- already (it happened), all ready (let's rumble)
- alright (frowned-upon variant), all right (preferred)
- altogether (entirely), all together (we gathered)
- awhile (stay awhile), a while (stay for a while)
- everyday (ordinary), every day (all the time)
- everyone (everybody), every one (each individual)
- into (a space), in to (give in to)

10. Cut the Syllables and Trim the Fat

You may recall Rudolf Flesch's readability studies about syllables and our suggestion to choose the short word over the long word when no meaning is lost. Well, here are some usage examples of what we meant. You can enjoy a full listing in **Appendix D, Brevity and Simplicity.** So for starters, consider using:

- about, *not* approximately
- give in, *not* acquiesce
- enough, *not* adequate *or* sufficient
- happen, *not* transpire
- use, *not* utilize

Sometimes you can drop unnecessary or redundant words by saying:

- after accepting the position, *not after having accepted the position*
- all the cookies, *not all of the cookies*
- death, *not tragic death*
- fact, *not actual fact*
- history, *not past history*
- murder, *not brutal murder*
- no, *not in the negative*
- opposed, *not diametrically opposed*
- yes, *not in the affirmative*

11. None of Us Agree on This One

Trigger warning: This core principle can hurt. Here's a crazy one for you—none. Do you say "none is" or "none are"? Answer: yes (lol), and you can decide.

Originally the word worked as a contraction ("no'ne") for "no one" or "not one." So start by trying to make none work as a singular meaning "it," as in:

None of the books is for sale.

None of the guests is leaving.

Now listen for how "none" can become a "they." How do these sentences sound to you?

None of the taxes have been paid.

None of the diplomats agree on what to do next.

Both are correct. The AP Stylebook entry **none** (AP, 206) says use a plural verb ("are," "were," "have") with "none" when it means "no amount" or "no two."

None of the taxes (no amount) have, not has.

None of the diplomats (no two) agree, not agrees.

The Chicago Manual of Style goes a little more technical in its explanation (5.250, 343) with a focus on the object of the preposition "of."

If it's singular, treat "none" like "it," as in:

*None of the **building** was painted.*

Or if it's plural, treat "none" like "they," as in:

*None of the **guests** were here when I arrived.*

Then the CMS says, "It is quite proper (though possibly stilted)" to write:

None of my suggestions was accepted. (as in not one of my suggestions)

We'll address that "stilted" thing in our last core principle. Now for something entirely different!

12. Break a Rule to Make a Mark or Set the Right Tone

Proper usage creates a serious and formal tone suitable for professional topics. But what if your topic is wacky? Then using standard English usage is like showing up to a beach party in a tuxedo.

Even one word—a purposeful mistake—can change the tone of your writing and get positive attention.

One of the longest-running usage debates in modern history erupted when a beloved rule went up in smoke. That's when R.J. Reynolds Tobacco Co. hired an advertising agency that brilliantly—and ungrammatically—coined this slogan in 1954:

"Winston tastes good like a cigarette should."

Shocking, right? You probably didn't even notice. But it created a scandal as schoolteachers for generations had pounded into kids' skulls that "like" is a preposition, not a conjunction.

First, a brief reminder: a preposition is a word that shows relationship ("between you and me") while a conjunction joins ideas ("comma-but," "and"). So add "like" to the long list of prepositions and add "as" to your roster of conjunctions.

Back to the slogan: Consider these "correct" sentences:

*Winston tastes good **as** a cigarette should.*

*Don't be **like** me and choose another brand.*

Not too snappy, eh? Winston added insult to usage injury by turning the slogan into a popular jingle. In 1999 Advertising Age included it among the Top 10 radio and television jingles of the 20th century (Garfield, 1999). So much for following strict usage rules.

The Chicago Manual of Style is still talking about it. Here's what the CMS entry for **like; as** (5.250, 340) says seven decades later:

"In Standard Written English, a conjunctive 'like' will still provoke frowns among some readers. But the objections are slowly dwindling."

Usage rules die hard, and the AP Stylebook isn't budging. Its **like, as** entry (AP, 175) is matter-of-fact: Use "like" as a preposition, and "as" is the "correct word" to use as a conjunction.

Finally, here's a game for you. As you read along, stop every time we use "like" as a conjunction, just to lighten the tone. Then add a count for when we use a sentence fragment (no subject and verb) to punch home a point consistent with a conversational tone. You can turn this exercise into a drinking game, nonalcoholic, of course—and no smoking.

Off you go, my students!

Read your required text, do your homework, then tackle the Appendix.

Class dismissed!

HOMEWORK

Assignment No. 1

Wow, that's a lot to keep straight, Part I. As you review all the various points packed into the 12 core principles, assemble your top 10 for a to-do list. Which are the ones that give you the most trouble? Then begin creating your first set of flashcards and test yourself a few times.

Assignment No. 2

Wow, that's a lot to keep straight, Part II. Which of the 12 entries made you think, "You know, I really had no idea." These are points about the niceties of the language that make you feel like a copy editor. You know they're good ones because you wanted to share the distinctions with family or friends—or maybe give them a quiz. Create your second set of flash cards, then test yourself a few times.

Assignment No. 3

The "hookup" example from the Urban Dictionary is one of many potentially embarrassing word choices that separate generations. Run a little experiment with friends your age, then parents and maybe even grandparents. You can ask innocently, "What does it mean to hook up?" Explain, then ask, "What other words or expressions have changed meaning over time?" See how many you can discover, then use them to create your next set of flashcards.

Assignment No. 4

We mentioned works by Shakespeare, a dictionary by Henry Fowler, books by Theodore Bernstein, Edwin Newman and Roy Peter Clark, and, of course, the AP Stylebook and the Chicago Manual of Style. But where do you go online to get advice on usage? Do a little analysis: Are you hearing the same points and getting the same kinds of advice? Where do your sources get their rules? Go with what works best for you.

REFERENCES

Bernstein, T.M. (1958). *Watch your language: A lively, informal guide to better writing, emanating from the news room of the New York Times*. Channel Press.

Bernstein, T.M. (1968). *The careful writer: A modern guide to English usage*. Atheneum.

Butterfield, J. (Ed.). (2016). *Fowler's concise dictionary of modern English usage* (3rd ed.). Oxford University Press.

Kottke, J. (2010). How many words did Shakespeare know? https://kottke.org/10/04/how-many-words-did-shakespeare-know

Spevack, M. (1974). *The Harvard concordance to Shakespeare*. Belknap Press of Harvard University Press.

FURTHER READING, RESOURCES

Barzun, J. (2001). *Simple & direct: A rhetoric for writers*. Scribner.

Bernstein, T.M. (1962). *More language that needs watching*. Channel Press.

Bernstein, T.M. (1971). *Miss Thistlebottom's hobgoblins: The careful writer's guide to the taboos, bugbears, and outmoded rules of English usage*. Farrar, Straus & Giroux.

Bernstein, T.M. (1975). *Bernstein's reverse dictionary* (2nd ed.). Times Books. Designed to help you find a word if you only know the definition.

Bernstein, T.M. (1975). *Dos, don'ts & maybes of English usage*. Times Books.

Clark, R.P. (2023). *Tell it like it is: A guide to clear and honest writing*. Little, Brown.

Clark, R.P. (2016). *Writing tools: 55 essential strategies for every writer* (10th anniversary ed.). Little, Brown.

Clark, R.P. (2010). *The glamour of grammar: A guide to the magic and mystery of practical English*. Little, Brown.

Gallix, A. (2013, May 23). The French protect their language like the British protect their currency. *The Guardian*. https://www.theguardian.com/commentisfree/2013/may/23/language-french-identity

Garfield, B. (1999, March 29). *Ad Age* advertising century: Top 10 jingles. *Ad Age*. https://adage.com/article/special-report-the-advertising-century/ad-age-advertising-century-top-10-jingles/140154

Library of Congress. (n.d.). *Urban Dictionary: Define your world*. https://www.loc.gov/item/lcwaN0004130

New York Times (1979, June 28). TM. Bernstein dies; language authority and ex-*Times* editor. https://www.nytimes.com/1979/06/28/archives/tm-bernstein-dies-language-authority-and-extimes-editor-tm.html

Newman, E. (1992). *Strictly speaking: Will America be the death of English?* Galahad Books.

Safire, W. (1981). *On language*. Avon Books.

Shakespeare Birthplace Trust. (n.d.). *Shakespeare's words*. https://www.shakespeare.org.uk/explore-shakespeare/shakespedia/shakespeares-words/

Showbiz Scene Archives. (n.d.). The century's top commercial jingles. http://www.archer2000.com/sbs/awardscj.html

EDITING NEWS ON DEADLINE.

As Rod Serling, creator of "The Twilight Zone," used to say, "You are about to enter another dimension. A dimension not only of sight and sound but of mind." He was known for his endings with a twist (MeTV, 2020). Talk about a twist: We're now delivering you to The Daily Journalism Zone.

Introducing **Section 2: Editing News on Deadline.**

In this section, we take off the training wheels, suggest some hacks to make deadline with quality content and introduce concepts that are unique to newsrooms. The evolution of editors tends to go like this: First, they are fast and bad, then they are slow and good, and finally they become fast and good.

We have structured our book to allow you to be slow and good, as you master the basics in **Section 1.** We can only imagine the reactions from daily deadline journalists to **Section 1**, particularly the three-part editing strategy: "That's nice, but …"

We hear you! That's because we, too, have worked on deadlines so tight that we hardly had time to think. In **Section 2**, like a carny working the stick on a merry-go-round at an amusement park, we will turn up the speed a few notches.

Welcome to Section 2

We start with **Chapter 2.1** by explaining "The Nature of News," first by comparing The New York Times with the New York Post, which have different target readers. Accordingly, they also have different formats, personalities and news philosophies. We then explain how news judgment operates on a macro level (story selection and placement) and on a micro level (word choice and story flow).

In **Chapter 2.2** we offer advice on "Writing Short: Posts, Titles and Headlines." For many readers, the headline "is" the story. The same goes for tweets, now called "posts" on X, the former Twitter. We offer you methods for dealing with straight news headlines ("skeleton" and "condense and patch") and light-hearted stories or advertising slogans ("seed approach").

In **Chapter 2.3: The Indispensable Image**, we provide a tutorial on photo selection, cropping and editing as well as advice on seeking permissions to use video from the source. In **Chapter 2.4**, we offer an antidote to math anxiety with "Stats, Graphs and Maps." In **Chapter 2.5**, we delve into the importance of quotations and sound bites with "Get Me a Quote!"

Chapter 2.6: Editing Crime Stories takes a sharp turn into dealing with serious matters in more ways than one—you can get sued. We wind down **Section 2** with **Chapter 2.7: Trimming Stories**, an essential and often difficult task, whether you're dealing with a long-form magazine article or a "PBS NewsHour" video package. In our **Epilogue,** we offer closing thoughts and best wishes as we say "bon voyage" as you will face a constellation of challenges on your journey to become a star editor.

Wait, look outside, it's now twilight. No better time to enter The Daily Journalism Zone!

—The Authors

REFERENCES

MeTV. (2020, June 8). The 10 most powerful closing statements from "The Twilight Zone." https://www.metv.com/lists/the-10-most-powerful-closing-statements-from-the-twilight-zone

THE NATURE OF NEWS

KEY POINTS IN THIS CHAPTER

1. Many elements factor into decisions about what stories are important and how to play them, including the personality of a news organization and an understanding of its audience. This is true whether the news lands on the front page of a newspaper or a magazine cover, as the lead story on a radio or television broadcast, or on the homepage of an online-only publication.

2. Traditional news values, such as timeliness, can provide some guidance in evaluating stories, but values such as conflict, celebrity or magnitude can lead editors to overestimate the importance of some stories. The result can be a turn-off, rather than a turn-on, for readers, listeners or viewers.

3. News meetings take on many forms depending on the news organization. Whether they are quick standup huddles, or long sit-down sessions in a crowded room, or Zoom meetings, the goal is the same—to get everyone on the same page.

4. The process of news judgment should be open and rational, centered on the best interests of readers and viewers. To address a lack of trust, editors will explain to their audiences why certain news judgments were made regarding coverage, headlines or photos in the interest of transparency.

> **"** *A good newspaper, I suppose, is*
> *a nation talking to itself."*
>
> —Arthur Miller, playwright

For nearly five years, Bill Horner III was something of a one-man band. He was listed on the contacts page of his newspaper's website as "publisher," but he also was the editor, writing coach and mentor, and lead columnist at the Chatham (North Carolina) News + Record.

Horner headed a staff of five at his award-winning weekly paper: two reporters who were recent college graduates, a sports editor, a photographer and himself. Currently he is executive editor of CityView, an online news organization serving residents of Fayetteville, North Carolina, and other communities in Cumberland County.

For Horner, news is what serves the reader.

"I want the story to provide a payoff for a reader," Horner said. "I ask my reporters, What's the payoff for the reader? What's the takeaway? What's the deliverable for the reader for the story?"

Those are good questions for any editor choosing stories and deciding what to change and what to leave alone. Horner would agree with playwright Arthur Miller's quote about what makes for a good newspaper. Good news judgment comes in knowing your readers, listeners and viewers and how to talk to them.

For many decisions, editors have hard-and-fast rules in their stylebook, a dictionary or other references.

But many decisions depend on good judgment related to news values. The editor must know what the story is about and what the writer is trying to accomplish. Is it hard news or a feature? News stories require a more formal tone, but many features are written in a casual tone where even the rules of grammar might be bent. Is the story noncontroversial or does it include potentially libelous material? Does it require a clever headline or a straightforward approach?

News judgment, then, includes good writing that makes a point readers can understand.

"When the story is not structured well, when it's not well-done, sometimes we just have to ask, Why are we writing this story?" Horner said. "Why are we doing this story now and not another story?"

Comparing Two Newspapers

News judgment is not guided by a set of concrete, universally held principles. It varies from person to person, from city to city and from publication to publication. At one end of the newspaper world is the community weekly with a circulation of a few thousand. At the other end, you find metro daily newspapers with circulations in the hundreds of thousands. Even in the same city, these heavy hitters can take radically different approaches to news.

Look at these front pages, from the New York Post (Figure 2.1.1) and The New York Times (Figure 2.1.2) from Wednesday, Nov. 4, 2020.

FIGURE 2.1.1   The New York Post uses a stock photo and a big, catchy headline "NAILBITER" on its front page. The Post, known for its partisan approach, offers a deck headline: "Trump defies polls, election on razor's edge."

The New York Times

VOL. CLXX ... No. 58,867   © 2020 The New York Times Company   NEW YORK, WEDNESDAY, NOVEMBER 4, 2020 $3.00

TURNOUT SOARS, ALONG WITH SUSPENSE, AS NATION IN TUMULT DELIVERS VERDICT

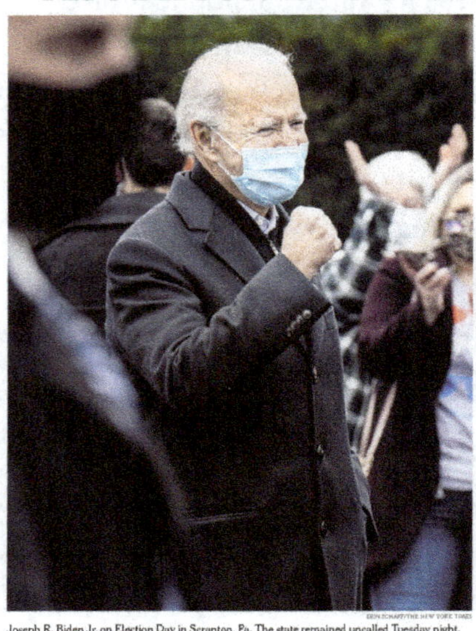

Joseph R. Biden Jr. on Election Day in Scranton, Pa. The state remained uncalled Tuesday night.

President Trump in Arlington, Va. Nationwide turnout was expected to top the record set in 2016.

Final Rush to the Ballot Box Is Smoother Than Forecast

This article is by Nick Corasaniti, Jim Rutenberg and Stephanie Saul.

The worst fears about a chaotic end to a chaotic campaign failed to materialize on Tuesday as the final day of voting went off with little more than sporadic glitches and confrontations even as the tension over the outcome and aftermath remained undiminished.

The most litigated, disrupted and polarized election in generations came to a close with voters who had not already cast their ballots by mail or in person during early voting trooping to the polls on an Election Day redefined by the coronavirus pandemic.

There were scattered problems and hints of battles still to be fought: The authorities in Michigan sought to hunt down the source of robocalls that warned voters to "stay home." A federal judge ordered the Postal Service to make an intensive sweep for mail-in ballots that had yet to be delivered. And legal skirmishes broke out in and around Philadelphia as Republicans sought to challenge votes in the critical Democratic stronghold.

With a record number of votes already having been cast, election

Limited Disruption — Counting Mail-In Votes Is Big Test

officials across the country reported relatively smooth operations on Tuesday, with nothing more than the usual long lines at polling places — made longer by social distancing — and machine malfunctions.

The scale of the turnout and the shift to mail voting led to slow counts in some major cities in battleground states. In Philadelphia, about 26 percent of the absentee ballots had been counted by 9 p.m. In Milwaukee, election officials said they would not be done until 5 a.m. on Wednesday at the earliest.

But much of what experts had feared might happen on a most unusual Election Day did not come to pass.

In the past several days and weeks, foreign countries interfered less than they had leading to the 2018 midterm elections, the director of the National Security Agency, Gen. Paul M. Nakasone,

Continued on Page A12

Key States Up for Grabs As Trump-Biden Battle Extends Late Into Night

By ALEXANDER BURNS and JONATHAN MARTIN

The 2020 presidential race remained shrouded in uncertainty deep into the night on Tuesday, as Joseph R. Biden Jr. failed to achieve any early breakthroughs that would have made him a strong favorite in the race and President Trump clung to a lead in a number of Southern states that Democrats had hoped to flip into their column.

None of the major swing states had been called for either candidate at 10:30 p.m., though Mr. Trump held a persistent edge in Florida with nearly all of the votes counted. The television networks and wire services were proceeding with great caution, handing each party only the most obvious victories in deeply partisan states like New York and Tennessee.

The prolonged suspense was, at least at the start, something of a victory for the president, who was at risk of being eliminated from contention if one of the big, historically Republican states of the Southeast had defected to Mr. Biden, the Democratic nominee. That was still a possibility in North Carolina or Georgia, where the vote tally was closely divided.

Vote-counting was moving relatively slowly in some battleground states on Tuesday night because of the scale of the turnout, a backlog of absentee ballots received by mail and scattered problems with processing the vote. And each state handled the counting and releasing of their ballots differently. Ohio, for example, released the results of all of its mail ballots after the polls closed — making the state seem to tilt toward Mr. Biden until more Election Day votes were cast. Similarly, Michigan released its day-of

votes in the first hours after polls closed, making it seem that Mr. Trump enjoyed a wide advantage in a hotly contested state.

The night unfolded after one of the most extraordinary election cycles in the nation's history, as Americans overcame their fears of the coronavirus, long lines at the polls and the vexing challenges of a transformed voting system to bring the race to a conclusion, with the fate of Mr.

Continued on Page A15

Mask? ✓ Sanitizer? ✓ Doing Their Civic Duty? ✓

By SARAH MERVOSH and MITCH SMITH

CLEVELAND — They voted from cars and at outdoor tables. They stood in lines spaced far apart. They strapped on masks and pumped sanitizer into their palms. All across America on Tuesday, voters cast ballots in a presidential election in which the uncontrolled coronavirus pandemic was both a top issue and a threat.

As millions of Americans turned out to vote, the nation was facing a rapidly escalating pandemic that is concentrated in some of the very states seen as critical in determining the outcome of the presidential race. From Wisconsin to North Carolina, infections were on the rise as the nation barreled toward 10 million total cases.

The virus that has left millions of people out of work and killed more than 230,000 people in the United States will be one of the most significant challenges for the winner of the presidential race, and it loomed over every chapter of the election, down to the final ballots.

In the last hours of campaigning, President Trump — who, regardless of the election outcome, will be in charge of the nation's response to the pandemic for the next two and a half critical months

Masks were Election Day attire on Tuesday in Las Vegas.

— was at odds with his own coronavirus advisers and suggested that he might fire Dr. Anthony S. Fauci, the nation's top infectious-disease expert. Former Vice President Joseph R. Biden Jr. told voters in a final pitch that "the first step to beating the virus is beating Donald Trump."

In Virginia, voters' tempratures were taken at some polling sites. In Wisconsin, the mayor of Wausau, a small city where cases are spiking and tensions are high, issued an order banning guns at polling places. And in Texas, an election judge did not wear a face covering, prompting accusations of voter intimidation and such intense heckling that the judge called the local sheriff to report that she felt unsafe.

The pandemic, which drove record numbers of Americans to vote early or by mail, rarely strayed far from their minds.

"I just don't want another shut-

Continued on Page A23

Dueling Ideas Of a President And a Country

By MATT FLEGENHEIMER

From the start of his 2020 campaign, Joseph R. Biden Jr. insisted that President Trump was an aberration, his norm-breaking, race-baiting tenure anathema to the national character. "It's not who we are," Mr. Biden often said, "not what America is." And at the end of the 2020 campaign, an anxious, quarrelsome country is turning a question back at him: Are you sure?

NEWS ANALYSIS

For millions of Trump supporters, the last four years have been a time when things changed for the better, when they felt they had a president who knew exactly who they were. They cheered pro-virus jobs success, shifts in the tax code, trade fights with China and the emerging rightward tilt of the Supreme Court. But they often responded more viscerally to the fury than the finer points: Mr. Trump's eager brawls against elites and institutions, against threats to conservatives' preferred social order, against shared enemies. For many Democrats, the

Continued on Page A14

Urging turnout in Milwaukee.

Trump's tumultuous White House reign hanging in the balance.

Turnout was expected to easily break the record of 139 million votes set in 2016, and the percentage of eligible Americans who voted might be the highest in

Continued on Page A15

ONLINE: ELECTION UPDATES

With millions voting by mail in a pandemic, this election has been like no other. For the latest news and results, go to nytimes.com.

FIGURE 2.1.2 The New York Times front page attempts to be nonpartisan with equal-sized pictures of both candidates and a straightforward informational headline: "Turnout soars, along with suspense, as nation in tumult delivers verdict."

The two pages are alike in few ways. Both presentations of the news, however, are valid, based on several factors.

Format. Don't discount the physical differences between a broadsheet paper like the Times and a tabloid like the Post. A 21st-century broadsheet is about 11 inches wide by 21 inches tall, not counting margins. A tabloid page is about half as big; it opens and reads like a magazine. The broadsheet editors have the luxury of hedging their bets with more stories on Page 1. That's what the Times did here, packaging several stories that give a thorough treatment of the election. The Post had to be decisive about the image and headline, relying on the reader to understand the meaning and turn inside for more news.

The webpages for these two newspapers retain many of the visual cues of the print editions.

An interesting development in broadcast news and web-based news is screen size. High-definition television sets provide more real estate for news organizations such as CNN or Fox News to load the viewer with text and graphic devices. Sometimes these can veer into the sensational (Figure 2.1.3).

Personality. The pattern for "tabloid journalism" was set in 1919 with the launch of New York's Illustrated Daily News. The traditional fare for the tabloid newspaper has been a sensational mix of crime, sex and entertainment; the New York Post has followed this pattern under the ownership of Rupert Murdoch's News Corp. Not all tabloids are as sensational as the Post. Many

FIGURE 2.1.3   War coverage lends itself to the sensational, particularly when reporting "on front lines," as the CNN chyron shouts.

display a "sophisticated sensationalism," the definition applied to modern tabloid journalism by newspaper and web designer Mario Garcia (2010).

Tabloid journalism has become the descriptive term for television shows such as "E!" and their accompanying websites.

Circulation patterns and audience. In the past, the New York Post took a large portion of its readership from within the New York metropolitan area while The Times marketed itself as a national newspaper. But print circulation for both papers has shrunk dramatically over the past 10 years, as it has for all mass-circulation newspapers. The Times, for example, once registered a print circulation of about 330,000 (Sheridan, 2022), down from about 1.3 million a decade earlier (Watson, 2023). Today, while it claims second place in the U.S. behind the Wall Street Journal for print circulation, the Times reports 9.7 million digital-only subscribers.

Website views for both papers have exploded. The nytimes.com "brand" is one of the fastest-growing websites in the country with 535.1 million visits in November 2022 compared with the Post at 143.2 million. Both newspaper brands showed double-digit growth year over year in 2022 (Majid, 2023).

While these newspapers see their audiences differently, both now consider themselves "national" newspapers. Although the print version of the Post does not travel as far from the city as the Times, both offer digital subscriptions across the country.

News philosophy. How does a publication position itself within the context of city, state and nation? The New York Times, with its reputation as a national newspaper of record, had placed a much higher value on national and international news than the Post. But with the shift to the web, national and international news is just as likely to show up on the Post's front page as New York City news.

News Judgments, Small and Large

News judgment comes into play with almost every decision an editor makes. Some decisions are on the micro level, where a single word choice is involved, and some occur on the macro level, where broad decisions are made about which stories should run, how big and in what place.

On the Micro Level

True story: Years ago in a game against the Detroit Lions, a Chicago Bears tackle named Dan Hampton laid a hard block on the Detroit kicker, Eddie

Murray. The Lions protested that the play was unnecessarily rough considering that Murray, perhaps the smallest player on the field, was hanging back after kicking off. The Bears were quick to point out that Hampton had acted within the rules in carrying out his blocking assignment.

In a follow-up story, a Chicago Tribune reporter wrote that the controversy arose when Hampton "blocked" Murray. When the story got to the desk, an editor changed "blocked" to "clobbered," believing the stronger word described better what had happened to the diminutive kicker.

At the Bears practice the next day, the reporter was confronted and criticized for his use of "clobbered" for what was, after all, a legal play.

In changing the reporter's word, the editor displayed poor news judgment. The reporter had carefully chosen a neutral word, "blocked," based on fairness to both sides. The editor chose his word based on the competing news value of conflict, accentuating the violent nature of the block.

Editors make dozens of decisions every day like the example above. It's news judgment at the micro level. For the editor, every story represents a series of small news decisions, any of which might be complex:

Is this the right word? This decision rests on knowing usage, on understanding what the story is about and on realizing the editorial angle the reporter wants to take. Sometimes reporters fall in love with a word without being quite sure what it means; editors are justified in correcting usage. But sometimes an editor can forget that writers today often are pushed by superiors to be more creative and entertaining. An editor who is too mechanical can deaden a writer's prose.

Is the sentence put together properly? This decision requires the editor to understand what element of the sentence is most important and deserves emphasis: who, what, when, where, why or how. The editor needs a firm grounding in grammar and a feel for clarity, simplicity and brevity.

Does the paragraph do its job efficiently? The editor must identify the topic of the paragraph and see to it that each sentence supports that topic. The editor needs an eye for composition. Editing at the paragraph level takes special care because fixing a paragraph often means making a substantial change in the writing. Editors must make sure they understand what writers are trying to do.

Does the story flow properly? The editor should err on the side of caution when it comes to moving paragraphs around. It takes an understanding of the subject matter and understanding what's most important. The editor must consult with a supervisor or the writer before making these major changes in a story.

On the Macro Level

Good editors soon find themselves invited into the next level of news judgment, where story selection and placement are decided.

The traditional process of news selection is a complex mix. Its ingredients include broad news values such as timeliness, proximity or oddity; the personalities and power relationships of those making the decisions; and a large measure of what longtime journalist Robert Giles called critical judgment. Giles, the late editor and publisher of The Detroit News, wrote that critical judgment involves gut instinct mostly based on experience tempered by a sense of fairness (Giles, 1990). At worst, gut instinct reflects the biases and interests of the individual.

The Challenge of News Judgment Today

As we explore the challenges of news editors today, it's helpful to take a brief look back to where we've been. David Brinkley, the legendary NBC and ABC newscaster, is widely quoted as saying, "News is what I say it is." And many news editors have believed they know what's best for readers and viewers. That formula might have worked when people had relatively few places to go for news, but that's the case no more. Ford Rowan, a former NBC correspondent and journalism professor, wrote more than 40 years ago, "The decision to publish should be an overt process rather than a submerged one" (Rowan, 1980, 236). Deciding what's news, he said, should be a conscious, rational process.

About 20 years later, Tom Bettag, the executive producer of ABC's "Nightline," wrote that the old style of news judgment—"News is what I say it is"—had been turned upside down by live coverage by networks such as C-SPAN, the need to program 24-hour cable news channels and the bottomless news hole of the internet.

"Small wonder that the American people have become cynical about the news media," Bettag wrote. "The only people more cynical are the journalists" (2000, 106).

Bettag suggests that the old way of deciding what was news held journalists accountable. But editors help themselves by having some idea of the things that interest readers and viewers. Traditional news values include concepts that are useful if editors employ them thoughtfully, out in the open and without personal bias.

"The story's got to deliver on the promise," Horner said about community news. "You've got to be able to walk away as a reader having been gifted something."

What follows are commonly accepted news values.

Timeliness

The news value of timeliness could be divided into two related elements.

The scoop mentality. If a news organization has a story first, its editors tend to overestimate the story's importance. The scoop mentality becomes damaging when scooping the competition overrides other news values. The result is that the trivial story might be overplayed. Scoop thinking also can be damaging when a news outlet rushes a story to publication, sometimes short-cutting normal reporting practices and ending up embarrassed.

Newspapers became less influenced by scoop thinking in the 1980s and 1990s as editors realized they could not beat radio and television to the punch. But as news organizations have concentrated on their websites as the first place news appears, scoop thinking has returned, thanks to social media.

Seasonal or recurring stories. The second component of timeliness has to do with seasonal stories. In this sense, timeliness requires editors and reporters to think ahead and anticipate events. A second challenge for editors and reporters is to freshen cyclical stories, such as during the holiday season, each time they come up.

Audience

Editors and reporters must keep in touch with the community where they work. They also need a general idea about what readers and viewers will or won't accept. Good taste is an important criterion where it involves pictures of gruesome scenes, stories about lewd behavior or writing that includes profanity.

For much of the history of newspapers, reporters and editors had a foggy notion of their audiences. Today with the rise of analytics, powered by artificial intelligence, editors can quickly see what interests their audience.

A long-held fear is that marketing steers reporters and editors away from printing what is in the public interest and directs them to print "merely what interests the public," as former FCC Commissioner Newton Minow put it (1961, May 9).

As Minow's words suggest, attention to audience has affected how broadcast newsrooms have operated. Television and radio stations have long been driven by ratings produced almost instantly by firms such as Nielsen Media

Research. The drive for higher ratings led television stations, beginning in the 1970s, to hire "news consultants," such as Frank N. Magid Associates. The consultants, using marketing techniques, affected judgments about news and how it was presented (O'Donnell, 1978). Magid is still a force today.

Magazines use marketing to tailor their product to a target audience, including how stories are selected and written. Those wishing to write for a magazine are advised to read the publication carefully and learn its "slant." For example, the writer's guidelines for Ms. magazine state:

> *Ms. is a multi-issue and globally-focused media outlet interested in a plethora of topics—from policy and politics to popular culture and the arts, from education to the environment, from violence to abortion. We consider reported pieces, features and social commentary rooted in an intersectional feminist lens. We do not consider articles on fashion, beauty, fitness, travel, food or of a "self-help" variety. (Ms., n.d.)*

The slant can be thought of as a point of view that guides editorial decisions with careful consideration of the magazine's readers.

Prominence

When important people are involved, insignificant details can take on great importance. In the 1950s, President Dwight D. Eisenhower suffered a heart attack. Because of Eisenhower's role as leader of the free world, every bit of news about his condition was important. His doctor, the eminent cardiologist Paul Dudley White, left few details out of his news briefings. He noted that Ike had had "a good bowel movement" in part, he said, because "the country is so bowel-minded anyway" (Lee, 2020). The tradition continued in November 2021 when the physician to the president delivered a letter addressed to President Biden's press secretary with a health summary referring to the "frequency and severity of 'throat clearing'" (O'Connor, 2021).

Celebrity

News about celebrities has taken on more importance with the rise of social media, but celebrities have long been important to readers and viewers. Whole magazines devote their pages to them. The E! cable channel reports mainly on the comings and goings of the rich and famous. When Oscar-winning actor Will Smith slapped comedian Chris Rock at the 94th annual Academy Awards on

March 27, 2022, on live television, the story instantly became an international phenomenon (Figure 2.1.4). The Gannett newspaper group, publisher of USA Today, made its own news with the hiring of a reporter to cover everything about just one celebrity, Taylor Swift (Willman, 2023).

Unlike prominence, fame is "manufactured," as Daniel Boorstin noted more than 60 years ago. Boorstin wrote that the media can "quickly and effectively" bestow fame on a person and that "we have willingly been misled into believing that fame—well-knownness—is still a hallmark of greatness" (Boorstin, 1987, 47). Note the difference: The pope, secretary of state and mayor of New York are prominent. Brad Pitt, Beyoncé and Jimmy Fallon are celebrities.

Will Smith's slap was heard all the way to China, where the actor is loved and ... humor is, well, different

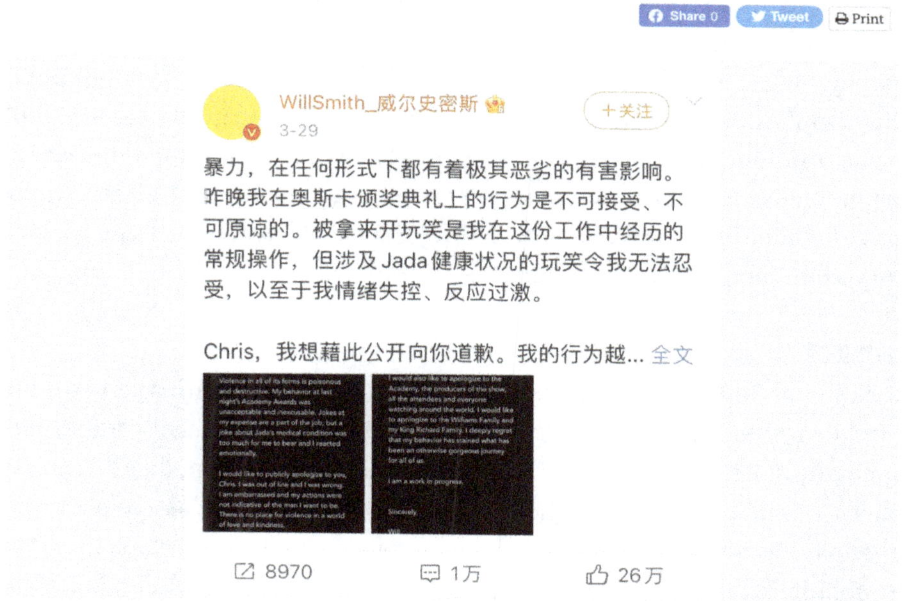

Will Smith's apology statement appeared simultaneously on his Facebook page and on Weibo, China's combination of Facebook and Twitter, both of which are blocked by the Chinese government.
SCREENSHOT

Posted Wednesday, April 20, 2022 11:10 am | Updated: Tuesday, May 31, 2022 5:51 pm

FIGURE 2.1.4   Celebrity news travels worldwide on social media as shown by this post from China about Will Smith slapping Chris Rock at the 2022 Oscars ceremony. Celebrity is a powerful news value despite its often frivolous nature.

Oddity

The "man bites dog" story continues to be standard fare for news organizations, and even more so if the story comes with pictures. Today, when cellphone cameras are everywhere, viewers are fed a steady diet of unusual happenings on the nightly news. The danger is that unimportant stories get major exposure merely because the television station has the video or the website has a photo.

Proximity

A Page 1 story in Chicago might be a brief news item in Miami. Many smaller newspapers and broadcast outlets pursue the "local angle" in almost every story they use; for them, news truly begins at home. The editors at these organizations realize that community news sells, and they strive for innovative ways to identify and present local stories.

Magnitude

Sometimes an event attracts so many spectators or participants that it must be covered. The Woodstock music festival in 1969 started out as a minor event that became a major story—and later an iconic piece of American history—when 400,000 or more spectators attended. The NFL's Super Bowl, now a global event with over 123 million viewers, began in January 1967 with a different, less-catchy name, "AFL-NFL World Championship Game." The danger is that editors and reporters will ignore stories rich in human interest that attract little attention. And the bandwagon effect can make a story seem more important than it is.

Impact

Stories affecting many people are important; that's why death and taxes are closely covered. But sometimes a story with impact is not easily identified, especially in its early stages. AIDS was treated as a minor medical curiosity when it was first diagnosed in the 1980s among what was seen as a select group of people. News organizations were slow to respond to it as a serious threat to the population at large. On Dec. 12, 2019, according to the CDC, an "atypical pneumonia-like illness" reported in China's Hubei Province became known as the worldwide COVID-19 epidemic (CDC, n.d.).

Conflict

Conflict is a key element in any drama, but sometimes those involved in a news story complain that only angry words get reported even if conflict was a minor part of a happening. Some editors have decried how news organizations cover public life as a game with everyone divided into winners and losers.

The public journalism movement, which debuted in 1989, arose in reaction to the "horse-race" coverage of elections that placed emphasis on who's ahead in the polls and who has the best campaign strategy. Public journalism, or civic journalism, sought to take election coverage back to a debate of issues relevant to the community by creating "a citizens agenda."

But horse-race coverage is easier to report and easier for readers to understand. **Chapter 2.4** discusses public opinion polls and their effect on election coverage.

Topics as News Values

News organizations realize that their readers and listeners have interests differing from the news values outlined above. News organizations today often organize news around topics they believe are important to their audiences. Go to the website of a major daily newspaper, television network or magazine and you'll likely see stories centered on some of these topics:

- **Education:** what's happening in the schools
- **Parenting:** family issues
- **Environment:** climate issues, quality of life, development
- **People:** stories about people like me
- **Career:** how to get ahead, successful people
- **Work:** issues of the workplace
- **Money:** how to make, save it
- **Time:** how to find it, spend it
- **Health:** fitness, nutrition, leisure
- **Consumerism:** getting value for your dollar

The News Meeting

News judgment on the macro level finds its expression in the news meeting, sometimes called a "budget" meeting or a news huddle. For morning newspapers, the first daily news meeting traditionally occurred in the morning with the last happening in the early evening, five or six hours before the last piece of copy was sent to the composing room. Some sections of the newspaper, such as features or special Sunday sections, were planned weeks in advance like the way magazines work. At broadcast stations, meetings began in the morning to plan coverage for the day; the final news meeting might have happened much closer to broadcast time.

The structure and timing of news meetings shifted as more news organizations changed their priority from the print edition or scheduled broadcasts to the 24-hour news cycle of the internet. The New York Times slimmed down its print-edition news meeting years ago. Massey (2015) writes, "The big daily free-for-all for editors to pitch their stories is no longer called the Page 1 meeting. It is the 4:30 news meeting, and the printed front page is not on the agenda." Instead, the main news meeting has as its task to respond "to the needs of a constant news cycle."

A newsroom might decide on news based on a vote by everyone in the news meeting or on a senior editor barking out instructions. The meeting can take place in a closed conference room, or out in the middle of the newsroom, or on Zoom. Those involved could be a small core of newsroom leaders or could extend to include readers or listeners.

News meetings have three goals:

1. **Decide on the all-important lead story and on other top stories.** Often the opinions of editors from other sections are valued.
2. **Avoid duplication between sections.** An important sports figure dies; does it go in the news section or sports? Do the news anchors report it, or does the sports anchor have the task?
3. **Discuss the competition:** What do other news outlets have? Has our story hit the news wires yet?

When editors meet to decide on news, the results depend on:

Who is calling the shots. When the editor-in-chief or the news editor presides over the news meeting, power is always part of the equation. By nature, news people are competitive types, and the news meeting might be their one chance a day to impress the boss. But news organizations today realize they must be open to new ideas. At The Economist, "The whole paper meets, and anyone—from the newest intern to the most senior editor—can put forward and write a leader [top story]. What matters is not a contributor's seniority, but the strength and quality of his or her arguments" (Coletta, 2018).

Who can make the best argument. Editors often succeed on charisma. Or sometimes it's just who can talk the loudest. Smart editors know that not every story they like can be the lead story. Instead, these editors push for stories that have real news value, gaining respect from others for their good news judgment.

Who owns the press, transmitter or website. The owners of news outlets vary from the starched-collar conservative to Barnum-like show people. News organizations do tend to lean conservative or progressive depending on their ownership. While outright partisanship is usually confined to the opinion sections, owners can skew what stories are emphasized and how they are presented. Google "Sinclair Media Group" for examples.

Right and wrong in news judgment used to be elusive because our tools were weak for measuring success defined as whether our audience is served by our decisions. Many editors preferred it that way, believing their job was to present news that readers needed, but in today's environment, editors must balance what they believe readers need to know with what readers want to know. That's because these days editors can see immediately through analytics what stories are getting the most attention from readers, listeners or viewers.

On Trust and Credibility

Sometimes feedback from the audience comes in the form of complaints, either through email, phone calls or social media posts, about news coverage, headlines or photos. In the interest of transparency, editors will publish explanations of their news judgment decisions, often thanking their readers for paying attention and caring enough to comment in a civil manner.

Being more transparent and explaining to people how news decisions are made are tools recommended by the Trusting News Project (n.d.), which encourages journalists to "follow along as we demystify trust in news and empower journalists to demonstrate credibility and actively earn trust." As public opinion polling, both nationally and internationally, continue to show a decline in people's trust in the news media, more and more studies and trust initiatives have emerged (Knight Foundation, 2023). This is really a call-to-arms for editors to sharpen their news judgment skills.

Changing Values

News organizations are moving away from classic standards of news judgment, spurred by increasing competition from new media. Editors, news directors, publishers and station owners realize that the traditional approaches to news judgment were formed in part by the biases of past editors and publishers rather than from a concern for readers. The only thing certain is that editors and reporters must expect change and handle it with an open mind. It's a bottom-line reality driving change as news outlets, particularly newspapers, face a grim financial outlook. It's also an opportunity for enterprising editors at specialty startup publications, some with nonprofit status, to increase diversity in the news media landscape.

HOMEWORK

Assignment No. 1

At the beginning of this chapter, we showed you front pages from The New York Times and the New York Post. We compared the news values displayed by the broadsheet Times and the tabloid Post. Now, go to the website of each newspaper (www.nytimes.com and nypost.com) and compare content from the same day. How do these news values relate to the internet versions? How do the websites carry over the visual cues from the print editions?

Assignment No. 2

Now go to the homepage of a news magazine such as Time, Newsweek or U.S. News & World Report. Compare the stories presented there with a magazine that engages in "long-form" journalism such as The Atlantic, The New Yorker or Mother Jones. In reading the titles on the homepage, note how the stories differ in their emphasis even though some of the same events are covered.

Assignment No. 3

Television newscasts have evolved from sober anchors reading from behind a desk to multimedia extravaganzas that border on the sensational. Tune into the national evening news from one of the major networks: ABC, NBC, CBS or FOX. How are the stories presented? Look for such things as the use of video clips, graphic devices, still images—and don't forget the music. What news values do you think are most important? Hint: weather. Does the newscast seem to sensationalize some stories? Why do you think that ABC News' "World News Tonight with David Muir" ranks No. 1 in the ratings so often?

Assignment No. 4

Do an online search for "trust in news media" and see what you can learn about the Trust Project, the News Literacy Project, the Trusting News Project, the Reuters Institute's Trust in News Project, the Pew Research Center's Trust in Media findings, the Knight/Gallup research initiative, and anything else interesting that pops up. What common denominators do you see? What would be your top five recommendations to regain trust if you were to draft a memo to a news staff?

REFERENCES

Bettag, T. (2000). Evolving definitions of news. *Harvard International Journal of Press/Politics, 5*(3), 105–107. https://doi.org/10.1177/1081180X00005003011

Boorstin, D. J. (1987). *The image: A guide to pseudo-events in America* (25th anniv. ed.). Atheneum.

Centers for Disease Control and Prevention. (n.d.). CDC museum COVID-19 timeline. https://www.cdc.gov/museum/timeline/covid19.html

Coletta, A. (2018, May 16). Inside *The Economist*'s editorial meeting. *The Economist on Medium.* https://medium.economist.com/inside-the-economists-editorial-meeting-961d1575f952

Garcia, M. (2010). One new platform for newspaper in Singapore: The sports pub. García Media. https://garciamedia.com/blog/one_new_platform_for_newspaper_in_singapore_the_sports_pub/

Giles, R. H. (1990). *Newsroom management: A guide to theory and practice.* Media Management Books.

Knight Foundation (2023, Feb. 15). *Gallup/Knight study offers new insights on why Americans' trust in news continues to decline.* https://knightfoundation.org/press/releases/gallup-knight-study-offers-new-insights-on-why-americans-trust-in-news-continues-to-decline/

Lee, T. H. (2020). Seizing the teachable moment—lessons from Eisenhower's heart attack. *New England Journal of Medicine, 383*(18). https://doi.org/10.1056/NEJMp2031046

Majid, A. (2023, October 13). Top 50 news websites in the US: AP and Axios among fastest-growing in September. Press Gazette. https://pressgazette.co.uk/media-audience-and-business-data/media_metrics/most-popular-websites-news-us-monthly-3/

Massey, K. (2015, May 13). The old page 1 meeting, R.I.P.: Updating a *Times* tradition for the digital age. *The New York Times.* https://archive.nytimes.com/www.nytimes.com/times-insider/2015/05/12/the-old-page-1-meeting-r-i-p-updating-a-times-tradition-for-the-digital-age/

Minow, N. (1961, May 9). Newton Minow: The "vast wasteland" of television speech. Terra Media. http://www.terramedia.co.uk/reference/documents/vast_wasteland.htm

Ms. (n.d.). *Writing for Ms.* https://msmagazine.com/submissions/

O'Connor, K. C. (2021, November 19). President Biden's current health summary. White House. https://www.whitehouse.gov/wp-content/uploads/2021/11/President-Biden-Current-Health-Summary-November-2021.pdf

O'Donnell, M. (1978). Newscast content of six Iowa television stations: News consultant-retaining stations vs. non-consultant stations, paper presented at the Association for Education in Journalism national convention, Radio-Television Division, Madison, Wis.

Rowan, F. (1980). News media responsibility: A program for improvement. *Willamette Law Review, 17*(1), 231–237.

Sheridan, D. (2022, August 30). August 30: Top 10 US newspaper circulations. Medium. https://medium.com/fact-of-the-day-1/august-30-top-10-us-newspaper-circulations-544544172a3f

Trusting News (n.d.). https://trustingnews.org/

Watson, A. (2023, Sept. 25). Weekday circulation of The New York Times from 2000 to 2022. Statista. https://www.statista.com/statistics/273503/average-paid-weekday-circulation-of-the-new-york-times/

Willman, C. (2023, Nov. 6). Gannett's Taylor Swift reporter, revealed: Meet Bryan West, the first full-time Swiftie journalist. *Variety.* https://variety.com/2023/music/news/taylor-swift-reporter-usa-today-gannett-hire-1235781178/

FURTHER READING, RESOURCES

Emery, M. C., Emery, E., & Roberts, N. L. (1996). *The press and America: An interpretive history of the mass media.* Allyn and Bacon.

New York Post. (2022, July 19). About *New York Post.* https://nypost.com/about-new-york-post/

The New York Times Company. (n.d.). Company. https://www.nytco.com/company/

WRITING SHORT

Posts, Titles and Headlines

KEY POINTS IN THIS CHAPTER

1. Writing short—headlines, titles, chyrons, tweets (now posts on X, the former Twitter)—has never been more important as the flood of news and information increases across today's media. For many readers, headlines and titles "are" the story as their time to read is short.

2. The "skeleton" and "condense and patch" methods can help you write headlines and titles for straightforward news items. These approaches begin with making sure a story's lede or nut graph is well-edited.

3. The "seed" method helps you twist a cliche when a clever title is needed, or for coming up with that great advertising slogan.

4. Short excerpts are a necessity for web-based publications and for posting on social media. Research recommends writing posts that can be digested in two seconds or less.

> **"** *The language of truth is unadorned and always simple."*
>
> —Ammianus Marcellinus

> **"** *Brevity is the soul of wit."*
>
> —Shakespeare

The ability to write clever, accurate headlines has long been admired in American newsrooms. In today's world, where social media sites are a primary path to news and social interaction, knowing how to write short, punchy titles and headlines is more important than ever. Multimedia storytellers, broadcasters, social media influencers and others follow the core principle of delivering the one-two punch of words and pictures.

Television broadcasts use the expanded real estate of high-definition screens to include "crawls" and "chyrons" with on-air reporters and live video. News websites rely on short titles and excerpts on their homepages to curate the day's content for busy readers. Clever storytellers twist a cliche to bring readers to their work through email digests.

Writing short has always been the hallmark of advertising, and the skill is vital to public relations as well.

Studies show that online and print readers scan headlines and titles for what interests them. But headlines are too important to leave until the last minute. In the Poynter Institute study "Eyes on the News" (Garcia & Stark, 1991), subjects were asked to read a newspaper prototype while their eye movements were recorded. The study found that 85% of headlines were "processed" by the readers. "Processed" meant that the subject's eyes stopped on that headline. By contrast, only 25% of the story ledes were processed, and many fewer ledes were actually read. Later studies confirm "readers" are "scanners."

Bloggers know the value of writing good entry titles to index information for their readers—and to attract search engine queries—putting an emphasis on search engine optimization (SEO). Facebook and X (formerly known as Twitter) act as news digests for a substantial portion of the U.S. public. The Pew Center for Research reports that for 2022, 31% of U.S. adults said they regularly get news from Facebook, which claims 3 billion daily users around the world. Meta, Facebook's parent company, announced in 2022 that it was "de-emphasizing its investment in news content" (Ingram, 2022). Other social media platforms such as X and Instagram provide news for smaller portions of the U.S. public (Pew Research Center, 2022).

TikTok is the latest social media app to claim extraordinary influence among consumers. For one example, sales of feta cheese at one grocery store jumped 200% after a pasta dish went viral on TikTok. The platform has spurred fashion and beauty fads and has helped songs reach the top of streaming charts. TikTok has become a conduit for political campaigns, and news organizations like The Associated Press have joined TikTok to reach new audiences (Thorbecke, 2022). These days TikTok is in the news as some states and the federal government have moved to ban the app from public officials' phones over cybersecurity concerns (Roush, 2022). Other popular social media outlets include LinkedIn, YouTube, Pinterest and Snapchat.

Many news organizations, advertising agencies and public relations firms have responded by putting more effort into writing short. Today, writers and editors must be skilled in creating headlines, titles and posts that are clever, direct and informative. Don't be annoying by "teasing" the reader. For most readers, the title or post "is" the story. Research suggests posts that take two seconds or less to absorb are very appealing (TwoSixDigital, n.d.).

Know Your Limits

Writing short today can mean writing to fit a space. A title for an online publication should sit comfortably on the page with no bad "splits." Newspapers and magazines have always placed a premium on brevity; headlines and magazine titles are written to fit a given space on the page—or a cellphone screen.

X presents its own special challenge. The maximum of 280 characters is short enough as it is, but those in the advertising and public relations business recommend writing much shorter to allow space for a link and an excerpt for a retweet (now repost).

Most print newspapers and magazines today rely on pagination, a system where entire pages are laid out on the computer and sent to an image setter as a complete, or composite, page. In these systems, the editor might be asked to write a headline or title with broad specifications so that final adjustments can be made by the makeup editor on the electronic page.

LATEST NEWS

St. Thomas seeks new local neighborhood liaison

December 12, 2022 1:59 PM

The University of St. Thomas is looking to hire a new neighborhood liaison as soon as possible after the previous liaison, Amy Gage, retired in August after eight years with the university. Karl Warner has the story.

LATEST SPORTS

Grad duo Miller, Bjorklund lead men's basketball past Green Bay 82-61

December 13, 2022 10:55 PM

Graduate forward Parker Bjorklund returned for his first game since Nov. 19 and knocked down 8 of 8 free throws, ending the night with 16 points in 15 minutes as the St. Thomas men's basketball team beat Green Bay 82-61 Tuesday at Schoenecker Arena.

FIGURE 2.2.1   Excerpts for webpages should be written carefully to tell the main point of the story. Don't rely on systems such as WordPress to generate excerpts automatically. Test headlines for "widows" to avoid one-word second lines.

Editors at web-based publications have added excerpts to their writing tasks to go with titles and captions. The excerpt appears on the homepage under the title, helping readers decide what to read (Figure 2.2.1).

Splits

Skillful writers know that headlines, titles, advertising copy, signs, billboards and the like must be well-written but also must sit nicely on the page or a screen. This means paying attention to "splits" when the writing extends over two or more lines. A skillful writer will keep a strong subject and strong verb together on one line.

Other splits to avoid include preposition-object, adjective-noun and verb-helping verb. Look at these two headlines:

**Car rams food
line; 1 killed**

**1 killed as car
rams food line**

Which is better? The first has a top line that sounds a bit silly until you read the second line, but overall, it flows better than the second headline. We like the second one better just because it prevents a reader with an odd sense of humor from laughing at a serious story.

Splits are a mistake when they cause the reader to do a double take, when they might confuse the reader or when they might be unappealing visually. Here's an example:

**Biden replaces Harris
aide in staff shake-up (NO!)**

**Harris aide replaced
as Biden shuffles staff**

The first headline suffers from a "modifier split," the type that is most easily misunderstood. Avoid modifier splits and avoid splitting names in general.

Another kind of split is the prepositional split between the preposition and its object. See the problem with Figure 2.2.2? The preposition "with" is split from its object "post." Figure 2.2.3 is much better, even though readers might not be able to say why. Ad designers give special attention to how type sits on the page or screen.

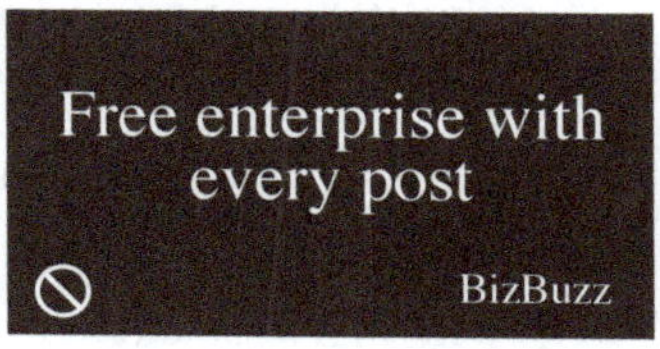

FIGURE 2.2.2   Designers carefully lay out text in ads. This example would never fly because of the prepositional split.

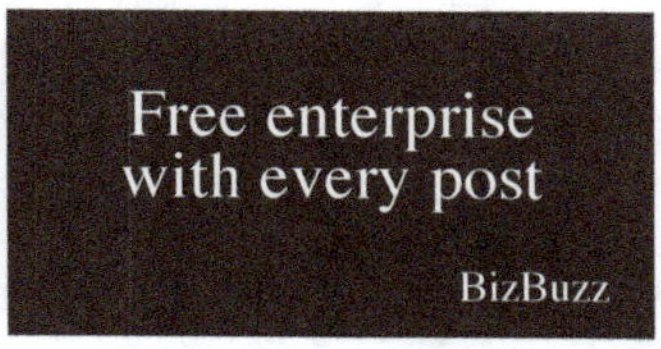

FIGURE 2.2.3   With the prepositional split removed, the copy in this ad is much crisper.

Figure 2.2.4 shows a WordPress title with a bad split. How would you fix it? You can't just make it two lines because of how WordPress titles work. The answer comes in writing tight just as newspaper copy editors have done since the beginning (Figure 2.2.5).

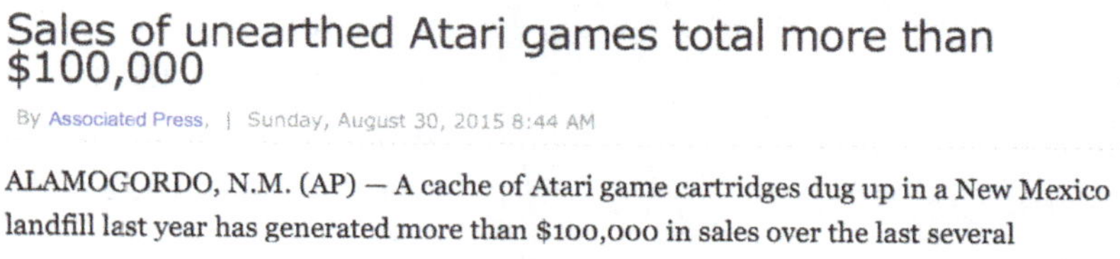

FIGURE 2.2.4   Title writers have much less control over how a content management system, such as WordPress, handles titles, but they can preview the page before publishing to eliminate splits like this.

Unearthed Atari games go for more than $100,000

By **Associated Press**, | Sunday, August 30, 2015 8:44 AM

ALAMOGORDO, N.M. (AP) — A cache of Atari game cartridges dug up in a New Mexico landfill last year has generated more than $100,000 in sales over the last several months.

FIGURE 2.2.5   By rewording the title, we can make it fit on one line and eliminate the split.

A third type of split is the verb split. The copy in Figure 2.2.6 fits in a neat shape, so the split is acceptable as a design consideration, but the helping verb "have" (part of the contraction "you've") is split from the main verb "got." This is not as serious as other types of splits, but it's often avoidable.

The fourth and final type is an infinitive split between "to" and the "verb." The ad in Figure 2.2.7 splits the infinitive "to eat." Again, given the layout of the ad, the split doesn't matter too much, but some designers would seek to fix it.[1]

FIGURE 2.2.6   This split between the helping verb "have," part of the contraction "you've," is acceptable in this tightly packed ad.

How to Write Short Display Type

This section outlines step-by-step approaches on how to write various types of short messages: headlines, titles, ad slogans and posts.

As you read through the rest of this chapter, keep in mind the golden rule of writing and editing headlines and titles: **Slow down!** Look at each word carefully before you pass it down the line. Headlines and titles are "big type" that draws attention. Errors here are especially damaging and might go viral.

On Page 3 of its sports section for June 6, 2015, the

FIGURE 2.2.7   Another example of an ad that packs a lot of type into a small space. The infinitive split could be fixed by moving "to" in the infinitive to the third line.

1   These are not real ads, and the products are fictional. They were put together for demonstration purposes only.

MLB

Amphibious pitcher makes debut

Venditte becomes first
pitcher in 20 years to
pitch with both arms
in MLB game

By HOWARD ULMAN
Associated Press

BOSTON — Pat Venditte took his warmup pitches in his major league debut with his right arm. And his left.

The ambidextrous pitcher entered the game against the Boston Red Sox at the start of the seventh inning after being called up Friday by the Oakland Athletics.

FIGURE 2.2.8   Oakland A's pitcher Pat Venditte was ambidextrous, not a cousin to frogs and salamanders. Images of the headline went viral and made the news nationally. Remember the golden rule of writing and editing headlines: Slow down! In this case, one misused word detracted from the remarkable feat of a pitcher.

East Oregonian of Pendleton, Oregon, ran the headline "Amphibious pitcher makes debut" (Figure 2.2.8). Oakland A's pitcher Pat Venditte had thrown right-handed and left-handed to Boston Red Sox hitters in a game the night before. Venditte was ambidextrous, not a cousin to frogs and salamanders. Images of the headline went viral and made the news nationally (Payne, 2015).

What follows is not only how-to but also hands-on, so before you read further, reach for a pencil. We'll start with headlines and titles.

The Skeleton Approach

The skeleton approach works best for the straight information we see in headlines and titles, and in posts from news organizations and public relations staff. Let's start with an assignment. What headline would you write for a story that begins with the following paragraph? You have just four words to do the job. Take a moment to think it through and jot down your answer.

> *The city's school board president was re-elected Monday in a close race that focused more on a textbook controversy than on the usual funding issues.*

The first step to writing a headline is to check the lede of the story, usually the first paragraph. If it is wrong, chances are the headline will be wrong. If its phrasing is weak, the headline probably will be weak. You must sweat every word of the lede to make sure it's the best summary for the story. The same goes for the nut graph of a news feature story.

We often err in short messages by reaching for ideas that don't relate to the main facts—in this case, the facts in the lede. Remember that the lede might be the first sentence or the first several paragraphs of a story. Anytime you write a headline that doesn't relate in some way to the lede, either the headline is bad or the lede is bad. For our example, let's assume that this lede is fine.

The second step is to look for the lede's skeleton. You identify the skeleton as the simplest form of the subject, verb and object in the main clause. Keep them in the same order. You just aren't picking out keywords; you're trying to write a scaled-down sentence that makes sense. By doing this, you are using the lede's structure to write the first draft. This first draft may be something you write out or just think through.

The full skeleton for this lede would be something like:

**School board president re-elected in close race
focusing on textbooks**

Note that in headline writing, we can leave out articles ("a," "an" and "the") and some verbs (in this example "is"). With a tight space, like the one here, only the skeleton's subject and verb may fit. In this case, your headline could read:

School board president re-elected

The last step is to ask whether your headline is really the best one for the story. A better idea may occur to you. Can you do better than "School board president re-elected"? Probably not.

Repeat After Me

Compare the challenge of writing the school board headline with this lede. You have two lines, and each line can hold only three or four short words. Remember to use the skeleton approach. Here's the lede, which you can assume is correct:

When it comes to securing a mortgage these days, homebuyers are facing a double whammy: Interest rates are high and lenders are scarce.

Applying the skeleton approach, you would focus on the main clause. The subject and verb would form the top line of the headline: "Homebuyers facing." The object would form the second line: "a double whammy."

"Double whammy" is the type of wording that a reader would notice, so we want to avoid repeating it in the headline. With the school board headline, the words were more routine, so repetition was less noticeable.

So what would be a good headline for this story? If the top line reads "Homebuyers facing" or "Homebuyers face," that's fine. The second line could just tell the story. Notice how a straightforward headline resulted from the skeleton approach (No. 1) and with a slight twist (No. 2):

1. **Homebuyers face**
   high rates, few lenders
2. **Homebuyers face**
   1–2 punch on loans

An editor concerned about reflecting the lighter tone of the lede would write headline No. 2.

Both headlines have their merits, and both arose from using a combination of the skeleton approach and another method, the condense and patch approach.

Condense and Patch Approach

To illustrate this approach, let's work through another example. What headline would you write for a story with the following lede? You have just five short words to do the job. As always, we'll start with the skeleton approach and see how far it can take us. Think it through and jot down your idea.

Three area residents were killed Monday when their car hit a telephone pole, skidded 50 feet and flipped over, police said.

First let's assume that the lede is correct. Now look for the skeleton:

Three killed when car hits pole, skids and flips over

The first five words of the skeleton will not work as a headline, so we turn to the condense and patch approach.

Weigh each idea to see if it absolutely must be in the headline. This is not always as easy as it seems. It requires good news judgment, and all good headline writers have that. Remember, every idea in a lede is good, or it wouldn't be in the lede. You have to decide which ideas must be represented and which would be nice to represent if you had room.

As you're weighing each word's value, you should look for ways to shorten ideas without losing meaning. Let's take the ideas one at a time.

"Three killed" is a must; it can become "3 killed" or "3 die" if you need to condense the idea. "Car" is a must, and you can't get any shorter than that. "Hits pole" and "flips over" are stronger than "skids"; most car wrecks involve skidding.

Now comes the moment of truth. You could liken this part to playing the parlor game "Lifeboat" in which you have to decide who in the boat deserves to live and who should be cast overboard for the good of the group. "Hits pole" seems more worthy than "flips over" because a car flipping over in a wreck is more common than a car hitting a pole.

Because of our five-word limit, we must deviate from the lede's structure and patch the headline together with a semicolon. Like so:

Car hits pole; 3 killed

Is it better to have active-voice verbs in headlines? Yes, most of the time. Then is "die" better here? Well, no. "Killed" is the stronger word. There isn't much action in dying; the idea of being killed is more vivid. With a tighter count, you could go with "Car crash kills 3."

Tightening the Grip

Sometimes the lede tends to defy headline writing. Take this example. What headline would you write for a story with this lede? You have only four words.

BUENOS AIRES, Argentina—The deadly rioting over economic austerity in Venezuela last week has sparked fears of similar social explosions across Latin America and has lent new urgency to calls for relief from the region's staggering foreign debt.

Assuming that the lede is accurate, we start with the skeleton approach and see how far it can take us. One obvious problem is that we're facing a "double-barreled lede." It introduces two different but complementary themes. The first skeleton would be this: "Rioting in Venezuela sparks fears across Latin America." The second skeleton would go something like this: "Rioting in Venezuela lends urgency to debt relief."

Now which do you pare down using the condense and patch approach? With a double-barreled lead, the first statement is usually the more important one, and the second provides a secondary idea. Sometimes the main idea goes in the main headline and the secondary idea goes in a "deck" headline. Because we have just four words, we'll concentrate on condensing the first skeleton.

"Rioting in Venezuela" can become "Venezuelan riots." "Sparks fears" is a classic case of a writer using "headlinese," those short words or expressions that headline writers must use because of tight counts. Writers should not use headlinese to replace simple, common language. Can you imagine flying in a plane, being jolted by turbulence and saying to the person next to you, "That sparked fear in me"? You would say "That scared me," or "frightened me," or "worried me," or something like that. So for the headline, let's say "worry."

This headline-writing task has come down to one challenge: How do you say "across Latin America" in one word. Here's where many headline writers stumble. They conclude it's impossible, begin tearing up what they've done and end up with a bad headline. The skeleton focuses the challenge. Headline writers succeed or fail based on their ability to condense ideas fairly and accurately. How do you say "across Latin America" in one word? How about "region" or "neighbors"?

Our headline for this story would be this:

Venezuelan riots worry neighbors

Now compare this with your idea. If you went with "Latin riots," you need to be more specific. If you tried to work in the debt angle, you probably didn't do either skeleton idea justice. You just didn't have enough room.

Writing short is labor intensive, but so is anything worth doing right.

Sizing Up Your Material

When we write headlines, titles and chyrons, we typically deal with three kinds of information:

1. **Serious topics.** They demand straight, serious treatment.
2. **Light, even humorous, topics.** They demand bright, clever treatment.
3. **Topics that can go either way.** They are the toughest and require good judgment.

The school board and car crash stories fall into the straight, serious category. The same goes for the Venezuelan riots story. The homebuyers story falls into the last category.

Although we will struggle with tight space, particularly those four- or five-word dandies, we can be excused for falling short of what needs to be said because we just did not have enough room.

The stories that demand bright, clever headlines, titles or chyrons, however, offer no easy way out. The same is true for advertising copy, where cleverness is a prized commodity. These types of messages also tend to render the skeleton approach and the condense and patch approach useless, so we need another strategy for them.

The Seed Approach

Let's say we're writing a title of 55–60 characters for this story on a webpage post. Jot down your idea.

> *Sally Johnson learned the hard way that love can hurt. This Valentine's Day, she sent her boyfriend a card expressing her affection, but the man's mother intercepted it. Now Johnson, beaten and bruised, lies in a hospital bed, and the man's mother is facing battery charges.*

Remember, the first step in writing short is to check your information. While this lede is factually correct, some might believe the light tone is inappropriate. But titles and headlines must reflect the tone and mood of the story. Consider how different the title challenge would be with a story like this:

> *A 53-year-old mother was charged Monday with battery in connection with the Valentine's Day attack on a woman who sent a message of affection to the older woman's son.*

Stories dealing with injury most often will demand a straight, serious title and should be written in a formal tone, but that's not always the case. Sometimes, a story becomes news because of the oddity involving the circumstances of injury, such as those in this case. We would have to take a sober approach if the woman had been killed. But she is alive and recovering, so let's go with the original lede.

Using the skeleton approach, you would end up with a headline like this:

Woman learns the hard way that love can hurt

That's exactly the point, but it's a bad idea for the title because you would be repeating the lede. The skeleton approach fails us here, so let's turn to the seed approach.

First, identify a word or idea that must be represented. This story would be timely around Valentine's Day, so an obvious seed would be "valentine."

Now brainstorm expressions that grow out of the seed, and then focus on ones that can be used to tell the story. Think of valentines—what ideas come to mind? Valentines are red. Turn over some expressions with red in them: *red hot, red sun, red sky at morning, seeing red.* Bingo. "Seeing red" is an expression for being angry, like the boyfriend's mother. You have a start on a title: "Son's valentine makes mother see red." That's 36 characters including spaces.

What other angles must be covered? For sure, the women's injury should be in the title. Playing off what you already have, you could write this:

**Woman sees stars after valentine
makes mother see red** (53 characters)

Keep going. Don't be satisfied with your first effort, although it might turn out to be your best. What else can you do with red? What about the Valentine's Day rhyme, "Roses are red, violets are blue"? With a twist, you could write this title:

Roses are red, valentine sender is black and blue (49 characters)

What if you can find a seed but get stuck thinking of expressions? Turn to a good dictionary and look up valentine, red or Cupid, then check for ideas from the definition. Or look for idioms at the end of the entries.

Another trick is to do a Google search of the terms "love," "valentine" and "quotations." Such a search turned up the proverb "All's fair in love and war." You can see where this might lead you.

The secret to success with the seed approach is to keep in mind that you need just one good idea to make a good title. Most of the expressions that come to mind will be bad ideas and should be discarded quickly. Don't waste time trying to force an expression into your headline. Look for another idea that will fit naturally.

The seed approach works well in writing advertising copy. Jeff Goodby used a process something like the seed approach when he came up with the "Got Milk?" campaign, recognized as among the greatest ad campaigns of all time (Kauffman, 2022). Goodby said that a woman in a focus group remarked, "The only time I notice milk is when I run out of it." Goodby and his associates homed in on "making people paranoid about running out of milk."

"The idea was to tell stories in which milk was the missing element," Goodby said, "and I thought the words 'Got milk?' would be a good punchline at the end" (Berger, 2004, 88).

Types of Headlines and Titles

The headline combinations being used in today's news environment are almost limitless. Print designers seek innovative ways to mingle headline type with pictures and graphics to create a layered, integrated look. In this regard, newspapers and magazines have become more alike in their use of display type. For social media examples, just check your Instagram news feed.

Design for online publications aims to serve the "scanner." Research by John Morkes and Jakob Nielsen (1997), the Poynter Institute (Outing, 2004) and others showed that readers scan a webpage for bold text, bulleted items and informative subheadings. Steve Outing (2004) writes that contrary to eyetrack studies on printed newspapers, online readers enter the page through the dominant title. "Text rules on the PC screen—both in order viewed and in overall time spent looking at it," Outing writes.

We can break headline combinations down into several broad categories.

Keep in mind as you read about headline and title types, and look at our examples, that the headline still must answer the reader's No. 1 question: What's this story about? In the examples that follow, note where that question is answered.

Kickers are small headlines of two to four words, usually about half the size of the main head. The role of the kicker is to provide contrast, introduce white space above the story and give the reader a quick, clever take on the story. Kickers focus on secondary elements in the story or something that emphasizes the main thrust of the story.

Or a kicker might index the topic of the story. In Figure 2.2.9, the kicker "Harry & Meghan" is in a bold sans-serif font to contrast with the serif font of the main headline, "Estranged royals vent anger in final Netflix episodes."

Don't use a kicker for an attribution, as in "Mayor alleges (kicker)," "City clerk stole funds (main head)." If the story is too long, the kicker might be cut, and the headline becomes unfair or even libelous.

'HARRY & MEGHAN'
Estranged royals vent anger in final Netflix episodes

FIGURE 2.2.9   This kicker, "Harry & Meghan," piques the reader's interest and ties the story to the title of the Netflix movie.

INSANE DEALS
Amazon scrambles to match prices from savings hack

FIGURE 2.2.10   The big, bold hammer headline grabs the reader's attention.

Hammers are about twice as big as the main headline and often much bigger. The hammer grabs the reader's attention; it hits the reader over the head. A well-written hammer leads the reader to read the "deck" head, where the theme of the story is found. Figure 2.2.10 takes two words from the story to make a point, then lets the deck explain the story. In this case, the deck is the main headline.

Hammers are bold. Sometimes special heavy-faced fonts are used. Hammers introduce white space and provide contrast. Hammers sum up a story in a word or in a phrase.

Readouts, sometimes called drop heads or decks, are smaller than the main head, usually about half as big. Readouts are in a contrasting type, usually a lighter face or in italics.

The type of readout in Figure 2.2.11 is called an underline. It extends the full width of the main headline.

Readouts often are set narrower than the main headline to fit on one column (Figure 2.2.12).

In writing a readout, look for a secondary element or theme that provides elaboration on the main head. Readouts get a separate headline order and must fit the column width. Readouts provide a visual transition; they take the reader from the big type of a main head to body type. Readouts direct the eye, serve as buffers and provide contrast.

Sidebar headlines go with a related story that runs with a main story and takes a separate headline.

Sidebar heads usually are set in a typeface that contrasts with the main head, either through size or weight, or by using a different typeface. Figure 2.2.13 is a sidebar head written to go on the same page as Figure 2.2.12.

In writing sidebar heads, look for elements in the story that do not echo the main story. Try not to repeat words in the main head or other heads on the same page, although some repetition is unavoidable.

Tripod heads are a variation of the hammer-main headline combination. Newspaper designer Mario Garcia (1993) gave the tripod its name.

The tripod head rests on three elements: a main headline, a hammer and a special display treatment of a key word or phrase. Figure 2.2.14 is an example.

Kentucky Supreme Court strikes down school choice program
Plan offered tax credits for private school tuition

FIGURE 2.2.11   An underline is a readout headline, also called a deck, that spans the full width of the main headline.

Kentucky Supreme Court strikes down school choice program
Plan would support
private school tuition
with tax credits

FIGURE 2.2.12   Readouts often are confined to one column under the main headline.

Private school vouchers open doors for underserved kids

FIGURE 2.2.13   A sidebar headline goes on a secondary story, usually on the same page as the main story.

75 AND STILL WORKING
Inflation is forcing seniors to return to the job market

FIGURE 2.2.14   The third leg of a tripod headline is the typographical treatment added to the main headline and the readout, or in this case, the hammer and the main headline.

The tripod is not new to magazines; it's almost a requirement for the two-page spread. Today, tripod heads show up on breaking news stories, made possible by computer programs that allow easy and quick manipulation of type.

The challenge for the designer is a display that is meaningful. Garcia (1993) advises that such headlines must be functional and easy to read.

Summary graphs add information to headlines and allow readers to get their news quickly as they scan print and web pages. Summary graphs, also known as "blurbs" or excerpts online, come in moderately large type, sometimes with bullets to attract the eye. A summary graph is similar to a readout, but it is written as a complete sentence with no missing words and with correct punctuation. Summary graphs can appear at the top of the story under a headline (Figure 2.2.15).

Adrift without sail or power

Two sailors who drifted in the Atlantic for 10 days are rescued after a storm dismasted their boat.

FIGURE 2.2.15   A summary graph is similar to a readout, but it is written as a complete sentence with no missing words and with correct punctuation.

The summary graph is like an excerpt on a webpage, written with complete sentences and with articles and all other words in place. An excerpt is important because it shows up on the homepage to summarize a story.

The key to writing summary graphs is to understand the story completely and to reveal the depth of that story. The mortal sin in writing summary graphs is to repeat what appears in the main headline.

The Seed Approach and Advertising

We often hear students say, "I'm just not creative." It's true that some of us have better memories than others; sometimes that can be mistaken for creativity. Some of us are more perceptive or have a more wicked sense of humor. But creativity also can be a process. The seed approach is one such process.

Gary Koepke, a creative officer at SapientNitro, said he invites all sorts of people from across the agency to come to brainstorming meetings—even people not with the agency.

Speaking to a panel convened by Advertising Week, Koepke said: "Ultimately what I like is **the random molecule idea.** Invite someone who maybe has nothing to do with anything. Maybe it's an artist or a musician. Maybe it's my mom. Anybody to say, 'Why are you doing that?' or 'What's this?' or 'You guys always do the same thing.'

"I believe everybody is creative, so it doesn't matter who's in the room, as long as they've been briefed properly and somebody is managing that process" (Nudd, 2013).

Developing an advertising campaign is an involved process that includes many participants. It starts with the brief, a statement from the client of what a product or concept is all about. Next comes extensive research on the client and its products, the audience, the competition. From this, a campaign plan arises through brainstorming, sketching, writing and rewriting. Execution of the plan comes next, then evaluation.

Somewhere in this process, a copywriter will try to come up with the exact right words, and the seed approach is one way to approach this task.

The Web Is Different: Writing Headlines for SEO

News organizations know that readers often find a story through a search engine, mainly Google. An editor might be asked to write two headlines, one for a print or email newsletter and one for online designed to attract search engines. Some tips (Morris, 2021):

- **Hold your title length to 50–60 characters.** Titles within these limits are more attractive to Google and can eliminate awkard splits on a search engine results page.
- **Write titles that are more direct.** Clever headlines are less attractive to search engines. This is where you might be asked to write two headlines, one for the website and one for the newsletter.
- **Write for readers:** Google ranks search results, but people choose where to click. Write understandable sentences or phrases, and don't overdo the keywords.
- **But use keywords:** Place keywords at or near the start of the headline. You can find ideas for keywords at trends.google.com.

A Little Bird Told Me

Facebook, X, Instagram, TikTok and other social media platforms have become important tools for journalists, advertisers, public relations people and anyone who likes to spread the news. For the journalist, posting during an event has become part of the job. In advertising and public relations, social media is a powerful tool in the hands of a skilled writer.

But for young people who have grown up with social media, common writing practices don't apply or can confuse those who aren't in on the lingo. Danielle Abril (2022) writes in The Washington Post that members of Generation Z, born roughly between 1997 and 2012, have their

(continued)

own way of communicating, something that "is creating a quirky challenge for multigenerational workplaces: the potential for confusing, anxiety-inducing and sometimes comical miscommunication."

Abril tells the story of a 23-year-old media relations specialist who said she had to adjust to seeing periods at the end of a sentence in Slack and email messages from her colleagues. For some young people, ending a text with a period is considered unfriendly (Feltman, 2015). She had to change her thinking about how to write on social media, as have her older colleagues who need to communicate effectively with Gen Z co-workers.

Follow these best practices for writing on social media:

- **Think like your readers.** Craft your message accurately to ensure that it will appeal to most readers. You probably are used to writing in acronyms (IMHO) or using emojis to get your points across. But in professional communication, these can slow down some readers or lead them to the wrong conclusions. You must know your audience.
- **Write clearly and concisely.** The limited space on social media platforms demands that you keep things short and to the point. Often your best results will come from writing shorter than the maximum allowed. For example, Stacey McLachlan (2022) writes that ideal length of a Facebook post is 80 characters or fewer. McLachlan notes that Facebook cuts off long posts using ellipses (Figure 2.2.16).

FIGURE 2.2.16   This Facebook post from The Atlantic magazine was too long and got cut off using an ellipsis.

- **Avoid sounding like a salesperson:** The goal is to sell while appearing to do something else, such as instructing someone on how to change the oil in their car. Morkes and Nielsen (1997) advise us to avoid "marketese," the hype that often finds itself in advertising: "Best ever!" "You won't find a better detergent!" "No. 1 across the board!"
- **Use correct, acceptable punctuation:** Poor punctuation—or nonstandard punctuation, such as leaving periods off the ends of sentences—distracts readers and reflects poorly on the writer. Use periods, commas and apostrophes in the right places and quote marks when needed. Avoid too many exclamation points.
- **Accept nothing less than flawless grammar and perfect spelling:** You can write your message in a word processor that has a grammar- and spell-checker, then paste it into your social media post. Avoid ALL CAPITAL LETTERS that look like shouting. Think twice about using LOL and other gems of social media.

HOMEWORK

Assignment No. 1

"Half your job as a copy editor is writing headlines," we were told at the Chicago Tribune. So one way to get the job in the first place was to rewrite headlines that had appeared in the newspaper. Try out that strategy for yourself. Pick up a publication or find a website that you would really like to work for, then go to work trying to improve the headlines. You can add that critique to your job application.

Assignment No. 2

Take a scroll through X, formally known as Twitter, and what do you notice? The headlines! A decision to drop them was reversed. Supposedly by stripping headlines from news-story links, the goal was to improve the look of posts. What do you think? Draft your own post on the topic. Then, if you have an X account, send your thoughts to your followers.

Assignment No. 3

Every year in California there's a big winner in the Safeway World Championship Pumpkin Weigh-Off. That's the perfect chance to flex "the seed approach" to headline writing. If you're thinking pumpkin seeds, you're our kind of person. If you enjoyed, "It's the Great Pumpkin, Charlie Brown," even more so.

The 2023 winner weighed 2,749 pounds, setting a record. You have four words: What's your headline? It was a big story for the Star Tribune of Minneapolis because the award-winning grower was from Anoka, Minnesota. For the jump headline, you have eight words: Go! (See the Star Tribune headlines below.)

REFERENCES

Abril, D. (2022, December 13). Gen Z came to "slay." Their bosses don't know what that means. *Washington Post.* https://www.washingtonpost.com/technology/2022/12/12/gen-z-work-emojis/

Berger, W. (2004, July). How I did it: Jeff Goodby. *Inc. 26*:7, 84–88.

Feltman, R. (2015, December 8). Study confirms that ending your text with a period is terrible. *Washington Post.* https://www.washingtonpost.com/news/speaking-of-science/wp/2015/12/08/study-confirms-that-ending-your-texts-with-a-period-is-terrible/

Garcia, M. R. (1993). *Contemporary newspaper design: A structural approach* (3rd ed.). Prentice Hall.

Garcia, M. R., & Stark, M. M. (1991). Eyes on the news. Poynter Institute for Media Studies.

Ingram M. (2022, July 28). Will Facebook changes leave news media out in the cold? *Columbia Journalism Review.* https://www.cjr.org/the media today/will-facebook-changes-leave-news-media-out-in-the-cold.php

Kauffman, J. (2022, December 1). Why "got milk?" is one of the greatest ad campaigns of all time. *Saveur.* https://www.saveur.com/culture/got-milk-greatest-ad-campaign/

McLachlan, S. (2022, August 2). Ideal length of social media posts: A guide for every platform. Hootsuite. https://blog.hootsuite.com/ideal-social-media-post-length/

Morkes, J., & Nielsen, J. (1997). Concise, SCANNABLE, and objective: How to write for the web. Nielsen Norman Group. https://www.nngroup.com/articles/concise-scannable-and-objective-how-to-write-for-the-web/

Morris, H. J. (2021, December 7). Write digital headlines both readers and Google will love. NPR. https://training.npr.org/2021/08/25/how-write-display-seo-headlines/

Nudd, T. (2013, September 25). Genius or process? How top creative directors come up with great ideas. *Adweek.* https://www.adweek.com/brand-marketing/genius-or-process-how-top-creative-directors-come-great-ideas-152697/

Outing, S. (2004, August 24). Eyetrack III: What news websites look like through readers' eyes. Poynter. https://www.poynter.org/archive/2004/eyetrack-iii-what-news-websites-look-like-through-readers-eyes/

Payne, M. (2015, June 9). Newspaper calls A's switch-pitcher Pat Venditte "amphibious." *Washington Post*. https://www.washingtonpost.com/news/early-lead/wp/2015/06/09/newspaper-calls-as-switch-pitcher-pat-venditte-amphibious/

Pew Research Center. (2022, December 14). Social media and news fact sheet. https://www.pewresearch.org/journalism/fact-sheet/social-media-and-news-fact-sheet/

Roush, T. (2022, December 23). Congress passes bill to ban TikTok from federal devices. *Forbes*. https://www.forbes.com/sites/tylerroush/2022/12/23/congress-passes-bill-to-ban-tiktok-from-federal-devices/

Thorbecke, C. (2022, December 16). TikTok might be too big to ban, no matter what lawmakers say. CNN. https://amp.cnn.com/cnn/2022/12/16/tech/tiktok-ban-users/index.html

TwoSixDigital (n.d.). 4 scientific reasons to keep social posts short and sweet. https://twosixdigital.com/4-scientific-reasons-to-keep-social-posts-short-sweet/

FURTHER READING, RESOURCES

Evon, D. (2015, June 9). Newspaper gave pitcher Pat Venditte a new talent. Snopes. https://www.snopes.com/news/2015/06/09/amphibious-pitcher/

Gianatasio, D. (2000). Rebels with a cause. *Adweek, 41*(26), 20.

Jorgenson, D. (2021). *Make a TikTok every day: 365 prompts for attention-grabbing TikToks*. DK.

Marshall, P., & Yu, D. (2022). *The definitive guide to TikTok advertising: How to access 1 billion people in 10 minutes!* Perry Marshall & Associates.

Moran, K. (2020, April 5). How people read online: New and old findings. Nielsen Norman Group. https://www.nngroup.com/articles/how-people-read-online/

Nielsen, J., & Pernice, K. (2010). *Eyetracking web usability*. New Riders.

Assignment No. 3: The reveal!

Main headline:

2,749-POUND PUMPKIN SQUASHES COMPETITION

Jump headline:

Anoka man's pumpkin the greatest of them all

THE INDISPENSABLE IMAGE

KEY POINTS IN THIS CHAPTER

1. All editors need to know how to select, crop and display images. While writers worry about what they will say in the lede of a story, readers will have already decided whether to look at the story based on the image and related headline, the one-two punch.

2. Photo editing requires a series of decisions about the quality and storytelling power of an image. Among the basic questions to be answered: Should we use it? If so, how big? Do we need to crop it or retouch it?

3. Caption writing aids the reader in understanding how the image connects with the story. Writing captions takes skill. The challenge is to add meaning rather than state the obvious. It's high stakes, as more captions will be read in their entirety than stories.

> **"** *I would willingly exchange every single painting of Christ for one snapshot."*
>
> —George Bernard Shaw

The Irish playwright George Bernard Shaw's wish for a snapshot of Jesus points to the power of photographic images. While paintings and drawings can portray angels and demons, a photograph or video must have a real subject in front of the lens.

Photographs and videos have never been more important in the media world. Technology enables us to transmit and process images instantly. Modern printing presses provide better reproduction of photos than ever before. Today's computer displays and high-definition television sets provide stunning detail and rich color. Not to mention that other screen—on your mobile phone.

Few events happen that aren't captured as an image or video, thanks to millions of people who always carry an excellent camera with them, one that doubles as a cellphone. Such images and video can spark profound change: In 2020, 17-year-old Darnella Frazier recorded Minneapolis police officer Derek Chauvin kneeling on George Floyd's neck (Hernandez, 2021). She was awarded a special Pulitzer Prize citation and award in 2021 for her courage in documenting the event.

Behind the rise in the importance of images are editors who appreciate the storytelling power of a picture. They know how best to deliver impact regardless of the medium, whether print, video or broadcast, or documentary.

At larger news organizations, the task of selecting photos and videos and preparing them for publication falls to specialized editors. They are involved in the process from making the assignment to archiving the finished product. At smaller publications, news editors or page designers often will double as their own photo and video editors.

The National Press Photographers Association today includes videographers and multimedia journalists among its membership. Photographers brought up on capturing still images have retrained themselves to shoot video, and the photo slideshow has breathed life into the time-honored photo story. Video editing for broadcast is still a specialized skill, but every journalist should have at least some training in video.

Editors need to know how to select, crop and display images, if for no other reason than to appreciate what the photographer and photo editor do. The editor might be working for an alumni magazine or newsletter or producing a slideshow for a radio or television news site to illustrate a story. Maybe the editor is working on the Friday Night Lights sports section for a newspaper's prep coverage or maybe just punching up a personal blog visually. Regardless of the media outlet, the editor needs to master a core set of principles. What follows is a simplified approach to photo editing.

Where Do Photos and Video Come From?

We are swimming in a sea of images thanks to the ever-present cellphone camera, sports action cameras and drones, and the ubiquitous surveillance camera. But finding and using just the right image requires knowledge of where to look, how to verify and how to get permission.

Large news organizations rely on their staff photojournalists and subscribe to news services such as the Associated Press, Reuters, Getty Images and Agence France-Presse. National news organizations such as The Washington Post and The New York Times also offer their photos and videos for reuse. These news services can be too expensive for small operations.

Many photos are available through Creative Commons licensing. Creators of photos and videos post their work on websites, such as YouTube, Vimeo and Flickr, among others, with a Creative Commons license specifying how the image or video can be used. Many are available for commercial use at no charge if attributed to the creator. Google Images provides an avenue for finding images; you can access it through the Creative Commons website. Wikipedia Commons offers millions of royalty-free images.

An image or video might not have a copyright notice attached, but that doesn't mean you are free to use it. Copyright law does not require that creators formally register their works. If you find an image that you believe will add to your story, follow these steps (Stim, 2021):

1. Decide if permission is needed.
2. Identify the owner.
3. Identify the rights needed.
4. Contact the owner and negotiate whether payment is needed.
5. Get your permission agreement in writing.

When searching these sites for images, be aware of stock photos and videos that will show up in your search. These are predominantly staged to produce ideal images. Stock images can be useful for advertising or for creating photo illustrations for news and feature stories if the final product is clearly labeled as an illustration.

Getting Down to Editing

Image editing involves five core decisions:

1. Should we use the image? Or as is often the case, which one?
2. How big do we run it, and where?
3. How do we crop it?
4. Should we retouch it?
5. What should the caption say?

These decisions have their parallels in video editing, too. A common practice for online organizations is to embed short video clips within text stories. These clips require no cropping but may need some type of caption.

1. Should We Use the Image?

The editor usually has more than one image or video to choose from. Professional photographers will return from an assignment with hundreds of frames or hours of video. The editor must decide on the relevance of any image chosen. The choice requires an appreciation for what makes a good image with storytelling power.

A good image makes the reader stop and think. Look for photos and clips with emotion that make the reader feel differently and with impact that make a strong statement.

Images should be informative. Two of the pioneers in this field are Sir Harold Evans, legendary editor of The Sunday Times of London, and Angus McDougall, inducted into the University of Missouri's Photojournalism Hall of Fame. Evans (1978) in his book "Pictures on a Page" wrote that news photos must have "relevant context." These are details that put the reader at the scene or help tell the story. McDougall and Hampton (1990) add that a good news photo makes a "clear statement." Its message is easily understood.

McDougall and Hampton also advise the editor to ask if the image is suitable for the audience and if it is fair to those who appear in it.

Figure 2.3.1 shows part of a photo shoot taken for a story about sardine fishing at Imperial Beach, California. The photo selected has details such as the clothing of the people, the fish in the sink and the ocean in the background. Those details help tell the story by providing relevant context. The editor has decided on ethe shot believed to be the best to tell the story. The editor also evaluated the shot for being in focus and well-exposed, allowing for the best reproduction.

FIGURE 2.3.1   The photo editor first chooses the most appropriate shot from the photo database. This example shows the available images taken at Imperial Beach in Southern California. The photo editor, using Adobe Bridge, has chosen a shot that includes "relevant context."

(Michael O'Donnell)

Editors must be sensitive to charges of sensationalism. They must draw the line between the image with unusual power and the image that turns off readers completely. But an editor can't be afraid to disturb people. Readers shouldn't be shielded from reality. Many American editors, unlike some of their international counterparts, draw the line at showing dead bodies and blood, even to the point of choosing a black-and-white photo over a color one showing red blood.

Newspapers and magazines can soften the blow of controversial images by not running them on Page 1 or on the cover. Web editors can place an image farther down the page and provide a warning before the reader scrolls through the story.

Editors should know when not to use an image. They should try to avoid staged shots, check-passing shots or group shots. A group shot of a choir is better if the people are singing. At least it has some action. That's not the case with check-passing shots where two people stand shoulder to shoulder holding the ends of a check as they stare into the camera. These cautions are just as important for choosing video.

The choice between two images can be critical, so always choose the one that best fits the story.

FIGURE 2.3.2   Front page of the St. Paul (Minnesota) Pioneer Press from September 13, 2001, with a picture showing a firefighter in agony being pulled from the wreckage of the World Trade Center on Sept. 12, 2001. While the photo is heart-wrenching, it has all the qualities of a great news shot: relevant context in the firefighters' gear and the destroyed building; emotion in the faces; and action in how the figures are posed. How big do you run it? The answer is as big as possible, as the example from the St. Paul Pioneer Press shows.

(Robert Mecea/Newsday via AP)

2. How Big Do We Run It?

When we speak of photo size, we mean in relationship to the page. Several factors go into how big a photo should run. Most important is the picture's newsworthiness. The first cloudy picture of Neil Armstrong on the moon, taken off a television monitor, covered the entire front of some newspapers in 1969. Despite a lack of quality, that picture was big news. Figure 2.3.2 presents another example. The editors of the St. Paul Pioneer Press had a great photo related to a huge story, and they ran with it.

Beyond newsworthiness, the photo editor must ask:

- **How much space is available?** A large, dominant image will get a reader into a story like nothing else. In dividing up scarce real estate on a printed page, editors and writers should be willing to balance text with good image play. Editors also should be willing to make the often-tough decision as to what image will dominate the page. The other photos must run smaller, no more than half as big. Web editors have different choices given the flexibility of the webpage. With responsive webpages, a photo or video can fill the computer screen in spectacular fashion (Figure 2.3.3), then adapt to a smaller screen, such as a smartphone or tablet. The editor must decide which image

FIGURE 2.3.3   The New York Times Magazine website ran this photo so that it covered the full screen on a laptop computer but resized automatically for tablets and smartphones. It shows police forcing people out of the Capitol building after confronting them in the Rotunda, 3:40 p.m. on Jan. 6, 2021, in Washington, D.C.
(Ashley Gilbertson for The New York Times)

appears first, what other photos are included down the page and whether enough good photos are available to create a photo slideshow.

- **Will the photo "read" if it runs small?** An image like a face that fills up the frame can run at a small size and still be recognizable. But pictures with a lot of small details must run larger, or readers won't be able to recognize what's in them.

- **Will the photo be too sensational if it runs big?** When photo editors have great shots, they want to run them as large as possible. But that zeal must be tempered with good taste. If the photo is gruesome but newsworthy, running it smaller will reduce its impact.

3. How Do We Crop It?

A good crop can help focus an image and enhance its size. When the photographer has processed an image, it will come to you already cropped. Photos presented on news service websites also have been cropped. Nevertheless, photojournalism professor Ken Kobré (2017) advises photo editors to "crop ruthlessly" while preserving the information in the image. Search out these targets when you crop:

- **Negative space.** The area of the image that adds nothing to the message is considered negative space or dead space (Figure 2.3.4). An expanse of

FIGURE 2.3.4. Photo of people cleaning sardines on the pier at Imperial Beach, California. The photo editor has cropped out "negative space" that adds nothing to the information in the picture. The crop also helps the reader to focus on the main subject while retaining relevant context.

(Michael O'Donnell)

space isn't always unnecessary. Some images are powerful for showing the emptiness of a scene (Figure 2.3.5).

FIGURE 2.3.5   Wide-angle shot of a surfer alone on the Pacific Ocean at Imperial Beach, California. Not all empty space is negative. Part of the power of this photo is the loneliness of the surfer on the ocean.

(Michael O'Donnell)

- **Peak emotion.** In selecting an image, look for human faces at their most expressive. The random people in Figure 2.3.6 add nothing to the story of having fun at a parade. The cropped area draws the reader toward the happy children.

FIGURE 2.3.6   Image of children watching a parade. The uncropped photo of a crowd watching a parade has no center of visual interest. Crop in on the children displaying peak emotion.

(Danielle Salazar)

FIGURE 2.3.7   This crop of a women's soccer game does two things: It focuses on the peak action and it eliminates the distracting player on the left.

(Josh Kleven/TommieMedia.com)

- **Peak action.** Images of action just before it resolves itself get readers deeply involved because they provide closure, completing the action. In Figure 2.3.7, the crop focuses on the collision between the goalie and player.
- **Key relationships.** When two people or objects in an image interact, crop tightly to emphasize the relationship. The equipment in Figure 2.3.8 is somewhat interesting, but the key relationship is the woman and her pig.
- **Distractions.** Often a full-frame image will include people or objects that draw attention away from the key parts of the story. In Figure 2.3.7 the player in the white uniform on the left adds nothing to the peak action and distracts the eye.
- **The redundant, mundane or repetitive.** We mentioned that group shots, check-passing shots or the classic shot of a person sitting at a desk, pen in hand, phone to the ear, are cliched images best avoided. But remember that some mundane shots take on importance when the story is important. The standard picture of a press conference might be a required image when the announcement is earth-shattering.

FIGURE 2.3.8   By eliminating the negative space in this photo, the editor has focused on the key relationship between the woman and the pig.

(Josie Donner)

Rule of Thirds

When cropping an image, use the rule of thirds. Imagine that the image is divided into nine equal parts by two equally spaced horizontal lines and two equally spaced vertical lines. Place your center of visual interest along these lines or where they cross. Doing this creates a more interesting and dynamic composition (Figure 2.3.9).

FIGURE 2.3.9   By following the rule of thirds, this photo has a dynamic quality that would be lacking if the young person had been placed dead center. *(Nolan Gutierrez)*

The key to getting a good crop is to let the photo play you; don't force a horizontal photo into a vertical shape or vice versa. Figure 2.3.10 shows a photo of a football team running on the field for its first practice. How would you crop it?

The original photo is a strong horizontal. Figure 2.3.11 shows a crop that forces the photo into a weak vertical shape. Besides changing the shape, and not for the better, this crop changes the information in the photo from a swarm of football players rushing onto the field to a few stragglers. This crop isn't honest.

In Figure 2.3.12 the photo is used full width, with some of the dead space cropped off the top. This crop strengthens the horizontal shape and focuses the photo on the players without losing information.

A Few Words About Mug Shots

A mug shot is a picture of a person's face. These small photos are regular items in most publications and are worth a little extra attention. Newspaper and web

FIGURE 2.3.10   In the unedited frame, the swarm of football players presents a horizontal shape. The bleachers above their heads create negative space and adds nothing to the content of the photo.

(Photos by Michael O'Donnell)

FIGURE 2.3.11   This crop forces the horizontal picture into a vertical shape. It is a dishonest crop because it changes the content of the photo from a swarm to a small group.

designer Mario Garcia says headshots alert readers to the "what" of the story (Garcia, 2002).

Mug shots often are cropped to a standard width and height. On a printed page, a one-column mug might be about 1.5 inches by 2 inches. A half-column mug could measure three-fourths of an inch by 1 inch. But mugs can run smaller thanks to the improved reproduction qualities of modern presses. A rule of thumb about the minimum size is that the mug shot should be big enough to match the size of your thumb placed over it. For a standard-size mug, the editor enters both dimensions into the computer rather than just the width. This means that sometimes a mug shot doesn't get the ideal crop.

On webpages, where space isn't as much of an issue, the "extended" mug shot is favored. An extended mug shows the subject with some context (Figure 2.3.13).

FIGURE 2.3.12   This crop retains the original information of the photo but focuses our attention on the players by eliminating negative space above them.

FIGURE 2.3.13   Web pages often use "extended" mug shots that provide some context for the subject. A full-width image works better when a webpage must be composed quickly or by using software.

(Rori West/TommieMedia.com)

Here are some tips on making the most of mug shots:

Fill the frame: Often photo editors give in to the temptation to squeeze or stretch a mug shot to save or take up space. The result is a mug that looks too loose or too tight. Follow these guidelines:

- A small amount of space should be left above the head and on each side of the ears. Generally, the space will be about a 10th of an inch for a standard mug.
- The bottom crop should be near the knot of a tie or just above where a woman's shoulders begin.
- Mug shots must be in balance. If several photos appear on the same page, all faces must be of the same relative size. If faces are side by side, then the eye level should be the same. Most publications have standard templates for mug shots.

FIGURE 2.3.14   The mugshot on the left is too tight. The one in the middle is too loose. The one on the right is spaced just right.
(Michael O'Donnell)

Figure 2.3.14 shows three crops. The crop on the right is most desirable. The one on the left is too tight; the one in the middle is too loose.

Profile shots: Mug shots often must be made from photos of people in profile. The secret is to avoid crowding the subject's face. Give the person somewhere to look.

Figure 2.3.15 shows with crop marks how a mug shot was carved out of a regular photo; no special portrait was taken. Notice also how the crop marks are arranged to "straighten" the mug shot.

The crop on the top right is too tight on the face. The one on the bottom right is better. To make a profile mug shot work, you might have to crop out some of the back of the head.

Intruding objects: What do you do when an object intrudes into the frame? Figure 2.3.16 shows two possible crops. You can:

- include the hand in the mug shot (left). When you do this, make sure that just enough of the object is in the frame to be recognizable.
- crop out the subject's hand altogether (right).

FIGURE 2.3.15   This image shows how a profile mug shot is cropped from the original photo. The bottom right crop is best because it doesn't crowd the person's face.
(Michael O'Donnell)

If the object is a hand, as in Figure 2.3.16, the reader should be able to tell whose hand it is. The danger is that to make room for the object, you'll reduce the size of the face too much. The crop with the hand in it will work better when the mug shot is used at a larger size, but either crop can be used.

4. Should We Retouch It?

In the early part of the 20th century, virtually every photo had to be retouched. This was because the technology for printing photos was new and crude, and photography itself was less exact.

As reproduction and photography improved, retouching became less necessary. But for the past 40 years, the retouching of photos has become a hot topic because of digital photo editing. Sophisticated computer programs make exotic alterations simple and easy.

FIGURE 2.3.16   Two possible crops of a mug shot with an intruding object. Either can be used.

(Michael O'Donnell)

Figure 2.3.17 shows a digital photo that was altered using Adobe Photoshop on a laptop computer. The surfer was "cloned" at different locations in the frame.

Professional photographers and photo editors are concerned that readers will begin to doubt the truthfulness of all photos if they suspect some have been altered. As a result, many professionals advocate no electronic retouching beyond what is needed to clarify a picture: removing dust and scratches, correcting color and tone, and restoring sharpness lost in the scanning process. Anything that might mislead readers should not be done; the credibility of the publication is at stake.

FIGURE 2.3.17   The surfer in this image has been "cloned" several times using Adobe Photoshop. When news organizations alter photos, even in the spirit of fun, they put their credibility at risk.

(Michael O'Donnell)

Some toning and retouching are almost always needed but only to improve image quality. The rule is to tone the photo so that it best represents what a person could have seen with the naked eye.

Professional photojournalists today capture images using RAW format where all the digital information in an image is preserved, unlike your cellphone images. The cellphone processes the image "on board" and compresses it into a JPEG format. The RAW image is unprocessed and not compressed. Adobe (2022) provides more insight into editing and toning RAW images.

5. What Does the Caption Say?

An image might be worth a thousand words, but usually a few words more are needed to explain the image, expand on its content and, most importantly, link the image to the story. That is the function of a caption, often called a cutline. Caption writing is high-stakes. Poynter eyetrack research (Garcia & Stark, 1991) revealed that readers are more likely to read a caption in its entirety than a story.

A caption briefly answers the who, what, where, when, why and how questions brought up by a picture. All the journalistic rules about brevity and precision apply with force to caption writing. In its most basic form, the caption identifies people or objects. Simple captions also can include the where and the when. But many photos need explanation and background. In such cases, a caption will place the event or action shown in context and sum up its significance.

An image should be analyzed to determine why it has been selected and what caption elements are needed. One way to decide what the caption needs to say is to look at the photo without any caption to see if the photo communicates on its own. If it does, the caption can be brief; if not, the caption must start out with the salient facts.

Each caption requires the writer to edit a mountain of facts down to only those that apply to the photo. This requires a careful reading of the story that goes with the photo. More tips:

The caption writer must avoid the obvious. When in doubt, let the picture do the talking. The caption is a selective writing job that demands clarity to help the reader understand the photo quickly.

The first sentence usually is cast in the present tense. The writer can shift to past tense in the following sentences. This use of the "historical present" is a long-standing practice. Some editors believe using past tense is more honest; follow your organization's style. In any case, don't hesitate to drop the present tense if it gives a false impression that something happened more recently than it did.

Writing in the present tense works with action photos but should not be done with file photos. Verbs are preferred, but a caption can be written without one if the action is obvious or the image is an illustrator that works best with a label caption.

COMMON TYPES OF IMAGES AND CAPTIONS

Images that go with feature stories require different treatment than for news. A picture retrieved from the archives to go with a story—what we call a "filer"—needs special handling. Stand-alone photos require different caption information than those running with a story and headline.

- **News images.** These need captions that contain facts and as many identities as possible. When a photo stands alone, without an accompanying story, a small headline called a "catchline" can state the facts or try to act as a bridge from image to caption. Tread on the side of caution when considering levity for a news catchline. Figure 2.3.18 shows a news image and caption.

- **Features.** Light features need a special writing touch with a witty catchline. Often, these images go with weather stories and caption writers make the mistake of repeating almost verbatim a forecast that is available in at least two other places in the publication. Serious features, such as the street department figuring out what to do about a pavement collapse, often work best with a witty catchline and a certain amount of flair in the writing. Figure 2.3.19 shows a feature photo with a catchline and caption.

- **Filers.** For many stories, images are retrieved from the reference library or another archive. These need special care so that the reader is not misled into thinking the image is current. The object of the caption should be to tie the image tightly to the story. The caption should alert the reader that the image is not current in as unobtrusive a manner as possible. One method is to handle the opening sentence as an explanation of the story's crux and not address the specific action of the photo (Figure 2.3.20). Caution is advised in using noncurrent images as generic illustrators, especially those showing identifiable people. And be careful of dead giveaways, such as a celebrity wearing a hairdo from the past decade.

FIGURE 2.3.18   Anglers clean sardines on the pier at Imperial Beach, south of San Diego. Sardines were rarely seen for decades due to overfishing, then rose and fell from 1990 to 2010. Now, their numbers again seem to be increasing.
(Michael O'Donnell)

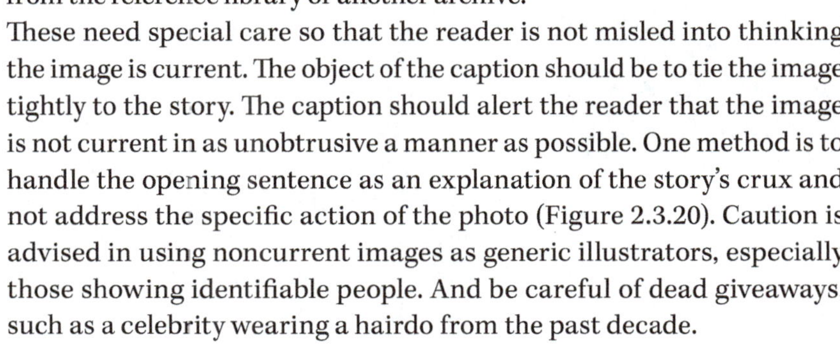

FIGURE 2.3.19. **Chill out, man:** Subzero temperatures and 2 feet of snow on Thursday could not force this Waldorf College student to don long pants. The forecast for Saturday promises temperatures that might get the job done.

(Michael O'Donnell)

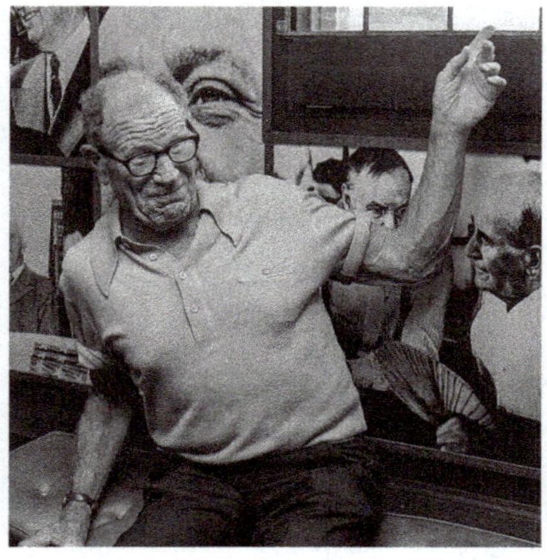

FIGURE 2.3.20   Bill Veeck will forever be remembered as the man who introduced the exploding scoreboard that shot fireworks after his Chicago White Sox hit a home run.

(File photo by Michael O'Donnell)

Filers often have nothing to do with the story. The caption must explain the connection. For example, the photo shows the mayor cutting a ribbon to a new shopping mall, but the story is about the mayor being charged with embezzlement. The charge must be included in the caption.

Often only a name line is necessary for a filer photo unless the photo is old and needs to be dated in the caption, or if obscure or secondary subjects in a story need to be identified. This happens often with mug shots on the business page, where a caption can add clarity by giving an executive's title.

- **Illustrators.** These often are environmental portraits of people, taken in their own surroundings. Many times, illustrators are set up; the action takes place for the camera. Do not lead readers into thinking otherwise. Illustrators include publicity shots, such as those received from a record company when a music group will perform.

  The easiest way to write a caption for an illustrator is to name the person and use a quote after a colon. Strive for something more, a mention of the surroundings or a contextual quote that contains no more than a phrase in direct quotes.

- **Combination captions.** When more than one image is used on a printed page, the best approach is to give each picture its own caption. An exception is when the photos are closely related, such as in chronological order.

Writing "combo" captions for several images requires care in guiding the reader around the page. Editors for web publications have the option of the photo slideshow; then, each image in the slideshow will have its own caption. Set the most important information in the first caption, then build on it.

Caption Writing Tips

Caption writing, like headline writing, has its own language. But unlike "headlinese," which is sometimes useful in tight spots, the much-used language of captions is riddled with cliches and weak verbs. Here's some advice:

- **Avoid empty verbs.** Use "poses," "stands," "waves," "sits," "points," "shares a laugh" and "looks on" only as a last resort. These verbs call attention to the weaknesses of a photo. If the caption can't be reworded, go without a verb:

  Tom Hanks and his wife, Rita Wilson, at the Golden Globe Awards. Not Tom Hanks and his wife, Rita Wilson, pose at the Golden Globe Awards.

- **Watch "stand."** If you must use the verb "stand," make sure the subject is standing with feet visible.
- **Don't state the obvious.** Describe the photo without stating the obvious. If the "when" and the "where" of an image are not apparent, make sure to clarify them for the reader. Here's an example for a file photo that went with a story about a lease dispute:

  Shoppers outside the Sears store at the Mall of America when it opened in August 1992. The retailer's exit from the mall in 2019 prompted litigation over the 100-year lease the two entities forged in 1991.

- **Explain before and after.** A good caption tells what happened before and after the action shown in the picture. If the action is obvious, telling the before and the after is often a way out of stating the obvious. This caption appeared under a video clip on The New York Times website:

  A blast at a Russian airfield came a day after Ukraine used drones to target two military bases deep inside Russia.

- **Name names.** The "who" is important even when it is obvious. A good example comes from The New York Times under a photo of President Biden giving a speech in November 2022:

  President Biden called on Americans to confront threats to democracy.

- **Connect meaning.** "What" and "how" should be obvious, visually or verbally, when someone is depicted making something.
- **Use only good quotes.** And make sure they help tie the photo to the story.
- **Don't assume.** And don't try to describe emotions or what a subject might be thinking. For example, if a person at a funeral is rubbing her eye, don't guess at what is going on and write "Judy Johnson fights back tears …"

Photographers are responsible for caption information, but often deadlines or other situations intervene, leaving many of the facts in question until the caption writer is involved. Similar situations arise with news service images. A call to the wire service, the assignment desk or a staff photographer might be able to clear up the problem, but if the problem cannot be ignored in the caption, sometimes a different photo can be used.

Identity Clues

Follow the style of your news organization for identity clues. Some place them in parentheses, others just within commas. Use as few as necessary. Often "(from left)" is all you need. More and more news organizations are using the convention of giving the reader a starting point then advising them to move clockwise or counterclockwise. The identity clue can be placed after a verb introducing a string of people or after the first name in the group (Figure 2.3.21).

FIGURE 2.3.21   The Mercury astronauts were the first Americans to go into space. Back row from left: Alan Shepard, Gus Grissom and Gordon Cooper. Front row: Wally Schirra, Deke Slayton, John Glenn and Scott Carpenter.
(NASA)

EDITING PHOTOS IN A SERIES

Once editors have processed individual images, they might have to take the added step of displaying them in a series. A few core principles can guide them whether they are designing a photo page, assembling a slideshow or producing a TV news package:

1. **Think 1–2–3**

   - **A "1-shot"** is also known as a wide shot or establishing shot. Typically, a photo page or a video package, even a documentary, will open with an establishing shot to help readers or viewers get their bearings on understanding the story about to be told. These wide shots provide a lot of context but often lack detail (Figure 2.3.22).

FIGURE 2.3.22   A 1-shot (establishing shot or wide shot) sets the scene. This image of Clara City, Minnesota, barber James R. Brown provides relevant context, but small details are lacking.
(Megan Brown)

   - **A "2-shot,"** also known as a medium shot, brings the audience closer to the scene. The medium shot has a strong center of visual interest and includes relevant context (Figure 2.3.23).
   - **A "3-shot"** is a close-up. On a page it can be the portrait of one person. In a video or film, it's accompanied by a sound bite. The 3-shot often needs other photos to make its meaning clear because it lacks context (Figure 2.3.24).

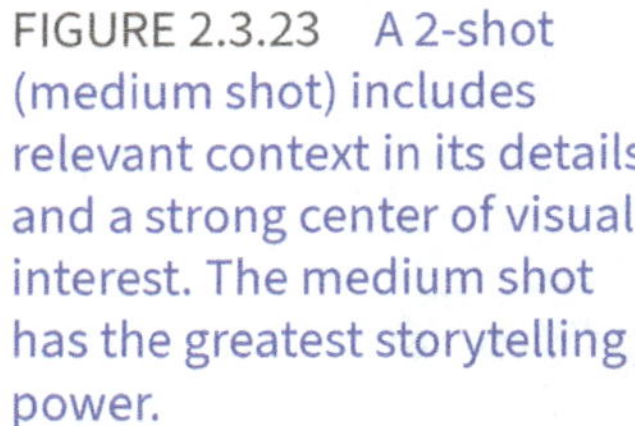

FIGURE 2.3.23   A 2-shot (medium shot) includes relevant context in its details and a strong center of visual interest. The medium shot has the greatest storytelling power.

(Megan Brown)

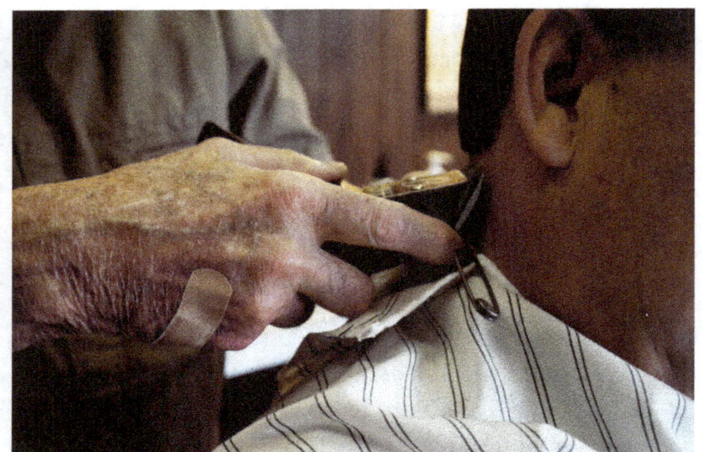

FIGURE 2.3.24. The 3-shot (close-up) homes in on an interesting detail. Close-ups add richness but often need other photos to provide context.

(Megan Brown)

2. **Find a rhythm**

- Think of photo editing like dance steps as you move through your storytelling: "1–2–3, 1–2–3."
- This works just as effectively in reverse: small, big, BIGGER. Even a close-up can have rhythm as the image changes from close, Very Close to EXTREMELY CLOSE.

3. **Variety and contrast**

- Storytelling comes alive through the variety of your images and the contrast they can provide in size (big and small), tone (dark and light) and content (serious and lighthearted).
- On a page an editor might choose to play one image more than twice the size of another. When the frame size is the same, as in a documentary or a TV news package, the variety comes from the size of the image within the frame.

Have Fun With All This

As George Bernard Shaw advised us, "We don't stop playing because we grow old; we grow old because we stop playing." Have fun selecting and editing photos. There's no better way to start storytelling on a page than with the one-two punch of a show-stopping visual and a large headline. In a documentary, it's that silent close-up that can make a viewer cry. Keep these core principles of photo editing in mind and enjoy the impact they can make.

HOMEWORK

Try these exercises at home to sharpen your eye for picture editing and caption writing.

Assignment No. 1

Go to The Associated Press webpage: apnews.com/photography.

You will find links to photos from the news stories of the day. Pick one image that you find especially compelling. What in the photo drew your attention? Remember the five questions a photo editor must ask about an image. If you had to choose one photo to run with a story, which would it be? You should be able to defend your choice based on the principles of photo editing from this chapter.

Assignment No. 2

Remember that a good photo has storytelling power. Visit the website of the newspaper or news organization in the largest city near you. Pick an important story that interests you and navigate through it. How are photos displayed with the story? Note which photo is displayed at the top and if other photos are included as you scroll down. Does the top photo help tell the story? What "relevant context" do you see in the photo that puts you at the scene? How does the caption link the photo to the story?

Assignment No. 3

Magazines use photos in different ways from newspapers, especially those magazines that specialize in feature stories. These stories center on people and how they live their lives. Pick a magazine such as Esquire, New York Magazine, Texas Monthly, Southern Living ... the list goes on. You might start with the American Society of Magazine Editors website for a list of award-winning magazines: www.asme.media/.

Choose a story that interests you. How might the photo with the story differ from what you saw on your newspaper website? Often, photos with feature stories are "setups," meaning that the photographer worked with the subject of the article to create a compelling image. What relevant context is present in the photo? How does the photo create an impression of the person? Note the caption: How is the magazine caption different from a newspaper caption?

Assignment No. 4

Go to your school library and visit the periodicals department. Examine a recent issue of a feature magazine. How does the experience of seeing images in print differ from seeing them on a website? What did you find interesting about how photos were displayed?

Look also at the print edition of a major newspaper, either a national newspaper such as The Washington Post or USA Today, or the newspaper from the largest city near you. Compare how photos are used in the newspaper with those in a magazine. What do you find interesting in how the photos are displayed? How are the captions different?

Assignment No. 5

You are editing a story about the Symbionese Liberation Army and the heiress Patty Hearst. The thrust of the story is about where Hearst is now. Go online and find two relevant images of Hearst then and now. What permissions are needed to use your two photos? What is the source of each?

REFERENCES

Adobe. (2022). Introduction to camera RAW. https://helpx.adobe.com/camera-raw/using/introduction-camera-raw.html

Evans, H. (1978). *Pictures on a page: Photojournalism, graphics and picture editing.* Holt, Rinehart and Winston.

Garcia, M. (2002, July 28). Head shots: Always a hit with readers. Poynter. https://www.poynter.org/reporting-editing/2002/head-shots-always-a-hit-with-readers/

Hernandez, J. (2021, May 26) Read this powerful statement from Darnella Frazier, who filmed George Floyd's murder. NPR. https://www.npr.org/1000475344

Kobré, K. (2017). *Photojournalism: The professionals' approach* (7th ed.). Routledge.

McDougall, A., & Hampton, V. J. (1990). *Picture editing & layout: A guide to better visual communication.* Viscom Press.

Stim, R. (2021, November 25). The basics of getting permission. Stanford Copyright and Fair Use Center. https://fairuse.stanford.edu/overview/introduction/getting-permission/

FURTHER READING, RESOURCES

Garcia, M. (2002a, July 27). Stand alone photos always rate high with readers. Poynter. https://www.poynter.org/reporting-editing/2002/stand-alone-photos-always-rate-high-with-readers/

Garcia, M. (2002b, July 27). The center of visual impact. Poynter. https://www.poynter.org/reporting-editing/2002/the-center-of-visual-impact/

Garcia, M.R., & Stark, M.M. (1991). Eyes on the news. Poynter Institute for Media Studies.

The Pulitzer Prizes (2021). *Darnella Frazier.* https://www.pulitzer.org/winners/darnella-frazier

More on Finding and Licensing Images and Video

Creative Commons: https://creativecommons.org/

Google Images: https://images.google.com/

Storyful: https://storyful.com/

Wikimedia Commons: https://commons.wikimedia.org/

STATS, GRAPHS AND MAPS

KEY POINTS IN THIS CHAPTER

1. Statistics show up in all types of media, starting with opinion polls and carrying over to business news and sports reports. Readers may cling to a particular figure and consider a poll "wrong" if editors do not explain the margin of error clearly enough. This is especially important in election coverage.

2. Editors should know enough about statistics to check the accuracy of percentages and how they are presented. A common mistake in stories is to mention a percentage of change without listing the numbers. A 100% increase sounds great until you see the change was to $2 a week from $1 a week.

3. Information graphics should be read and edited carefully for accuracy and relevance. Part of media literacy is the ability of a reader to follow and understand a chart. This is a skill that should not be overestimated—the more explanation the better.

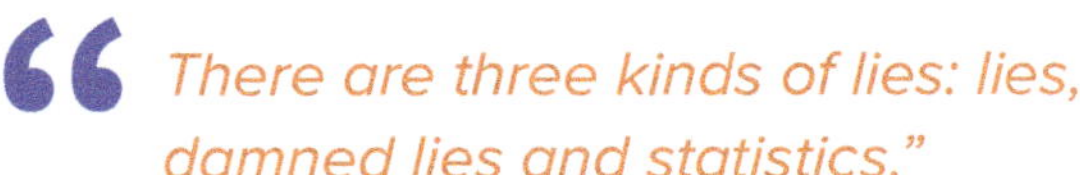

> *There are three kinds of lies: lies, damned lies and statistics."*
>
> —Benjamin Disraeli, former
> prime minister of the United Kingdom

Editors run into statistics constantly. They show up in stories based on polls, in graphics summarizing financial data and in baseball stories on the sports pages. Stories containing statistics require careful editing for content and for accuracy because, as twice British Prime Minister Benjamin Disraeli knew well in the 19th century, numbers are only as good as the person interpreting and reporting them. Then, as we know from teaching editing to college students over four decades, there's one more great challenge: math anxiety. Don't worry, we're here to help.

Information graphics go hand in hand with statistics. Visual representations of data help readers make comparisons and grasp significant differences in numbers. Maps fall into the category of infographics, especially when a map is combined with data.

The basic core principles of statistics and graphics are important for any editor. The challenge is two-fold—helping editors understand the basics but also keeping in mind readers' media literacy skills, as Americans are known to struggle with understanding graphs (3iap, 2023).

Surveys and Polls

Being skeptical about election polls is nothing new. Let's go back in the time machine to relive two cautionary tales about surveys:

In 1936, Alf Landon, the Republican governor of Kansas, ran for president against Franklin D. Roosevelt, the incumbent Democrat. The Literary Digest, as it had done successfully since 1916, conducted a poll of voters. The magazine sent 10 million ballots to two groups: a list of "prospective subscribers" who were mostly upper- and middle-income people, and a list of people selected from telephone books and motor vehicle registrations. This second group was chosen to "correct for bias" from the first list. About 25% of the ballots (2.4 million) were returned, with Landon predicted to win by a huge margin of 57% to 40% for FDR (Squire, 1988).

FDR won with about 60% of the vote, and the Literary Digest soon went out of business.

FIGURE 2.4.1   A victorious Harry Truman holds up the edition of the Chicago Daily Tribune that declared Thomas E. Dewey the winner of the 1948 presidential election. Truman won, defying opinion polls that had him losing in a landslide.

(Wikipedia.com)

The 1948 presidential election pitted New York's Republican governor, Thomas E. Dewey, against Harry S. Truman, who had become president when Roosevelt died in 1945. The Gallup organization conducted a poll on the election, as it had done for every presidential race since 1936. Gallup used a representative sample of about 3,000 voters based on geographic location, community size, socioeconomic level, gender and age. Gallup went to press six weeks before the election with the prediction that Dewey would win. The message was echoed on election night by the banner headline DEWEY DEFEATS TRUMAN in the early editions of the Chicago Daily Tribune. The photo of the victorious Truman holding the newspaper aloft (Figure 2.4.1) has become an enduring icon of journalism history (Campbell, 2020).

Both cases still receive attention today in college courses and scholarly journals.

In 1936, the Literary Digest used what would be a huge sample by today's standards. But the magazine made two mistakes:

- In the group of "prospective subscribers," Republicans were heavily overrepresented. And in 1936, voters in Roosevelt's Democratic coalition of workers, farmers and minorities did not own telephones, did not drive cars and did not subscribe to literary magazines.

- The respondents were self-selected; ballots were returned only by those who cared enough to do so (Campbell, 2020).

Gallup's sampling methods in 1948 were much more reliable, but Gallup made two crucial mistakes:

- The organization stopped polling too soon. In the last six weeks of an election, voters can change their minds.
- Gallup assumed that "undecided" respondents could be split between the two candidates because they were, after all, undecided. But voters who report themselves as "undecided" often have strong leanings one way or the other (Campbell, 2020).

Organizations that conduct surveys today remain undaunted if more cautious, and the poll story is a staple of the election season. News organizations also use survey research methods to gather information and opinions on the issues of the day, a practice described by Philip Meyer (1991) as "precision journalism."

The problem is, public opinion polls in elections continue to miss the mark, including the 2020 presidential election (Clinton, 2021). As the November 2023 election for Kentucky's governor approached, the prevailing view expressed in the Commonwealth's leading newspaper, the Louisville Courier Journal, was "new poll has Andy Beshear, Daniel Cameron tied," both with 47% of the vote (Aulbach, 2023). That was quite a shift, as the same polling outfit, Emerson College Polling, a month earlier had Beshear leading by 16 percentage points. As this was a nationally watched race, other publications echoed the new view of a "dead heat."

Election Day results, however, showed Beshear winning handily (52.5% to 47.5%) with a 5-percentage-point margin. So was the latest poll "wrong"? It had a margin of error of plus or minus 3 percentage points, which is considered highly reliable. If Beshear was polling at 47% at the time, then his Election Day total could have been as high as 50% with a win or as low as 44% in a loss. The charge has been made that the polls sometimes drive events. In the Kentucky case, the news media's playing up a close race was good for business—and voter turnout.

But was this the case, as we warned in **Core Principle No. 4,** of the news media "getting played"? Hard to tell, but one thing is for sure, journalists—and citizens—should read political polls with a healthy dose of skepticism.

The notion that polls can drive events is nothing new. More than 25 years ago the focus was on the impeachment and Senate trial of President Bill Clinton, a Democrat. Polls conducted in December 1998 through February 1999 by The New York Times and CBS News were typical of many surveys concerning the president's problems. Clinton's approval ratings reached a high of 72% in late December 1998. At the same time, 60% of respondents said the vote by House Republicans to impeach Clinton was not impartial. Clinton was acquitted on Feb. 12, 1999 (Kagay, 1999).

The president's high approval ratings during the impeachment process were cited in the press as a strong influence on the Senate leadership to seek an exit strategy. Did opinion polls influence the Senate's outcome? Kagay (1999, 462) wrote that "public sentiments surely acted as a brake on some members of Congress," leading several Republican senators to defect and allowing all 45 Democratic senators to stay the course.

The key takeaway wasn't Clinton's guilt or innocence but rather how Republicans were going to deal with poll results. These polls took on the qualities of self-fulfilling prophecies.

Editors need to slow down when reading stories about survey results.

Some Things to Consider About Polls

The source. Large newspapers and magazines often conduct surveys in partnership with academic institutions. Sometimes print media outlets and broadcast outlets will form alliances. This is necessary because a well-conducted poll is expensive.

Editors should make sure that the participants in the survey and the poll's sponsors are included with the results. Sometimes this is done as part of the graphics package. PBS partners with NPR and the Marist Institute for Public Opinion. For a story posted Jan. 19, 2021, on the PBS website, the editors added this paragraph:

> "PBS NewsHour," NPR and Marist Poll conducted a survey Aug. 29 – Sept. 1 that polled 1,236 U.S. adults (margin of error of 4.1 percentage points), 1,151 registered voters (margin of error of 4.3 percentage points), 697 adults working for pay (margin of error of 5.5 percentage points) and 261 adults working for pay who changed jobs (margin of error of 9.0 percentage points). (Montanaro, 2021, Jan. 19)

Be careful of polls conducted for industry groups, political parties or individual candidates. If the story is about research into road wear, and the research is paid for by Citizens for Better Roads, that fact should be reported. If Citizens for Better Roads is a coalition of paving companies, that should be reported, too. Know the people you are dealing with.

The sample. Survey research relies on sampling to make its methods affordable. Researchers interview a manageable number of people, then apply the results to the population at large. In the "PBS NewsHour"/NPR/Marist poll mentioned above, the researchers interviewed 1,236 U.S. adults. While it might seem risky to let those people speak for the adult population of the United States, 1,236 is a large sample, statistically speaking.

If you ask 10 people which candidate they will vote for, those 10 probably don't represent the views of the millions of Americans of voting age. The odds of getting it wrong shrink dramatically as the sample size increases.

Researchers will increase the reliability of a survey by using a "systematic" or "stratified" sample. They will divide respondents by gender, marital status, age, income, education and party affiliation, then choose randomly from within those groups in proportion to the population as a whole. The results also can be reported by demographic group where comparisons are meaningful. In the "PBS NewsHour"/NPR/Marist poll mentioned above, researchers divided responses by Democrats, Republicans and Independents, and by college graduates and nongraduates. Another key factor is whether or not you are surveying "likely voters," people who have a history of going to the polls.

Margin of error. Even using a large sample, a survey can produce the wrong conclusions. Researchers know how to calculate the likelihood of being wrong as a statistical probability. For opinion surveys, the "margin of error" is stated as plus or minus percentage points. A typical figure for a political poll is plus or minus 4 percentage points. When the results are conclusive, the margin of error is not significant. But let's say a poll finds that one candidate is leading another 52% to 48%, with a margin of error of plus or minus 4. The result has to be interpreted as a virtual tie.

Note that in the "PBS NewsHour"/NPR/Marist poll, the margin of error increased as the sample size got smaller, from 4.1 percentage points for the largest sample to a whopping 9.0 percentage points for the smallest sample of 261 respondents.

A scientific study will report a "confidence level," the probability that the results are due to chance rather than a real effect. The confidence level is stated as a decimal, such as .95, meaning the result could be expected happen by chance only five out of 100 times. In the social sciences, studies witn a confidence level of equal to or greater than .95 are considered "statistically significant," and the results are considered valid.

Healthy Skepticism

Victor Cohn, in his book "News and Numbers," says reporters and editors must ask questions about statistical stories (Cohn et al., 2012). The two questions he suggests are "How do you know?" and "Have you done a study?" The first question concerns the methods by which reporters come to their conclusions. The second asks if that method follows the rules of a formal study, including scientific sampling, pretesting of questions and proper statistical analysis.

Other questions always worth asking: "Compared to what?" "Have other studies been done and are the results consistent?" and "Have the results changed over time?"

If editors maintain a healthy skepticism, questions will come to mind as they read the statistical story. An editor should never be afraid to ask such questions of reporters and other editors.

Checking the Numbers

Here are a few notes to help you edit statistical stories (be sure to use your calculator):

- To **figure a percent**, divide the small number by the larger and multiply by 100. For instance, to find what percent 15 is of 60, divide 15 by 60 to get .25, then multiply by 100 to get 25%.
- When **calculating percentage of increase or decrease**, remember it's always difference/original. So moving from 1 to 2 is a 100% increase (1/1), or you can say it doubled. Dropping from 2 to 1 is a 50% decrease (1/2), or you can say cut in half. Remember to include the numbers as well as the percentages.
- Got it? Now try the next example. Remember, to figure the percent of change between two numbers, find the difference between the two numbers and divide by the original. So what would be the percentage of increase if the numbers moved to 6 from 4? Answer: The difference between the numbers is 2. Because you started with 4, it is the original number, so 2 divided by 4 equals .5. Multiply by 100 and you have an increase of 50%.

- Often you'll see the phrasing **"one out of 80"** or words to that effect. To figure this out, divide the larger number by the smaller number. For 15 out of 60, divide 60 by 15 to get 4; 15 out of 60 can be stated as one out of four.
- Beware of the difference in **"five times more than"** and **"five times as much."** For example, if a building is worth $10,000 and you paid five times "more than" it's worth, you paid $60,000, (the $10,000 plus five times $10,000). If a building is worth $10,000 and you paid five times "as much as" it's worth, you paid $50,000.
- In stating an increase, use phrasing such as "the sales tax increased **to 6% from 1%."** The phrasing "from 1% to 6%" might be misinterpreted as anywhere between 1% and 6%. Likewise for a decrease: **to 1% from 6%.**
- Beware of the **phrasings "more than" and "less than."** Check them out. For instance, let's say a story claims, "More than 17% said they preferred chocolate chips." You work out the arithmetic and get .1699999. That figure would round off to .17, but it is not "more than" 17%. You can state it simply as "a total of 17%."
- The percent of increase often can be **more than 100%.** If the hotel tax goes to $9 from $3, then the difference between the numbers is 6; the original number is 3, so divide 6 by 3 to get 2.00. Multiply by 100 to get **an increase of 200%.**
- For a decrease, it works the same. If the number of doctors in a county goes to 10 from 20, the difference is 10. Divide by 20, the original number, to get .50 or **a 50% decrease.**
- A breakdown of percentages should **add up to 100**. If not, check the original figures to find the mistake. Don't guess! A number could be wrong or a category could be missing.

If you calculate a group of percentages, watch out for **rounding errors**. First you'll decide on how many decimal places you'll want to report. For most purposes, one decimal place is usually enough. Second, follow the rule of rounding upward from 5 or more. Let's say you figure percentages and get these three numbers: .45455, .36364 and .18182. You round them off and multiply by 100 to get these percentages: 45.5, 36.4 and 18.2. You add them up and get 100.1%. To fix this problem, you could adjust one or two of the numbers. If the difference from 100% is large, more than 1%, then you might consider carrying the percentages out to another decimal place. Some publications simply report that the percentages add up to **more than 100 "due to rounding errors."**

- Be aware of the difference between a **"10% increase"** and **"an increase of 10 percentage points."** If government spending for space programs increases to 20% of the budget from 10%, that's an increase of "10 percentage points," or a "100% increase."

When numbers are presented visually, editors can choose from a menu of information graphics.

Information Graphics

An information graphic is any visual representation of information. This broad definition includes tables, charts, pictographs, "how-to" graphics describing a process and maps with data. A well-done information graphic allows readers to make visual comparisons and to interpret differences in numbers in meaningful ways. The best graphics present more than one variable, such as oil production over time by country.

In its simplest form, the information graphic contains four parts: the **headline,** the **chatter** explaining the graphic, the **body** of the graphic, and the **source and credit lines** (Figure 2.4.2). Editors should read graphics like any piece of copy, checking for inconsistencies, misspellings and factual errors.

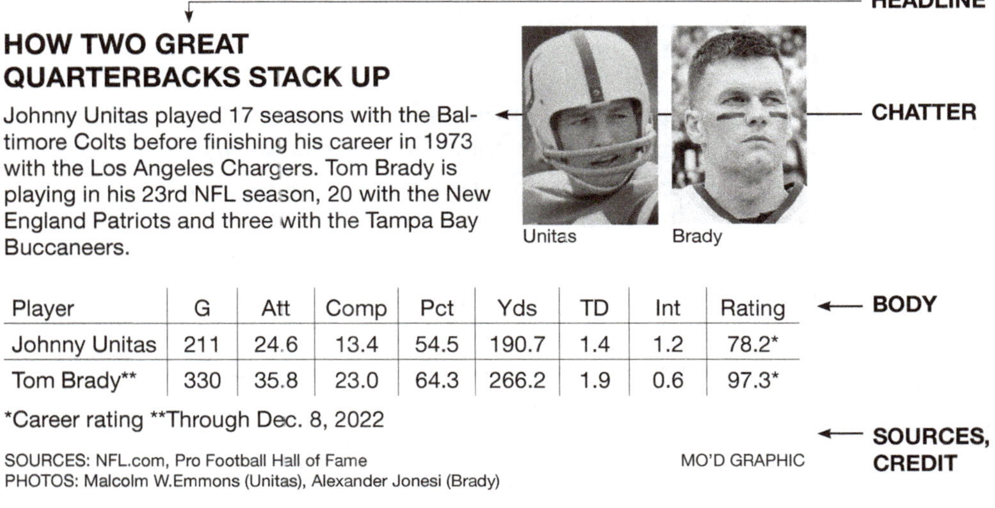

Player	G	Att	Comp	Pct	Yds	TD	Int	Rating
Johnny Unitas	211	24.6	13.4	54.5	190.7	1.4	1.2	78.2*
Tom Brady**	330	35.8	23.0	64.3	266.2	1.9	0.6	97.3*

*Career rating **Through Dec. 8, 2022

SOURCES: NFL.com, Pro Football Hall of Fame
PHOTOS: Malcolm W.Emmons (Unitas), Alexander Jonesi (Brady)

FIGURE 2.4.2   An information graphic contains four parts: the headline, the chatter explaining the graphic, the body of the graphic, and the source and credit lines. Brady retired in February 2023.

Tables

A table (Figure 2.4.3) is the simplest information graphic, one that editors or reporters may be called upon to produce. It lists figures by categories in columns and rows, allowing the reader to make comparisons. Tables can be built using the newspaper or magazine's text editing system without resorting to special graphics software.

EDUCATIONAL ATTAINMENT

2021 American Community Survey 1-Year Estimates

Measure	Kentucky	Virginia	U.S.
High School or equivalent degree	32.7%	23.9%	26.3%
Some college, no degree	19.3%	18.0%	19.3%
Associate's degree	9.0%	7.7%	8.8%
Bachelor's degree	15.9%	23.5%	21.2%
Graduate or professional degree	11.1%	18.3%	13.8%
Other	12%	8.6%	10.6%

SOURCE: U.S. Census Bureau   MO'D GRAPHIC

FIGURE 2.4.3   A table is the simplest information graphic. Editors or reporters might be called upon to produce tables.

Here are four reasons tables are the best choice for an information graphic. Use tables when …

- **the range of numbers would make another type of chart impractical**. For example, a series of numbers that begins with 5 and ends with 5 million could not be represented in a meaningful way with a bar chart or line chart.
- **a plotted chart turns out to be a tangled mess.** Often this is related to information overload, and space may be saved by setting numbers in type as a table.
- **the exact numbers are important**. In Figure 2.4.2, the exact percentages are not critical, but they do provide a fine level of detail.
- **the numbers do not represent the same thing**—the "apples and oranges" situation. Figure 2.4.3 presents various levels of education.

Make sure the numbers are aligned correctly. Note in Figure 2.4.3, percentages align right, meaning the ones and 10s are aligned in columns. For dollar amounts, align the numbers on the decimal point.

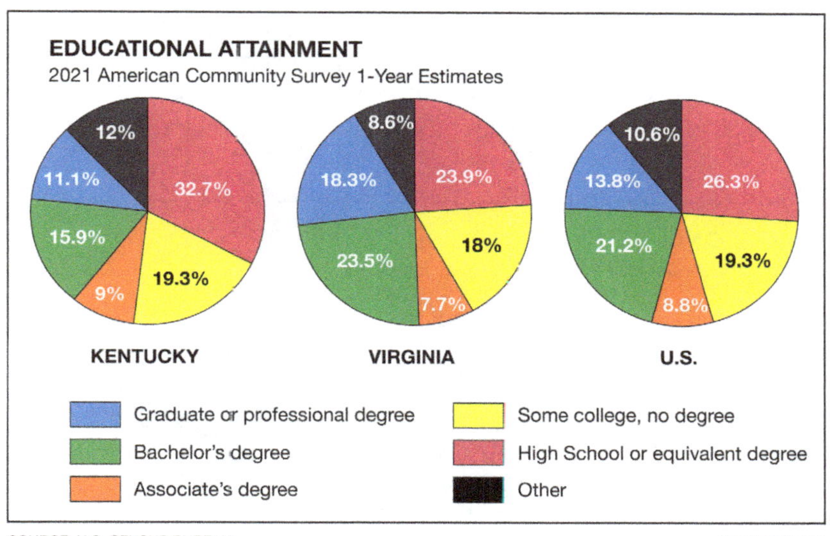

FIGURE 2.4.4   A pie chart, like other types of charts, is valuable for providing a visual representation of data.

Pie Charts

The first and most important rule for using a pie chart is that each pie must represent 100% of the data. In Figure 2.4.4, the educational levels are expressed in percent, but numbers could be used if segments still include all the categories. A pie chart, like other types of charts, is valuable for providing a visual representation of data. But note how this pie chart requires more work of the reader than did the simple table.

Look for these problems with pie charts:

- **Segments too numerous or extremely small.** One common guideline is that a pie chart should be limited to a maximum of seven segments. In Figure 2.4.4 you'll see six segments. The graphic remains readable because of the limited number of slices. When the slices become very small and numerous, consider combining categories.
- **Segments don't match the data.** When editing pie charts, try to gauge the proportion of each slice with its percentage. It's not as hard as you might think. In Figure 2.4.4, the slices for "high school or equivalent degree" are about a third for Kentucky and about a fourth for Virginia and the United States. Other slices can be compared according to similarity. The slices for "some college no degree" are all about 18%, so they should be similar.

- **Segments distorted by perspective.** Graphic artists use foreshortening to give charts a 3D quality. In Figure 2.4.5, perspective has been applied to the education chart. While a chart using perspective can be eye-catching, always ask, Do the segments maintain the proper proportions? The visual honesty of a chart should not be sacrificed for attractiveness.

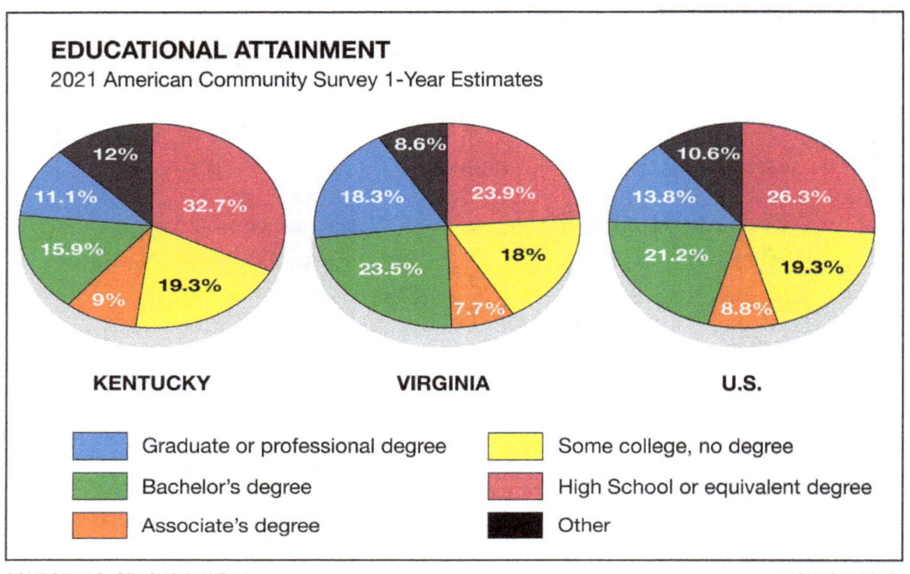

FIGURE 2.4.5   While a chart using perspective can be eye-catching, do the segments maintain the proper proportions? The visual honesty of a chart should not be sacrificed for attractiveness.

Bar Charts

Use bar charts to show comparisons between individual numbers within a series. Bar charts can be used when some numbers are missing or when the time periods are irregular. Figure 2.4.6 uses a bar chart to compare educational attainment by state. This chart provides a visual comparison that is easier to digest.

When many data points are available, the bar chart may become impractical, and a line chart can be used.

Line Charts

Line charts also are known as fever charts or trend charts. Use them when the data are charted over a period of time. The emphasis is on movement rather than the individual numbers. For an issue so often in the news—climate change—there's a vast set of examples of line charts on the Environmental

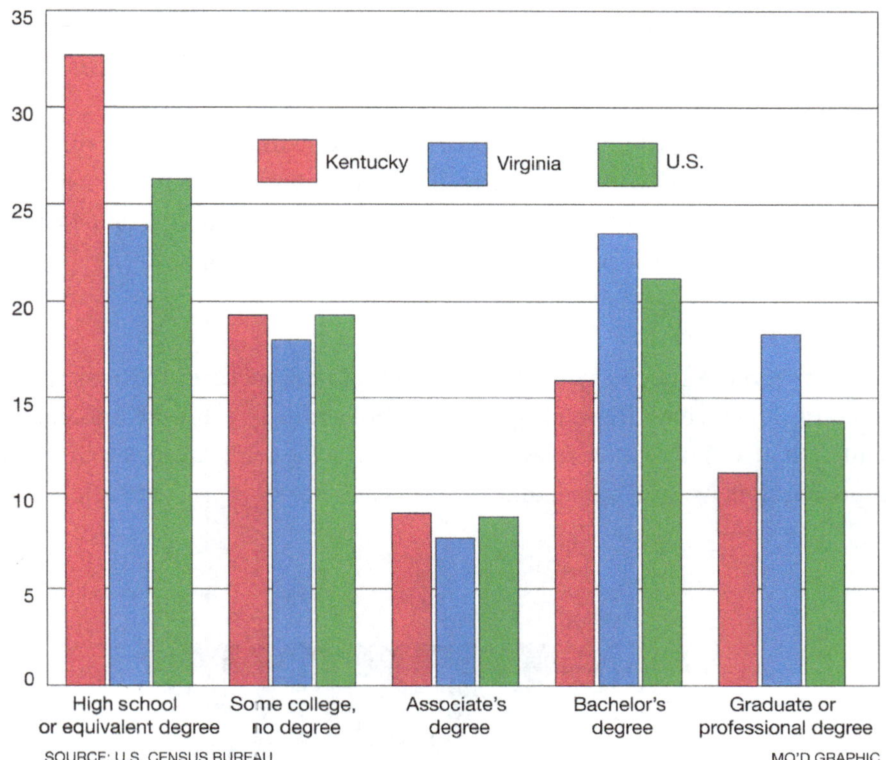

FIGURE 2.4.6   Use bar charts to show comparisons between individual numbers within a series. Bar charts can be used when some numbers are missing or when the time periods are irregular.

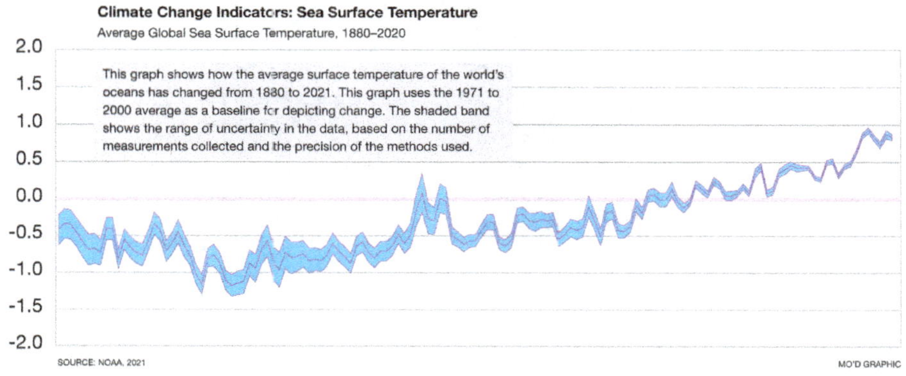

FIGURE 2.4.7   Line charts also are known as fever charts or trend charts. Use them when the data points are charted over time.

Protection Agency's government website (EPA, 2023). Sometimes a line chart can show projected data. Line charts are especially good for showing seasonal changes or for comparing trends over the same time periods, as Figure 2.4.7 does.

Avoid making too many comparisons on one line chart, the "spaghetti bowl" syndrome. As with bar charts, line charts are not practical when the data jumps from a small amount to a huge amount. Finally, line charts aren't valuable if they show just random variation or no variation.

Pictographs

A pictograph is a special type of bar chart that uses pictures to dress up statistical information. The pictograph symbol should be simple and easy to identify. It also should have relevance to the data. Figure 2.4.8, a pictograph for oil production, uses oil barrel images with each barrel representing a million

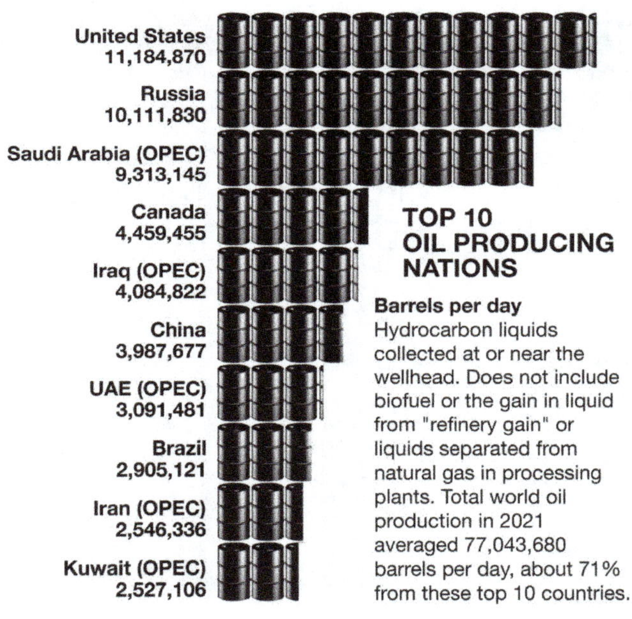

FIGURE 2.4.8   A pictograph is a special type of bar chart that uses pictures to dress up statistics. The pictograph symbol should be simple and easy to identify. It also should have relevance to the data.

barrels per day. Because comparisons may be more difficult to make visually than with a plain bar chart, numbers often are included.

Edward Tufte (1983) cautions against using "non-data ink" in graphics merely to decorate them visually. At its worst, this sort of decoration devolves into what Tufte calls "chart junk."

"How-to" Graphics

"How-to" graphics, or process graphics, use pictures and diagrams to describe a process or show how something works or how something is done. Often these involve "cutaway" drawings to reveal the inner parts of an object. Figure 2.4.9 shows a complex process graphic rendered in a computer drawing program.

An editor who is proofing a process graphic must pay attention to visual detail. Here's an example: Many newspapers have used graphic "depth charts" for previewing important sporting events. These charts often were done as miniature playing fields with miniature players representing the two teams.

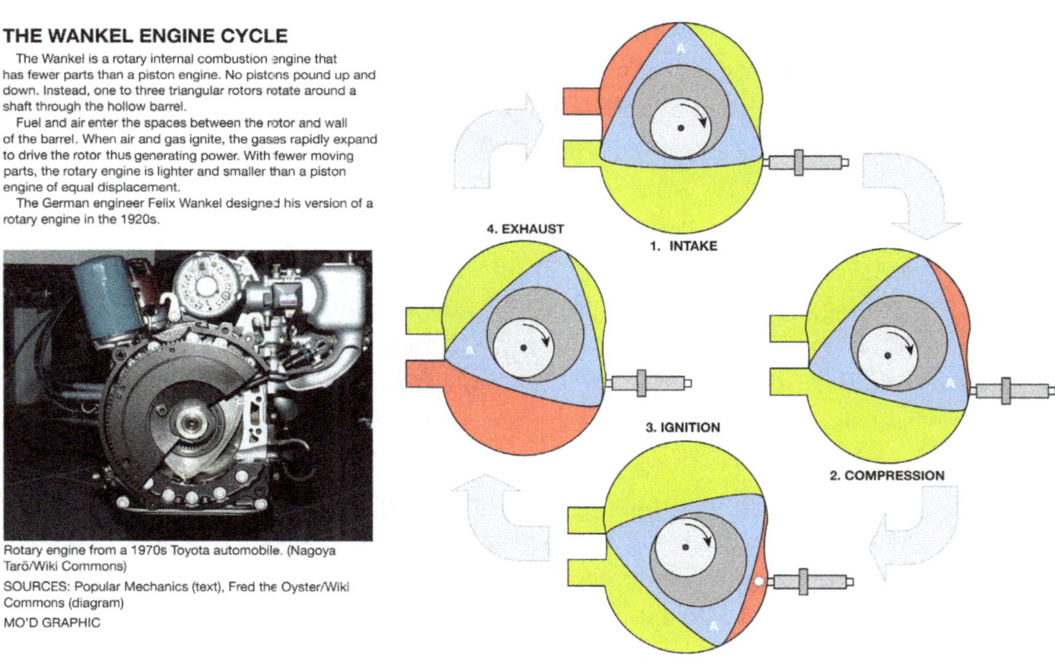

Rotary engine from a 1970s Toyota automobile. (Nagoya Tarō/Wiki Commons)

SOURCES: Popular Mechanics (text), Fred the Oyster/Wiki Commons (diagram)

MO'D GRAPHIC

FIGURE 2.4.9   Process or "how-to" graphics use pictures and diagrams to show how something works or how something is done.

Graphic artists produce these charts by drawing one figure, say, a baseball player in fielding position, then copying and pasting it to fill in all the positions. But what if some of the players are left-handed? What if some of them are Black? When the chart goes out to thousands of readers, you can be sure more than one will notice these mistakes—and let you know about it.

Maps

In his book "Maps With the News," Mark Monmonier (1989) wrote that The Times of London began using a daily weather map in 1875 with the New York Herald following a year later. When USA Today debuted in 1982, its full-page weather map set a new standard and received the highest compliment—it seemed to be copied everywhere.

The introduction of computer graphics into the newsroom eased the way for increased use of maps, for two reasons: First, maps, once drawn, can be stored electronically and easily altered to serve new stories. Second, maps can be downloaded from graphic services and altered to fit a publication's style for typography, color and texture.

The Persian Gulf War of 1990–91 produced an explosion of maps, along with other information graphics, because access to the battle zone was tightly controlled by the Pentagon and because many readers were unfamiliar with the Middle East. In an informal analysis of 50 or so newspapers, we found that the same base maps, weapons graphics and charts appeared in almost all the papers. They were downloading from the same graphic services, mainly the AP. But the newspapers varied in how they recombined the images, altered the typography and mixed in color. More than 30 years later, with the Hamas-Israel war of 2023, readers and viewers are seeing Middle East maps again in print, on network and cable television, on news websites, and on social media.

Maps range from small "locator" maps (Figure 2.4.10) to full-pagers that include demographic data or show the progress of a news event. Adding data to a map can result in a satisfying graphic that allows readers to make comparisons at the macro and micro levels. Figure 2.4.11 shows a map of the United States overlaid with data about flood disasters. Readers taking the macro view can quickly see areas prone to flood disasters. On the micro level, readers can pick out individual states. The federal government keeps track of billion-dollar disasters related to weather and climate. It identifies sites with eight different

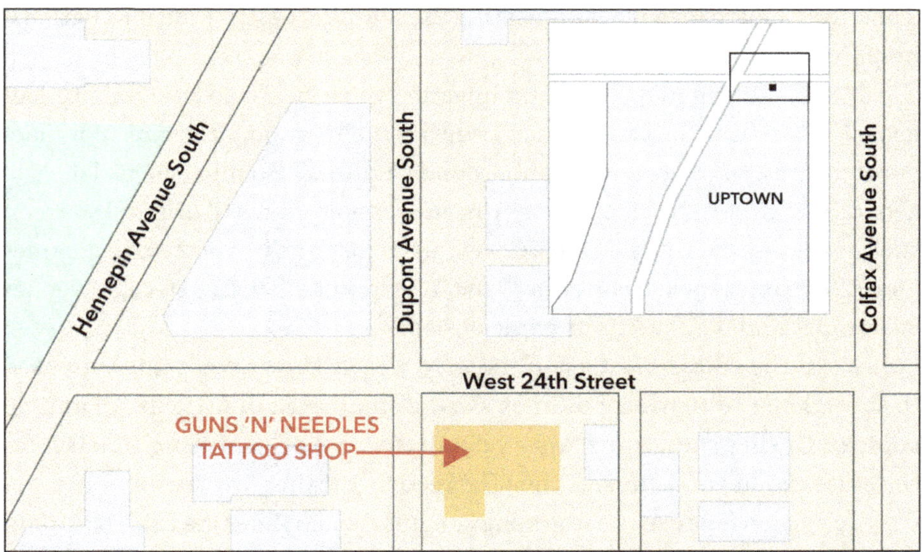

FIGURE 2.4.10   A small locator map helps readers picture the location. Often they are inset into a map of a larger area for context.

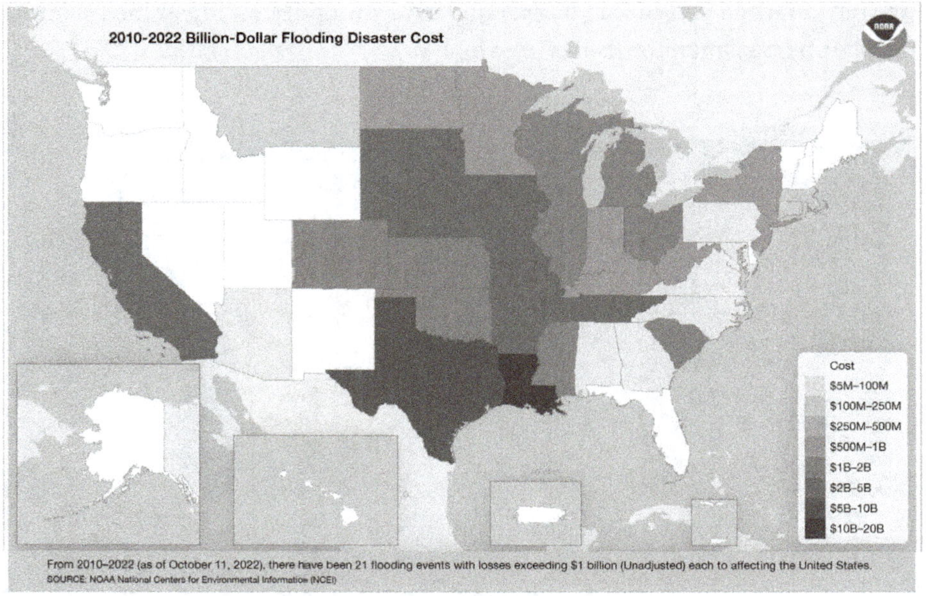

FIGURE 2.4.11   Adding data to a map can result in a satisfying graphic that allows readers to make comparisons at the macro and micro levels.

icons, from hail to tornadoes, indicating the source of destruction on a national map (NOAA, 2023).

When editing maps, the first question must be, "Does the map reflect geographic reality?" Savvy editors know their cities and often can spot inaccurately drawn streets and neighborhoods. Editors also must check labels of geographic landmarks. Sometimes this means going back to original sources, such as the atlas or Google Maps. Other questions to ask: "Are the street names and other names spelled correctly?" and "Are streets labeled as streets, avenues as avenues and boulevards as boulevards?"

Next, the editor must ask if the map clearly shows what it is supposed to show. Locator maps sometimes show a small area in little detail and no context. Or they show unnecessary detail that can be confusing. The test for the editor is, "If I'm confused, then the reader certainly will be."

Television newscasts use graphics regularly, and the same rules of careful editing apply on the screen, too. See if you can spot the embarrassing mistake on this map from Nov. 19, 2020, on Fox News (Figure 2.4.12).

A picture may be worth a thousand words, but the few words in a graphic need to be sweated letter by letter. We know statistics can be daunting, and this may be one chapter you'll need to read again and again. But the studying will pay off when you catch an error and save your publication or media outlet from embarrassment or loss of credibility.

FIGURE 2.4.12   The same rules of careful editing apply on the screen, too. See if you can spot the embarrassing mistake on this map from Nov. 19, 2020, on Fox News.

HOMEWORK

Try these exercises at home to explore how statistics and graphics are used in today's media.

Assignment No. 1

Sports and business reporting are two areas where statistics appear in many stories. Find a source such as the business or sports section of a newspaper like The New York Times, or a television channel like ESPN or Fox Business. You can access these media through their websites. Look at two or three stories, text or video. How are statistics used in the reports? If you look at video, pay special attention to graphics and "the crawl"—the text that scrolls across the bottom of the screen.

Assignment No. 2

For all sorts of stories using statistics, visit the website **projects.fivethirtyeight. com/polls**. This website analyzes opinion polls and grades their accuracy based on how close the poll came to predicting actual results. In the search box, type in NPR to access the ratings for the PBS/NPR/Marist poll cited in this chapter. How accurate was this poll in predicting the latest national elections? Now search for Gallup. Do the accuracy ratings surprise you? Why or why not?

Assignment No. 3

Go to The New York Times website and explore its use of graphics. You can find the latest stories using graphics at **www.nytimes.com/spotlight/graphics**. What types of graphics does the Times use? Look for interactive graphics, such as the fire tracker map (www.nytimes.com/interactive/2022/us/fire-tracker-maps.html). Is the interactive map effective for telling the story?

Assignment No. 4

This chapter presents three graphics using data on educational attainment for Kentucky, Virginia and the United States as a whole: a table, a bar chart and pie charts. Decide which one is most effective and explain your choice. Was your choice based on visual interest, accuracy or ease of understanding the numbers?

REFERENCES

Aulbach, L. (2023, November 3). With Kentucky governor election days away, new poll has Andy Beshear, Daniel Cameron tied. *Louisville Courier Journal.*

Campbell, W. J. (2020). *Lost in a Gallup: Polling failure in U.S. presidential elections.* University of California Press. https://doi.org/10.2307/j.ctv153k69w

Clinton, J. (2021, January 11). Polling problems and why we should still trust (some) polls. Vanderbilt Project on Unity & American Democracy. https://www.vanderbilt.edu/unity/2021/01/11/polling-problems-and-why-we-should-still-trust-some-polls/

Cohn, V., Cope, L., & Cohn Runkle, D. (2012). *News & numbers: A writer's guide to statistics* (3rd ed.). Wiley-Blackwell.

Environmental Protection Agency. (2023, September). Climate change indicators in the United States. https://www.epa.gov/climate-indicators

Kagay, M. R. (1999). Presidential address: Public opinion and polling during presidential scandal and impeachment. *Public Opinion Quarterly, 63*(3), 449–463. https://doi.org/10.1086/297734

Meyer, P. (1991). *The new precision journalism.* Indiana University Press.

Monmonier, M. (1989). *Maps with the news: The development of American journalistic cartography.* University of Chicago Press.

NOAA National Centers for Environmental Information (NCEI). (2023). *U.S. 2023 billion-dollar weather and climate disasters.* https://www.ncei.noaa.gov/access/billions/, DOI: 10.25921/stkw-7w73

Squire, P. (1988). Why the 1936 *Literary Digest* poll failed. *Public Opinion Quarterly, 52*(1), 125–133. https://doi.org/10.1086/269085

3iap (2023). Americans struggle with graphs. 3iap.com. https://3iap.com/numeracy-and-data-literacy-in-the-united-states-7b1w9J_wRjqyzqo3WDLTdA/

Tufte, E. R. (1983). *The visual display of quantitative information.* Graphics Press.

FURTHER READING, RESOURCES

Evon, D. (2020, November 20). Did Fox News map mislabel Michigan as Canada? Snopes. https://www.snopes.com/fact-check/fox-news-michigan-canada-map/

Fineman, H., & Klaidman, D. (1999). With foes like these: Clinton's the one in the dock, but he's got the Republicans on the run. Where does the GOP go from here? *Newsweek, 133*(5), 22.

Lusinchi, D. (2012). "President" Landon and the 1936 *Literary Digest* poll: Were automobile and telephone owners to blame? *Social Science History, 36*(1), 23–54. doi:10.1017/S014555320001035X

Lusinchi, D. (2018). "The Great Fiasco" of the 1948 presidential election polls: Status recognition and norms conflict in social science. *Annals of Science, 75*(2), 120–144. https://doi.org/10.1080/00033790.2018.1466194

Sonner, M. W., & Wilcox, C. (1999). Forgiving and forgetting: Public support for Bill Clinton during the Lewinsky scandal. *PS: Political Science & Politics, 32*(3), 554–557. https://doi.org/10.1017/S1049096500049982

Thomas, E. (1999). Why Clinton won: What saved the president at trial? An intriguing mix of polls, senatorial pride and, as usual, the excesses of his enemies: The inside story of Clinton's acquittal. *Newsweek, 133*(8), 24.

GET ME A QUOTE!

KEY POINTS IN THIS CHAPTER

1. Quotes and their electronic counterpart, sound bites, are indispensable to news stories because they lend authority and connect readers and viewers with the speakers.

2. Quotes should be strong and advance the story. Quotes from news releases are suspect, and video news releases (VNR) should be used cautiously. Weak quotes are often used out of desperation.

3. Strong quotes arise when someone important says something newsworthy, when someone says something truly new or when someone expresses something with a special flair.

4. A quote is enclosed in quote marks and is attributed to a speaker. What appears within the quote marks should be considered the exact words of the speaker, so tread carefully in your editing. And never add quote marks to copy even if it looks like a quote.

5. Use snippets, ellipses and brackets to save quotes that have value but are wordy or that contain irrelevant material. When that proves awkward or

impractical, remove the quote marks and paraphrase. Delete the quote when it is dumb or libelous.

6. When a quote contains profanity, you must know the policies of your news organization. Times have changed since 1972, when George Carlin performed his routine "Seven Words You Can Never Say on Television"—and was arrested on disorderly conduct charges. But make sure profanity in a story is necessary for telling the news.

> " *By necessity, by proclivity and by delight, we all quote. … In fact it is as difficult to appropriate the thoughts of others as it is to invent."*
>
> —Ralph Waldo Emerson

> " *I never said most of the things I said."*
>
> —Yogi Berra

Take note of the title for this chapter: "Get Me a Quote!" Those who have spent any time in a daily newspaper newsroom probably have heard that order barked out more than once by an editor seeking to liven up a story. Those editors agree with Emerson, the philosopher and poet, who said we take special delight in hearing directly from other people.

Editors need to take special care when handling quotations. For the reader, the quote marks signal a speaker's exact words, whether they are exact or not. For many news people, quotes are untouchable, and editing them is considered a grave mistake in some newsrooms. We have seen someone fired for messing with a quote.

When you take your place as an editor, make sure you are aware of your organization's policy on quotes before you do anything. The freelance editor, book editor or newspaper or magazine editor should know the writer's expectations as well. The No. 1 rule: Don't change what's between the quote marks without checking with the writer.

When a news source's words create controversy, they often resort to the charge, "I was misquoted!" That's one more reason for careful editing. Broadcasters, with their time pressures, must be vigilant against what the late CBS anchorman Walter Cronkite called the "malquote." That's a sound bite taken out of context or without explanation of what question the speaker was answering.

So what is a quote? It is:

- any part of the copy that is enclosed in quotation marks
- attributed to a source

This is not a fine distinction. No quote marks? No quote. An editor might choose to remove the quote marks. Then the copy becomes a paraphrase and can be edited as usual.

Because of newsroom policy that discourages editing quotes, many editors feel uncomfortable doing anything when they see quote marks. But many stories can be improved when editors read quotations with the same critical eye they use on other copy.

We would be naïve to think that what reporters present as quotes are always the exact words of the speaker. Some reporters will read back from their notes to their sources to confirm quotations. Other reporters will write their best representation of what a speaker said. The exact words of the speaker are filtered by the reporter's sense of hearing, note-taking ability, cellphone recording quality, attention to detail, news judgment, typing skills and language skills. Even so, the editor must defer to the writer when handling quotes.

What the editor does with a quote requires good judgment and a thorough understanding of the story. For attribution use "said," not loaded words like "admitted" or "claimed." Feature writers may use "says."

Quotes: The Few, the Strong

- Quotes should be strong.
- Quotes should advance the story.
- Quotes should not repeat what's in the paragraphs preceding them.
- Quotes should be consistent with the content of the story.

As editors, you need to understand how quotes get into a story before making changes.

The Origins of Weak Quotes

Publicists love quotes. Smart publicists use long quotes in their press releases because they know writers and editors are hesitant to dig in and cut quotes. In targeting broadcasters, publicists know the value of actualities, recorded sound bites that the newscaster can insert into the broadcast. Television producers see more and more "video news releases" with ready-made "interviews" that come from the public relations arms of major corporations. Researchers for the Center for Media and Democracy found that many news producers succumbed to the temptation to use these interviews as if they were real news without disclosing the source (Farsetta & Price, 2012).

Although quotes in news releases often are attributed to people in high positions, the quotes likely were written by the publicist and approved by the person "quoted." The quotes become their words. The same goes for recorded actualities; the questions asked offer no surprises to the interviewee and result in scripted responses. For these reasons, sometimes quotes from press releases, typed or taped, are empty of real news value.

Lazy writers love quotes. A story filled with quotes requires less thinking on the part of the writer. Some reporters practice "tape-recorder journalism." By letting the audio recorder run and by using the quotes at length, the writer lets the story write itself. The reporter becomes a stenographer rather than a reporter. This often results in meaningless and repetitive quotes, or paragraph after paragraph of unbroken quotes.

Quotes are used in desperation. Some writers will use a quote because they got it right. It might not say much, but it's right. Writers often are under pressure to produce quotes in the story. The days of news editors barking, "Get me a quote!" are not dead. For the same reasons, short, nearly meaningless sound bites sometimes show up in TV news reports.

The Indispensable Quote

Quotes are considered mandatory in news stories of any length. Here's why:

Quotes lend authority. The quote marks say to the reader, "Here are the exact words." Along with this sense of authority comes the appearance of accuracy, even though the reporter might not get all the words right.

Quotes give visual or audio relief. Just as a long, unbroken series of quotes can be boring, so can the long story unrelieved by quotes. In printed matter, quotes relieve grayness in copy. A full quote should begin with a new paragraph. In one newswriting formula, the first paragraph is the lede, the second paragraph sets up a quote and the third paragraph delivers.

In broadcasting, too, quotes provided welcome relief from news being read as voice-overs by reporters. The popularity of the sound bite comes in part from this ability to add variety.

Quotes draw in readers. Quotes make the story feel more human; they put the reader in touch with the speaker. Quotes are an excellent way to characterize a subject and are much better than a description.

When to Quote

Not all quotes are created equal. A quote usually is worth keeping if:

Someone important says something newsworthy. The emphasis is on **who and what**. The Washington Post offered this quote from Justice Ketanji Brown Jackson at a celebration of her investiture as the Supreme Court's first Black female member: "I have a seat at the table now," she said at the Library of Congress event. "And I'm ready to work" (Barnes & Marimow, 2022).

Someone says something truly new. Often the quote will be a straightforward, newsworthy statement. The emphasis is on **what** is said.

News conferences often produce routine material not worth quoting. Such is not the case when the news conference is used to announce a rare occurrence with real news value. When Michael Jordan retired from basketball for good in 2003, his news conference was totally predictable, and the conference went as expected. Nevertheless, Jordan's words were quoted at length in newspapers and magazines and on radio and television. Even National Public Radio used actualities of Jordan's news conference on its news show "All Things Considered" (Goldman, 2003). The unique quality of the event made the routine news conference newsworthy.

Someone says something with a special flair. When a source has a way with words, good quotes result. Hall of Fame catcher Yogi Berra was famous for saying things such as, "When you come to a fork in the road, take it."

Often such a quote brings out the human dimension of an otherwise complicated or dull story. The emphasis is on **how** someone speaks.

In its Dec. 29, 2022, edition, the Star Tribune of Minneapolis ran a front-page story about efforts in Colorado to fix a broken juvenile justice system. The story began dramatically with teenage boys, wearing ankle monitors listening to a mother, Sharletta Evans, talk about losing her son Casson in a gang crossfire when the boy was 3. The first two paragraphs set up a dramatic quote:

> *"Tonight, the mother in me is rising up, because I hear too many of you making excuses," Evans said. "You have to understand that children are dying, that my beautiful baby boy is never coming back and your life is at risk because of your choices." (Sawyer & Serres, 2022)*

In its print edition, the Star Tribune ran Evans' quote highlighted in large type as a "pull quote" (Figure 2.5.1). Such is the power of a well-spoken quote.

JUVENILE INJUSTICE • A SPECIAL REPORT

LAYING DOWN THE LAW FOR TROUBLED YOUTH

Colorado diverts youths from detention — and new crimes

Last in an occasional series by CHRIS SERRES, LIZ SAWYER and MARYJO WEBSTER • Photos by JERRY HOLT • Star Tribune

DENVER

Six teenage boys dressed in hoodies and wearing ankle monitors sat in silence as they passed around a photograph of a 3-year-old named Casson, who was killed in the crossfire of a gang shootout 27 years ago.

The photo of the toddler made its way back to the boy's mother, Sharletta Evans. She described the final, agonizing moments of Casson's life, of crying out for help as she cradled her bleeding son in her arms.

"Tonight, the mother in me is rising up, because I hear too many of you making excuses," Evans said. "You have to understand that children are dying, that my beautiful baby boy is never coming back and your life is at risk because of your choices."

"You have to understand that children are dying, that my beautiful baby boy is never coming back and your life is at risk because of your choices."

Sharletta Evans, speaking to troubled teens about her son Casson. He was killed at age 3 in the crossfire of a gang shooting.

FIGURE 2.5.1   When the speaker has a unique way of expressing herself, the quote can be worthy of larger display, as in this quote highlighted in large type from a mother who lost her child to gun violence.

The Importance of Quote Marks

Words contained within quote marks have special status, so be careful.

Never add quote marks. In editing quotes, the editor has one hard-and-fast rule that must never be violated: Don't add quote marks to something just because it sounds like a quote. Here's an example from the days in Iraq before the fall of Saddam Hussein:

Baghdad will fire on warplanes violating Iraqi airspace,
Vice President Taha Yassin Ramadan said.

The novice might make it:

"Baghdad will fire on warplanes violating Iraqi airspace,"
Vice President Taha Yassin Ramadan said. (NO!)

Even if the sentence is essentially what Ramadan had said, placing it in quote marks allows the charge to be made that the vice president wasn't quoted accurately. Sources sometimes make such charges to discredit stories critical of them.

Strategies for Handling Quotes

Some quotes have important or unique thoughts contained in complex, dull paragraphs. Saving a quote means that the editor preserves at least part of what was said in quote marks. Sometimes this means removing material and using the partial quote. Sometimes this means adding explanatory words in brackets.

Here are ways to save quotes:

Use Snippets

A snippet is a partial quote, sometimes as short as one word, as opposed to a full quote. Note that when we say "full quote," we mean a quote that can stand alone as a full sentence.

A full quote can contain more words than it's worth but still have critical language that must be quoted. On Jan. 7, 1999, Chief Justice William Rehnquist of the Supreme Court delivered this oath to members of the U.S. Senate:

> *"Do you solemnly swear that in all things appertaining to the trial of the impeachment of William Jefferson Clinton, president of the United States, now pending, you will do impartial justice according to the Constitution and laws: So help you God?"*

An Associated Press story for afternoon papers of Jan. 7 boiled that down to this:

> *Senators today were taking an oath to "do impartial justice," and Chief Justice William Rehnquist was assuming his role as presiding officer for Clinton's trial on charges of perjury and obstruction of justice. (Margasck, 1999)*

The language "do impartial justice" was considered important because of the political nature of the Clinton impeachment, and in fact, the Senate vote largely followed party lines. The AP writer probably considered the rest of the oath dull and legalistic.

Don't overuse snippets; they can make the reader eye-weary. See below:

Original

Sen. Trent Lott of Mississippi said the best way for senators to remain "cool and calm" would be to "hear each other" and to "talk to each other," adding that the Senate was in "uncharted waters." At the White House, Joe Lockhart, Clinton's press secretary, said the president's lawyers would make a "compelling case" for acquittal.

Edited

Sen. Trent Lott of Mississippi said the best way for senators to remain "cool and calm" would be to hear and talk to each other, adding that the Senate was in "uncharted waters." At the White House, Joe Lockhart, Clinton's press secretary, said the president's lawyers would make a compelling case for acquittal.

Be careful not to introduce an ungrammatical or awkward shift in pronouns when you use a snippet. Look at these sentences:

In a brief statement issued by the association, Lang said he was quitting for health reasons. His doctor "has recommended that I immediately discontinue all stressful activity. Therefore, I hereby resign as president of the Smith Mountain Lake."

Note how the second sentence shifts from third person "his" to first person "I." Here's how we would edit it:

In a brief statement issued by the association, Lang said he was quitting for health reasons. He said his doctor had recommended that he "immediately discontinue all stressful activity."

"Therefore, I hereby resign as president of the Smith Mountain Lake," Lang said.

Take note that the full quote beginning with "therefore" starts a new paragraph. Also take note of how the two paragraphs are punctuated with period and comma inside the end quote marks.

Use Ellipses ...

Ellipses signal that words have been removed from the quotes. A good quote with a stretch of useless or repetitive information in the middle can be shortened with an ellipsis. Be aware, however, that ellipses serve two purposes: to mark where material is missing or to indicate a pause.

Here is a confusing use of ellipses:

> *On the day he stabbed bus driver Luther Crowder, Edmonds said,*
> *"Queen Isabella stomped me with her foot to my mind … there was*
> *no way to base my mentality … no way to survive …"*

In this example, ellipses serve only to draw attention to what's missing. The edited version with just one ellipsis:

> *On the day he stabbed bus driver Luther Crowder, Edmonds said:*
> *"Queen Isabella stomped me with her foot to my mind. There was no*
> *way to base my mentality … no way to survive."*

The best practice would be to discuss the change above with the writer.

An ellipsis is unnecessary at the beginning of the second sentence in the quote below, too.

Original

> *"The safest thing will be to bow out now and let everyone know," said*
> *Bill Houck, vice president in charge of public relations for Festival*
> *Park. "…A lot of people probably put a lot of time into it, and we*
> *know they'd like to be in that water, but it's just too dangerous."*

Edited

> *"The safest thing will be to bow out now and let everyone know," said*
> *Bill Houck, vice president in charge of public relations for Festival*
> *Park. "A lot of people probably put a lot of time into it, and we know*
> *they'd like to be in that water, but it's just too dangerous."*

If you believe that more of a break is needed where the ellipsis was placed in the original, you can start a new paragraph and repeat attribution:

> *"The safest thing will be to bow out now and let everyone know," said*
> *Bill Houck, vice president in charge of public relations for Festival*
> *Park.*
>
> *"A lot of people probably put a lot of time into it," Houck said, "and*
> *we know they'd like to be in that water, but it's just too dangerous."*

Use Brackets

Sometimes one or two words of explanation in brackets or parentheses can save a quote from being meaningless or hard to understand. The most common practice is to use brackets [ ] for adding words to quotes, but some news organizations use parentheses ( ).

Original:

"He is making a mockery of the United States immigration system," the senator said.

Edited:

"[Mayorkas] is making a mockery of the United States immigration system," the senator said.

Notice that the pronoun "he" is not included in the edited version.

Watch the Grammar

It's not fair to hold people to mistakes in grammar; people don't talk as neatly as they write. Mistakes get in the way of what is being said and distract the reader. Rather than quote a grammatical mistake that makes someone look bad, consider just paraphrasing the sentence.

Sometimes grammar has a bearing on the story. For example, consider a story written about a man who wanted to educate his son at home and was being prosecuted under state truancy laws.

Here is one of the few quotes from the story:

"My son won't go to these schools," Hermanstyne said. "They cannot teach him nothing in the sciences."

Should the editor change it to "anything about the sciences"? NO!

The editor checked with the reporter. The reporter said the man used atrocious grammar for two hours. The quote was fair, and because grammar had a bearing on the story, it was left as written.

The AP Stylebook states: "Never alter quotations even to correct minor grammatical errors or word usage" (AP, 242). Know the policy of your organization and proceed with caution!

Phonetic Spelling

When the emphasis is on who is speaking, leave grammar alone. In feature stories about people, quotes often are used to characterize the subject, bad grammar and all. But be careful of phonetic spellings used to convey dialect. Consider this quote:

> *"I'm gonna draw my pay and then I'm takin' me a little vacation," Bonner said.*

Are the phonetic spellings necessary or fair? Many of us drop our g's or say "gonna" instead of "going to." One of our former presidents used to talk about "the zekative branch of gummint," but writers always translated it into "executive" and "government." Writers seem to use dialect only when the speaker is from a rural area. Be fair, and don't perpetuate stereotypes. If this is a one-time quote to characterize the speaker, then the editor can let it pass.

A problem arises when writers aren't consistent with phonetic spellings. Consider this:

> *"I'm gonna draw my pay and then I'm takin' me a little vacation," Bonner said. "Upon my return, my wife and I will look into buying the quaint English Tudor on the hill."*

How do you fix the inconsistency? Bounce it back to the writer for advice on what to do next. One idea is to keep the first sentence and paraphrase the second one or use a snippet.

When a Quote Can't Be Saved

In sizing up a quotation, an editor might decide that the information is valuable but that too much needs to be done to correct problems. In this case, the editor can paraphrase the quote. At other times, the editor may decide to delete the quote.

Paraphrasing

Remember that paraphrasing is not a way to save a quote. The first step is to remove the quote marks. In doing so, the editor is saying, "These are no longer the exact words of the speaker. It is no longer a direct quote." In this regard, paraphrases are sometimes called "indirect quotes." After you remove the quote marks, you can edit the words like any other piece of copy.

Paraphrasing is often the best way to deal with jargon.

Original

"On subsequent investigation of the terrain, CENCOM determined that a vertical insertion of troops would best facilitate success of the planned interdiction," Ridgeman said.

Edited

After mapping out the terrain, the central command decided that using paratroopers would be the best way to make the attack a success, Ridgeman said.

Paraphrasing also is a useful tool when a writer lets quotes run for several paragraphs. After the quote runs for two or three paragraphs, the editor can look for a change of direction or a change of subject, then paraphrase a sentence or two. This adds variety and can supply a valuable transition to the story.

A good paraphrase will maintain the meaning of the quote but not mimic the speaker's exact words. Paraphrasing, then, requires sensitivity to what a speaker means.

Deleting the Quote

If you can't paraphrase the quote, or if it's not worth saving, strike the quote. Anything dumb, wrong, libelous, unnecessary or inconsistent should be cut.

How would you handle this quote?

"We nailed the rapist," an unidentified bystander said. "Now, we just hope some do-gooder judge doesn't let him go."

This quote is libelous because the person arrested in the case is being convicted in print as a rapist—and by an anonymous person. It also expresses an extreme opinion of the court system that might not be fair. The best thing to do would be to delete the quote.

One More Time: Be Careful

Because people don't speak as neatly as they write, virtually every quotation you see published could be said better in a paraphrase. Keep in mind the importance of having quotes and that the editor's first approach is to try to save them.

Your two most common mistakes:

- You'll make too many attempts with ellipses or brackets to save a quote.
- You'll kill a quote worth saving.

Finally, context is sometimes as important as what a person said. Consider this excerpt from a Newsweek story about radio personality Don Imus:

> *Does Imus go too far? "I'm the f---ing I-man!" he explodes. "What do you mean too far! What, are you crazy?"*

The quote above is just as it was written except some of the context has been removed. It makes Imus seem like an egomaniac. But here's the quote as the reporter, Evan Thomas, actually wrote it:

> *Does Imus go too far? "I'm the f---ing I-man!" he explodes, **or pretends to**. "What do you mean too far! What, are you crazy?" (Thomas, 1999)*

The quote as Thomas wrote it takes on a playful nature and tells us much more about the personality of the speaker. Context makes the quotes mean different things.

A Few Words on Profanity

In 1950, the actor Jack Webb created a sensation when he said the word "damn" during an episode of the police drama "Dragnet." Today, profanity is inescapable, on street corners, in television episodes and in the news.

Reporters more and more will find sources who use profanity in answering even routine questions. In the quote above from Don Imus, it's instructive that he dropped the f-bomb without hesitation on a reporter from a national news magazine.

When a reporter runs into a source who swears, the reporter might believe that the profanity must be included if quotes are to be accurate. Then the editor must decide whether to cut out the swearing or leave it in. How does an editor decide?

Know the Publication

In deciding about profanity, the editor must respect the news organization's policy. Most newspapers see themselves as family publications and forbid most profanity.

When a newsmaker utters a profanity that is important to the story, the editor must find a way to convey that to readers without offending them. In the Imus quote, Newsweek attempted to soften the force of Imus' profanity by making it "f---ing" while leaving the word in to retain Imus' irreverent nature. Some media outlets would just bleep the offending word, if spoken. Print and online journalists know using hyphens doesn't really hide the word from readers.

Some media outlets have no reluctance to let profanity stand in all its glory if it is important to the context of the story. The New Yorker, considered one of the more dignified magazines on the newsstand, routinely allows all varieties of profanity to appear in its pages—when the profanity is relevant to the story.

Know the Speaker

The New York Times found profanity inescapable during the four years of the Trump administration. In July 2017, Anthony Scaramucci, newly appointed White House communications director, gave a profanity-laced interview with Ryan Lizza of The New Yorker magazine. Because of Scaramucci's position in the government, the Times felt compelled to report his crudities and profanities verbatim (Baker & Haberman, 2017).

Many readers were appalled, of course. In an editorial page statement, Cliff Levy, deputy managing editor for digital, explained the decision:

The Times published Mr. Scaramucci's profanity after top editors, including our executive editor, Dean Baquet, discussed whether it was proper. We decided that it was newsworthy that a top aide to President Trump used such language.

We also knew that many of our readers would want to know what Mr. Scaramucci said, and we did not want them to have to search elsewhere to find out. (The New York Times, 2017)

In January 2018, the Times faced a similar dilemma when Trump was quoted as saying Haiti and African nations were "shithole countries." With the words coming from the president of the United States, the Times editors again believed they had no choice but to use the exact words (De Greef & Chan, 2018).

Know the Writer

Columnists, especially highly paid stars, are allowed to take their writing where other reporters can't. Often they are encouraged to be controversial and to take risks. Editors might warn their supervisors about what a columnist has written, but the editor can't make even small changes without the columnist's consent.

Sometimes the columnist will use profanity, usually in a quote. Mike Royko, The Chicago Tribune columnist who died in 1997, had a more colorful style than most; his columns were occasionally questioned by editors. In the vast majority of cases, Royko won because, well, he was Royko.

The danger is that other writers will see the columnist using profanity and sneak some into their writing. Feature writers often try this, and because features tend to be looser and freer with the language, editors sometimes let the swearing stand.

Broadcasters have the added burden of the Federal Communications Commission. For much of broadcasting's history, the FCC allowed no profanity on the airwaves and had elaborate procedures a station must perform if one of George Carlin's "seven words you can never say on television" were spoken into a live microphone (Bella, 2012). The seven words were vulgarities for bodily functions or referred to sexual practices.

A study of American books from 1950 to 2008 (Twenge et al., 2017) found that books published from 2005 to 2008 were 28 times more likely to include swear words than books from the early 1950s. As seen above, some of those seven words now appear in family newspapers when they are newsworthy.

Today, in the age of deregulation and cable television, broadcasters feel much freer to use profanity to the point where two of the seven deadly words, "piss" and "fart," pop up regularly on talk shows and entertainment shows. News shows can't be far behind.

Don't Go Out of Your Way to Offend

When profanity is necessary, don't rub the reader's nose in it. It's one thing to use profanity in a story; it's quite another to put that profanity in a headline, a repeated broadcast teaser or a pull quote set in larger type.

Make sure something inoffensive doesn't become offensive when it is removed from the context of the story. Remember that many readers scan these pieces of larger type and never get to the story. Here's an example:

Years ago a travel writer at The Chicago Tribune told about a trouble-filled trip he took to England. In the story, he quoted a British cabbie as saying, "Keep your pecker up, sir," carefully explaining that "pecker" to the British means chin, as in "Keep your chin up, sir." The pull quote, in 14-point bold type, set smack in the middle of the page, used the quote without the context, running the risk of unnecessarily offending readers.

On the other hand, when American Media Inc., publisher of the National Enquirer, threatened Amazon founder Jeff Bezos with release of pictures of him in the nude, Bezos blew the whistle. The headline in the Huffington Post was "BEZOS EXPOSES PECKER," referring to AMI CEO David Pecker. The New York Post followed the next day with the same headline (Lach, 2019).

Bob Dylan had it right: The times, they are a-changing.

HOMEWORK

Assignment No. 1

Quotes often serve to elaborate on a point made in a story. Go to the website of a large news organization. This might be a newspaper such as The New York Times or The Washington Post, or it might be an online-only operation such as Politico or HuffPost. Seek out a longer story that includes some analysis. How are quotes used? As main points? As explanation? Or as elaboration? Explain what led you to this conclusion.

Assignment No. 2

Look for a story with a "delayed lede" such as the Star Tribune story about juvenile justice cited above. The story starts with an anecdote about a person, followed by a background graph that sets the stage for a mother's voice, then a powerful quotation. In the story you found, what role did the quote play in the lede? Was it a strong quote? Did it display emotion?

Assignment No. 3

Let's turn to broadcast, either television or radio. Start with a network newscast. Look for sound bites, the electronic version of the quote. Were the sound bites short or long? What do you think was left out? Would you say the sound bites were strong and advanced the story?

Assignment No. 4

Public broadcasting, such as the "PBS NewsHour" or NPR's "All Things Considered," takes a different approach in part because these shows have fewer time restraints. How do the interviews and sound bites compare with network news? Which is most effective in your judgment? Explain your answer.

REFERENCES

Associated Press. (2022). *The Associated Press stylebook: 2022–2024* (56th ed.). Basic Books. The entry **quotations in the news** is well worth reviewing, pages 242–244.

Baker, P., & Haberman, M. (2017, July 27). Anthony Scaramucci's uncensored rant: Foul words and threats to have Priebus fired. *The New York Times.* https://www.nytimes.com/2017/07/27/us/politics/scaramucci-priebus-leaks.html

Barnes, R., & Marimow, A. E. (2022, October 15). New Supreme Court Justice Ketanji Brown Jackson makes herself heard. *Washington Post.* https://www.washingtonpost.com/politics/2022/10/15/kentaji-brown-jackson-talkative/

Bella, T. (2012, May 24). The "7 dirty words" turn 40, but they're still dirty. *The Atlantic.* https://www.theatlantic.com/entertainment/archive/2012/05/the-7-dirty-words-turn-40-but-theyre-still-dirty/257374/

De Greef, K., & Chan, S. (2018, January 15). Trump comments, infuriating Africans, may set back U.S. interests. *The New York Times.* https://www.nytimes.com/2018/01/15/world/africa/trump-shithole-africa.html

Farsetta, D., & Price, D. (2012, December 15). Fake TV news: Widespread and undisclosed. PR Watch. https://www.prwatch.org/fakenews/execsummary

Goldman, T. (2003, April 16). *Michael Jordan retires, again.* NPR. https://www.npr.org/templates/story/story.php?storyId=1234171

Lach, E. (2019, February 8). The story behind the instant classic "Bezos exposes Pecker" headline. *The New Yorker.* https://www.newyorker.com/news/current/the-story-behind-the-instant-classic-bezos-exposes-pecker-headline

Margasak, L. (1999, Jan. 7). Senate opens historic trial of Clinton. *SouthCoast Today / The Standard Times.* https://www.southcoasttoday.com/story/news/1999/01/07/senate-opens-historic-trial-clinton/19848945007/

The New York Times (2017, July 28). Why the Times published Scaramucci's profanities. https://www.nytimes.com/2017/07/28/reader-center/times-published-scaramucci-profanities.html

Sawyer, L., & Serres, C. (2022, December 29). Laying down the law for troubled youths. *Star Tribune.* https://www.startribune.com/juvenile-youth-justice-system-reform-minnesota-colorado/600237479/

Thomas, E. (1999). The ringmaster. *Newsweek, 133*(3), 27. https://www.newsweek.com/ringmaster-165502

Twenge, J. M., VanLandingham, H., & Campbell, W. K. (2017). The seven words you can never say on television: Increases in the use of swear words in American books, 1950–2008. *SAGE Open, 7*(3). https://doi.org/10.1177/2158244017723689

CREDIT

Fig. 2.5.1: Chris Serres, Liz Sawyer, MaryJo Webster and Jerry Holly, Selection from "Laying Down the Law for Troubled Youth: Colorado Diverts Youths from Detention – and New Crimes," *Star Tribune of Minneapolis.* Copyright © 2022 by StarTribune.

EDITING CRIME STORIES

KEY POINTS IN THIS CHAPTER

1. Anytime a story turns negative or accusatory, that should be a stop sign for editors. They should put themselves in the place of the accused and ask, "Is this right? Is it fair?" Double down on fact-checking, particularly the legitimacy of sources, and be sure the attribution is clear.

2. When someone is accused of a crime, editors need to handle the report with extra sensitivity. Above all, they should remember that someone is innocent until proved guilty. The focus should not be about how to win a libel lawsuit; the focus should be on how to be so fair that your news organization doesn't get sued in the first place.

3. To ensure fairness, separate the names of suspects from a retelling of the crime. Attribute circumstances regarding a crime to authorities. It's not your story to tell, and the worst thing you can do is "convict" someone in print or on the air. Use passive voice to avoid assigning blame.

4. Turn to resources such as the Associated Press Stylebook with its "Briefing on media law" (now online) when in doubt about how to handle a sensitive story. The stylebook offers many related entries for you to review.

> **"** *It has long been an axiom of mine that the little things are infinitely the most important."*

> **"** *It is a capital mistake to theorize before one has data."*

—Sir Arthur Conan Doyle

Innocent Until Proved Guilty

As Sir Arthur Conan Doyle, creator of Sherlock Holmes, knew well, stories about crime attract readers. So it is today with newspapers, magazines, websites, broadcasts and podcasts (Dickson, et al., 2022).

Crime stories at all levels demand careful treatment from writers and editors. Both must be aware of the potential for libel or slander and must know how to avoid it. Writers and editors should strive for fairness in any story where a person is accused of a crime.

The AP Stylebook in its "Briefing on media law" states:

Libel is one side of the coin called "defamation," slander being the flip side. At its most basic, defamation means injury to reputation. Libel is generally distinguished from slander, in that a libel is written, or otherwise printed, whereas a slander is spoken.

The stylebook notes that even though broadcast reports are spoken, in many states, spoken defamation is still called "libel."

When we say "libel," we mean any statement that is potentially libelous. The legal definition of libel, including topics such as public figures vs. private individuals or actual malice, is important, but we're not focused on how cases are argued in court. We're trying to keep you out of court in the first place. The AP Stylebook is a great source for legal information.

Guilty or Liable

One important distinction is the difference between the words "guilty" and "liable." It depends on whether you're dealing with a case that ends up in **criminal court** (how do you plead, guilty or not guilty?) or **civil court** (held liable or not). Someone found guilty may end up in prison; someone found liable may end up paying damages. Note the "s" in the word. Paying thousands of dollars if you lose a civil lawsuit may damage your pocketbook, but the term applies to either **compensatory damages** (a dollar amount trying to make someone whole) or **punitive damages** (levied as a punishment).

Some other basics to keep in mind:

Criminal law and civil law differ with respect to **how cases are initiated** (who may bring charges or file suit), how cases are decided (by a judge or a jury), what kinds of **punishment or penalty** may be imposed, what **standards of proof** must be met and what **legal protections** may be available to the defendant (Duignan, n.d.).

Here's where we're headed in this chapter in a nutshell: When you make missteps in covering a crime that ends up in criminal court, you may find yourself sitting next to a lawyer defending you in civil court over a libel lawsuit.

Fairness Goes Beyond Libel

We're concerned with truth and accuracy, the ultimate defenses in an actual libel or slander trial, but we want to go beyond that to fairness. Objectivity is impossible, so fairness is our standard. When you judge the fairness of a crime story, ask yourself how you would feel reading it if your name were inserted in place of the suspect's.

When a news organization is sued, it loses even if it wins in court. It loses in the form of legal fees, reporters' lost time, and most of all, respect in the public eye. Yes, news organizations can pay for libel insurance, but the best way to win a libel suit is not to be sued in the first place.

Not all news organizations agree on how some things should be handled, but here are a few ideas about how to avoid libel suits.

Don't Convict Someone in Your Report

The courts have the job of deciding guilt or innocence. We must always assume that someone arrested is innocent until proved guilty.

One way to be fair is to separate the suspect from the crime. Treat the suspect and the perpetrator as two different people; that's one good way to ensure fairness.

What Can We Say About the Suspect?

Identity. Some news organizations will not identify a suspect until a person has been charged with a crime. Other organizations believe all arrest information is public record. Know your organization's policy.

Address. Use a simplified form to identify suspects: "John Smythe of Bloomington was arrested ..." In the largest cities, news organizations might use full addresses to avoid misidentification. But avoid giving a victim's address when it can cause harm. Consider this lede:

> *A disabled man was beaten and his apartment at 1234 Main St. was burglarized Monday for the third time this month.*

What will happen when this gets published? He'll probably be robbed a fourth time. Just a legal vocabulary note: a **burglary**, or break-in, happens to a home or a business; a **robbery** happens to a person in the face of violence or some kind of threat. However, AP says a home can be robbed, and we'll still refer to a bank robbery. When something is stolen, that's **theft**, or a legal term for the same thing is **larceny**.

Circumstances of arrest. Often this is incriminating, so it needs to be attributed to a privileged source, such as to police or other authorities. Here's an example:

> *Smythe was arrested with a diamond bracelet in his pocket, police said.*

Because this incriminating detail comes from police, either a spokesperson or a police report, it is fair and not libelous.

Personal details, including criminal history. Be careful here. Personal details such as "the suspect lived alone" seem to imply something suspicious but usually are irrelevant. Some publications refuse to use a suspect's criminal history, or "rap sheet." Others go with it only when they believe it is pertinent. Always err on the side of fairness.

Unconfirmed allegations. These should never make the news.

What Can We Say About the Perpetrator?

In assuming that a suspect is innocent, we create another unknown person who committed the crime. The court decides if the suspect and that other person, the perpetrator, are one and the same. Because we make no attempt to identify the perpetrator as a real person, we have more freedom in what we can say.

Description. News organizations routinely use descriptions of perpetrators: what they look like, what kinds of vehicles they drive, their clothes. The more complete the description, the more useful it is. Often police are seeking the public's help in trying to arrest a suspect.

Race is a sensitive issue in a description. Use race in a description of a perpetrator only when the description is thorough and complete. Otherwise, the information serves only to point the finger at a large group of people. If all you have is that the perpetrator was a Black teenager or a Hispanic man, how many people do you put on the spot by including such information in a story? It doesn't narrow anything down and may cause more harm than good.

The circumstances of the crime. The imaginary construct of the perpetrator is most useful in describing the crime; it keeps the suspect out of things. Consider this:

> *An assailant attacked a businessman on the elevated platform, and a suspect was arrested two blocks away, police said.*

The sentence is thorough and yet fair to the suspect. Remember, our goal is to separate the suspect from the crime as reasonably as possible.

All circumstances of the crime must be attributed to privileged sources.

Attribute Hot Information

Attributing information to a privileged source protects the news organization from libel suits. An attribution such as "a police spokesperson said" tells the audience that this is not our interpretation of the facts but one from the authorities.

Privileged sources include:

- the police, sheriff, FBI
- prosecutors
- court records and testimony
- regulatory agency proceedings
- Congress in session

How do you know if an unattributed statement came from the police? If you have doubts, you must ask your supervisor, a source editor or the reporter.

All "hot" information must be attributed to authorities. Hot information is anything that is incriminating or tends to implicate a person in a crime, including accusations, evidence, charges or claims. Anything that makes it look like the suspect is guilty must be attributed.

This applies to quotations. "A witness who refused to be identified" is not a solid attribution. "A witness told police" is usable. This is an especially important distinction because "a witness who told your reporter" some incriminating information is a lot different from "a witness who told police" something. The first one, taken at face value, can get your news organization in trouble, as unfortunately people lie. Sadly, there are pathological liars who get wrapped up in crimes. But reporting on what a witness told police, as filed in an official police report, is a much safer and more responsible way to handle crime stories.

Who Is Doing the Alleging?

"Alleged" is overworked; sprinkling the word "alleged" liberally in a news story won't protect you from libel suits. The story must state clearly who is doing the alleging, and often that person must be a privileged source. The more complete the attribution, the better. If you have a police official releasing information, use his or her full name.

Use the word "alleged" with reference to crimes, not ordinary things or occurrences. "Alleged" is nonsensical in the phrase an "alleged gun." Either it's a gun or it's not. But it would be OK to say the "alleged murder weapon." Consider this sentence:

The alleged meeting of organized crime bosses took place on Jan. 7.

Either the meeting took place or it didn't. Maybe the point is more like: "Police are investigating whether the organized crime bosses met on Jan. 7." But "alleged meeting" doesn't make much sense. The word works, however, when it's attached to a crime. Take this example:

The alleged embezzlement took place Friday after bank hours.

This phrasing is OK if all you know is that money is missing and police are investigating the crime as a possible embezzlement. It doesn't accuse anyone. If money exchanges hands and you call it a "bribe," then you've convicted someone of a crime. Make it: "alleged bribe."

It's also correct but not advisable to call someone an "alleged accomplice" or an "alleged killer" if you state that a privileged source is doing the alleging. But what happens if "alleged" is accidentally deleted? Or in a broadcast, the reporter or anchor accidentally skips the word? Big trouble.

Let's talk briefly about grammar: What's the difference between calling someone "an accused killer" and "a murder suspect"? If you put the emphasis on the noun "killer," then you are less fair than if you emphasize the noun "suspect." Do everything you can, especially with word choice, to be fair. This also applies after a conviction. Compare these phrases: "convicted murderer" and "man convicted on a murder charge." We prefer the latter because we have seen so many cases of people serving long prison terms for crimes they did not commit.

At the Chicago Tribune back in the day, with two full-time investigative reporters working the organized-crime beat, it was "local style" to call a mobster a mobster. Elsewhere in the world, the least you would do is identify someone as a "reputed mobster."

Avoid Words That Assign Blame

Strike "arrested for …" and "indicted for …" from your vocabulary. That word "for" assigns blame. It's the same as saying the suspect committed the crime and was arrested for it. Instead, write that the suspect was arrested "in connection with …" or "arrested on a charge of …" if charges have been filed.

Passive voice is useful to avoid convicting someone in print. This sentence convicts the suspect:

> *A St. Paul man was arrested after he shot a woman to death on Saturday in a bar. (NO!)*

This sentence using the passive voice "was shot" separates the suspect from the crime:

> *A St. Paul man was arrested after a woman was shot to death on Saturday in a bar.*

Note that many often-used words, such as "hit," tend to assign blame. If we say "a car hit an oncoming truck," the car's driver seems to be at fault. If we say "a car and a truck collided," blame isn't assigned to either one. "Collide" means both vehicles were moving. "Hit" is OK when blame is obvious, as in "a car hit a utility pole." The pole wasn't going anywhere.

Follow the Process

Just to get you square on word choice, let's follow an arrest story. OK, someone is **arrested** in connection with a crime. The next formal step is to be **charged**. Sometimes activists, especially celebrities, may go to a protest and get arrested or taken into custody. But then they are let go down at the police station without ever getting formally charged, or "booked." Celebrities may wear an arrest record as a badge of honor, but a criminal record is a different story—it may cost them their jobs.

Let's say our unlucky fellow gets charged. If it's a really complex case, then the fellow might be **indicted.** That means the same thing as charged, though indicted sounds worse. In complex cases, a grand jury may hear evidence and deliver the indictment.

The next step is to be **arraigned** before a judge who asks the fellow whether he pleads **guilty** or **not guilty**. A journalistic convention, though not legally correct, is to use the words "pleaded innocent." It's an attempt to avert trouble if the "not" gets dropped in print or overlooked in a script. We're fast-forwarding now: The case goes to trial and the fellow is **acquitted** by a jury of his peers. Do you see why we have been so careful in the first place? AP's 57th edition advises that if you are unlikely to cover an outcome, consider not naming the subject or not writing a story at all.

There's an old journalistic expression worth remembering: "There are not always two sides to a story. There are always at least three: what one person says, what the other person says and the truth." Showing humility will serve you well in dealing with crime stories.

Consult the Stylebook

The AP's media law section in the 56th edition is supplemented with many style entries to guide an editor working on crime stories. Here are some entries worth reviewing. In the 57th edition, most of these are clustered in the **Criminal Justice** chapter:

- **accused, alleged, suspected** (4)
- **allege** (11–12)
- **anonymous sources** (17–18). See news values in 57th edition.
- **arrest** (22)
- **assassin, killer, murderer** (22)
- **assault, battery** (22)
- **burglary, larceny, robbery, theft** (36)
- **civil cases, criminal cases** (48)
- **court names** (65)
- **felony, misdemeanor** (108–109)
- **habeas corpus** (132)
- **homicide, murder, manslaughter** (141)
- **judge** (164)
- **juvenile delinquent** (166)
- **police department** (227–228)
- **prison, jail** (235–236)
- **weapons** (307–310)

As much as you might admire Sir Arthur Conan Doyle and his detective Sherlock Holmes, it's not your job as an editor to solve a crime. Leave that to the professionals, just as you wouldn't turn over your editing tasks to a police officer.

HOMEWORK

Assignment No. 1

Sharpen your eye by reading two or three crime stories from a nearby newspaper or on a website. You can access the stories online or in print. What does the paper do right in reporting a crime? Zero in on the word "alleged." Does the story tell you who is doing the alleging? Does the story separate the suspect from the perpetrator?

Assignment No. 2

Now sharpen your ear by watching the news on TV. Often this also can be done on the station's website. Remember that broadcast stories of 30 seconds to a minute must be economical with words. Do the news anchors and reporters follow this chapter's guidelines for handling crime stories? What do their reports get right and where do they come up short?

Assignment No. 3

Often police and prosecutors have the upper hand in shaping news coverage of a crime. Why might this be so? Look again at your crime stories and see who is quoted and in what way. What does that suggest? Following a case to its final conclusion can take a long time, even years. Compare coverage of when someone is acquitted with someone convicted and sentenced. If someone is acquitted, do you see why we were so careful in the first place?

REFERENCES

Associated Press. (2022). *The Associated Press stylebook: 2022–2024* (56th ed.). Basic Books. The section titled "Briefing on media law" is well worth studying.

Associated Press. (2024). *The Associated Press stylebook: 2024–2026* (57th ed.). Basic Books.

Dickson, E. J., Ehrlich, B., Garber-Paul, E., & Marks, A. (2022, June 3). The 25 best true-crime podcasts of all time. *Rolling Stone.* https://www.rollingstone.com/culture/culture-features/best-true-crime-podcasts-all-time-1292829/

Duignan, B. (n.d.). What is the difference between criminal law and civil law? Britannica. https://www.britannica.com/story/what-is-the-difference-between-criminal-law-and-civil-law

FURTHER READING, RESOURCES

Digital Media Law Project. (n.d.). http://www.dmlp.org/

McBride, K. (2020, June 4). Did George Floyd die or was he murdered? One of many ethics questions NPR must answer. NPR. https://www.npr.org/sections/publiceditor/2020/06/04/868969745/did-george-floyd-die-or-was-he-murdered-one-of-many-ethics-questions-npr-must-answer. We can't casually refer to a crime as "embezzlement" or "murder" until a formal charge has been filed. The George Floyd case offered special challenges in that the incident was caught on video and widely distributed. Read this analysis from National Public Radio.

TRIMMING STORIES

KEY POINTS IN THIS CHAPTER

1. Story length is a function of the type of publication—from long (magazine, documentary) to medium (newspaper) to short (radio or television). Even news organizations engaged in "long-form" journalism must trim stories.

2. The challenge of trimming stories is easier with inverted pyramid ledes. They are often seen in breaking news stories designed to be trimmed from the bottom while making sure no information important to your audience gets lost.

3. Narrative stories present a more difficult challenge for trimming. They should be analyzed and broken down into their various parts: delayed lede, nut graph, main points with support and elaboration. Trimming focuses first on the elaboration.

> 66 *Read your own compositions, and when you meet with a passage which you think is particularly fine, strike it out."*
>
> —Samuel Johnson, (1709–84), English author, lexicographer

> 66 *I have only made this [letter] longer because I have not had the time to make it shorter."*
>
> —Blaise Pascal (1623–62), French scientist, philosopher

Down to the Minute

Simeon Lancaster had a problem: A story he helped produce for the "PBS NewsHour" was too long. It was about prison inmates going to law school remotely.

"We're supposed to be submitting pieces between five and seven minutes," Lancaster said, "and our first cut was like nine and a half, and we're like, damn, it's hard to cut anything out. Even our first news editor said, 'It's too long, but I don't see anything you can cut, either.'"

He and correspondent Fred de Sam Lazaro make up the Under-Told Stories Project. They work independently to produce long-form video reports for the "NewsHour." The two eventually trimmed the story to 8½ minutes and turned it over to PBS editors.

Lancaster feared editors would cut a "really great segment" featuring Albert Woodfox, who spent 44 years in solitary confinement in the Louisiana State Penitentiary at Angola, Louisiana.

"He's been a huge activist and a big inspiration for this movement," Lancaster said, "and he died a couple of weeks after we interviewed him. It's like his stuff is so good, so compelling, but also if anyone's going to get cut …"

In the end, Woodfox appeared in the story, but his interview was cut (Under-Told Stories Project, 2022).

"I believe his section saved us about 45 seconds," Lancaster said, "and with a couple additional trims we shaved off the full minute we needed."

As editors, we often must trim stories to fit a specification. Magazines budget by word count, especially for standing features in the "front of the book" (Bugeja, 1997). Online news stories are kept short in the belief that readers on smartphones and tablets don't want to deal with large blocks of text (Fischer, 2021). Print editions of newspapers have always specified story lengths, stated in "column inches." And as we have seen with Simeon Lancaster's experience, broadcast stories must meet a specified time limit.

Important Elements

Our approach to trimming stories is dictated by:

Who wrote the story. A news organization will make room for its best writers and take care in trimming their work. In part this is because the best correspondents receive the most important assignments. Length and display (photos, drawings, charts) are planned well in advance. Mutual respect is important here. Simeon Lancaster noted that Fred de Sam Lazaro has worked with the "PBS NewsHour" "for longer than any of the editors have been there, so they respect him and his choices as well."

What use is made of the story. Some stories are centerpieces, taking up several pages of a newspaper or magazine, along with photos. The cover story in the October 2022 issue of The Atlantic by CNN's Jake Tapper (2022, November) covered 12 pages, including a two-page graphic display and photos. The article was more than 10,700 words. This contrasts with standing features at the front and back of the book. The regular feature "Dispatches," for example, usually runs over two pages, about 1,200 words, and no more than four pages.

Remember that in **Chapter 2.1: The Nature of News,** we mentioned that a big story in one part of the country is a "brief" somewhere else. A story from the Associated Press (2022, Dec. 31) told of extensive flooding after heavy rain and snow in California. The AP story was short—330 words. The Star Tribune of Minneapolis cut this to 75 words for a "Nation & World" digest in its print edition (Star Tribune, 2022), although it ran the entire AP story on its website, where news organizations enjoy a "bottomless news hole." A story in the Los Angeles Times about the same weather incident was staff-written and took up 625 words (Smith, 2022).

What type of story. At one end of the spectrum is the **inverted pyramid** story. These stories often are used in a digest along with other short items, as with the California flooding story in the Star Tribune print edition. In news broadcasts, these stories might run from 10 seconds to a minute. Inverted pyramid stories can be trimmed to just the most important or interesting facts, most often from the bottom up.

At the other end is the complex feature story written by a staff member or in-depth pieces such as those produced by the Under-Told Stories Project. These stories often take a prominent place on the front of a newspaper section or as a spread in a magazine or as a centerpiece story on television.

In between are a variety of stories and the many ways they are used. Sometimes we must take a more complex story and trim it severely, as in a package of news briefs. At other times, we might take a story carefully written by a staff member and cut it down for a different edition.

The Inverted Pyramid

Hard-news stories from news services such as the Associated Press are written to accommodate trimming from the bottom up. This inverted pyramid style came about with the invention of the telegraph and the coming of the wire services (Figure 2.7.1).

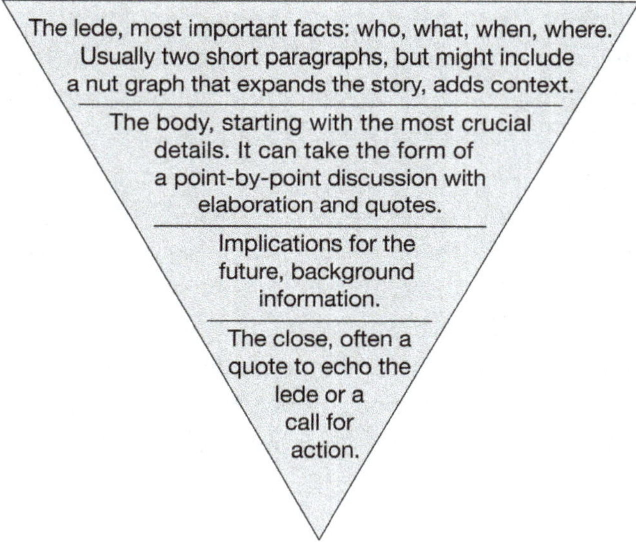

FIGURE 2.7.1   Inverted pyramid stories are designed to have the most important information at the top. They can be trimmed from the bottom, but look for important buried details.

Chip Scanlan of the Poynter Institute for Media Studies writes that the expense of using the telegraph caused newspapers to develop "a new kind of writing that departed from the flowery language of the 19th century; it was concise, stripped of opinion and detail."

The fledgling Associated Press incorporated the style of writing stories that "would be brief, tailored for a national audience and deliberately stripped of the partisanship that characterized American newspapers until that time," Scanlan writes.

Scanlan discounts the idea that reporters used the inverted pyramid because they were afraid the telegraph wire would be cut off before they were done transmitting. A more flowery style of writing continued during the Civil War (Scanlan, 2003).

When editors trim an inverted pyramid story, they should read the copy to make sure nothing important is near the end. For example, in a story about Congress passing a bill, the votes of representatives from the news organization's state might be buried. These should be salvaged and moved up.

Narrative Stories

Stories written in a narrative style are harder to trim and require careful news judgment. To do this, you must know how to break down a story. Nan Asimov (2017, February 12), longtime education reporter for the San Francisco Chronicle, writes that longer news stories follow a pattern of talking points and quotes.

In the story outlined below (Kauffman, 2022), notice the rhythm as the story makes a point, supports that point, then adds elaboration, often in the form of a quote. As we size this story up for trimming, we must identify each main point. Eventually we might have to use our news judgment to decide if a point stays or is cut, as in the Under-Told Stories Project piece on prisoners earning law degrees.

First paragraph or paragraphs make up the delayed lede. The first sentence is often the news, as it is in an inverted pyramid story. A news lede tells who, what, when and where, and it isn't overloaded with details. The lede must never be cut from the story. This story takes a more stylish approach than an inverted pyramid story by using a delayed lede:

When Robert Vischer arrived at St. Thomas as an associate professor of law in 2005, he had no aspirations beyond being a "contributor" in the school's journey.

Second sentence gives more details and supports the lede. Good writers save details for the second sentence and avoid packing them into the opening line:

> *Now, as the university's second lay president and 16th president overall, he will have the opportunity to contribute on a much larger scale.*

A quote elaborating on the first two paragraphs usually ends up in the third paragraph. This quote illustrates the points made in the opening:

> *"This is the university where I've developed as a teacher and scholar, and I think we have a distinctive mission that the world needs more than ever," Vischer told TommieMedia in an exclusive interview Monday as his hiring was announced. "I'm unbelievably humbled and honored to be tasked with leading us into the next chapter."*

The second sentence and the supporting quote constitute what we call **the "nut graph."** A nut graph summarizes the point of a story and sets the stage for the rest of the writing. It provides essential information, definitely not something to trim.

An important connection lies between **the nut graph and the headline**. For this story, the editor played the main headline straight: "St. Thomas names Robert Vischer as 16th president." If there were a subhed or deck, then a likely candidate would be: "Second lay president says, 'This is the university where I've developed as a teacher and scholar.'"

The story continues with **a background graph** to provide context. It tells how the current news fits into the larger picture and begins a series of points about the **new president's qualifications**:

> *Vischer took over as interim president earlier this year following then-president Julie Sullivan's departure to become president of Santa Clara University. During Vischer's 18-year tenure at the St. Thomas School of Law, he moved from associate professor to associate dean, later taking over as dean from 2013–22.*

A summary of what's to come often follows the nut graph. Such a summary lays out the varying points of view, foreshadowing the details of the rest of the story. In a severe trim, if this paragraph isn't present, the editor might write one that condenses much of what follows.

The story about Vischer continues to outline his qualifications, taking **a step back into his history**:

Before coming to St. Thomas, Vischer graduated summa cum laude from the University of New Orleans, later graduating cum laude with a Juris Doctor from Harvard Law School.

While serving as dean at St. Thomas, he was lauded for his work in diversity, equity and inclusion, which is something Vischer said he wants to focus on in his tenure as president. In 2017, Vischer won the inaugural Minnesota Lawyer Diversity and Inclusion Award, which recognizes a Minnesota lawyer's contributions to the advancement of diversity and inclusion in the practice of law.

Supporting quote comes next. This quote supports the point made in the previous graph:

"It (diversity) has to be a focus for us because it's at the heart of our mission," Vischer said. "It's because we're a Catholic university that we have to be committed to making sure that our community reflects the diversity of the communities we aspire to serve, and that the diversity is matched by a relentless commitment to inclusion."

The story might go on for some length with a transition **introducing another point, followed by supporting quotes**. Quotes from two people should never be back-to-back. A transition is needed as a bridge from one speaker to another. Quotes are usually in a separate paragraph to set them off. Notice how a snippet introduces a full quote.

Vischer also believes in increasing St. Thomas' local and national visibility, saying St. Thomas' size and the quality of education it has to offer allow it to provide a liberal arts education in "a way that has been elusive to large state universities."

"We should be and we need to be better known outside Minnesota, and that's a journey that's already begun," Vischer said, "both with athletics and with academics and really being a little bit louder about our distinctives in the communities outside Minnesota, and we're going to continue even intensifying our forward momentum on that."

Here's another transition, then its supporting quote:

During his six months as interim president, Vischer focused a lot on building a "culture of encounter" at St. Thomas, which he described as being the opposite of self-absorption and indifference.

"We want to do everything possible to make sure that every student who sets foot on our campus is seen, known and valued," Vischer said.

A reporter might add real-time color, anecdotes and examples. This need not be confined to this section. "Color" means brief descriptions of sights, sounds and mood. It can be condensed or trimmed, but often it is important to the story.

The past, or background information, might be necessary. Be careful that you don't eliminate something that is a key to understanding the story. This background information should not be trimmed or condensed:

Vischer was selected by the St. Thomas Board of Trustees by a unanimous decision. He will officially start his new position on Jan. 1, 2023.

Well-crafted news stories usually end with a "kicker"—a short high-impact sentence or a telling quote. In some stories, the kicker can be something that brings the reader back to an idea or anecdote told at the beginning. Or it could be a great quote. Stylish writers often save their second-best quote for the end:

"I couldn't imagine a more exciting place to have a leadership opportunity," Vischer said.

A look to the future often comes toward the end of a story. Simeon Lancaster says that the Under-Told Stories Project often ends a piece with a look forward. What is the next step? If an anecdote is used up toward the top, a useful technique is to refer to the beginning, or to the anecdote, in a way that looks to the future.

A Strategy for Trimming

Most wire stories are written in an inverted pyramid format. These are easily trimmed from the bottom, taking care that no important buried information is lost.

With a more complex story, the idea is to condense the piece, as opposed to cutting it. Follow these steps:

STEP 1: Identify the lede and the nut graph. It might be just the first sentence, or it might extend across more than one paragraph, as in many magazine stories. These cannot be cut, although they might be condensed.

STEP 2: Identify the main points of a story. For the university president story, these could be:

1. Vischer will be the school's 16th president and second lay president (nut graph).
2. Vischer took over as interim president after a long tenure at the St. Thomas law school.
3. Vischer graduated with honors in earning a bachelor's degree and a law degree.
4. As dean of the law school, he received an award for his work on diversity.
5. He believes in increasing the university's local and national exposure.
6. He worked to create a "culture of encounter" as interim president.
7. The university regents voted unanimously to hire him as president.
8. Final quote expresses his enthusiasm for the university.

STEP 3: Spare the nut graph. The delayed lede and the nut graph cannot be trimmed.

STEP 4: Scan the story for elaboration, often in the form of quotes. This would be the fat of the story, and as such, it is the first candidate to be trimmed. Note that while quotes are prime targets to be trimmed, you will make a mistake by just randomly trimming every quote. Remember that quotes serve many purposes; some are fat and some are meat.

STEP 5: If you have trimmed all the "fat" and the story is still too long, you must decide which of the major points of the story must go. Remember the example from the Under-Told Stories Project. When Simeon Lancaster got down to needing one more minute to cut, the interview with Albert Woodfox was taken out.

As we mentioned in **Chapter 1.1: The Core Principles of Editing,** the best results happen when an editor works collaboratively with a writer. Nowhere is this more important than in trimming a long narrative. In **Chapter 1.4: The Good Writer,** we noted in a segment titled "Prepare for the Haircut" that sometimes writers can help themselves by marking certain paragraphs as "optional trims." Whatever the method, your audience—the reader, listener or viewer—is best served when writers and editors get on the same page, working as a team, to enhance the impact of a good story by showing "less is more."

HOMEWORK

Assignment No. 1

Do an online search for an Associated Press story about the death of Pope Benedict XVI with the headline, "Benedict XVI, reluctant pope who chose to retire, dies at 95." You can find a link in the references (Winfield, 2022, Dec. 31). The article is about 2,115 words, long for an AP story. Use your analytical skills to map out the story: lede, nut graph, main points with support and elaboration. If you had to cut this down to 1,000 words, what would you eliminate? What main points can be summarized? Which would you cut entirely? Be able to defend your answer.

Assignment No. 2

Most newscasts begin with a "headline" opener, quick takes on the day's stories, each one maybe 10 seconds long. Watch the opening for a nightly news broadcast on ABC, NBC, CBS or FOX. Compare that with the opening news segment on NPR's "All Things Considered" or the "PBS NewsHour." How do they differ in length and in style? If you have a cellphone, use the stopwatch function to time a few network stories. Do two or three, then average them out. What is a typical length? Compare that with NPR or PBS.

Assignment No. 3

Visit the Associated Press news website (apnews.com) and call up some of the top stories. What types of ledes do you see? Can you identify a pattern as to when the AP uses an inverted pyramid lede and when it goes to a more complex narrative with a nut graph?

REFERENCES

Asimov, N. (2017, Feb. 12). Asimov's dirty dozen elements of a standard news story. Studylib.Net. https://studylib.net/doc/8421391/asimov-s-dirty-dozen-elements-of-a-standard-news-story-by

Associated Press. (2022, Dec. 31). Storm brings flooding, landslides across California. https://apnews.com/article/weather-sports-storms-natural-disasters-california-e57e078d2b03f4d5019a95a885c77014

Bugeja, M. (1997). *Guide to writing magazine nonfiction*. Allyn & Bacon.

Fischer, S. (2021, March 9). The new era for long-form journalism. Axios. https://www.axios.com/2021/03/09/journalism-podcasts-longreads-phones-word-count

Kauffman, C. (2022, Dec. 19). St. Thomas names Robert Vischer as 16th president. https://www.tommiemedia.com/st-thomas-names-robert-vischer-as-16th-president/

Scanlan, C. (2003, June 20). Birth of the inverted pyramid: A child of technology, commerce and history. Poynter. https://www.poynter.org/reporting-editing/2003/birth-of-the-inverted-pyramid-a-child-of-technology-commerce-and-history/

Smith, H. (2022, Dec. 30). Miracle or mirage? Atmospheric rivers end California drought year with heavy snow and rain. *Los Angeles Times*. https://www.latimes.com/california/story/2022-12-30/atmospheric-rivers-end-california-drought-year-with-storms

Star Tribune (2022, Dec. 31). Nation and World.

Tapper, J. (2022, Oct. 12) This is not justice: A Philadelphia teenager and the empty promise of the Sixth Amendment. *The Atlantic 330*(4), 28–41. https://www.theatlantic.com/magazine/archive/2022/11/campaign-to-free-incarcerated-philadelphia-teenager-sixth-amendment/671527/

Under-Told Stories. (2022, December 14). The legal revolution. https://www.undertoldstories.org/2022/12/14/the-legal-revolution/

Winfield, N. (2022, Dec. 31). Benedict XVI, reluctant pope who chose to retire, dies at 95. AP News. https://apnews.com/article/pope-benedict-xvi-a-life-remembered-ed6ddf20f696d84ffe0680e1ef0bab0f

EPILOGUE

At ease, mates!

We salute you for navigating from "The Core Principles of Editing" in **Chapter 1.1** to "Trimming Stories" in **Chapter 2.7**, then in between earning a gold medal in our Language Skills Olympics.

Let's close this chapter with another quick quiz. Ready? A show of hands, please.

How many of you are interested in doing a podcast? Or maybe having a career in daily or weekly newspapers? Or magazines? Wait, maybe something in broadcasting, either sports or TV news, possibly the "PBS NewsHour"? Or perhaps a newsletter or a news website?

The answer: Over the years, those distinctions have disappeared as the news media world has blurred the lines across print, broadcast and online.

We've seen a weekly newspaper that does podcasts, something akin to radio news. The demand for newsletter editors has been rising ever since newsletters became a profitable way to collect email addresses for marketing (Burns, 2020).

For the first time in 2024, broadcast and audio companies with digital news sites competed for a Pulitzer Prize, the crowning achievement once restricted solely to print journalism. "There's no such thing as newspaper and broadcast anymore," said Brian Carovillano, senior vice president and head of news standards at NBC News (Bauder, 2023).

We suggest you call up "The Good Writer," **Chapter 1.4,** because there's a catch: Entries must show a substantial amount of good writing. We could see this change coming.

In 2022 the New York Times won a duPont-Columbia Award for audio and video journalism for its 40-minute documentary "Day of Rage" about the Jan. 6 riot at the U.S. Capitol (duPont-Columbia Awards, 2022).

In 2020 Time magazine earned a nomination for an Emmy—that's another broadcast award—for a multimedia project with Univision that qualified as a documentary (Time, 2020).

In 2014 two photojournalists at the Cincinnati Enquirer won awards as the only newspaper to be nominated for an Emmy, or more precisely the

National Academy of Television Arts and Sciences' Ohio Valley Regional Emmy Awards (Marotti, 2014).

And in 2010, MediaStorm, founded by Brian Storm, became the first organization of its kind to win a duPont-Columbia Award, honoring public service through excellence in broadcast and digital journalism (Stuart, 2010).

MediaStorm, a web-based production company, says it publishes "diverse narratives" and offers advanced storytelling training. It has won Webby Awards, Emmy Awards and an Edward R. Murrow Award from the Radio Television Digital News Association.

In some ways, 21st-century journalism has adopted a routine reminiscent of 1846 with the founding of The Associated Press. Get a story out quickly with a "flash," or a few words like *"Pope shot."*

Your co-author was working on the copy desk of the Chicago Tribune when the world's first Polish-born pope, John Paul II, was shot at 5:17 p.m. Rome time on May 13, 1981, in St. Peter's Square in Vatican City (Vögele, 2022). Following the flash came a lede, then multiple "write-thrus" being typed out on an AP wire machine.

Today we can easily imagine how those same few words would appear on X (formally known as Twitter), TikTok, Facebook or Instagram, then in broadcast bulletins and longer stories on news websites around the world.

The process is the same: writing and editing at full speed. As stories grow from small to extra large, we can only hope writers and editors channel Joseph Pulitzer, who delivered this exhortation to his staff: "Accuracy! Accuracy! Accuracy!"

We wish this book can serve you well as a writer and an editor in the future. We understand if you choose not to apply your newfound editing skills as a journalist. We're fully supportive of you however you choose to make the world a better-edited place.

Bon voyage!

—The Authors

REFERENCES

Bauder, D. (2023, November 6). Broadcast, audio companies will be eligible for Pulitzer Prizes, for work on digital sites. Associated Press. https://apnews.com/article/pulitzer-broadcast-digital-journalism-0e956c1063d0e88fb6c0c20a210987b4

Burns, S. (2020, April 18). 6 ways to cash in on a small email list. Forbes. https://www.forbes.com/sites/stephanieburns/2020/04/18/6-ways-to-cash-in-on-a-small-email-list

duPont-Columbia Awards (2022.) 2022 Winners—DuPont-Columbia Awards. https://dupont.org/day-of-rage-credits

Marotti, A. (2014, August 3). Enquirer photojournalists bring home Emmys. cincinnati.com. https://www.cincinnati.com/story/news/2014/08/03/enquirer-photojournalists-bring-home-emmys/13543745/

Stuart, J. (2010, January 14). Intended Consequences named as first web winner of Alfred I. DuPont-Columbia University Awards. MediaStorm. https://www.mediastorm.com/blog/2010/01/14/intended-consequences-named-as-first-web-winner-of-alfred-i-dupont-columbia-university-awards/

Time. (2020, August 7). *Time* earns Emmy nomination for multimedia project in partnership with Univision. https://time.com/5877685/time-emmy-nomination-multimedia-project-univision/

Vögele, M. (2022, May 13). "Everyone was crying": An eyewitness recalls the attempted assassination of St John Paul II. Catholic News Agency. https://www.catholicnewsagency.com/news/251224/everyone-was-crying-an-eyewitness-recalls-the-attempted-assassination-of-st-john-paul-ii

THE LANGUAGE SKILLS SURVIVAL KIT!

I t's our version of a Swiss Army knife that you can use to do battle with editing any kind of prose. We start with a handy guide, then dive deeper into the rules of grammar and punctuation, then swing into ways to increase readability through brevity and simplicity, and wrap up with commonly misspelled words.

No better way to start than to introduce you to the first of our five-part appendix—The Fixtionary. It's something like a *dictionary,* but that doesn't tell you how to fix a problem. It's no substitute for a good stylebook, such as the Associated Press Stylebook or the Chicago Manual of Style, though it's built something like one.

The main difference is The Fixtionary's blunt advice, cautionary tales and tips with humor. It can give you a memory trick, or deliver a fun fact, or issue a warning to keep you from getting sued. Rather than give you a full recitation on passive voice, for example, The Fixtionary asks you to stop on the word "by" and see if you can drop it and flip the sentence.

We believe good editors have an internal system of bells that tell them when to stop on a word. These bells are cast in mental molds over years of studying various stylebooks, having different and brilliant bosses, and suffering a lot of on-the-job mistakes. In this way The Fixtionary is a carillon that can help you tune in to editing problems like a pro.

Did you just hear that bell? It's time to go! Now, introducing, The Fixtionary.

THE FIXTIONARY

A

a—Or do you mean **an?** Show us "a historic building" and we'll show you "an honorable architect." It's not the letter of the word that follows—it's the sound. Use **an** if it's a vowel sound like "on" (**an** honorable woman) or "ay" (**an** 1898 war battle). See? Don't go British on us and drop the consonant "h" sound. Don't say "an historic"; it's **a historic**, you Yankee Doodle Dandy!

accommodate—The word is big enough to accommodate two c's and two m's.

accusative—Yes, making accusations is dangerous business, as you can read in **Chapter 2.6: Editing Crime Stories**, but we offer you a fun fact here: **accusative** is another term for objective case (*me, him, her, us, them*). We don't use the term, as we're trying to keep grammar simple. But if you ever get into an argument with a grammar know-it-all, you can toss out the term to strut your stuff.

adviser—The AP Stylebook still sticks with **-er** for "adviser"—not "advisor"—as the preferred spelling. "Advisor" becomes the most "misspelled" word on college campuses with journalism schools.

affect—Or do you mean **effect?** This one drives writers and editors crazy. We suggest a simple solution—use the plug-in test. Substitute the word that **affec**t and **effect** mean when they are used as nouns (add **the** in front) or verbs (add **to** in front). Then see if you're using the right word. So here's the list to keep in mind:

> **the affect**—*emotion*
>
> **to affect**—*influence*
>
> **the effect**—*result*
>
> **to effect**—*bring about*

So repeat after us:

> *The **effect** (result) of the tax policy **affected** (influenced) my vote.*
>
> *The **affect** (emotion) of the trauma **effected** (brought about) great change in me.*

Got it? Weep no more!

aggravated—Or do you mean **annoyed**? It's a matter of degree. The first alarm "annoyed" me; the second and third "aggravated" me.

alleged—It's the alleged **murder weapon**, not the alleged **gun**. It's the alleged **mobster**, not the alleged **man.** There has to be a crime or criminal involved to use the qualifier **alleged.**

ALL CAPS—A way to shout your message, but we think the strong, silent type is more convincing.

a lot—Two words. It gets misspelled a lot, so allot more time to studying spelling.

alluded—Or do you mean **referred**? Use **refer** for a direct mention; use **allude** for an oblique reference. So you would say: *The wife **alluded** to her husband's illness **without directly mentioning** a stroke.*

&—Don't use the ampersand for "and" willy-nilly. Check the formal name to be sure it's properly used, as in P&G for Procter & Gamble.

and—Check your comma supply. Either use one before "and" in "red, white, and blue" (Oxford comma, Chicago style) or not in "red, white and blue" (AP style). Just pick a style and be consistent. When you see a second subject, no comma if the ideas are closely related, as in: *We walked to the store and I bought milk.* If you shift gears with the second subject, then a comma is a good signal, as in: *We walked to the store, and when we got there, we saw it had burned down.*

B

badly—Do you mean **bad**? You feel **bad** (sick). If you feel **badly**, you've lost your sense of touch.

basis—Usually can be deleted. So don't say *on a one-to-one basis*; just say *individually*.

Because—Starting a sentence with **Because** is frowned upon because … it makes more sense to state a point first before you explain the reason for it. Because you may want to separate cause and effect for emphasis, we never say never.

between—Ay yai yai, don't end the prepositional phrase with "I." It's *just between you and me*, not *you and I*.

both—Can you drop it? Usually the "and" is enough to say two are involved. So you can say just *you and me*, not *both you and me*. If there was some surprise involved, then "both" works for emphasis, as in: *Both the Jets and the Patriots will make the playoffs. One week ago, neither qualified.*

busses—Kisses, not vehicles (**buses**).

but—Think comma-but when you see a second subject, even if it's the same one, as in: *I really studied hard, but I still flunked.* If **but** means **except**, then no comma. You would say, *Everyone but me passed the test.*

by—Can you drop it and flip the sentence? So not: *The examination was given by the doctor*, but rather: *The doctor gave the examination*, or better: *The doctor examined the patient.*

C

Canada goose—Not "Canadian." It hardly ever comes up, except in crossword puzzles or tests for jobs, but it's one of our favorite fun facts.

canceled—One "l." It's pronounced CAN-cel (accent on first syllable), so single letter with -ed.

catholic—This means universal, not particular to the Roman Catholic Church. The Apostles' Creed, spoken in Roman Catholic, Anglican and many other Protestant churches, expresses belief in "the holy catholic church" (lowercase "c").

cemetery—Three "e's"—ghosts go "eee" in a cemetery.

Christmas—Dec. 25, right? A Facebook post from one of our former students, now supervising editor for NPR's "Morning Edition," reminded us that Jan. 7, 2023, was "the day many Orthodox Christians around the world celebrate Christmas." Then she delivered this observation from Lviv, Ukraine, where she was covering the war: "In an attempt to move away from Russia culturally, some Ukrainians celebrated Christmas on December 25th this year" (Loboda, 2023). It's a big world out there, and the more contacts you have—around the country and around the globe—the clearer and more informed your worldview becomes.

Colombia—The South American country (with an "o"), not "Columbia," the university, the river or the District of (with a "u").

compliment—Think of the "i" as in *I praise you*, and you won't confuse this word with **complement**.

comprise—Means "embrace," so you would say "composed of," not embraced of. *The zoo **comprises** many animals*, or *The zoo **is composed of** many animals.*

committed—Two t's. It's pronounced co-MIT (accent on last syllable), so double letter with -ed.

completely destroyed—"Destroy" means complete destruction, so you can just say "destroyed" or maybe "devastated" is what you mean.

coordinate—This is the term for adjectives of equal weight, so you use a comma to separate them, whether two (the *cold, wet* breeze) or more (the *simple, mind-numbing, contemporary* novel). Equal weight means the order doesn't matter and the comma replaces an *and*. Now check out these two adjectives: the *gentle verbal* warning. No comma because they are not coordinate.

couple—A word desperately clinging to its noun status, as it relentlessly gets misused as an adjective: *a couple people, a couple bets, a couple drinks.* To save the noun, add "of"—more than *a couple of times.*

covfefe—If we ever needed a crazy way to tie lessons from **Chapters 1.4** (zingers) and **2.5** (quotes) together, it came six minutes after midnight (EDT) on May 31, 2017, when then-President Trump tweeted a lament about constant negative press coverage (Estepa, 2018). Only he coined a new word—covfefe—in a quote that went viral because someone important said something with a special flair.

D

definitely—Not "definately."

democracy—"Our democracy is at stake!" Millions in political donations have flowed from that outrage, but we hate to break this to you—the U.S. never had a democracy. No, this is not a politically charged statement, just a historical note. Since the Constitutional Convention of 1787, we've had a "republic," or more precisely a "constitutional federal republic." If the will of a majority of citizens prevails in a democracy, why do we have laws that defy public opinion? Because we don't have a democracy; instead, we turn over these decisions to elected representatives. Every time you hear an emotional appeal, such as "Our democracy is at stake!" review **Chapter 1.3, 1st Sweep, Point No. 6. Getting played.** And always question your sources.

democratic—This refers to democracy, not the Democratic Party (capitalized).

didn't think—The "not" is in the wrong place in this sentence: *We didn't think it was correct.* Better: *We thought it was not correct.*

discreet—This one works for a secret; **"discrete"** means separate. Think of the "ee" like "shh"—you want to keep this quiet.

Disney—The legal department makes it the unhappiest place on earth over the sale of unauthorized Disney merchandise. Be warned if you're thinking about using any copyrighted material—the names, characters' images or music—in your latest creative endeavor. You'll very likely hear from Disney's attorneys.

due to—Or do you mean **because of**? Think of "due" as an adjective that works backward to modify a noun: *The paper (noun) was due (adjective).* So you would say, *The postponement (noun) was due (adjective) to rain.* But, if an action verb is involved, then you need the adverb phrase: *The game was canceled because of rain.*

E

either—What follows **either** should be in the same form as what follows **or.** So you would say, *Either **the** boy or **the** girl.* Don't say, *Either the Bills or Bengals will win.* Keep words the same on **each** side; don't say *on either side.* "Either" refers to one of two options.

embarrassing—Two r's, two s's. An embarrassing word to misspell.

examination—Shun the -tion word. See if you can resurrect the verb "examine" from the noun in this sentence: *The Realtor will conduct an examination of the property.* Easy! *The Realtor will examine the property.*

F

fact that—Let a bell ring every time you read that phrase. It's a signal to edit. Take this sentence: *It's a fact that some birds can swim.* Instead simply say, *Some birds can swim.* Now consider this sentence: *Given the fact that it snowed all weekend, we had to cancel the game.* Better: *We canceled the game because it snowed all weekend.*

familiar—Two i's. Think "family," and change the *y* to *i.*

famous—If the person is truly famous, then you don't need the word. So not, *the famous comedian Jerry Seinfeld* or *the famous author Ernest Hemingway.*

But if you use the word "famous" for someone well-known to only a subset of society, then you just make your readers or listeners wonder, or feel stupid. *Ah, yes, the famous Vinny Magliulo!* We know Vinny; he's a legendary oddsmaker in Las Vegas. Chances are you never heard of Vinny, so it's better to explain his fame than hang it all on one word.

firsthand—One word like **secondhand**.

foreword—Opening for a book, not to be confused with **forward**.

frisbee—No, **Frisbee**. The great fear of any brand is that it becomes generic, as was the fate of aspirin, which originally was spelled Aspirin as a registered trademark by Bayer, its manufacturer, in 1899. Frisbee's origin story dates back to pie tins being tossed around from the Bridgeport Frisbie Pie Co., founded in 1871 in Connecticut (History.com, 2022). The Wham-O toy company launched the Super Flyer Frisbee, then Mattel bought Wham-O in 1994. It was about then that we began seeing letters from Mattel's legal department circulating on the Chicago Tribune copy desk anytime we dropped the uppercase "F."

G

genocide—This is a scorching hot political term that should not be used lightly or even go unchallenged. Be careful when somebody works it into a quotation to score political points.

gerund—Just a fancy name for an "-ing" word serving as a noun, as in *Learning is fun!* It looks like a verb, but it's not. The verb form would be *I am learning*.

given—Watch out for human sacrifices! When you start a sentence with *He was given*, it sounds like *he was given up to the gods*. Make it *He received the prize.*

good—Do you mean **well**? You can feel **good** (happy and strong) and you can feel **well** (not sick).

goodness' sake—Yep, that's right—you need an apostrophe. Like for *heaven's sake* and *a day's pay for a day's work*.

grammar—It ends with **-ar**, not **-er**. So don't write "grammer," for goodness' sake.

guerrilla—Two r's and two l's for the rebel; just one "r" in **"gorilla"** for the primate.

H

Hamas—In the 56th edition, the AP Stylebook tells you **Hamas** (AP, 133) is "a Palestinian Islamic political party, which has an armed wing of the same name." That sounds like an understatement given the horrific events of Oct. 7, 2023, which launched a Mideast war involving Hamas and Israel. Israel is more likely to define Hamas as an extremist fundamentalist Palestinian Islamic organization whose goal is to destroy Israel through "holy war." The point is, if you ask Palestinians, they may give you different definitions. Words matter, and politically charged words matter even more. So just be careful when you define things, especially from conflict zones. If you're going to take sides, that's fine; just be upfront about it. Inexplicably, the AP dropped its **Hamas** entry in the 57th edition.

Harvard—As in *the Harvard of…* Jump down to the entry on **Yo-Yo Ma** and you'll see where we're going with this caution about overworked or inappropriate analogies. Harvard University, founded in 1636 as the first college in the colonies—or 140 years before the Declaration of Independence—has a $50 billion endowment compared with $1.6 billion on average for the 379 ranked national universities (Wood, 2023). In other words, there's really no comparison. On the evil side, the same goes for **Hitler**.

hell—As a swear word, this one used to give editors pause. Not just editors, but mothers, too. We have a friend whose mother never let her swear, so when shocked our friend would exclaim: "What the Helen Keller!!!" We'll spare you a list of other curse words—you know them all—and just say, before you want one published, ask yourself, "Is this really necessary?"

Hezbollah—The AP's 56th edition tells you **Hezbollah** (AP, 137) is "the Lebanese Shiite Muslim political party, which has an armed wing of the same name." The word translates to "Party of Allah" in Arabic. Israel might say it's out to get them. Whereas Hamas operates in the Gaza Strip, on Israel's southern side toward Egypt, Hezbollah operates to Israel's north toward Lebanon and Syria. Editors need to know their geography to help readers, listeners and viewers understand complex issues.

Hi, comma!—We can tell a lot about a person who uses a comma for direct address and someone else, sadly, who does not. It's amazing how that little comma can scream, *I'm educated!* So cheers to all you who send us notes that read: *Hi, Buck!* or *Good morning, Mike!*

his or him—It depends on where you put the emphasis. Compare these two sentences: *Did you like his singing?* and *Did you like him singing?* The first puts the emphasis on singing: *Did you like his singing—or do your ears hurt like mine?* The second puts the emphasis on the person: *Did you like him singing or do you prefer Sally?*

historical fact—History is not "the truth," so don't fall into that mind trap when telling a story. Better to keep Napoleon Bonaparte's definition in mind: "History is a set of lies agreed upon." Or Winston Churchill: "History will be kind to me for I intend to write it." Storytellers have great power to decide when to start a tale. Take America, for example. Do you begin with 1492, 1619, 1776 or some other date? The point is, anytime you see "a historical fact" to support an argument, keep looking because you're likely to find another fact to dispute it.

hopeful—Don't say, *She is hopeful for success*; just *She hopes for success.* A news tradition makes it: *She **says** she hopes*, just like *She **says** she thinks.* That's because journalists refrain from reporting from people's heads; they prefer to document what people say or write.

hung—Do you mean **hanged**? Use **hung** for a picture on a wall. Use **hanged** for suicides or executions.

I—We know it's you talking, so just let it rip. No need to say, *I believe that voting is important.* You can just say, *Voting is important.* When you read, or hear, a commentary with a lot of *I-I-I-I-I-I*, the repeated use of the personal pronoun starts to distract. Less is more.

i.e.,—Note the periods and comma. Means *for example,* though it's actually an abbreviation from Latin meaning *that is.*

impostor—Note the "or," as in one person or the other.

include—Use with a partial list. If you list everything, try "consist of."

infinitive—The "to-form" of a verb. Impress your friends with this crazy grammar rule: *The subject of an infinitive is always in the objective case.* In this sentence, *She wanted me to tell the truth*, we have the subject (*me*) before the infinitive (*to tell*).

in order to—Just say "to." So not: *I study hard in order to accomplish my goals.* Rather: *I study hard to accomplish my goals.*

insure—Do you mean **ensure** for guarantee? Reserve the "in" for insurance. We **assure** you, that's the thing to do.

intention—Say *she intended* rather than *It was her intention.* Shun the -tion words.

irregardless—It means "not without regard." Just say **"regardless."**

ISIS—Do you mean **ISIL** or just **IS** or maybe **Daesh?** Welcome back to the Middle East. In the AP Stylebook the entry **Islamic State group** (AP, 161) gives this warning: To avoid giving the impression that it is a nation, do not refer to it as the "Islamic State"; it is the "Islamic State group."

It—Bad start to a sentence. See if you can drop it. So not: *It is really hot in Miami right now.* Better: *Miami is really hot right now.*

-ize—Go easy on the "-ize" verbs. See if alternatives can work for you, such as "use" for "utilize" and "picture" for "visualize." Beware of real stretches like "Americanize." The more you ask a word to do, the less clear it becomes.

J

Jay-Z—Wait, Jay Z. No, it's now **JAY-Z.** You know you're big when dropping a hyphen in your name makes the news. Then you're really big when you insist on ALL CAPS in your name and bring back the hyphen. That's how awesome Shawn Carter really is. The point is, people have the right to spell their names however they want, and even change how they wish to be identified. A common journalist's question is, "How do you spell your name?"

judgment—Just one "e."

just—Be careful, it's an opinion. Often it's a misplaced modifier like its cousins **nearly**, **almost** and **barely**. Remember, keep words close to the ones they modify. So you would not say, *Alice just (nearly, almost, barely) found a quarter when she needed a dollar.* Instead: *Alice found just a quarter. … You get the idea!*

K

Kenneth, what's the frequency?—As the great Milt Hansen, night city editor at the Chicago Tribune, used to say: "Sometimes fact is stranger than fiction." In 1986 Dan Rather, the CBS anchorman who succeeded Walter Cronkite, was attacked on the streets of New York City by a guy repeating inexplicably: "Kenneth, what is the frequency?" A year later, in 1987, songwriter Scott Miller of Game Theory produced, "Kenneth, What's the Frequency?" as reported by Rolling Stone (Ehrlich, 2019). The story did not end there. In 1994, R.E.M. put the "alternative" in rock music yet again by releasing its song "What's the Frequency, Kenneth?" It's an expression that continues to live on in popular culture, so if you hear it, don't be confused.

kindergarten—It's German with a teaching philosophy: *kinder* means children and *garten* means garden. Teaching techniques should help the kids bloom.

Kitty Litter—A brand name for cat litter.

Kleenex—A brand name for tissue.

kudos—Looks plural, but you'll see: *Kudos (praise or credit) is in order for the director.* Simpler is better: *Kudos to the director!*

L

lay—The use of "lie" or "lay" can be tricky. Substitute "reclined" (*I **lay** on the couch all day)* for the past tense or "place" (*Just **lay** the book on the shelf*) for the present tense.

La-Z-Boy—Although the generic term is "recliner," this company makes a lot of different furniture.

lectern—Or do you mean **podium**? You stand *behind* a lectern and stand *on* a **podium**.

lede—The start of a news story or news release. Also, "lead" (pronounced LEED).

lets—Or do you mean **let's?** "To let" is a housing term, as "to rent out" an apartment. "Let's go!" means *let us* rock on!

liaison—Don't forget the middle "i," which acts as a liaison between "Lia" and her "son."

lightning—No "e."

liter—Gas prices in Europe, Asia and other parts of the world will look cheap if you forget we price our gasoline by the gallon, not the liter. Multiply the liter price roughly by four, then calculate the currency exchange.

literally—This literally gets misused all the time when **figuratively** is meant.

longtime—Right, no hyphen, for "a longtime copy editor" or for someone who spent a long time on a copy desk.

low man on the totem pole—Using a cliche is bad enough, but this expression is upside down. For many totem poles, the lowest figures are considered the most prestigious, not the least powerful like a new hire.

M

manner—Usually can be deleted. So don't say *in an adept manner;* just say *adeptly.*

mantel, mantle, Mantle—a shelf, a cloak, a Hall of Fame baseball player.

marshal—Do you mean **martial**? You **marshal** (muster) your forces when faced with **martial** (wartime) law.

media—Journalists get touchy on this point, insisting to say the news media "are." In other words, don't lump us good journalists in with the quasi-ones. Nonetheless, you have readers and listeners who believe: "The media is biased." So think twice before you apply a verb to "media," either in its plural meaning or collective sense.

mens room—Don't go there—it's dangerous grammatically. Enter only the "**men's room**" or "men's clothing store."

middle initial—Names in casualty lists include middle initials for clarity, but that's not always enough. Even full names for the living and the dead can be identical, so include whatever other information you have, such as hometowns and occupations, if it's available.

millions, billions, trillions—The late Republican Sen. Everett Dirksen, who was U.S. Senate minority leader from 1959 to 1969, supposedly said about the federal government's overspending, "A billion here, a billion there, and pretty soon you're talking real money." One billion in 1959 is the inflation equivalent of $10.3 billion today. That same year, 1959, Ralph Wilson bought the Buffalo Bills for $25,000; in 2014 the NFL franchise sold for $1.4 billion (King, 2014). The national debt in 1959 was $285 billion; today it's more than $34 trillion. The point is, tossing around big numbers can be mind-numbing, especially if you don't account for inflation. Try a little humor. "What do you call a billionaire who buys a newspaper?" A millionaire.

minuscule—It's something small and sounds like *mini-school,* so it's often misspelled with an "i" rather than a "u."

minute—It can mean a long time, as in *It's been a minute,* as spoken by a former NFL player about his role in Super Bowl III in 1969. For a full explanation, return to The Zinger Factory in **Chapter 1.4** under **No. 6, Coin a Word or Phrase.** This is an example of creating a new meaning for an existing word.

mishap—Something minor. People die in "accidents."

misspelled—Two s's, two l's. An embarrassing word to misspell.

Moby-Dick—Yep, there's a hyphen there. Just like the metaphor for a goal impossible to attain, you will endlessly struggle to get names correct.

M&Ms, Diet Sprite, the "Mexican Revolution" omelet—Details, details, details. They make for great writing. Don't be the kind of editor who deletes them. Instead, be like the editor who asks, "Did you get the dog's name?" Here are a few examples:

In the we-can't-make-this-up category, we share this news item (Ganz, 2012):

This rock 'n' roll legend turned out to be true: In the 1980s, the party-rock superstars in Van Halen demanded, via a clause embedded in their tour rider, that no brown M&Ms be allowed backstage at their concerts.

Back in the day, there was this report about Dick Cheney's hotel room requirements (NBC News, 2006):

The vice president also requires that all televisions be tuned to Fox News, and a pot of decaf coffee and four cans of "Diet Caffeine Free Sprite" be in the room.

The late, great Angelo Henderson, then a Wall Street Journal reporter working on what would become a 1999 Pulitzer Prize-winning feature story, insisted on the name of a breakfast dish—*a "Mexican Revolution" omelet*—be preserved in his story (Pulitzer Prizes, 1999).

Muhammad—The most popular baby name for a boy in the United Kingdom (Bell, 2022). It translates to "praiseworthy." The tricky part for name counters is there are so many variations of the phonetic spelling from Arabic.

Muhammad the Prophet—Be careful of depictions. A New York Post article told the story of a Hamline University professor in St. Paul, Minnesota, who was fired for showing images of Muhammad in class. When the Post published an image with its news story, it blurred out the prophet's face (Lee, 2023). In 2015 a series of terrorist attacks in Paris killed 11 journalists and six others over the depiction of Muhammad in the satirical magazine Charlie Hebdo (Petrikowski, 2023). In **Chapter 1.3**, our editing philosophy begins with "First, do no harm." That requires cultural sensitivity.

myriad—No "of"—the word means *several*. It's misused myriad times.

myself—I myself think the **reflective pronoun** is usually overkill. Same goes for *himself, herself, yourself, themselves*—you get the idea. Pick your spots if you think the amplification is really necessary.

N

neither—See **either** entry—same rule, only use "nor." *Neither this nor that …*

No. 1—Not *Number One*. Better to say: *We're No. 1!*

none—If you can read it as *not one* or *no one*, then it's singular: *Many fell, but none was injured.* If that doesn't work, then it's plural. See if it means *no amount* or *no two*: *None of the leaves were raked. None of the teens agree on which film to watch.*

not guilty—You'll see: *He pleaded innocent.* Though technically not correct (the choices are "guilty" or "not guilty"), the fear is that the "not" will get lost or go unheard. Making it "innocent" is a journalistic safeguard.

not only—It usually takes a "but" or "but also," with no commas, as in: *There's not only a rule involved but also a lot of good advice.* If you start a sentence with "Not only," it can get tricky, but don't sweat it. You can say, *Not only is the professor giving us good advice, but he's also keeping us sane.*

nut graph—A good one summarizes the point of a story and sets up the rest of the writing with words or phrases that create a kind of outline for what gets covered later. Think of the word "nut" as delivering the "kernel" of truth.

O

occurred—Two c's and two r's, as it's pronounced oh-CUR (accent on the last syllable). Watch for the expression "it occurred to someone." Take this sentence: *Suddenly it occurred to Nancy that the ringmaster was the thief.* Make it: *Suddenly Nancy realized the ringmaster was the thief.*

of—See if you can drop it and flip the phrase. *The monarch of Spain* can be simply *Spain's monarch.* How about this one? *Sales from the month of January set a record.* Yep, you can make it *January sales set a record.*

only—Be careful, it's an opinion. If "only two people" showed up, they might be your best friends. If you use *only*, be sure to place it next to the word it modifies. So don't say, *There only was one choice*; make it instead: *There was only one choice.*

Osama bin Laden—That's the spelling according to AP style (AP, 21). You would think the U.S. government would be the final arbiter on how to translate the name phonetically from Arabic, but no—not for journalists. The official 9/11 Commission Report spells it "Usama Bin Ladin," calling him "UBL" for short.

owing to the fact that—Just say "because."

P

paid—Not "payed."

past—Do you mean **passed**? If you **passed** our grammar test, all your worries are in the **past**.

%—It's OK to use this for "percent" (one word), not "per cent."

pore—You **pore** over your books as you **pour** your coffee.

press—You'll still see "press release," but you'll hear a preference for "news release," especially for broadcast outlets or online publications. The same goes for "press conference"; the AP Stylebook (AP, 234) says "news conference" is preferred.

principal—Or do you mean **principle**? The first one is tricky because it can be both a noun and an adjective. *The school **principal** is your "pal"* (noun). If something is important, it's a "principal" concern (adjective). If your point is about rules or values, then you use **principle**. *She is a woman of **principle** who taught her children to live according to the highest principles.*

prior to—Just say "before."

professor—Lowercase as a job description (professor John Chatham) but capitalize as a formal title (Associate Professor John Chatham).

pull a Charissa—Make something up. When NFL sideline reporter Charissa Thompson admitted in 2023 that she invented quotes from coaches, there was a minor earthquake. Former "Monday Night Football" sideline reporter Lisa Guerrero, who said she was fired 20 years earlier for an honest mistake, told NPR that Thompson's confession was "like she threw a verbal Molotov cocktail." In that way, she said, Thompson blew up the credibility of not only all women sideline reporters but all journalists in a world where "fake news" claims persist (NPR, 2023).

 Q

Q—Just inadvertently dropping a capital letter like that into your prose can get you accused of being a conspiracy theorist. We're talking about QAnon and its secret codes. God forbid your cat sits on your keyboard and tweets, "WWG1WGA." It's important to stay hip to what's in the news (Rosen, 2022), so you don't innocently say or write something that causes you a headache.

R

Realtor—Not all real estate agents are Realtors, who have joined the National Association of Realtors and pay dues.

receive—Remember, i *b*efore e except after c. "Thief" is correct.

refute—You won the argument! If not, you just **disputed** something.

republican—This refers to republican ideals, not the Republican Party (capitalized).

rock 'n' roll—But it's the Rock & Roll Hall of Fame in Cleveland, Ohio.

S

S-sound—Stop on the s-sound: don't confuse "it's" for "its." Write "teacher's pet" but "teachers strike"—both are correct: one possessive, the other not. Do you mean the "candidate's progress" (one person) or the "candidates' progress" (multiple people)? Slow down for plurals and possessives, and exaggerate the "s" when reading your writing to focus your attention.

science—It's one word whose value dropped like the Dow Jones Industrial Average in the 2020 pandemic. Your readers and listeners can be defined by which group thinks "Follow the science" is a joke and which does not. It's a cautionary tale for writers and editors about sources, attribution and, ultimately, credibility.

sex—You probably mean "gender."

split infinitive—Some split infinitives are famous, such as ***to boldly go*** from "Star Trek" fame. Others, not so much: ***to quickly go*** can easily become ***to go quickly***.

stationery—Note the *-er* as in **paper.**

style—Don't confuse a writer's style, or voice, with style rules in a stylebook.

swum—Some perfectly correct words—a past participle in this case—just look and sound so weird they get misused. *I **swim** today, I **swam** yesterday, I have **swum** every Sunday for a week.* Yes, *swum.* You'll hear and read *have swam* instead—just as incorrectly as *have ran* rather than *have run.* Here's where a good dictionary comes to the rescue, conjugating verbs in the present and past tenses, then listing the past participle used for the present and past perfect tenses.

T

that—Do you mean **who**? Take this sentence: *Democracy relies on journalists that are honest.* True dat, but it should be journalists "who" are honest. Use "who" for people and pets; "that" for things and the horse with no name.

that, no comma—Listen to this: *The story that I'm writing with a manual typewriter is a deep-sea fishing tale. The one that I'm writing by hand is more romantic.* No commas with **that.** Just get to the point of the different stories and writing methods.

that with verbs—Some verbs have a built-in *that—assert that, contend that, declare that, estimate that.* Even *said* takes a *that* when it's used with a day of the week: *The mayor said Monday that property taxes must decline.*

the—Do you mean **a** or **an?** If you're using "the," then you've already used an "a" or "an" with the noun. So you wrote, *A dog just ran in front of my car.* Then you add: ***The dog is just fine, but I'm not.*** When you say **the** first, then you're making a definitive statement, such as: *Aaron Rodgers is the greatest quarterback who ever lived.*

their—Give them **their** money. Not **there** or **they're.**

their opinion—When you're talking about more than one person, you need to add an "s"—**"their opinions."**

then—Do you mean **than**? These two get confused in an autocorrect-mispronunciation haze. Just remember to use **then** for time and **than** to compare. If you think one word is better **than** the other, **then** you're crazy.

There—Bad start to a sentence. See if you can drop it. So not: *There are three killer bears stalking their prey.* Better: *Three killer bears are stalking their prey.*

too—There's "too much" difference between this word and the word **"to,"** yet they get confused.

try and find—No, **"try to find."** You're not taking separate actions.

U

Ukko-Pekka Luukkonen—Sometimes getting a name straight requires double-checking your math. For the Buffalo Sabres' Finnish goalie, that's six *k's,* three *u's,* two *o's, e's* and *n's,* one *a*—and don't forget the hyphen. As we advised in our editing strategy, SLOW DOWN for NAMES.

unique—Only one of its kind. If there's more than one, then it's **rare,** not unique. Sadly, AP's 57th edition says writers can use "very unique" to mean rare.

United States—When AP style overthinks something, feel free to ignore the entry, such as the one on **United States** (AP, 298). For some odd reason, the stylebook says it's **U.S.** in text and **US** in headlines (no periods). We prefer that you stay consistent using **U.S.,** whose periods AP requires in headlines for push alerts. Crazy, we know.

V

very—Try to delete it and find a stronger word. So, for example:

- very beautiful—exquisite
- very fine—superb
- very rich—wealthy
- very smart—brilliant
- very tasty—delicious

W

Washington—Big difference between Washington State and Washington, D.C., so be clear about which one you're writing about.

well—Means both "not sick" and "effectively." So you can say, "I am well" and "I work well."

which—Think "comma-which-comma," as in: *The environmental program, which was approved on a 10-3 vote, will reduce the city's carbon footprint*. Or use comma-which as a tipoff to tighten: *The environmental program, approved on a 10-3 vote, will reduce the city's carbon footprint*.

who—Or do you mean **whom**? Figuring this out gets easier if you remember a few basics: 1) Every verb has a subject; 2) **who** is a subject like *I, he, she, they*; and 3) if you can't match **who** with a verb, then you use **whom** as an object. The same goes for **whoever** and **whomever**.

who, comma—Take this sentence: *Charlie Murphy, who ran for mayor in 2022 and lost, announced he is entering the priesthood*. We use commas around the "who ran" clause because it's considered nonessential. It reads more like, "Oh, by the way …"

who is, who was—See if you can drop them. For example, *I received the gift from someone who is (was) familiar with my family*. This can be: *I received the gift from someone familiar with my family*.

who, no comma—Note this sentence: *The man who rescued me is next to the man who sank my canoe*. There are no commas because "who" introduces essential clauses that define the different men.

X

Malcolm X—Assassinated in 1965. Nearly 60 years later, this NPR headline: "The men exonerated in the Malcolm X killing will receive $36 million" (AP, 2022). We devote an entire chapter in **Section 2** to dealing with crime stories. The wrongful convictions in the Malcolm X case help us summarize the chapter in six words—don't convict someone in your report.

X-rayed—Weird, we know, but it's correct.

Y

year—Use commas around a year with dates, as in: *On May 13, 2026, the mayor will turn 100 years old.*

Yo-Yo Ma—Great name, great cellist. Some writers will make the mistake of trying to compare "a virtuoso" in one field with this virtuoso cellist: *She's the Yo-Yo Ma of quiltmakers.* Please don't.

Z

Zelenskyy—Yes, two y's—that's the way Ukraine's president, Volodymyr, wants it spelled.

REFERENCES

Associated Press (2022, October 31). The men exonerated in the Malcolm X killing will receive $36 million. NPR. https://www.npr.org/2022/10/31/1132757141/the-men-exonerated-in-the-malcolm-x-killing-will-receive-36-million

Bell, S. (2022, November). Top baby names of 2022. Babycentre. https://www.babycentre.co.uk/top-baby-names

Ehrlich, B. (2019, November 1). Flashback: Dan Rather's 'Kenneth, what is the frequency?' assault inspires R.E.M., Game Theory. *Rolling Stone.* https://www.rollingstone.com/music/music-news/kenneth-whats-the-frequency-rem-game-theory-906518/

Estepa, J. (2018, May 31). Covfefe, one year later: How a late-night Trump tweet turned into a phenomenon. USA Today. https://www.usatoday.com/story/news/politics/onpolitics/2018/05/31/covfefe-one-year-anniverary-donald-trumps-confusing-tweet/659414002/

Ganz, J. (2012, February 14). The truth about Van Halen and those brown M&Ms. NPR. https://www.npr.org/sections/therecord/2012/02/14/146880432/the-truth-about-van-halen-and-those-brown-m-ms

History.com (2022, January 20). 1957, January 23, Toy company Wham-O produces first Frisbees. https://www.history.com/this-day-in-history/toy-company-wham-o-produces-first-frisbees

King, P. (2014, March 26) R.I.P. Ralph Wilson. *Sports Illustrated.* https://www.si.com/nfl/2014/03/26/ralph-wilson-buffalo-bills-dies#:~:text=Buffalo%20never%20had%20a%20major,settled%20for%20an%20AFL%20team.

Lee, M. (2023, January 8). Hamline University professor fired for showing images of Muhammad had warned students in syllabus. *New York Post.*

Loboda, A. (2023, January 7). Ashley Westerman Loboda is with Anton Loboda in Lviv, Ukraine. Facebook post.

NBC News (2006, March 23). Site reveals Cheney's hotel requirements. https://www.nbcnews.com/id/wbna11975731

NPR (2023, November 20). Colleagues say it's a firing offense when a sideline reporter makes up quotes. *Morning Edition.* https://www.npr.org/2023/11/20/1214109137/colleagues-say-its-a-firing-offense-when-a-sideline-reporter-makes-up-quotes#:~:text=Hourly%20News-,Colleagues%20say%20it's%20a%20'firing%20offense'%20when%20a%20sideline%20reporter,she%20was%20a%20sideline%20reporter.

Petrikowski, N. P. (2023, January 1). *Charlie Hebdo* shooting, terrorist attacks, Paris, France [2015]. Britannica.

Pulitzer Prizes (1999). Angelo B. Henderson of the *Wall Street Journal.* https://www.pulitzer.org/winners/angelo-b-henderson

Rosen, J. (2022, September 24). Trump signals affinity with QAnon followers in social media post, at rallies. CBS News. https://www.cbsnews.com/news/donald-trump-qanon-followers-social-media/

Wood, S. (2023, October 2). 15 national universities with the biggest endowments. *U.S. News & World Report.* https://www.usnews.com/education/best-colleges/the-short-list-college/articles/10-universities-with-the-biggest-endowments#:~:text=The%20average%20endowment%20at%20the,size%20is%20about%20%241.6%20billion.

FURTHER READING, RESOURCES

Meek, A. (2022, May 14). Ukraine stories podcast: NPR veterans deliver a tour de force of narrative journalism. *Forbes.* https://www.forbes.com/sites/andymeek/2022/05/14/ukraine-stories-podcast-npr-veterans-deliver-a-tour-de-force-of-narrative-journalism

Rashida (n.d.). Why does Disney sue everyone who uses its brand? Content Cucumber. https://www.contentcucumber.com/blog/why-does-disney-sue-everyone-who-use-its-brand

Willett, J. (n.d.). Get the name of the dog: How thinking like a journalist leads to better content. Influence & Co. https://blog.influenceandco.com/get-the-name-of-the-dog-how-thinking-like-a-journalist-leads-to-better-content

DEEP GRAMMAR

Introduction

> **"** *I am this old; therefore, I must know grammar."*

Nope, the life of a writer or an editor doesn't work that way. Grammar is learned.

It's best learned over time with great instruction and plenty of reinforcement.

Sadly, that hasn't been the case for many writers and editors. No worries, we're here to help. Just lift your tray tables and move your seat to the upright and locked position. A grammar oxygen mask is about to appear before your very eyes. Get ready for Part II of **The Language Skills Survival Kit: Deep Grammar**.

After teaching language skills for four decades, we understand that not all minds think alike. The core concepts of editing may resonate with "global thinkers," who like to see the big picture first, more than "sequential thinkers," who prefer a more logical and orderly approach.

That's why we offer the survival kit either to supplement what you have read so far or to provide a launching pad for you to start gaining confidence with your writing and editing. We hope that if you are a visual learner, the parsing of sentences will help you understand our points more easily.

In this section we'll focus on grammar vocabulary and concepts that will help you better understand our advice in the next section, which focuses on punctuation. A person might write with good grammar based on years of hearing it spoken correctly, but that takes editors only so far. They need to understand the rules so they can explain any changes they make. That's why we stress knowing the rules and how they work.

The Right Tone

We made this point before, but it bears repeating: Writing rules begin with tone. Most news stories and news releases require a formal tone, meaning painfully correct grammar. Feature stories, columns or opinion pieces, and advertising copy can take an informal tone. That means grammar rules can be relaxed and sometimes even broken. Writers and editors first need to know the rules before they can know when to bend or break them.

Ready for takeoff? Here goes!

Parsing, Parts of Speech and Functions

When we "parse" a sentence, we determine what part of speech each word plays, and then we label each word as such. Parsing parts of speech is the first step to understanding the language, then comes an understanding of the functions words perform. Together these exercises can help you build confidence as a writer or editor. First, a quick review of **The First Step** sidebar in **Chapter 1.7**, then we'll build on your knowledge. Here goes:

Parts of Speech (9)

n   **noun** is the name of a person, place or thing.

pro   **pronoun** takes the place of a noun.

v   **verb** can be an action verb ("write," "edit," "parse") or a linking verb ("to be," "to feel").

adj   **adjective** modifies a noun ("happy person") or pronoun ("she is happy").

adv   **adverb** modifies a verb ("work quickly"), adjective ("really smart") or other adverb ("very effectively").

prep   **preposition** shows relationship ("to," "from," "over," "between").

con   **conjunction** joins ideas ("and," "but," "or").

I   **interjection** shouts ("yikes!").

a   **article** sets up a noun ("a," "an," "the").

Functions in a Sentence (8)

s   **subject** is the doer that usually starts a sentence.

p   **predicate** is the verb, only with a new name, that connects with the subject to create a clause. A phrase does not have a predicate.

op   **object of the preposition** is the noun or pronoun that follows a preposition.

do   **direct object** is what an action verb delivers.

io   **indirect object** is the receiver of the direct object.

pa   **predicate adjective** follows a linking verb and modifies the subject.

pn   **predicate nominative** is a noun or pronoun that follows a linking verb and relates to the subject.

inf   **infinitive** is the "to" version of a verb ("to write," "to edit," "to retire") that is not conjugated ("she writes," "I edited," "they will retire").

The Difference Between Clauses and Phrases

Clauses have subjects and predicates; phrases do not. Let us explain by trying out this parsing thing. Take a look at this sentence:

They paid John under the table.

OK, we have both a clause and a prepositional phrase. Can you tell which is which?

Let's parse it first for parts of speech:

pro	**v**	**n**	**prep**	**a**	**n**
They	paid	John	under	the	table.

Now for functions:

s	**p**	**do**	**op**		
They	paid	John	under	the	table.

The clause is "They paid" and the phrase is "under the table." The prepositional phrase doubles as an adverb telling where. Good so far, right?

Now how would you parse this sentence?

The man John thanked shook his hand.

Now we have two clauses—"The man shook" and "John thanked"—and no phrases. Right? Phrases typically begin with prepositions, but there are no prepositions here. See?

a	**n**	**n**	**v**	**v**	**pro**	**n**
The	man	John	thanked	shook	his	hand.

Note: "Man" is a common noun. "John" (capitalized) is a proper noun.

But just as the prepositional phrase "under the table" also acted as an adverb, one of the clauses here acts as an adjective. Do you see that, too?

	s	**adj**	**p**		**do**
The	man	John thanked	shook	his	hand.

Yep, sometimes clauses, like "John thanked," can act as adjectives, in this case modifying the noun "man." Adjectives answer the question, "Which one?" Or, in this case, "Which man?"

If you marked "John" as a subject and "thanked" as a predicate, you're not wrong. It's just not their main functions in the sentence. "The man shook" is the main clause and "John thanked" is a subordinate clause.

Here is an example of a prepositional phrase acting as an adjective:

	s	**op** **p**			**do**
The	man	in the **booth**	took	John's	money.

The preposition "in" starts a phrase that answers the question, "Which man?" There's just one main clause here: "the man took."

In the old days, we would "diagram" sentences as a way, like parsing, to help you see the syntax of how sentences are built. This brings us back to the **Chapter 1.7** analogy about the difference between taking a driving lesson and learning auto mechanics. You are now learning the mechanics of the language.

The more familiar and comfortable you are with the vocabulary of grammar, the more the rules will make sense. Let's take a deeper look at the nine parts of speech.

Parts of Speech, Take 2

We just gave you the skinny on the nine parts of speech. It's worth taking a little more time to explain them. Here goes.

NOUN

The word "noun" comes from Latin meaning "name." That's why we say a noun is the name of a person, place, thing, idea or quality. We have **common nouns** (lowercase like this), **proper nouns** (capitalized) and verb forms that acts as nouns (**gerunds**).

Those gerunds tend to be "-ing" words, such as "writing" in this sentence: "Writing is fun." Be careful because the same word can be used as a verb ("she was writing") or an adjective ("the writing guidelines").

Parsing tip: Nouns answer the question **"who?"** or **"what?"** A tipoff to a noun is that an **article ("a," "an," "the")** precedes it.

PRONOUN

A pronoun takes the place of a noun. The noun it replaces is called the "antecedent." Take this sentence:

Eric has no money because he gave it away.

The pronoun is "he" and the proper noun that gives it meaning is "Eric," the antecedent.

You'll recall from **Chapter 1.5: Style** that a lot has been written about the need to be respectful when it comes to someone's preference on the use of **pronouns** and **gender-neutral language**. We, as a culture, are in transition from historical definitions.

A note to the wise: We know some of you may be seeing missing, or misplaced, pronouns here. We understand both the power of history and the pursuit of social change and justice. We're on your side if you wish to create a local style sheet that adds to, or changes, what is advised about the **use of pronouns** in the AP Stylebook, the Chicago Manual of Style or any other stylebook for your organization. Here is what tradition tells us:

Personal pronouns come in three persons, are declined as they would be used as subjects, objects and possessives, and may be singular or plural, like so:

Person, number	Case		
	Nominative	Objective	Possessive
First, singular	I	me	my, mine
First, plural	we	us	our, ours
Second, singular	you	you	your, yours
Second, plural	you (y'all)	you (y'all)	your, yours
Third, singular	she, he, it	her, him, it	her, hers, his, its
Third, plural	they	them	their, theirs

A tip of the hat to those of you who use "y'all" for the plural "you," bless your heart.

Interrogative pronouns give writers heartburn: **"who," "whom," "whose."**

Pronouns used as subjects are in the **nominative case**, as in: "She is happy." You'll remember under "Functions in a Sentence," we mentioned

predicate nominative. That's when the pronoun "she" follows a linking verb. So the phone rings, the person asks for her and she says, "This is she."

Pronouns used as objects are in the **objective case**, as when the pronoun is used as a direct object, an indirect object or an object of a preposition. More on this in a bit, but the subject of an infinitive is also in the objective case.

Pronouns in the **possessive case** create autocorrect spelling problems because unlike nouns that add an "apostrophe-s" to become possessive, these personal pronouns do not. So don't confuse them with **contractions**:

its not **it's** (it is or has)
their not **they're** (they are)
your not **you're** (you are)
whose not **who's** (who is or has)

VERB

A verb can be an **action verb** (She "painted" the barn) or a **linking verb** (She "is" a painter), also called a "state-of-being verb" (a version of "to be").

A verb may be in one of **six tenses**:

present	She "paints" today.
past	She "painted" yesterday.
future	She "will paint" tomorrow.
present perfect	She "has painted" often.
past perfect	She "had painted" before.
future perfect	She "will have painted" for 10 years.

Or **two voices**:

active voice	She "painted" the room.
passive voice	The room "was painted" by her.

Or **three moods**:

indicative	She "painted" using watercolors.
imperative	"Paint" the walls, please.
subjunctive	Her boss demanded that she "paint" faster.

That's if the verb is conjugated. Otherwise, you're dealing with an **infinitive** ("to paint"). You can read more about infinitives under **Functions in a Sentence.** They fit into a larger category called **verbals.**

ADJECTIVE

An adjective can be a word, a phrase or a clause used to modify a noun or pronoun.

First, a little story: You're minding your own business, when all of a sudden you see two cats—a pretty one and a mangy one—confront two mice. One mouse gets frozen stiff and the other runs away. So you tell your mother:

The pretty cat chased the mouse that ran.

Parsing time! Can you identify the adjectives?

Parsing tip: An adjective answers the questions **"which one?" "what kind?" "how much?"** or **"how many?"**

Time's up! Here are the two adjectives:

"pretty"—a word that modifies the noun "cat," telling what kind.

"that ran"—a clause that modifies the noun "mouse," telling which one.

Hope you were two-for-two. Getting good at parsing takes time. Let's go to our next part of speech.

ADVERB

An adverb is a word, a phrase or a clause used to modify a verb, an adjective or another adverb. Sometimes an adverb can modify an entire sentence.

Parsing time again: Can you identify how many adverbs are in this sentence?

The very cute dog wandered slowly into the store when the owner arrived.

Parsing tip: An adverb answers the questions **"how?" "when?"** or **"where?"**

OK, here are the four adverbs:

"very"—a word that modifies the adjective "cute," telling how cute.

"slowly"—a word that modifies the verb "wandered," telling how fast.

"into the store"—a prepositional phrase that tells "where" the dog wandered.

"when the owner arrived"—a clause that tells "when" the dog entered.

You're seeing it now, we hope. Here are examples of how an adverb can modify an entire sentence:

> **Seriously**, I will never go into that school again.
> **Fortunately**, I have friends I can count on.
> **Accordingly**, the defendant will be held without bail.

PREPOSITION

A preposition is a word that shows relationship. It's followed by an object, which can be a noun or pronoun. For example:

"He runs **like** me." (preposition "like," object the pronoun "me")

"He ran **toward** the exit." (preposition "toward," object the noun "exit")

So far we have seen a prepositional phrase used as an adverb. It's important to keep those modifiers close to the words they modify to avoid confusion. There's a big difference between these two sentences:

Running into the house, the woman saw the deer.

The woman saw the deer running into the house.

Parsing tip: The English language has 150 or so prepositions. To give you feel for the way the word shows relationships, here are some frequently used ones:

aboard	beside	outside
about	between	over
above	beyond	since
across	by	through
after	down	throughout
against	during	to
along	except	under
amid	for	underneath
among	from	unto
around	in	up
at	into	upon
before	of	with
behind	off	within
below	on	
beneath	out	

A note about "to": Don't confuse the preposition "to" with an infinitive ("to run," "to jump," "to write," "to edit"). The infinitive "to" is part of the verb.

CONJUNCTION

A conjunction connects words, phrases or clauses. There are three types: coordinating, subordinating and correlative.

a. Coordinating conjunctions

The most common ones are **"and"** and **"but."** These conjunctions connect two words, two phrases or two clauses, as in:

You and I are twins. (words)

She went to the doctor but not to the dentist. (phrases)

I'll bring milk and you bring flour. (clauses)

The key is that the elements connected are of **equal rank**. One does not depend on the other for meaning. Other coordinating conjunctions include **"for," "or," "nor," "so," "yet."**

Conjunctive adverbs also are used to connect clauses of equal rank. Examples: "however," "then," "therefore," "thus" (use rarely).

b. Subordinating conjunctions

These connect independent clauses, which can stand alone as sentences, with dependent clauses, which cannot. Take this sentence:

I went first through the door because she was too scared.

Can you identify the independent clause?
Right: "I went first through the door."
Why is the second clause dependent? Well think about the reaction if you said: "She is too scared." Someone would ask, "Too scared about what?" The answer—too scared about what's outside—is dependent on the meaning of the first clause.

Subordinating conjunctions include not only **"because"** but also **"as," "as if," "before," "if," "since," "that," "till," "unless," "when," "where," "whether."**

Relative pronouns, such as **"who," "whom," "whose," "which," "what"** and **"that"** also can be used as subordinating conjunctions.

c. Correlative conjunctions

Correlative conjunctions are used in pairs, such as **both/and, either/or, neither/nor, not only/but also, as (so)/as.**

The key is that whatever word or phrasing is on one side of the conjunction should be the same on the other side. So, for example:

Both a strong leader and a fine person (a=a)

Either the Yankees or the Red Sox (the=the)

Neither England nor France (country name=country name)

Not only hot but also spicy (adjective=adjective)

She is as tall as he is (She is=he is)

The mother is not so tall as the father (the mother=the father)

A negative word like "not" or "never" turns the first "as" into "so."

INTERJECTION

An interjection expresses strong feeling, such as **"oh!" "hurrah!" "wow!"**

    Parsing tip: Look for an exclamation point following the words.

ARTICLES

The articles—**"a," "an," "the"**—are considered to be adjectives as they typically modify nouns. But for us they feel different enough that we put them in a separate category for parts of speech.

Articles fall into two groups. We know there's a difference between saying "a religion" and "the religion," so grammatically the terms are indefinite ("a," "an") and definite ("the") articles.

The **indefinite articles** are used to refer to an unknown member of a group or to an example of something. The **definite article** refers to something known to the writer and reader, or something previously mentioned in the story.

Compare these two sentences:

***A** woman walked into the bank and began shouting.*

***The** woman walked into the bank and began shouting.*

Both are correct if the articles are used properly. The first says a woman we don't know walked into the bank. The second refers to a specific woman, probably mentioned earlier in the story.

Functions in a Sentence, Take 2!

We just gave you the skinny on the eight functions in a sentence. It's worth taking a little more time to explain them. Here goes.

SUBJECT

A subject does what the predicate expresses; it's the **"who"** or **"what"** that goes with the predicate. Generally, the subject comes before the predicate.

PREDICATE

Predicate is another term for a verb, either **action (transitive)** or **linking (intransitive).** "Predicate" is a useful term because a predicate can include more than one verb. For example:

*The guitar **can be played** with a pick or **strummed** with fingers.*

A transitive verb is an action verb, such as **"fix,"** that takes a direct object. For example:

Jim fixed his car.

An intransitive verb is often a linking verb such as **"is."** For example:

Jim is a car mechanic.

A transitive verb may or may not carry a **direct object**. For example:

Larry played the fish like an expert. (direct object "fish")

Susan played alone in the sand. (no direct object)

An intransitive verb may be followed by a **predicate adjective,** as in:

Susan was lonely.

An intransitive verb may be followed by a **predicate nominative,** too. Let's say Jill sees Susan playing alone and goes over to play with her. The teacher notices the kind gesture, asks Susan about who befriended her, and Susan points to Jill and says:

This is she.

DIRECT OBJECT

We can say this now to you with confidence: the direct object receives the action expressed by the transitive verb. A direct object may be a noun or a pronoun. There's news in this example:

*The mail carrier bit the **dog.***

In a follow-up story about the dog, if it was a pet, then you would use the pronoun "him" or "her" as the direct object. Otherwise, if the poor dog were a stray and available for adoption, then you would use the pronoun "it" until it got a name.

INDIRECT OBJECT

The indirect object receives the direct object. Like the direct object, it can be a noun or pronoun. Can you identify the indirect object in this sentence?

The mail carrier gave George the letter.

Right, the indirect object is "George," who was eyewitness to the carrier-dog altercation. In a recap, you could say:

The mail carrier gave him the letter before the dog approached.

Indirect object "him," direct object "letter."

OBJECT OF THE PREPOSITION

A noun or pronoun that follows a preposition in a phrase is called the object of the preposition. The nouns are not a problem, but ay yai yai, watch out for "I." Please don't disappoint your old professors by being caught saying:

walking toward him and I (nope)

giving a gift to her and I (nope)

a difficult time for Steve and I (nope)

And, of course, the insidious:

Just between you and I (nope)

We're sure you're not the selfish type, but when it comes to these objects of the preposition, it's all about me, me, me, me.

PREDICATE ADJECTIVE

The predicate adjective reaches back from a linking verb and modifies the subject, which may be a noun or pronoun. It typically arises after a form of the verb "to be," as in:

*The mayor was **funny.***

*She is **smart.***

But there are other linking verbs at work, often ones related to the senses, as in:

*Damar feels **ill**.*

*The banana tastes **bad**.*

*The research paper looks **good**.*

PREDICATE NOMINATIVE

The predicate nominative works just like the predicate adjective only what follows the linking verb is a noun or pronoun. So, for example:

*He is the **president**.*

*The suspect is **he**.*

The correct form sounds so weird that you'll see this written instead:

The suspect is him.

Grammatically incorrect, but acceptable.

Be careful about using "I'm him." The Urban Dictionary points out "h-i-m" is a slogan used by musician Kevin Gates to mean "his (or her) imperial majesty." Trash-talking athletes on the basketball court or football playing field will declare, "I'm Him."

Once you get fully comfortable with your knowledge of grammar, feel free to declare yourself, "I'm him," "I'm her," "I'm them," or the objective pronoun of your choice.

INFINITIVE

Just as we departed from grammatical tradition by adding articles in our **Parts of Speech**, we end this segment on **Functions in a Sentence** with the infinitive, which we addressed briefly under verbs. Here's why: Take a look at this sentence and tell us how many clauses you see:

He thought her to be me.

Answer, two: "He thought" and "her to be." You see "He" as the subject of the predicate "thought," right? Here's the tricky part about subjects and verbs when you're dealing with infinitives:

The subject of an infinitive is always in the objective case.

In this sentence, the subject of the infinitive "to be" is "her." The linking verb remains an equal sign, so what's on one side, the objective case "her," is parallel to the "me" on the other side. So, for the record, look at another sentence:

He thought the woman in the back of the limo to be a movie star.

The subject of the infinitive is "woman" and the object is "movie star"—both in the objective case. Nouns don't show their case so clearly as pronouns.

Congratulations, you're now fully up to speed on all things parsing!

A Dozen Tips for the Serious Writer and Editor

"I'm looking for the right word," your friend says, seeking advice about her writing. Now you can really help. As we said in **The First Step** sidebar in **Chapter 1.7**, it's not so much the word as its use in a sentence that makes it a part of speech.

When in doubt about what part of speech a word is, consult your dictionary.

The dictionary might list several parts of speech for the same word, so be guided by how the word is used in the sentence. Now that you're feeling more confident with your grammar vocabulary, we're pleased to offer a little more technical advice.

1. Know Your Adjectives from Your Adverbs

Do you see anything wrong with this phrase?

a real nice surprise

It should be "a really nice surprise." "Real" is an adjective and "nice" is an adjective; it takes an adverb like "really" to modify nice, formally speaking.

2. Use Adverbs as a Tipoff to Editing

The verb-adverb combination is one to watch. Often it's a tipoff to a weak verb, or at least a challenge to find a more forceful or precise one. So:

*ran quickly—***raced**

*ran really quick—***sped or dashed**

*moved extremely slow—***crawled**

3. Avoid Turning Perfectly Good Nouns into Awkward Verbs

You hear someone say something that sounds forced, such as:

The president tasked an aide to deliver the bad news.

Now you know why: "task" is a noun that's being twisted into a verb. A more natural verb might be "asked" or "assigned." A dictionary will list "task" first as a noun, then as a verb. Good writers hold words to their primary use.

Here's another example out of left field:

The Cubs downed the Dodgers.

Yes, we know the word "down" can serve many roles. But what's its primary use? Well, if you go to a dictionary, you'll see it listed as an adverb, a preposition and an adjective long before it's defined as a verb. That's a tip that a more natural verb might be "defeated."

4. Adjectives Aren't Verbs and Conjunctions Aren't Prepositions

A variation of this game of Twister is the use of the adjective "best" as a verb, as in: "The Cubs bested the Dodgers." This is not what's meant by clever writing or sentence variation; it just leads to misguided cliches.

Readers or listeners are used to having the conjunction "but" serve as a directional signal toward a new idea, as in:

The lawmakers say they are concerned about climate change, but their policies speak to something else.

Then a writer will switch gears and use "but" as a preposition:

The lawmakers lined up to vote, all but the New York senator.

It sounds a little jarring because "except" is the more natural preposition. By natural we mean if you go to your dictionary, you'll see "except" listed as a preposition first and "but" listed first as a conjunction—not a preposition.

5. The Right Way Follows the Right Tone

In **Chapter 1.4** we advised you to **Watch Out for False Passives** ("he was given") and **Stop on "It" and "There"** (expletives, not a pronoun or an adverb). We suggest that you reread those passages now that you have a tighter grasp on parts of speech and functions in a sentence.

But the key point now, which returns us to **the Right Tone** segment, is never say never. You'll see stylebook entries that use the word "always," but now that you are learning the rules, you are also earning the license to break them. As we said, we have rules for a formal tone and reasons to stretch those rules to create an informal tone. Starting a sentence with "It" or "There" just might fit the right tone for a feature story.

6. Use Contractions Wisely

Contractions often contain two parts of speech. For example, the contraction "it's" contains a pronoun ("it") and a verb ("is" or "has").

Contractions lend an informal tone to a story. Avoid their use in serious stories, but always keep them in quotes: "The president was not happy when he said, 'I can't accept this.'"

7. Keep Track of Pronouns and Their Antecedents

Use pronouns sparingly, especially "it"; pronouns can lead to confusion. For example:

The dog dragged in the cloth, and it was muddy.

Question: Is the "dog" or the "cloth" muddy?

8. Verbals Can Be Various Parts of Speech

Verbals are forms of verbs often used as other parts of speech. The verbals are the infinitive, the gerund and the participle.

- The **infinitive** is the "to" form of a verb. The present infinitive would be "to go." The perfect infinitive would be "to have gone."
- The **gerund** is a verbal noun. It can be used as a subject: **Reading** is fun. And it can be used as an object: Doug enjoys **reading**.
- The **participle** is a verbal adjective. It can be the present participle, the past participle or the perfect participle. This sentence uses a present participle as an adjective:

Sitting here, we saw the parade. ("Sitting" modifies "we.")

As we highlighted in **Chapter 1.7, Beware the -ing Ding and the -ed Dud**, a common error is the dangling participle. The noun or pronoun modified by the participle must immediately follow the phrase containing the participle. So this would be a mistake:

Sitting here, the parade passed us by.

This sentence uses a past participle as an adjective:

The terms suggested by the committee were fair. ("suggested" modifies "terms")

This sentence uses a perfect participle as adjective:

Having finished the work, I left. ("Having finished" modifies "I")

9. Pronouns Before Gerunds Can Get Tricky

Remember, a gerund is the "ing" form of a verb used as a noun. Sometimes you'll see a possessive noun used before a gerund, as in:

John's playing the tuba was obnoxious.

Other times you'll have to decide whether to use a possessive or not. Take these two sentences: Do you see a difference?

Did you enjoy his playing the guitar?

Did you enjoy him playing the guitar?

Yes, there's a difference between a focus on "playing" and a focus on "him." Consider these follow-up sentences:

Did you enjoy his playing the guitar? I thought his performance was much better than his tuba playing.

Did you enjoy him playing the guitar? I thought Julie was better.

10. How to Navigate Who or Whom, Good or Well, Lie or Lay

Now that you're hip to grammar lingo, some word choices will be easier for you to make. Hear us now:

Who is a subject or a predicate nominative.

Whom can be a direct object, an indirect object, an object of a preposition or the subject of an infinitive.

Get that? Wow, how far you've come!

Here's where parsing really helps. When you're trying to figure out **who** or **whom,** or **whoever** and **whomever**, start with the verbs. How many verbs are there in this sentence?

Give the package to whoever comes to the door.

Two, right. That means you must have two subjects, and they are **(you) give** and **whoever comes.** The entire clause ("whoever comes to the door") acts as the indirect object.

This is tricky because two things point to using "whomever": 1) the object of the preposition "to" and 2) a clause as an indirect object. But in grammatical tug-of-wars like this, verbs take precedent. That's why we say start with the verbs and match up their subjects.

Now compare that sentence with this one:

Give the package to whomever.

Here you have subject ("you"), verb ("give"), direct object ("package"), object of the preposition "to" ("whomever").

Here are other examples and explanations:

Who is there? ("who" as **subject***)*

Bill is who? You mean he's the club president. ("who" as **predicate nominative***)*

You hit whom? That's the principal, for goodness' sake. ("whom" as **direct object***)*

You gave whom the gift? ("whom" as **indirect object***)*

The race is now between you and whom? ("whom" as **object of the preposition***)*

You thought whom to be me? She's a movie star—thanks a lot! ("whom" as **subject of the infinitive***)*

Good is an adjective, which modifies nouns and pronouns.
Well is an adverb, but it also can be an adjective meaning "not sick."
So you would say correctly:

She's a **good** *musician. (adjective meaning impressive)*

I am **good***. (adjective meaning fine)*

I feel **well***. (adjective meaning not sick)*

I work **well** *in teams. (adverb meaning effectively)*

"Well" is often used to create a double negative, and that's OK, too:

I don't feel **well***. (I'm sick)*

Some grammarians are reluctant to say, "I feel well" because it might be confused with "I have a good sense of touch." That's overthinking, we believe, so no worries.

Lie means to "recline" or "fib."

Lied means to tell a fib in the past.

Lay means to "place," but it's also the past tense of "lie" to mean "reclined."

So you would say correctly:

*Don't **lie** to me. (tell me the truth)*

*Are you just going to **lie** there all day? (or are you going to get up?)*

*On vacation I just **lay** around the house all day. (sometimes in a recliner)*

***Lay** the book on the shelf. (place it there)*

11. Let's You and Me Watch Out for Reflexives

When you see a personal pronoun followed by another word for emphasis, you're probably looking at a reflexive. They are the "self" forms of pronouns. So, for example:

*I **myself** will take on the challenge.*

*You **yourself** should stay out of the matter.*

*They **themselves** will attend the protest.*

The great Chicago columnist Mike Royko used to refer to the all-powerful Mayor Richard J. Daley simply as "**Himself**."

There are rare moments when the reflexive feels right and necessary. The test is always to drop them and see if it feels like something important is missing.

Something akin to "-self reflexives" occurs in a sentence like this:

Let's you and me look for the dog.

It makes you stop because you see "me," not "I," in front of the verb "look." But it's correct. Parsing helps:

Subject: you (understood)

Verb: "let"

Direct object: "us"

So the phrase "you and me"—both objective case—is merely clarifying "us."

Here's another example: What do you think?

It was we editors who made the difference.

This takes us back to the predicate nominative discussion. "We" is correct, as both "we" and "editors" are predicate nominatives. Sometimes correct sounds too weird, so keep you audience in mind on making a final decision.

This next example is easier:

The teacher gave us students the answers.

Yes, this is correct. Again parsing helps:
Subject: teacher
Verb: gave
Direct object: answers
Indirect object: students
"Us" and "students" are both objective case.
Let us rejoice that you now see why we needed to explain parsing.

12. Hmm, Is That Conditional or Subjunctive?

Subjunctive mood is one of the subtleties of the English language that often get lost on writers. That's too bad because one word can make a big difference to a sentence's meaning, whether something is a fact or not. Subjunctive mood has to do with the way verbs are conjugated differently from the matter-of-fact indicative mood.

As we'll see, one of the many times that subjunctive mood applies is when you are making **a statement contrary to fact**. It's the difference between saying **I was** and **I were**. More on this in a moment, when we compare conditional statements with ones in the subjunctive mood.

For now, know that you conjugate a verb in the subjunctive mood when you are expressing:

A doubt: "I wonder if it **be** true." In the subjunctive mood, "be true" is correct rather than the indicative "is true."

A wish: "I wish I **were** a rock singer." Use "were" rather than "was."

A prayer: "Peace be with you." Use "be" rather than "is." Subjunctive mood is used in other idioms: **"if need be," "God bless you," "God forbid," "so be it."**

A demand: "I insist that he **go**." Use "he go" rather than "he goes."

A necessity: "The board had no choice but that she **be** dismissed." Use "she be" not "she is."

A resolution or motion: "I resolve that he **investigate** the matter." It's not "he investigates." "I move that the meeting **be** adjourned." It's not "is adjourned."

And now back to this one:

A condition contrary to fact: "If I **were** you, I would go." Use "were," not "was."

Don't confuse this last use of the subjunctive mood with conditional statements using indicative mood.

The subjunctive mood is used in clauses introduced by "as if" and "as though." This is correct, in the subjunctive mood:

*She yelled as if she **were** hurt. (not was hurt)*

Conditional statements also use the word "if," but the meaning is entirely different. Let's say a friend was at a party, and you did not see him. You might say:

*If he **was** there, I didn't see him.*

You are making a simple statement not contrary to fact, so use the indicative "was." Now let's say your friend couldn't make the party and you had a lousy time. Then you might say:

*If he **were** there, I would have had a great time.*

In this case, use the subjunctive "were" because your friend was not there; you are stating a condition contrary to fact. **One word makes the difference.**

Here are other examples of conditional statements in the indicative mood:

*If I **was** there, I don't remember.*

*If you **are** telling the truth, I will apologize.*

Knowing the difference between the subjunctive and the indicative in the last example could save you a punch in the nose. Compare it with this:

*If Jack **were** telling the truth, I would apologize.*

You are calling Jack a liar. And that's about as serious as grammar gets.

We hope you enjoyed this deep dive into the do's and don'ts of grammar. We know this has not been exactly a day at the beach. Sometimes you need to let these rules wash over you like waves. Before long you will increase your strength and confidence, and your writing and editing will show improvement. Stay tuned for exercises to help you build those grammar muscles. Take the rest of the day off—you deserve it!

DEEP PUNCTUATION

Introduction

Punctuation rules can seem complicated, but they all fall under one broad guideline: Punctuation should add clarity.

Good writers use punctuation to show relationships clearly. They join related ideas with commas and semicolons, add emphasis by setting off ideas with colons and dashes, and separate unrelated ideas with periods and parentheses. When in doubt about a punctuation mark, ask if it helps make the writing clearer.

In this deep dive into punctuation, we will focus on just six of the most used and abused pieces of punctuation. We start with the grandaddy of them all—the poor comma. Editor's note: We're using AP style here.

The Comma

Commas are used for clarity; they stop your eyes from running into trouble. Take this sentence:

Ever since the boy has been better.

Put a comma after "since," and you have a sentence. Without it, you have a run-on mind-boggler. We'll parse sentences to help explain the punctuation rules. Here's a reminder on what the abbreviations mean:

Functions

s	subject (usually starts a sentence)
p	predicate (verb)
op	object of the preposition
do	direct object
io	indirect object
pn	predicate nominative
pa	predicate adjective
inf	infinitive

Parts of Speech

con	conjunction (joins ideas in a sentence)

Conjunctions

Commas are used with conjunctions to join related clauses. We'll focus on four types of conjunctions.

AND

Here are some punctuation rules to keep in mind for the conjunction "and":

1. If no subject follows "and," then no comma should come before it. Take this sentence:

I finished studying and went to a movie.

Let's parse the sentence for functions:

s	p	do		p		op
I	finished	studying	and	went	to a	movie.

You have one subject with two predicates, known as a "**compound verb.**" Why is that important to know? Because there's no comma between a subject and a verb, so no comma before "and." Now compare this sentence:

I finished studying, and Sally went to a movie.

Why the comma? Now the conjunction "and" is joining two clauses ("I finished," "Sally went") with different subjects. Let's parse the sentence for functions:

s	p	do		s	p		op
I	finished	studying,	and	Sally	went	to a	movie.

2. If the subjects of clauses joined by "and" are the same, and the clauses are closely related, then don't use a comma before "and."

s	p			op		s	p		do
We	walked	to	the	store	and	we	bought	some	groceries.

3. If the subjects of clauses joined by "and" are different, use a comma before "and."

s	p		do		s	p	do
I	wrote	the	paper,	and	my	roommate edited	it.

BUT

Here are some punctuation rules to keep in mind for the conjunction "but" when it joins two clauses:

1. Use a comma before "but" if a second subject, different or same, is stated after "but."

<pre>
s   p   op   s   p   op
Charles   ran   for   president,   but   I   did   not   vote   for   him.

s   p   op   s   p
Charles   ran   for   president,   but   he   did   not   win.
</pre>

2. If no subject follows "but," then no comma should come before it.

<pre>
s   p   op   p
Charles   ran   for   president   but   did   not   win.
</pre>

OR AND FOR

Here are some punctuation rules to keep in mind for the conjunctions "or" and "for" when they join two clauses:

1. Use a comma before "or" when the second subject is different.

<pre>
s   p   pn   s   p   io   do
June   is   the   best   teacher,   or   St. Thomas   wouldn't   her   a   fellowship.
                                                      have given
</pre>

2. When the subjects before and after "or" are the same, no comma should come before it.

<pre>
s   p   pn   op   s   p   s   p
Roger   is   the   star   on   the   team   or   he   thinks   he   is.
</pre>

3. Always use a comma before the conjunction " for" to show that it is not a preposition.

<pre>
       s   p   do   inf   con s   p   s   p
The   pirate   told   them   where   to look,   for   he   knew   where   the   treasure   lay.
</pre>

COMMAS AND RHYTHM

Using simple sentences in a series adds rhythm to writing, and light punctuation can set the tone. Use commas when semicolons would interrupt the rhythm.

Just as you would use a comma to separate a simple series of words such as "red, white and blue," use a comma to separate simple sentences in a series:

In San Diego it was sunny today, it was sunny yesterday, it will be sunny tomorrow.

The Bucs won the Super Bowl, the Lightning won the Stanley Cup and the Florida Marlins won the World Series.

INTRODUCTORY WORDS

Use commas after introductory clauses or phrases. If the phrase is short, the comma can be omitted. The longer the introductory statement, the more you need a comma. Consider these sentences:

In 1999 he left for the circus.

In the bright summer of 1999, he left for the circus.

When he finally returned home after many years, we celebrated like clowns.

Sometimes clarity dictates a pause.

No*: When we ate the cow mooed.*

Yes*: When we ate, the cow mooed.*

Otherwise*: The job being done, we went home.*

Use commas after "yes" and "no":

Yes, you may go to the show.

No, not that guy again.

Use commas after interjections not requiring an exclamation point: "ah," "oh," "well," "why." For example:

Oh, well, we'll survive.

ESSENTIAL AND NONESSENTIAL

Set off nonessential clauses and phrases, and parenthetical words, with commas. "Nonessential" doesn't mean unnecessary; it's a grammatical term. Remember, commas come in pairs, one before and one after the clause or phrase.

Keanu Reeves, who starred in "The Matrix," is my favorite actor.

Reese Witherspoon, my favorite actor, has starred in many movies.

In this sentence, "seeing" introduces the nonessential phrase:

The soldier, seeing the grenade, ducked.

When a state or a year is parenthetical, then set it off with two commas, as in:

He came from Tempe, Arizona, to see us.

She was born on March 10, 2010, in New York City.

If it's just a month and year, then no comma: "May 2021."

In the following sentence, "Harry" is considered nonessential because his sister has only one brother, so there's no confusion. You can cover up the word "Harry" with your finger and there's no problem:

Her only brother, Harry, helped.

In the following sentence, "Linda" is considered essential as Harry has two sisters.

Harry gave his sister Linda a gift.

If you cover up the word "Linda" with your finger, there would be confusion. A friend would ask, "Which sister?" That's what we mean by essential, so no commas. Get right to the name.

Likewise, omit the commas with essential clauses beginning with "who" or "that."

Students who come to class get good grades.

The rare bird that landed in my backyard gave me joy.

Essential clauses, also known as restrictive clauses, restrict the meaning. So with the first sentence it's only the students who come to class, not those who skip. In the second sentence, the rare bird that landed in the backyard is different from all the sparrows in the front yard.

Also no commas with essential phrases, as in:

The man throwing the popcorn is my father.

"Throwing" introduces the essential phrase identifying the embarrassing father.

QUOTATIONS

Use commas to set off simple quotations:

The runner said, "Ah, well, I'll win next time."

"Ah, well, I'll win next time," the runner said.

"Ah, well," the runner said, "I'll win next time."

In quotations of more than one sentence, attributions should be placed at the first logical break, usually at the end of the opening line.

If it's a full sentence that opens the quotation, then use a period rather than a comma:

"We must go now," she said. "I have to get up very early tomorrow."

No comma is needed when a quote in a sentence is closely related to the rest of the sentence:

His reaction was always "ah, well, maybe next time."

He said the "time is now" for action.

COORDINATE ADJECTIVES

Adjectives having the same weight are joined by commas. These are "coordinate adjectives":

The tall, agile girl entered the room without a sound.

The kind, graceful gymnast signed an autograph.

To test if adjectives are coordinate, substitute the conjunction "and" for the comma. If it makes sense, the adjectives are coordinate:

The gaunt, anxious man laughed.

The gaunt and anxious man laughed.

Another test is to see if you can switch the adjectives, like so:

The anxious, gaunt man laughed.

If those tests don't work, then the adjectives are not coordinate, as in:

The desperate Harvard man winced.

No comma, as these don't make sense: "the desperate and Harvard man" or "the Harvard, desperate man."
The adjective "Harvard" carries more weight.

The Semicolon

The semicolon is one of the most underused and misused punctuation marks. Get used to it and use it freely. Use semicolons to link ideas to show direct relationship or contrast.

The semicolon replaces a conjunction when two sentences are joined:

They asked many questions; he answered them all.

John liked the show; Bill was bored.

Using a comma would be wrong. It is called a "comma splice." So don't write this:

John liked the show, Bill was bored.

Semicolons lend clarity by setting off elements separated by commas in complex constructions.

The survivors included his wife, June; two sons, Walter and Theodore; and a brother, Harold.

Note the semicolon before "and." Here's another example:

The speakers at the meeting were Hiram Hills, president of the company; Mitch Pickett, chairman of the board; and Isaac Inman, corporation counsel.

Use semicolons to separate sentences joined by conjunctive adverbs, such as "therefore," "however," "hence," "nevertheless," "accordingly," "thus," "then." For example:

The team did not block well; therefore, it could not expect to win.

We laughed until our stomachs hurt; however, the best was yet to come.

Use a semicolon before "as," "namely" or "thus" when introducing examples:

Three singers signed for the concert; namely, Elton John, Bob Seger and Elvis Costello.

When only one example follows, a comma suffices:

Only one fruit was eaten, namely, apples.

The Colon

The colon is a useful yet underused punctuation mark. Use colons to introduce or emphasize words or ideas, such as:

She suggested three colors: blue, green and red.

He had only one idea in mind: eating.

When a complete sentence follows a colon, the AP Stylebook says the first word is capitalized, as in:

She left us with this promise: All will be well tomorrow.

Other stylebooks recommend a lowercase "all." The Chicago Manual of Style's 18th edition changes to follow AP on this rule.

Use a colon rather than a comma to set off long quotations, especially if they run more than one paragraph. For example:

John Glenn, who resigned from NASA in 1964 after years of frustration, said: "It was only years later that I read in a book that [John F.] Kennedy had passed the word that he didn't want me to go back up.

"I don't know if he was afraid of the political fallout if I got killed, but by the time I found out, he had been dead for some time, so I never got to discuss it with him."

Note that no end-quotation mark is needed after "back up."

The Hyphen

Hyphens are used primarily for clarity and sometimes for conciseness. If confusion would result, use a hyphen to join compound modifiers. For example:

He went to the modern-art museum.

That's something different from an art museum that's modern.

She had four great-grandchildren.

Whether they were great kids or not, we don't know.

The senator was soft-spoken.

This is different from being soft, as in soft on crime. Other examples of hyphens needed to avoid double takes:

The comic was quick-witted.

The team was second-rate.

Some compound modifiers take hyphens, but when the phrasing is reversed, the hyphens are dropped. For example:

She has a full-time job.

She works full time.

The 2-year-old child cried.

The child was 2 years old.

Hyphens are not needed to join adverbs to adjectives, as in:

It is a specially manufactured product.

Her hobby is making uniquely crafted face masks.

Do not make these "specially-manufactured" or "uniquely-crafted."
One exception is the adverb "well." Then you would hyphenate these modifiers:

She is a well-known woman.

He also is well-known.

Sometimes a hyphen is a must for clarity:

He covered the roof and re-covered it.

That's different from being "recovered" after he fell from the roof. And this next example is "really" different:

The NATO nations need to re-ally their forces.

Suspended hyphenation is used for brevity. Just be sure to provide a space to show the suspension:

Change came at 10- to 20-year intervals.

Two- and three-bedroom apartments are available to low- and middle-income families.

The Dash

Beware of the dashers. Those writers use the dash when a colon or comma would do, or when they want to pack as many ideas as possible into one sentence. So don't write:

The mayor proposed a tax hike—it was unprecedented—to bail out the schools.

Make it:

The mayor proposed an unprecedented tax hike to bail out the schools.

Another example:

She listed the qualities—small, cute, playful and loyal—that she liked in dogs.

Make it:

She listed the qualities she liked in dogs: small, cute, playful and loyal.

One more example:

Sally Weathers—the new Senate majority leader—arrived at the state Capitol.

Make it:

Sally Weathers, the new Senate majority leader, arrived at the state Capitol.

Occasionally a dash may be used to set off a word or phrase for emphasis. Such a sentence often ends with an exclamation point:

We will vacation in Monaco—if I get a raise.

She found the perfect gift: small, charming, exotic—and cheap!

The Parentheses

Parentheses within a sentence usually are a good sign that the sentence should be recast. They often interrupt the flow of ideas. For example:

Neil Armstrong (he never went back into space after being the first man to walk on the moon—for 2 hours and 14 minutes) declined to run for public office.

Make it:

Neil Armstrong declined to run for public office. He never went back into space after being the first man to walk on the moon for 2 hours and 14 minutes.

Sometimes parentheses are an acceptable way to tighten writing. They work best for information that is short and succinctly answers a question on the reader's mind.

Hall of Fame quarterback Dan Marino played in one Super Bowl (he lost) and never made it back to the championship game.

Sharpening Your Tools

Punctuation marks are like tools in your toolbox as a writer or an editor. There's an old expression: If the only tool you have is a hammer, everything looks like a nail.

As you've seen in this deep dive, you have six tools—the comma, the semicolon, the colon, the hyphen, the dash and the parentheses. We hope that this section of **The Language Skills Survival Kit** can help you make your writing easier to read and, most of all, clear.

BREVITY AND SIMPLICITY

Introduction

We'll keep this brief. Ernest Hemingway said the best dialogue is good conversation only better. We should write the way we talk but, as Hemingway said, only better. That is, keep the simple tones but clear up any ambiguity that may arise in imperfect speech.

Clarity can be achieved by keeping writing brief and simple, and in that spirit we welcome you to Part IV of **The Language Skills Survival Kit**. Redundant expressions and superfluous words in copy are like weeds in a garden, obscuring vision and choking vitality. We begin with brevity as we teach you to use some gardening tools. Then we turn to simplicity where the work will be more along the lines of trimming syllables.

If gardening is not your thing, think about it this way: Time is money. If a reader can save time by getting the same meaning from reading one word rather than four, or one syllable rather than three, then your writing is more profitable. The term we use for this in the third sweep of our editing strategy is "tightening." See how many words and syllables you can save in our Brevity and Simplicity hit lists. Here goes.

Brevity

The wordy constructions come first, then we suggest something briefer.

A

absolutely complete: **complete**
abundance of caution: **caution**
adequate enough: **enough**
advance planning: **planning**
ahead of schedule: **early**
a large proportion of: **many**
along the lines of: **like**
am in possession of: **have**
and moreover: **moreover**
and so as a result: **so**
angry clash: **clash**
a number of: **several**
any and all: **any**
a percentage of: **some**
appear to be: **appear**
appointed to the post of: **appointed**
are currently or are now: **are**
as a matter of fact: **in fact**
as far as she is concerned: **as for her**
ask the question: **ask**
as of this date: **today**
assembled together: **together**
as to: **about**
as to whether: **whether**
as yet: **yet**
at an early date: **soon**

atop of: **atop**
at some time to come: **at some point**
at the present time: **now**
at this point in time: **now**
awkward predicament: **predicament**

B

be in a position to: **can**
best of health: **well** or **healthy**
big in size: **big**
biography of his life: **biography**
blue in color: **blue**
both of them: **they**
but nevertheless: **nevertheless**
by means of: **by** or **with**
by the name of: **named**

C

call a halt to: **stop**
Capitol building: **Capitol**
caused injuries to: **injured**
christened as: **christened**
classified into groups: **classified**
close proximity: **close**
collaborate together: **collaborate**
commute to and from: **commute to**
completely destroy: **destroy**
connect together: **connect**
consensus of opinion: **consensus**
continue on: **continue**
cooperate together: **cooperate**

D

damaged by fire: **burned**
dates back from: **dates from**
depreciate or appreciate in value: **drop in value** or **rise in value**
descend down: **descend**

doctorate degree: **doctorate**
draw the attention of him: **show, point out**
during the time that: **while**

E

each and every: **each**
eliminate altogether: **eliminate**
enclosed herein: **enclosed**
end result: **result**
entirely complete: **complete**
every now and then: **occasionally**
exactly identical: **identical**

F

fellow colleagues: **colleagues**
few in number: **few**
filled to capacity: **filled**
final completion: **completion**
follow after: **after**
for the purpose of: **for**
for the reason that: **because**
from a commercial standpoint: **commercially**
frown on his face: **frown** (same for **smile**)

G-H-I

gather up, gather together: **gather**
general public: **public**
give due consideration to: **consider**
give rise to: **cause**
good benefit: **benefit**
graceful in appearance: **graceful**
had occasion to be: **was**
hurry up: **hurry**
in a number of cases: **some**
in advance of: **before**
in connection with: **in, on, of, about**

in order that: **so**
in order to: **to**
in possession of: **have**
in relation to: **to, about, toward**
in spite of the fact that: **although**
in the amount of: **for**
in the case of: **about**
in the case of workers who are late: **for late workers**
in the event that: **if**
in the matter of: **in**
in the nature of: **like**
in the near future: **soon**
in the vicinity of: **near**
in this day and age: **today**
in view of: **because**
invited guest: **guest**
in view of the fact that: **as**
is located on: **on**
I would like to: **I want to**

J-K-L-M-N

join together with: **join**
join up: **join**
joint cooperation: **cooperation**
knots per hour: **knots**
last of all: **last**
little duckling: **duckling**
made a statement saying: **stated, said**
made good an escape: **escaped**
made out of: **made of**
major breakthrough: **breakthrough**
more superior: **superior**
mutual cooperation: **cooperation**
never at any time: **never**
new beginning: **beginning**
new innovation: **innovation**

O

of a similar nature: **similar**
old adage: **adage**
on a few occasions: **occasionally**
on behalf of: **for**
on the basis of: **by**
on the grounds that: **because**
on the occasion whenever: **whenever**
on the part of: **for, by, among**
on the subject of: **about**
one and the same: **the same**
original source: **source**
over and done with: **over**
owing to the fact that: **because**

P

pair of twins: **twins**
passing phase, passing fad: **phase, fad**
past history: **history**
penetrate into: **penetrate**
persist still: **persist**
place under arrest: **arrest**
plan in advance: **plan**
prejudge in advance: **prejudge**
present incumbent: **incumbent**
present in greater abundance: **more**
prior to: **before**
proposed plan: **plan**
put in an appearance: **appear**

Q-R

quite unique: **special, unique**
recoil back: **recoil**
remand back: **remand**
render assistance: **help**
repeat again: **repeat**
results so far achieved: **results**

retain position: **remain**
revert back: **revert**
root cause: **cause**

S

self-confessed: **confessed**
separate and distinct: **distinct**
separate entities: **entities**
serious danger: **danger**
shuttle back and forth: **shuttle**
sink down: **sink**
skirt around: **skirt**
sparsely scattered: **scattered**
strangle to death: **strangle**
subsequent to: **after**
suburban area: **suburbs**
succumbed to injuries: **died**
surgeon by occupation: **surgeon**
surrounding circumstances: **circumstances**
swoop down: **swoop**

T-U-V

take action on the matter: **act**
take into consideration: **consider**
tender his resignation: **resign**
termed as: **called**
the reason why: **the reason**
total annihilation: **annihilation**
total destruction: **destruction**
total extinction: **extinction**
true facts: **facts**
undergraduate student: **undergraduate**
under the circumstances: **because**
usual customs: **customs**

W-X-Y-Z

was of the opinion that: **said, thought**
was witness to: **saw**

weather conditions: **weather**
when and if: **if**
with a view to: **to**
with reference to: **about**
with regard to: **about**
with the result that: **so that**
young infant: **infant, baby**
zigzag all over the place: **zigzag**

Simplicity

The following list of words, moving from multiple syllables to fewer ones, is designed to get you to think about your word choice. Don't get the idea that a particular word is wrong; all these words can find their places in good writing. But if as a writer you start to utilize "finalize" as you conversationalize, then we'll be concerned that your editor will be forced to put you out to pasture—or shall we say, "pasteurize" you!

Have fun taking up the challenge of choosing the short word over the long word when no meaning is lost. Feel free to add your own words to fill out the alphabet.

A

accumulate: **gather**
acquaint with: **talk about**
additional: **added**
advise: **tell**
aggregate: **total**
ameliorate: **improve**
apparent: **clear**
approximately: **about**
ascertain: **find out**
assist: **help**
assistance: **aid**

C

cognizance: **knowledge**
commence: **start**
commitment: **promise, vow**
compensation: **pay**
construct: **build**
contribute: **give**
cooperate: **help**

D

deceased: **dead**
demonstrate: **show**
desire: **want**
determine: **find out, figure**
disclose: **show**

E

encounter: **meet**
equivalent: **equal**
expedite: **hasten**
explicit: **plain**

F

facilitate: **make easy**
failed to: **didn't**
forward: **send**

I-L-M

inconvenience: **trouble**
indicate: **show**
initial, inaugural: **first**
locality: **place**
materialize: **appear**
modification: **change**

O

objective: **aim, goal**
obligation: **debt**
optimum: **best**

P-R

participate: **take part**
proceed: **go**
procure: **get**
purchase: **buy**
reimburse: **pay back**

S

submit: **give, send**
subsequent: **later, next**
substantial: **big**
sufficient: **enough**

T-U-V-Y

terminate: **end, stop, fire**
transmit: **send**
transpire: **happen**
utilize: **use**
vehicle: **car, truck**
visualize: **picture, see**
youth: **boy, girl**

COMMONLY MISSPELLED WORDS

Introduction

Let's have a spelling bee!

When your co-author was in St. Patrick's grade school, the nun would line up the kids and randomly ask each one to spell a word. If you missed the word, you would suffer the public humiliation of having to return to your seat. If you spelled the word correctly, then you stayed for the next round.

After spelling a word correctly, in a daring act of passive aggressiveness, one young student would reach back to pull out his handkerchief and dab his brow. At the end of the spelling bee, one student—the top speller—remained. No prize was awarded, or anything like that. The real prize was missing a word that you would never again misspell.

So please line up against the wall, easy now, and we'll give you a spelling test. Actually it's more a spelling study guide. We've collected the top 150 words we think you should know by heart.

Caution: These are not what one enterprising reporter cited as "the most commonly misspelled words in the U.S.," including the most misspelled word state-by-state (Miller, 2022). Just so you know, the most misspelled word in 47 countries is "coolly," according to WordTips (Iancu, 2023).

"Why test us," you ask, "when we have spell-check?" Well, if spell-check worked so great, and writers actually used it, why do you think these words get misspelled so often? We're guessing you noticed them yourself in articles, in tweets or posts, on lower-thirds ("chyrons") for videos or TV news stories, and even in (gulp) books.

Remember, in **Appendix A: The Fixtionary**, we talked about bells going off in editors' heads. Studying spelling and taking quizzes are ways to help cast those bells. You can help each other, either with one-on-one quizzing or by holding your own spelling bees. Why not offer exciting prizes for the winners!

What's missing in this guide—pronunciation tips—is something H.W. Fowler tried to address in 1926 with his dictionary. Sometimes it's not enough that you know how to spell a word; you also need to know how it's pronounced.

True confession from a co-author: One day riding shotgun on a car trip in college, he pronounced "epitome" as "ep-pee-TOME." Once the driver looked askance at him, he quickly regrouped with an "aw-that-was-just-a-joke" smile, did a panicked brain scan and realized for the first time, oh, that's pronounced "uh-PI-tuh-mee." How embarrassing. We know what you're thinking—there's an app for that! And there is, so by any means possible, if one of our top 150 words throws you, please search for its definition and proper pronunciation.

OK, let the studying begin! As you know by now, the "correct" spelling is found in your stylebook. If there's a discrepancy between the AP Stylebook and the Chicago Manual of Style, we'll note that. Here goes.

A

1. accommodate
2. acquitted
3. advisable
4. adviser (AP), advisor (CMS) (Ticak, 2021)
5. African American
6. afterward (not afterwards)

7. a lot
8. apparent
9. argument
10. Asian American
11. assassination

B

12. backward (not backwards)
13. basically
14. believe
15. bizarre
16. Black (African American)
17. broccoli
18. bureaucracies

C

19. calendar
20. canceled
21. cannot
22. Caribbean
23. cemetery
24. colleague
25. Colombia (South American nation)
26. Columbia (District of, river, university)
27. connoisseur
28. conscientiously
29. conscious
30. consensus
31. convenient
32. copyright
33. counterproposal

D

34. definitely
35. desperate
36. dietitian
37. dilate

38. disastrous
39. do's and don'ts (AP), dos and don'ts (CMS)
40. drunkenness

E

41. embarrass
42. entrepreneur
43. environment
44. epitome
45. exonerate

F

46. familiar
47. fluorescent
48. foreign
49. forty
50. fuchsia

G

51. gauge
52. grammar
53. grateful

H

54. habeas corpus
55. Hajj (AP says capitalize in 57th edition)
56. Hanukkah
57. harass
58. hemorrhage

I

59. impostor
60. incidentally
61. independent

62. Indigenous Peoples Day
63. ingenious
64. interrupt
65. irresistible

J

66. jack-o'-lantern
67. Jacuzzi
68. jewelry
69. judgment

K

70. kibbutz
71. kindergartners
72. knowledge
73. K-pop

L

74. liaison
75. license
76. lightning
77. liquefy
78. longtime

M

79. maneuver
80. medieval
81. memento
82. minuscule
83. misspell
84. Muhammad
85. Muslim

N

86. naloxone
87. nauseous
88. nickel
89. noticeable

O

90. occasionally
91. occurred
92. occurrence
93. OK
94. orangutan
95. ordinance (legislation)
96. ordnance (artillery shells)

P

97. paid
98. paraphernalia
99. Ph.D.
100. Philippines
101. playwright
102. possession
103. precede
104. preferable
105. preferred
106. Presidents Day (AP), Presidents' Day (CMS)
107. privilege
108. pronunciation
109. protester
110. publicly
111. pursue

Q

112. questionnaire
113. Quran (AP), Koran or Qur'an (CMS)

R

114. Realtor (certified real estate agent)
115. receive
116. recreation (have fun)
117. re-creation (create anew)
118. referred
119. referring
120. regardless (not irregardless)
121. responsibility
122. restaurateur
123. rhythm
124. rock 'n' roll

S

125. sacrilegious
126. secede
127. separate
128. sizable
129. slough
130. succeed
131. succinct
132. supersede
133. surprise

T

134. tendency
135. toward (not towards)
136. truly

U

137. unfortunately
138. unnecessary
139. usable

V

140. V8 (juice)
141. V-8 (engine, AP style)
142. vice versa
143. volunteerism

W

144. wartime
145. weird
146. willful

X

147. Xbox

Y

148. yearlong
149. year-round

Z

150. zeros (noun), zeroes (verb)

REFERENCES

Iancu, M. (2023, April 21). The most misspelled English word in every country and state, based on two billion tweets. Wordtips. https://word.tips/most-misspelled-words-map/

Miller, D. (2022, October 13). The most commonly misspelled words in the US. How many can you get right? Fox4 KDFW. https://www.fox4news.com/news/the-most-commonly-misspelled-words-us

Ticak, M. (2021, August 17). Advisor vs. adviser. Grammarly. https://www.grammarly.com/blog/advisor-vs-adviser/

GLOSSARY

ABCs of Editing: Editors need a reason to change copy. The top reasons are accuracy, brevity and clarity. But we'll add three more for good measure: coherence, consistency and simplicity.

Académie Française: In France the official custodian of the language, the *Académie Française*, dates to 1635 to counter foreign influences. You can read about French laws trying to stop the "veggie burger," for example. For English we don't have an official authority on the language, only self-appointed guardians to guide us on standard English usage.

accept, except: Yes, they sound similar, but don't confuse *"accept"* (receive) with *"except"* (exclude, other than).

accordion: The fourth of five steps in "The What?! Approach to Writing" (**Chapter 1.4**), the *accordion* (a "4") follows the nut graph (a "3") in more ways than one. As the nut graph summarizes the point of a story, it also sets up the rest of the writing. That segment is called the accordion because it can be long or short depending on length limits. If the nut graph addresses three points, as in a, b and c, then the accordion will elaborate on those points in that order.

adjective: An *adjective* modifies a noun (*"good"* guy) or a pronoun (she is *"nice"*). It tells which one, what kind or how many.

adverb: An *adverb* modifies a verb (run *"quickly"*), adjective (*"really"* nice) or other adverb (*"very"* slowly). It tells how, why, when, where and to what extent.

adverse, averse: Be careful: *"adverse"* (bad) doesn't mean *"averse"* (opposed).

advice, advise: Careful pronunciation helps so you won't confuse *"advice"* (tips) with *"advise"* (consult).

affect, effect: No problem, just substitute what the word means as a noun to see if you're using it properly: the *"effect"* (result), the *"affect"* (emotion). Do the same as a verb: *"effect"* (to bring about), *"affect"* (to influence).

African American or African-American: Should it be hyphenated? That's a matter of style. The Associated Press and other publications changed their spelling to drop the hyphen after a top editor at the Los Angeles Times wrote an essay arguing "Hyphenated Americans" are second-class citizens.

aid, aide: Don't confuse *"aid"* (help) with *"aide"* (person).

alleged: An overworked word in crime stories. Sprinkling the word *"alleged"* liberally in a news story won't protect you from libel suits. The story must state clearly who is doing the alleging, and often that person must be a *"privileged source,"* ranging from police to members of Congress.

allot, a lot: There's a lot of difference between *"allot"* (give out) and *"a lot"* (much).

already, all ready: Big difference here: *"already"* (it happened), *"all ready"* (let's rumble).

alright, all right: You perk up when you see *"never"* in an AP entry. There it is: Never *"alright."* We think it's more about tone: *"all right"* is preferred, especially with a formal tone. You'll see *"alright,"* the frowned-upon variant, used in writing with an informal tone.

altogether, all together: There's a difference: *"altogether"* (entirely), *"all together"* (we gathered).

amount, number: Be careful you don't talk about the *"amount of people,"* as their volume is difficult to assess. Remember: *"amount"* (of courage), *"number"* (of people or things).

analytics: *"Analytics,"* or *"data analytics,"* uses computer science to sort through data gained from users of apps, websites, search engines or social media. The goal is to gain insights and knowledge used to sharpen messages. Google Analytics, for example, provides free tools to help you understand what's working and what needs to be improved on your website.

anxious, eager: The child was *"eager"* to get an ice cream cone, not *"anxious."* Don't let these two words melt together. Remember: *"anxious"* (anxiety), *"eager"* (hurry up).

AP style: The rules set out in the Associated Press Stylebook. Journalists and public relations writers in the field of media relations will most likely adhere to these rules.

APA style: The rules set out in the American Psychological Association stylebook.

apostrophe: The *apostrophe* is tricky because sometimes it is used for plurals (*"do's and don'ts," "p's and q's"*) and for contractions like *"it's"* (*"it is"* or *"it has"*). But mostly the apostrophe is used to show possession, either with singular nouns (*"the boy's teddy bear"*) or plural ones (*"the girls' toys"*). It's missing in signs like *"Mens Room"* (should be *"Men's"*). It's even needed where you'd think it doesn't belong (*"for appearance' sake"*), and sometimes you think you need an apostrophe, but you don't (*"teachers strike"*).

arraignment: An *arraignment* is an appearance by a suspect before a judge who asks the suspect to plead guilty or not guilty. Once the legal process begins, a *"suspect"* may be called a *"defendant."*

arrested for and **indicted for:** Strike these terms from your vocabulary. It's the same as saying the suspect was arrested *"for committing the crime."* Instead, write that the suspect was arrested *"in connection with ..."* or *"arrested on a charge of ..."* if charges have been filed.

article: As a grammatical term, an *article* is a modifier that sets up a noun (*"a," "an," "the"*). It may be considered an *adjective* or a separate part of speech.

Asian American or Asian-American: No hyphen. The Associated Press and other publications changed their spelling to drop the hyphen after a top editor at the Los Angeles Times wrote an essay arguing "Hyphenated Americans" are second-class citizens.

Associated Press Stylebook: The Associated Press Stylebook calls itself "the journalist's bible." Its core section, listed on the Contents page simply as "Stylebook," covers 322 pages from entries **a-** (the prefix) to **zip line** in its 56th edition. The other 21 headings include these titles: "Punctuation," "Business,"

"Inclusive storytelling," "Religion," "Sports" and "Briefing on media law," which was dropped in the 57th edition and moved to online only.

assume: You can't expect that everything you read is correct. "Never '*assume*,'" the crusty city editor told the cub reporter, "or you'll make an '*ass*' out of '*u*' and '*me*.'" That same crusty old guy also warned: "If your mother says she loves you, check it out."

attribution: *Attribution* is the practice of identifying the speaker of a quote. In print, attribution most often follows the quote in the form of *"he said," "they said," "Jones said."* In audio broadcasts, attribution often comes first in the form of introducing a speaker before a sound bite. In video broadcasts, attribution often is stated in a graphic, such as a chyron, as a person speaks before the camera. In stories about crime, attribution to a *"privileged source"* is a protection against a libel suit. *"A witness who refused to be identified"* is not a solid attribution. *"A witness told police,"* as filed in an official police report, is a much safer and more responsible way to handle attribution in crime stories.

audience: One of our news values, *audience*, requires editors to be in touch with the community where they work. They also need a general idea about what readers and viewers will or won't accept. Marketing employed by news organizations using *analytics* can help form an accurate view of the audience, or a target reader, listener or viewer.

audience growth manager: An *audience growth manager*, also known as an *audience development manager*, typically uses social media to create content for different audiences to gain the most reach, then works closely with a digital *audience-analytics team* to understand a website's level of engagement.

average: Watch this word, especially the article before it, when considering subject-verb agreement. The AP Stylebook sees a difference whether the subject is *"the" average* or *"an" average*. Both these sentences are considered correct: *"The average **is** 74* (singular)." and *"An average of 100 new jobs **are** created daily* (plural)."

awhile, a while: This is subtle: *"awhile"* (stay awhile), *"a while"* (stay for a while). If you think of *"while"* as a noun (a period of time), then you can see it more clearly as the object of the preposition *"for." "Awhile"* is an adverb: *"We ate awhile, then talked."*

Axios: A news site that embraces brevity and simplicity in a *"bullet-proof"* approach to writing and editing as described in the book "Smart Brevity: The Power of Saying More With Less."

B

background: *Background* is information on past developments relevant to the story. In an inverted pyramid story, background most often comes at the end. In trimming background, be careful not to eliminate something that is a key to understanding the story.

bar chart: A *bar chart* shows comparisons between individual numbers within a series by the length of horizontal or vertical bars. Bar charts can be used when some numbers are missing or when the time periods are irregular. When many data points are available, the bar chart may become impractical, and a *line chart* can be used.

because, since: The shorthand difference: *"because"* (cause and effect), *"since"* (time). *"The jar smashed **because** the cat knocked it over. She's done things like that **since** she was a kitten."*

beside, besides: These aren't interchangeable, as they mean different things: *"beside"* (next to) is not the same as *"besides"* (also).

bias: Every aspect of your life—age, gender, race, ethnicity, nationality, class, religion, sexual orientation, political affiliation, ability or disability—creates an opportunity for bias to blur your vision and miss truth.

big type: Headlines, titles, chyrons and excerpts are considered *"big type"* because they draw attention to a story and are often all that is read. Always slow down for the big type. Errors here are especially damaging and might go viral.

Black: Capitalize *"Black"* but not *"white,"* the AP Stylebook says. One thing that's consistent about the English language is there's no consistency.

blurbs: *Blurbs*, also called *summary graphs*, are short paragraphs that add information to headlines and allow readers to get their news quickly as they scan print and webpages.

brackets: *Brackets* [ ] are not the same as parentheses ( ) in look or purpose, though transmission problems with the Associated Press make them interchangeable or something to be avoided. The Chicago Manual of Style distinguishes brackets from braces { }. The most common use of brackets comes within parentheses (when something [new] is enclosed). They are used to insert words into a quote and signal to the reader that the words are not the speaker's. The most common practice is to use brackets for adding words to quotes, but some news organizations use parentheses.

breath, breathe: Careful pronunciation helps so you won't confuse *"breath"* (mouth) with *"breathe"* (lungs).

brief: A short story, called a *brief*, is sometimes just one paragraph in a news digest. What might be a major story in one newspaper, such as local flooding, might be a brief in a distant publication.

broadsheet: A *broadsheet* is the largest newspaper format with tall, vertical pages that allow for several stories per page. Editors use their news judgment to allot space to each story, determine a headline size and place each story on the page. The more important stories go near the top of the page, or *"above the fold."* These decisions can carry over to the newspaper's web page, including what the viewer sees before scrolling down. The New York Times has a typical broadsheet page size of 12 x 22 inches.

budget: A *budget* is a schedule of stories for an edition of a newspaper, a magazine or a news broadcast. Each story comes with a length or time limit.

bugaboo: Some matters of style, grammar, punctuation and standard English usage become personal for writers and editors because they feel so important. A good example is the Oxford comma, which is life-or-death for some people and no big deal for others. Writers are wise to know their editors' *bugaboos* so as not to drive them crazy.

C

can, may: Big difference in asking, *"May I go to the bathroom?"* Remember, *"can"* (ability), *"may"* (permission).

canon, cannon: Don't confuse *"canon"* (rule or book) with *"cannon"* (gun).

capital, Capitol: Don't confuse *"capital"* (city) with *"Capitol"* (building).

caption: Also called a *cutline*, a *caption* briefly answers questions raised by a picture. All the journalistic rules about brevity and precision apply with force to caption writing. Present tense verbs are often used for a sense of immediacy. Some captions serve "stand-alone" pictures and might take a short headline called a *"catchline."*

catchline: A *catchline* is a short headline with bigger type than the caption it complements. Catchlines usually are "catchy," as they strive to appeal to readers by catching their attention with a clever word or phrase.

celebrity: *Celebrity,* a news value, is "manufactured" through public relations and the media. Historian Daniel Boorstin wrote that the media can "quickly and effectively" bestow fame on a person, and that "we have willingly been misled into believing that fame—well-knownness—is still a hallmark of greatness."

center on, revolve around: The discussion didn't *"center around"* the eligibility issue. Better to say *"center on"* or *"revolve around."*

centerpiece: A *centerpiece* is a complex feature story written or produced by a news organization staff member. In a broadcast sense, it is an in-depth story package like those produced by the Under-Told Stories Project for the "PBS NewsHour." These stories often take a prominent place on the front of a newspaper section, as a spread in a magazine or as a lengthy segment in a television news program.

charges: When people are arrested, they might be released without being charged with a crime. Police might file *charges* against a suspect, or the charges could come from a city, county or district attorney. Once a suspect is formally charged, or *"booked,"* that person has entered the criminal justice system.

chart junk: Statistician Edward Tufte cautions against using "non-data ink" in graphics merely to decorate them visually. At its worst, this sort of decoration devolves into what Tufte calls *"chart junk."*

Chicago Manual of Style: The Chicago Manual of Style, 17th edition (2017), is almost double the size of the AP Stylebook. "Part I, The Publishing Process," offers guidelines on editing books and journals. "Part II, Style and Usage," more closely relates to the contents of the AP Stylebook, though not all the rules agree. "Part III, Source Citations and Indexes," reflects the academic orientation of Chicago style. The rules are preferred by many magazine and book editors. The 18th edition (2024) promises "the most extensive revision in two decades."

chicken Kiev: This dish inadvertently got caught in the crossfire over the Russia-Ukraine conflict. Using *"Kiev"* for that dish is generally accepted. Spelling and saying *"Kyiv"* for the city favors the view that Ukraine is an independent country.

chyron: An electronically generated headline or caption superimposed on a television screen. *Chyron* is the name of the company that produced the software for adding words, phrases and images to broadcasts.

cite, site, sight, sights: Don't confuse *"cite"* (mention), *"site"* (place), *"sight"* (vision) or *"sights"* (for tourists; set your *"sights"* on).

clarifier: The second of five steps in "The What?! Approach to Writing" (**Chapter 1.4**), the *clarifier* (a "2") is a kind of decompression chamber that has two jobs: first, to relieve the anxiety raised by a clever opening line and, second, to set up the nut graph (a "3"), which carries the point of the story.

clause: A *clause* is a statement with a subject and a verb.

clever opening line: The first of five steps in "The What?! Approach to Writing" (**Chapter 1.4**), the *clever opening line* (a "1") is the first line you write, which is 10,000 times more important than the second line. You have some people who won't even get to the second line. Make the readers or listeners say, "What?!" Now you have their attention.

cliche: A worn-out expression you've heard many times before: *I'm busy as a bee, there are plenty of fish in the sea, think outside the box.* Twist *cliches*, as in you're busy as a *"B" student*, there are plenty of *phish* in the sea of email, think outside the *box office.*

coin a word or phrase: This is the sixth technique listed in The Zinger Factory (**Chapter 1.4**) and it's considered the granddaddy of them all because it affords you the chance to change the dictionary. New additions for 2023: *"rage farming," "petfluencer," "nearlywed," "adorkable"* and *"janky."* Rather than create a new word, you can take an old word or phrase and give it new meaning just like this sports jargon for something good or impressive: *"nasty," "ridiculous," "break his ankles."*

"Collegiate": If you're using the Chicago Manual of Style and you discover a discrepancy between the Webster's Third New International Dictionary and Merriam-Webster's Collegiate Dictionary on how to spell a word, you should follow the *"Collegiate"* (or its online counterpart) "since it represents newer lexical research."

colon: Quietly, the *colon* introduces an idea. It may be one word: *"Stop!"* Or it may be a list: *"apples, bananas and cherries."* Or it may be a sentence: *"Stylebooks disagree about whether the first word after a colon is capitalized or not."* The AP says use a capital letter for a full sentence, as we've done here. Chicago style is changing its lowercase rule to align with AP's approach.

color: *Color* is a term used to describe sights, sounds and moods that bring a story to life. Color can be condensed or trimmed, but often it is important to the story.

column inches: A common way for newspapers to specify story length is through *column inches*, which are based on standard column widths. Other news media may rely on a *word count* to determine length.

combo captions: When more than one image is used on a printed page, the best approach is to give each picture its own caption. An exception is when the photos are closely related, such as in chronological order. Writing *combo captions* for several images requires care in guiding the reader around the page. On the web, a photo slide show requires the caption writer to tie the photos together without unnecessary repetition.

comma: A *comma* may take the place of *"and"* in a phrase like *"the tall, lean man."* The most common mistake with commas is to forget that they come in pairs. In these cases, the first comma is like opening a door. Be sure to close the door with a second comma. For example: The date *Sept. 11, 2001,* will live in infamy. The boy, *who is only 4 years old,* played the piano magnificently. She's the first in her family, *and believe me not the last,* to graduate from college.

comma-and: When joining two sentences together, you use a *"comma-and"* when you're shifting subjects: *"He entered the store, and she went home."* If the ideas are closely related, then no *"comma-and"* is needed: *"He entered the store and the prices shocked him."*

comma-because: No comma is needed before *"because"*; that would slow down the cause-and-effect. You would say, *"She ran for president because our nation is in trouble."* You might see a comma before *"because"* when it closes the door on a parenthetical statement: *"She ran for president, the highest office in our land, because our nation is in trouble."*

comma-but: Use a comma before the conjunction *"but"* when it joins two clauses: *"The wolf pack got close to the school, but no child was injured."* Don't be fooled by *"but"* as the preposition meaning *"except."* In that case, no comma is needed. For example, *"All but one parent escaped the wolves."*

comma-which, that-no comma: Use commas to set off internal *"which"* clauses but not *"that"* clauses. You would write, *"The mayor's proposal, which would increase taxes 50%, was dead on arrival at the city council."* But then, *"The mayor's proposal that would increase taxes is more radical than her proposal to increase green spaces."*

complement, compliment: Don't confuse *"complement"* (complete) with *"compliment"* (praise).

complex series: There's no question about the need for a comma before *"and"* in a complex series, as in *"She ordered coffee, orange juice, and ham and eggs."* Remember, the rule above all rules is to avoid possible confusion. You want your readers to skate along, then slow down with a comma, so they don't trip on thinking about *"juice and ham."*

comprise, compose: The best way to keep these straight is to substitute in your mind the words they mean: *"comprise"* (embrace all), *"compose"* (make up).

condense and patch approach: The *condense and patch approach* to headline or title writing works best with straight news stories. It's a way of shortening a headline or title by turning phrases into words or by finding shorter words (condensing). Key parts of the headline are then patched together to form the final headline. The condense and patch approach works off the *"skeleton"* of a lede or nut graph for a story, but then shrinks words like *"investigation"* to *"inquiry"* or *"probe."* The order of key words will change, too, as in: *"Car hits pole; 2 die"* from a lede that begins, *"Two people were killed early Monday when. ..."*

conditional: A *conditional* verb form is used to express a hypothetical or an unlikely situation. Conditional verbs can be in the present, past or future tense, and tipoffs will be the use of the helping verbs *"will"* or *"would,"* *"can"* or *"could,"* *"may"* or *"might."* Typically, the sentences are in an *"If-comma-then"* construction, like so: *"If I **can go** to the party, then you **will be** the first to know."*

confidant, confident: Big difference here: *"confidant"* (companion), *"confident"* (certain).

confidence level: The probability that the results are due to chance rather than a real effect. The *confidence level* is stated as a decimal, such as .95, meaning the result could be expected to happen by chance only five out of 100 times. In the social sciences, studies with a confidence level of equal to or greater than .95 are considered *"statistically significant,"* and the results are considered valid.

conflict: *Conflict*, a news value, is a key element in any drama, but sometimes confrontation is reported while other aspects of an event are downplayed. Some editors have decried how news organizations cover public life as a game with everyone divided into winners and losers.

conjunction: A *conjunction* is a word, such as *"and," but," "or,"* that joins words, phrases or clauses.

connote, denote: They're opposites: *"connote"* (oblique mention), *"denote"* (direct mention).

conscious, conscience: Remember the difference: *"conscious"* (awake), *"conscience"* (voice in your head).

context: Providing *context* with information surrounding a quote helps explain the speaker's situation or character. A quote without context can be misconstrued in what legendary CBS anchorman Walter Cronkite called a *"malquote."*

continual, continuous: These mean different things: *"continual"* (brief interruptions), *"continuous"* (no interruptions).

convince, persuade: The shorthand difference: *"persuade to," "convince that."* You *"persuade"* someone *"to do"* something. But you're *"convinced that"* something is true, or convinced *"of"* it.

copy: A story or text created by a writer is called *copy*; that's why we have copy editors who need reasons to change copy.

copy flow: *Copy flow* is the rate at which stories begin the editing process. Editors set staggered deadlines for writers to achieve a manageable copy flow. Otherwise, a crash of copy at the last minute would leave them little time to edit. Copy flow might also refer to the many steps in publishing, including writing, editing, production and proofreading.

copyright: Any image that has a *copyright* cannot be used without permission. A copyright notice does not have to be attached to the photo. Copyright law does not require that creators formally register their works. If you want to use an image that is under copyright, identify the owner and get permission in writing.

core, corps: Don't confuse *"core"* (center) with *"corps"* (Marine Corps).

council, counsel: A *"council"* (board) may have a *"counsel"* (attorney).

courtesy titles: Also known as *honorifics,* they include *"Mr.," "Mrs.," "Miss," "Ms.," "Rev.," "Dr. (Ph.D.)," "Dr. (medical)."* Stylebooks offer different rules on their use for first or second reference to a person, or no use at all.

crawls: *Crawls* are a text-based display typically in the lower third of a video screen, but they may be horizontal or vertical depending on a language's writing system. They are also called a *"crawler," "news ticker," "slide," "zipper"* or *"ticker tape."* The text typically scrolls right to left and provides story summaries and breaking news. It can be a vertical device, running up a screen.

Creative Commons licenses: *Creative Commons licenses* provide a standardized way for image creators to grant the public permission to use their creative work under copyright law. The six CC licenses range from unlimited use to noncommercial use only, with other qualifications. A lot of content is available on Wikipedia, Google, YouTube and Flickr under CC licensing.

cropping: *Cropping* is the art of eliminating parts of an image that don't contribute to the message you want to convey. A good crop focuses on key relationships, peak emotion or peak action and eliminates distractions and redundant elements.

cq: It's an abbreviation for *"checked"* that writers will use when they anticipate that their editors will ask about a name's unusual spelling. It typically is used in parentheses after the name, as in *"Jon Smyth (cq)."*

currently, presently: Big difference: *"currently"* (now), *"presently"* (soon).

D

damage, damages: *Damages* is the remedy that an injured party requests in a civil suit, usually in the form of money. Note the word ends in *"s."* A windstorm causes *"damage"*; a civil court awards *"damages."*

dash: A *dash* works best when it's used rarely and when what follows is a short burst like a shout, maybe even ending with an exclamation point. Beware the dashers who cram sentences into sentences.

data: Some words, like *"data,"* can be singular or plural depending on their meaning: *"The data* (it) *is available." "The data* (they) *do not add up."*

datelines: Under **international datelines**, the AP Stylebook lists 49 cities, out of 4 million in the world, whose countries are so obvious they don't need to be mentioned. Under **domestic datelines,** it lists 30 U.S. cities out of more than 100,000 that don't need their state added. Local style applies if you live in Paris, Kentucky. Remember, the rule above all rules is avoid possible confusion.

deadline: How much flexibility you have as an editor to meet a deadline depends on the medium. The meaning of *"deadline"* ranges from a drop-dead moment, as in the beginning of a live newscast, to a time-management marker, such as one in a series of deadlines in producing a film or documentary, or in publishing a book. Even with the same medium, such as a newspaper, a deadline can vary greatly whether you're publishing a metro daily or a weekly. Regardless, as **Core Principle No. 2** states, "Know the Deadline."

declining: *Declining* an adjective means moving from the positive (*"good"*) to the comparative (*"better"*) to the superlative (*"best"*).

defamation: *Defamation* involves injury to a person's reputation either through writing (*"libel"*) or speaking (*"slander"*).

deliverables: The term *"deliverable"* refers to the finished version of a puzzle piece needed to complete an overall product, such as a book's cover used for promotions before the actual book is in hand. Deliverables will have various deadlines. In filmmaking deliverables may include 10- to 30-second promos and closed captioning. Advance deadlines for deliverables can range from eight to 16 weeks before a film's release.

description: News organizations routinely describe perpetrators: what they look like, what kinds of vehicles they drive, their clothes. The more complete the description, the more useful it is. *Race is a sensitive issue in a description.* Use race in a description of a perpetrator only when the description is thorough.

desert, dessert: You can taste the difference: *"desert"* (sand), *"dessert"* (yum!).

dictionary: Not all dictionaries are alike. When it comes to spelling, check your publication's stylebook first, not the dictionary. Not all stylebooks agree on how to spell a word nor do all dictionaries. Go with your organization's stylebook and the dictionary it recommends. The AP is switching from Webster's New World College Dictionary to Merriam-Webster for its stylebook's 57th edition. The Chicago Manual of Style recommends Webster's Third New International Dictionary, Merriam-Webster's Collegiate Dictionary or the American Heritage Dictionary of the English Language.

different: Something is *"different from"* another thing, not different *"than,"* because the adjective *"different"* is in the positive form, not comparative form. To make it comparative, you need to add *"more,"* so you would say *"more different than."*

digest: A *digest* is a grouping of brief stories related in some way, such as by locale (nation, state, local) or topic (celebrities, politics, health news).

digital first: *Digital first* applies to a news media outlet that begins storytelling immediately online, either with a social media post or a brief website story, then compiles information and refines the story for publication, such as in a newspaper or on a television news program.

direct address: Use a comma before someone's name, as in *"Hi, Buck,"* or *"Happy Birthday, Mike,"* or any form of direct address, such as, *"Now, dear reader, listen up."*

direct object: A *direct object* is what an action verb delivers: *"He gave the **gift**."*

disbursed, dispersed: Yes, they sound similar, but don't confuse *"dispersed"* (smoke cleared) with *"disbursed"* (a loan).

discreet, discrete: Don't confuse *"discreet"* (*shh*) with *"discrete"* (separate).

disinterested, uninterested: Big difference: *"disinterested"* (impartial), *"uninterested"* (bored).

display type challenge: When we write headlines, titles and chyrons, we will deal with *three types* of information: 1) Serious topics demand straight, serious treatment; 2) light, even humorous, topics demand bright, clever treatment; 3) topics that can go either way; these are the toughest and require good judgment.

dispute, refute: Be careful, one says a lot more than the other: *"dispute"* (question or challenge), *"refute"* (prove wrong).

distractions begone: When cropping a full-frame image, you may notice people or objects that draw attention away from the key parts of the story. Crop out *distractions* that add nothing to the information in the image.

E

echo or kicker: The fifth and last step in "The What?! Approach to Writing" (**Chapter 1.4**) is the *echo* (a "5"), which repeats a word or phrase from the clever opening line. The echo provides a sense of closure, tying the ending to the beginning. A short, high-impact sentence or a telling quote that puts a clear ending on the story is called a *kicker*. An *echo* is something that brings the reader back to an idea or anecdote told at the beginning. Stylish writers often save their second-best quote for the end of a story.

edit in the air: When an editor can work closely with a writer on an assignment, one key to success in interpersonal editing is to *"edit in the air,"* meaning to talk through possible *ledes* or transitions before writers put words on a page. Once writers have invested a lot of time and energy in their writing, then it's more difficult and time-consuming to change the focus of a story.

editing strategy: Beginning editors tend to dive into stories and begin changing things. Often mistakes get overlooked and writers' egos get bruised in the process. That's because *editors can't think big and small at the same time.* Instead, we suggest that editors have an editing strategy for interpersonal exchanges with writers and for addressing three levels of mistakes: big, embarrassing and tedious. An editing strategy on deadline may allow just one quick sweep through a story. But ideally an editor can make more than one sweep, and there's great value in allowing writing to sit for a while, if possible, then return to it with fresh eyes.

elaboration: Stories are built in three tiers: *points, support* for those points and *elaboration.* When trims are necessary, the *"fat"* in a story is often found in the elaboration, which adds color or depth often in the form of quotations.

ellipsis: An *ellipsis* is the formal name for that dot-dot-dot or three periods (...) that you'll see to indicate something is missing (as in a quote) or represent a voice trailing off or a pause. Don't overuse them (plural *"ellipses"*).

em dash: A technical note from the old typesetting days: Another name for the dash is *em dash* because it's the width of a capital *"M."* Leave a space before and after the dash, according to the AP Stylebook. You may see the term *"en dash,"* which is half the width of an *em dash* and almost the size of a capital *"N."* But it's not quite the same as a hyphen, which is shorter. AP does not use the *"en dash."*

empathy, sympathy: Both deal with emotions, but don't confuse them. Think *"empathy"* (I feel your pain), *"sympathy"* (I pity you).

english, English: Don't confuse *"english"* (put a spin on the ball) and *"English"* (the language).

essential and nonessential: Rather than use the traditional grammatical term *"restrictive"* to describe phrases and clauses, the AP Stylebook uses *"essential."* It distinguishes between *"essential"* and *"nonessential"* phrases and clauses, while the Chicago Manual of Style uses the traditional terms *"restrictive"* and *"nonrestrictive."* Basically, no commas are needed with restrictive (essential) phrases or clauses, such as *"The woman **who complimented me** sat next to the fellow **who hit me.**"* Commas are typically used around nonrestrictive (nonessential) phrases or clauses, such as *"The woman, **who is a Taylor Swift fan,** won the grand prize."*

et al., etc.: Both are Latin abbreviations for expressions with similar meanings. The Latin *"et alia,"* meaning "and others," applies to a list of names, such as other authors. The Latin *"et cetera,"* meaning "and the rest," works best when you have already stated a long list and now you are recapping a few items, then adding *"etc."*

etymology: The source of many usage rules is *etymology,* the study of word origins from their Latin and Greek roots and how the meanings have changed over time. Good writers and editors try to keep words to their original meanings but must be aware of their current usage to avoid distraction or confusion.

everyday, every day: This is extra subtle: *"everyday"* (ordinary) is an adjective; *"every day"* (all the time) is an adverb.

everyone, every one: We wish to thank *"every one"* of you for paying attention. With proper usage, *"everyone"* wins. The shorthand: *"everyone"* (everybody), *"every one"* (each individual).

excerpt: An excerpt, a short summary of a story, appears on the home page of a news organization's website. Platforms such as WordPress will create these automatically, but the result can be confusing or incomplete. Excerpts are similar to *summary graphs* on a printed page.

exclamation point: *"Oh my gosh!!! Wasn't that exciting!!!"* The more you use *exclamation points,* the less impact they have. Try using them rarely and one at a time. OK? *OK!*

F

fairness: While truth and accuracy are the ultimate defenses in a libel or slander trial, *fairness* is our standard. To judge the fairness of a crime story, ask how you would feel reading it if your name were inserted in place of the suspect's.

Falkland Islands: You are taking the British side when you use this term rather than *"Islas Malvinas,"* which is how Argentina refers to the islands. War has a way of forcing writers and editors to take sides. In 1982, when England engaged in a 10-week undeclared war with Argentina in the South Atlantic over the *Falkland Islands,* editors in the Western news media chose not to use "*Islas Malvinas.*"

family newspaper concept: Whereas the Federal Communications Commission (FCC) focuses on obscene, indecent and profane language or depictions, and may issue fines for offenses, some print and online publications decide what's appropriate based on the *family newspaper concept.* Just as FCC rules apply between 6 a.m. and 10 p.m., when "there is a reasonable risk that children may be in the audience," publishers keep kids in mind. Under **obscenities, profanities, vulgarities,** the AP Stylebook advises using only the first letter, then hyphens ("f---," "s---"). Other times, it says, you might just replace the curse word with a generic word in parentheses, like *"(expletive)."*

farther, further: One you can count, the other not so much. Don't confuse "*farther*" (distance in miles) with "*further*" (more).

fault lines: A concept from the Maynard Institute's newsroom training that helps journalists understand their unconscious bias in seeing a world aligned across five *fault lines:* race, gender, class, generation and geography.

feature captions: Stories about people are a staple of the features section of a newspaper or website, and there you find the challenge of writing *feature captions.* Feature images often work best with a witty catchline and a certain amount of flair in the writing.

fewer, less: One deals with numbers, the other amounts. Don't confuse "*fewer*" (dollars) with "*less*" (energy).

file photo captions: Many images are retrieved from a reference library or another archive to run with a story. *File photo captions* need special care so that the reader is not misled into thinking the image is current. The caption's goal is to tie the image tightly to the story.

film producer: For films, the title "*producer*" applies to someone involved with the movie's script, casting, directing and editing, as well as finances, marketing, release dates and distribution.

Fixtionary: *The Fixtionary,* found in **Appendix A,** is the start of **The Language Skills Survival Kit**. It's like a dictionary but with an action plan.

Flesch test: It's a readability formula developed by Rudolf Flesch to assess a score for "reading ease" and "human interest." The formula's steps include figuring average sentence length (ideally 20 words or so), calculating the number of syllables per 100 words (fewer the better) and counting the number of "personal words" (pronouns, identifiers like *"father"* and *"sister"* and words like *"people"* and *"folks"*).

foreign names: You'll see multiple spellings of names, places and words translated to English phonetically from foreign-language alphabets. Be careful because not only phonetics but also politics can be involved. Check your stylebook for the preferred spellings.

foreshadowing: *Foreshadowing* is typically a paragraph or two near the beginning of a news story that hints at what's to come. If length is a problem, an editor might write a foreshadowing graph to condense much of what follows if such a paragraph isn't present.

foreword, forward: A *"foreword"* (introduction) can move a book *"forward"* (onward!).

format: The physical layout of a newspaper or web page, or the presentation style of a news broadcast, is known as the *format*. Print examples include broadsheet or tabloid newspapers, magazines and newsletters. Broadcast examples include headline news, news magazine ("60 Minutes") and tabloid news ("E! News").

G

gantlet, gauntlet: You run the *"gantlet"* and throw down the *"gauntlet"* to issue a challenge, not the other way around. As the AP Stylebook maintains: *"gantlet"* (ordeal), *"gauntlet"* (glove). But these days, you may see only "run the gauntlet" as the expression in common usage.

general audience: A concept in journalism that dates to the "penny press" newspapers of the 1830s for maximum circulation. It affects an editor's approach to storytelling, including adherence to general style rules, such as AP style.

gibe, jibe: Don't confuse *"gibe"* (insult) with *"jibe"* (fit neatly).

good, well : *Good* is an adjective; *well* can be either an adjective or an adverb. So you would say: I feel *"good"* (happy, adjective). I feel *"well"* (not sick, adjective). Those two adjectives are stated *"well"* (skillfully, adverb).

grammar mistakes in quotes: *Grammar mistakes* in quotations get in the way of what is being said and distract the reader. Changing a quote, however, can be a fireable offense at your news organization, so know the rules. Sometimes grammar problems are retained as they provide characterization of the speaker. When in doubt, consider paraphrasing the quote.

guilty or liable: In criminal court, a defendant pleads *"guilty"* or *"not guilty."* In a civil suit, the defendant, or the one being sued, can be *"held liable"* or not. Someone found guilty may end up in *"prison"*; someone found liable may end up paying *"damages."*

H

hammers: Big, bold headlines, called *hammers*, attract readers with one to three words. A second headline, called a *subhed* or *readout*, provides relevant information to explain the story.

hangar, hanger: Don't confuse *"hangar"* (airplanes) with *"hanger"* (clothes).

hanged, hung: These are easily confused, with deadly consequences. Remember, *"hanged"* (executed), *"hung"* (your clothes).

here, hear: Don't confuse *"here"* (arrived) with *"hear"* (ear).

Hippocrates: Hippocrates, a physician in ancient Greece, wrote something in his classic work "Of the Epidemics" that can be adapted as an editing philosophy if you just replace *"patients"* with *"readers"*: *"I will follow that system of regimen which, according to my ability and judgment, I consider for the benefit of my patients, and abstain from whatever is deleterious and mischievous."* In other words, first, do no harm.

hissing sound: Anytime you see an *"s"* or an *"apostrophe-s,"* hear the *hissing sound "ssss"* and STOP! Ask, is this a plural word or a possessive? Use an apostrophe with an implied *"of,"* but no apostrophe if *"by"* or *"for"* is implied. For example: *My teacher's pet peeve* (the pet peeve of my teacher). *A teachers* *union* (a union for teachers). Maybe it's a contraction you're hearing: *"There's a problem"* (there is), *"but the problem is theirs"* (possessive form of "they"). Autocorrect makes *"it's"* or *"its"* a common mistake.

hyphen: *Hyphens* often take two or more words and turn them into one modifier to avoid possible confusion. So you would write, *"The 13-year-old girl was well-known as a small-business owner."* Yes, she was *"well"* (not sick) and *"small"* for her age, but that wasn't the point here.

identity clues: Images of more than one person require captions with *identity clues*, such as *"from left."* Follow the style of your news organization.

illustrators: Illustrator photos show some important aspect of a story. These often are environmental portraits of people taken in their own surroundings. Many times *illustrators* are set up; the action takes place for the camera. Illustrators include publicity shots, such as those received from a record company when a music group will perform. The *illustrator caption* cannot mislead the viewer into thinking the photo shows action when it really doesn't.

image search engines: Two of the most popular sources for images are Google Images and Wikipedia Commons. These *image search engines* provide access to millions of images and can be found on the Creative Commons website.

impact as a news value: The greater the impact the more news coverage you will see. Stories affecting many people are important, but sometimes the impact is not easily identified, especially in the early stages.

impact as a noun: Don't use as a verb. Be specific: Say *help* or *hurt*, or just *affect*.

imply, infer: These are easy to remember if you substitute in your mind the words they mean: *"imply"* (speak), *"infer"* (hear).

include, comprise, composed of: Use *"include"* only with partial lists. Don't say, *"The trio included a guitarist, a drummer and a banjo player."* Instead: *"The trio, which **included** the tavern owner's wife, was **composed of** a guitarist, a drummer and a banjo player."* Or *"The trio comprised a guitarist, a drummer and a banjo player."*

incriminating details: Statements with details that seem to incriminate a suspect must come from a *privileged source*, such as a police spokesperson or police report, formal charges in a document or trial testimony.

indicted: Being *indicted* means the same as being *charged*, though indicted sounds worse. In complex cases, a grand jury may hear evidence and deliver the indictment.

indirect object: An *indirect object* is the receiver of the direct object: *"He gave her the gift."*

information graphic: An *information graphic* is a visual representation of data that helps readers to compare numbers and grasp significant differences. This broad definition includes charts, tables, maps, pictographs and "how-to" graphics describing a process (see **Chapter 2.4**). A well-done information graphic allows readers to compare data visually and to interpret differences in numbers in meaningful ways. The best graphics present more than one variable, such as oil production over time by country.

interjection: An interjection shouts with a word (*"wow!"*) or phrase (*"holy cow!"*).

into, in to: There's a difference, either a preposition or a verb phrase: *"into"* (a space), *"in to"* (give in to).

inverted pyramid: Stories written in the *inverted pyramid* form put the most important facts in the lede, followed by facts in descending order of importance. Inverted pyramid stories can be trimmed to just the most important or interesting facts, most often from the bottom up. Be sure to read the whole story to make sure nothing important, such as the names of local legislators, is near the end.

its, it's: Don't confuse *"its"* (possessive) with *"it's"* (it is or it has).

J

jargon: Specialized language used by certain professions, such as the military, medical personnel, academics and law enforcement, is called *jargon*. Paraphrase jargon into language that is easily understood without losing meaning.

JPEG format: An image in the *JPEG format* compresses the data in the image file to save disc space and allow for faster transmission of the image.

K

key relationships: When two people or objects in an image interact, crop tightly to emphasize the *key relationships.*

kickers: *Kickers* are small headlines of two to four words that provide contrast, introduce white space above a story and give the reader a quick, clever take. Kickers focus on secondary elements, not something that emphasizes the main thrust of the story.

killer mistake: A *killer mi*stake is one that kills your credibility. For example, misspell or mispronounce a name and you've made a killer mistake. Never commit the *killer mistake* of taking a paraphrased statement with attribution and turning it into a quotation. Adding those quotation marks can get you fired.

Koran, Quran: For years the AP Stylebook listed the correct spelling for the Muslim holy book as *"Koran."* In the 56th edition, the entry **Koran** says use *"Quran"* in all references except when preferred by an organization or in a specific title or name.

Kyiv: This spelling and its pronunciation *(KEEV)* shows favoritism to Ukraine as a sovereign country. When the war in Ukraine broke out (again) on Feb. 24, 2022, writers were confronted with the decision to call the capital either *"Kiev" (kee-EV)*, a bow historically to Russia, or *Kyiv,* a nod toward an independent Ukraine.

L

lede: This unique spelling for *"lead"* (pronounced *LEED*) refers to the start of a story, which may be the first sentence, the first few sentences or a few introductory paragraphs in a narrative article. The *lede's* purpose is to summarize what's most important about a story, and a good lede includes key words and phrases that are explained in the rest of the story. A news lede typically tells who, what, when and where; a news analysis tends to focus on why and how. A news lede isn't overloaded with details, and it must never be cut from a story.

lets, let's: Don't confuse *"lets"* (to rent out an apartment) with *"let's"* (let us go!).

levels of mistakes: Not all mistakes carry the same weight. In some cases, what editors consider "mistakes," such as style errors, many readers won't notice. Other mistakes might even make someone in a story look good. When mistakes are a real problem, they come in three levels: killer, embarrassing and tedious.

libel: *Libel* is defamation of a person's reputation through something written or printed. "Libel is generally distinguished from slander, in that a libel is written, or otherwise printed, whereas a slander is spoken," according to the Associated Press Stylebook.

lie, lay: The tricky thing is *"lay"* means both to *"place"* (present tense) and *"reclined"* (past tense of *"lie"*). Keep these sentences in mind: *"Lay the book on the table—just place it there." "I lay on the beach all day—just reclined in my chair until sunset."* We won't lie: It doesn't always sound right. Here's a shorthand: *"lie"* (recline, fib), *"lay"* (reclined, place).

like, as: *"Like"* works best as a preposition (*"like"* me). Use *"as"* a conjunction (*"as"* I do).

line charts: *Line charts* also are known as *fever charts* or *trend charts*. Use them when the data is charted over a period of time. The emphasis is on trends rather than the individual numbers. Sometimes a line chart can show projected data. Line charts are especially good for showing seasonal changes or comparing more than one trend over the same time periods.

listening sessions: Small groups of a media outlet's listeners, viewers or readers are convened in *listening sessions,* where researchers can hear what story ideas and ways of presentation are most preferred. Also called *focus groups*, listening sessions help editors fine-tune their understanding of the target audience.

literally, figuratively: Big difference: *"literally"* (actually), *"figuratively"* (not actually).

local style sheets: Also known as *house rules, local style sheets* cover issues specific to a local community or to a particular publication and may contain exceptions to the official stylebook in use.

locator maps: *Locator maps* are small maps that help readers place an event at a location in the community. Locator maps often are used with crime stories because the location of a crime is of high interest to readers and viewers.

logline: A *logline* meets the challenge of telling the whole story of a film, documentary or television program in one sentence. It may be a required part of a grant application for funding or something used to make a pitch to investors.

lose, loose: Careful pronunciation helps so you won't confuse *"lose"* (sorry!) with *"loose"* (not tight).

M

macro and micro comparisons: Good information graphics present an overall impression of data on the *"macro,"* or wide, view, then allow for closer inspection on close, or *"micro,"* viewing.

macro-level news judgment: *Macro-level news judgment* involves story selection and placement. Its ingredients include broad news values (*timeliness, proximity* or *oddity*), the personalities and power relationships of those making the decisions, and critical judgments by editors based on their experience tempered by a sense of fairness.

maestro: The term for an editor leading a Maestro Concept story planning session. The maestro leads with questions for writers, beginning with *"Can you summarize your story in 30 words or fewer?"* and then, *"Why should I care?"* The answers to those questions create the first draft of a headline and the story's nut graph. A third question—*"What is the most interesting part of the story?"*—inspires a powerful visual to go with the headline to create a one-two punch to stop readers and entice them to read.

Maestro Concept: The original *Maestro Concept* (1993) was defined like so: *"A time-management, teamwork intensive approach to story planning that brings reporters, editors, designers and photographers together as a team after* *preliminary reporting but before any writing, editing or design. At this point you have a story; now the challenge is figuring out the best way to present it."* That version of the concept is still at play in one way or another from high school journalism classes to newspapers here and abroad. Author Buck Ryan, who created the concept and introduced it to the American Society of Newspaper Editors in a video and report, recommends an updated Media Maestro approach that adds journalists working in audio and video as well as social media to the storytelling team.

magnitude: *Magnitude,* a news value, can be seen in an event like the Super Bowl that attracts millions of spectators. The danger is that editors and reporters will ignore stories rich in human interest that attract little attention. And the bandwagon effect can make a story seem more important than it is.

malquote: A *malquote,* something other than a misquote, is a term coined by the late CBS anchorman Walter Cronkite meaning a sound bite taken out of context or without explanation of what question the speaker was answering.

mantra: A mental checklist to keep editors focused on the BIG MISTAKES—names, titles, numbers, locations, quotations, bias, libel.

maps: *Maps,* once drawn in a computer program, can be stored electronically and easily altered to serve new stories. Maps can be downloaded from graphic services and altered to fit a publication's style for typography, color and texture. Adding data to a map can result in a satisfying graphic that allows readers to make comparisons.

margin of error: With a *margin of error,* researchers calculate the likelihood of being wrong as a statistical probability. For opinion surveys, the *margin of error* is stated as plus or minus percentage points. A typical figure for a political poll is plus or minus 4 percentage points. Margin of error decreases as the sample size increases.

medal, meddle: Don't confuse *"medal"* (award) with *"meddle"* (interfere).

media: The word *"media"* can be singular or plural depending on its meaning. The key to finding the right verb for subject-verb agreement is to ask yourself, *Does the word mean **it** or **they**?* Both the AP Stylebook and the Chicago Manual of Style consider these sentences correct: *The media is biased!* (singular, one monolithic group). *The media are largely misrepresenting the event.* (plural, many outlets)

metal, mettle: Getting hit with a *"metal"* pipe will really test your *"mettle."* Remember: *"metal"* (steel), *"mettle"* (your character).

metaphor: *Metaphors,* like *similes,* compare something new with something familiar. The difference is a metaphor does this without using *"as"* or *"like."* It's the second figure of speech listed in The Zinger Factory (**Chapter 1.4**). For example: *Grammar is a sore tooth. His temper is a volcano.*

micro-level news judgment: For the editor, every story represents a series of small news decisions, any of which might be complex: *Is this the right word? Is the sentence put together properly? Does the paragraph do its job efficiently? Does the story flow properly?* These questions relate to *micro-level news judgment.*

MLA style: The rules set out in the Modern Language Association stylebook.

mood: Verbs have three *moods*: *"indicative,"* telling it straight (*"I **am** a superstar"*); *"imperative,"* delivering a command (*"**Be** a superstar!"*); and *"subjunctive,"* for example, making a demand (*"My ballet instructor insisted that I **be** a superstar"*).

more than, over: Some editors still insist on using *"more than"* for numbers (*"more than"* 10%) and reserving *"over"* for spatial relationships (*"over"* the moon). Both the AP and Chicago style now say *"over"* is fine for both.

mug shot: A picture of a person's face, called a *mug shot,* is often used at a small size as an identifier. Mug shots often are cropped to a standard width and height, for example, 1 column (about 1.5 inches) wide by 2 inches tall or half the size as a *thumbnail.*

N

narratives: Stories written as *narratives* are literary, like a short story or a novelette, carefully constructed with a beginning, middle and end. Such stories are harder to trim and require careful news judgment.

nat sound: The use of *natural sound,* or background noise, in a podcast or radio news package makes images come to life in a listener's mind.

negative space: The area of an image that adds nothing visually is sometimes called *dead space*. If it serves no purpose, you can crop it out. But sometimes an expanse of *negative space* helps to tell the story, for example one about loneliness.

news captions: For photos or video of current events that accompany stories, *news captions* should contain facts and as many identities as possible. Tread on the side of caution when considering levity for a news *catchline*, which attracts attention with larger type to accompany a caption.

news hole: *News hole* is the available space for stories on a publication's pages around advertising, which pays for production costs. In general, the more advertising, the bigger the news hole. One exception is the TV news broadcast bound by a set time, usually 30 minutes. Another is the *bottomless news hole* of the online news publication not confined to the dimensions of a printed page.

news meeting: News judgment on the macro level often takes place in a *news meeting*, sometimes called a *budget meeting* or a *news huddle*. The structure and timing of news meetings have shifted as more news organizations changed their priority from the print edition or scheduled broadcasts to the 24-hour news cycle and a digital-first approach to coverage on the internet.

news philosophy: *News philosophy* refers to how a media outlet positions itself within the context of city, state and national issues. Once-local organizations are affected by the international reach of the internet.

news release: A *news release* is a ready-made story written by a public relations specialist and distributed to news organizations. These often include quotations that editors might be reluctant to cut. Treat a news release like any other story that needs to be fact-checked and edited.

news service photo: *News services*, also called *wire services*, are organizations that provide hundreds of images a day for their subscribers. These organizations include the Associated Press, Reuters, Getty Images and Agence France-Presse. National news organizations such as The Washington Post and The New York Times also offer their photos and videos for reuse at a price.

NFT: *NFT*, or *non-fungible tokens*, is a term coined in 2017 but just added as an entry to the AP Stylebook (2022-2024), which provides a detailed explanation as part of a longer entry titled **Cryptocurrency, blockchain, bitcoin, NFT,**

Web3. An NFT is like a one-of-a-kind trading card that can be anything digital, such as an artwork or piece of music.

nose axis: The *nose axis* is an invisible line between two subjects connecting their noses when a videographer is lining up a shot, usually in an interview setting. It is also known as the *axis of action* or the *180-degree rule,* and it is one of the core principles of cinematography. Staying on one side of this line keeps backgrounds and angles uniform. Crossing this line breaks the continuity of a scene.

noun: A *noun* is the name of a person, place or thing. Common nouns are lowercase. Proper nouns are capitalized. Meanings change, of course: *"Catholic,"* as in the Roman Catholic Church, is different from *"catholic,"* which means universal.

number: *Number* is the grammatical term for whether a word is *singular* (it is) or *plural* (they are).

nut graph: A *nut graph,* like a *lede,* serves two purposes: It summarizes a story's point and sets up the organization for the rest of the writing. The third of five steps in The What?! Approach to Writing (**Chapter 1.4**), a nut graph (a "3") usually follows an interesting anecdote, or *clarifier* (a "2"), that grabs readers' attention, serving as a kind of decompression chamber from the *clever opening line* (a "1"). The anecdote combines with the nut graph to create what's called an *anecdotal lede.* The writer steps back from the immediate events to provide context, so the nut graph can explain how the current news fits into a larger picture.

O

objectivity: A term of neutrality. Journalists who claim it, in fact, make a series of *subjective* decisions.

object of the preposition: The *object* is the noun or pronoun that follows a preposition. Remember, prepositions like *"over"* and *"out"* show relationship. Note their objects in this sentence: *"The deer jumped over **you** and **me**, then fled out the **door.**"*

oddity: *Oddity*, a news value, involves stories about unusual people or happenings. These stories are standard fare for news organizations, and even more so if the story comes with pictures. Today, when cellphone cameras are everywhere, viewers are fed a steady diet of unusual happenings on the news.

1-shot: A *1-shot* is also known as a *wide shot* or *establishing shot*. Typically, a photo page or a video package, even a documentary, will open with an establishing shot to help readers or viewers get their bearings on understanding the story about to be told. These wide shots provide a lot of context but often lack detail.

one-two punch: Busy readers need a reason to stop and pay attention. A large, strong visual is a good place to start, but when that visual is combined with a *hammer headline,* or typography that's BIG and BOLD, then you deliver a one-two punch to attract attention.

ou: Playwright George Bernard Shaw's quote that England and America are "two countries separated by a common language" is true when it comes to spelling. We consider all those *"u's"* in proper British spellings, such as *"colour,"* *"favour"* and *"labour,"* to be superfluous.

Oxford comma: Also called a serial comma or a Harvard comma, it's the one before "and" with simple words in a series, such as *"red, white, and blue."* The same punctuation rule applies to phrases, as in *"through the yard, over the fence, and into the forest."* And even short sentences, as in *"He walked into the classroom confidently, he picked up a pen, and he flunked the test."* Not all stylebooks agree it's necessary. The Chicago Manual of Style calls for the Oxford comma, but the AP Stylebook does not.

P

page proofs: A *page proof* is the next-to-final version of how a publication will look. It provides editors with the last chance to make any changes, hopefully small ones, before publishing. A *proofreader* is a person who uses a full set of marks on *"hard copy,"* or printed pages, to indicate what changes need to be made before actual printing. PDFs of pages may be circulated to copy editors, who then can make changes electronically.

pagination: *Pagination* is a system where entire pages are laid out on the computer and sent to an image setter as a complete, or composite, page. In pagination systems, an editor might be asked to write a headline or title with broad specifications, then final adjustments are made by the makeup editor on the electronic page.

parallel construction: *Parallel construction* is the use of the same word or phrase in a series for consistency and coherence, sometimes to assist with transitions. In a travel story for people "on the go," for example, the writer might advise travelers on where *"to go fishing, hunting and camping."* The three "-ing" endings keep the sentence parallel. The authors used the word "On" to begin sections on editing in sweeps *(On the first sweep ..., On the second sweep ..., On the third sweep ...).* This is an example of using parallel construction for transitions.

paraphrase: To *paraphrase* means to remove the quote marks and restate the information in a more concise or understandable way. Sometimes called an *indirect quote*, a paraphrase still requires an attribution. A good paraphrase will maintain the meaning of the quote but not mimic the speaker's exact words. Paraphrasing requires sensitivity to what a speaker means.

parentheses: *Parentheses* present information with a whisper often in an aside, as in *"She was invited to the prom by five young men (accepted none) and spent the night reading a good book in her room."* Parentheses work best when the information inside is short and to the point, as in *"The university is ranked first in the nation (25th last year) and now is the odds-on favorite to win the national championship."* The longer the contents in parentheses, the more the writer should consider commas or a separate sentence.

passive voice: *Passive voice* is useful to avoid convicting someone in print. Passive voice consists of a form of the verb *"to be,"* a past participle and a prepositional phrase beginning with *"by,"* stated or implied. When the *"by"* phrase is not included, we can avoid assigning blame as in this sentence: *"A St. Paul man was arrested after **a woman was attacked** Saturday in a nightclub."*

peak, peek, pique: Don't be fooled by words that sound alike but are spelled differently, such as *"peak"* (mountaintop), *"peek"* (look) and *"pique"* (stimulate).

peak action: Images of action just before it resolves itself, known as *peak action*, get viewers deeply involved because they must provide closure, completing the action. Think of the diver at the top of her arc before she starts to descend.

peak emotion: In selecting an image, look for human faces at their most expressive. Crop out negative space and distractions to focus on *peak emotion*.

pedal, peddle: Don't confuse *"pedal"* (by foot) with *"peddle"* (by selling).

percent: A *percent* is a proportion stated as a number per hundred. To figure a percent, divide the small number by the larger and multiply by 100. For instance, to find what percent 15 is of 60, divide 15 by 60 to get .25, then multiply by 100 to get 25%.

periods: The more *periods* the better to lower your average sentence length and improve your writing's readability. See if what you have between commas, dashes or parentheses just might work better as separate sentences. Unless there's a clear connection between statements, a period might work better than a semicolon.

perpetrator: Use the term *"perpetrator"* for an unknown person who committed a crime. A court decides if a suspect and a perpetrator are one and the same. Because we make no attempt to identify the perpetrator as a real person, we have more freedom in what we can say about details of the crime.

personality: The *personality* of a news organization goes hand in hand with its news philosophy. The personality is shaped by how a publication or news organization thinks of itself in relation to its audience: feisty voice of the people, or sober national newspaper of record, or stalwart community member.

personification: *Personification* involves attributing human qualities to inanimate objects. It's the third figure of speech listed in The Zinger Factory (**Chapter 1.4**) and another way to create a memorable line. For example: *The siren slapped us across the face.* AP's 57th edition says don't ascribe human emotions to AI models or use gender pronouns for AI tools.

phonetic spelling: Nonstandard spelling is sometimes used in quotes to mimic regional accents or dialects: *"We're gonna give it our best." Phonetic spelling* can make a quote hard to read. Be careful, as writers who use phonetic spelling to characterize people might be promoting stereotypes unfairly.

photo illustrations: News organizations will sometimes combine a photo with other photos or artwork to create a striking image for a story. These *photo illustrations* must be clearly labeled as such to prevent duping the viewer into thinking the image reflects reality.

phrase: A *phrase* is a statement without a subject and a verb.

pictograph: A *pictograph* is a special type of bar chart that uses pictures to dress up statistical information. The pictograph symbol should be simple and easy to identify. It also should have relevance to the data, such as oil barrel images with each barrel representing a million barrels of oil per day. Because comparisons may be more difficult to make visually than with a plain bar chart, numbers often are included.

pie chart: A *pie chart* is a circular graphic divided into pie-shaped slices, each proportional to a percent of the total. The first and most important rule for using a pie chart is that each pie must represent 100% of the data.

PinkNews: This is an online newspaper founded by Benjamin Cohen in 2005 in the United Kingdom. It finds its target reader in the gay, lesbian, bisexual and transgender community worldwide. It's an example of an editing success story when people can see themselves in a publication.

play on a name: It's the fifth technique listed in The Zinger Factory (**Chapter 1.4**) as a way to create a memorable line. This one is tricky because you need to start with a famous name. If it's Malcolm X, then you can wonder if the movie about him was *"Malcolm X-rated."* Do we cheat them and how? Just ask the law firm of *Dewey, Cheetham & Howe.*

poll sources: Organizations that conduct public opinion surveys, such as newspapers, magazines and broadcast networks, often partner with academic institutions. Partnerships are necessary because a well-conducted poll is expensive. Be wary of polls conducted for industry groups, political parties or individual candidates. These *poll sources* may be less reliable.

pore, pour: If you *"pour"* a drink, it may spill on the papers you're trying to *"pore"* over. Remember: *"pour"* (spill), *"pore"* (look over).

precision journalism: *Precision journalism,* as defined by the late Philip Meyer, is applying social and behavioral science research methods to the process of journalism.

predicate: A *predicate* is another name for a verb.

predicate adjective: A *predicate adjective* follows a linking verb (*"to be," "to feel," "to smell"*) and modifies a subject (*"pork chop"*) in this example: *This pork chop smells **bad**—don't eat it.*

predicate nominative: Two word clues here: first, *"predicate,"* which means a verb like *"to be"* (*"am," "is," "are"*). Second, *"nominative,"* which is the case of pronouns used as a subject (*"he," "she," "they"*). So here are examples of predicate nominatives: *"I am **he**." "This is **she**." "The winners are **they**."*

preferred spelling: The way a word is listed in a stylebook is called the *preferred spelling.* It is derived from a particular dictionary that lists the word first among options and provides a full definition of the word. If you find a word in the dictionary and it doesn't have a full definition, keep looking. That's not the preferred spelling. For instance, *"usable,"* the preferred spelling, is also listed in Webster's New World College Dictionary, 5th edition, as *"useable"* but with no definition. Merriam-Webster lists "useable" as a variant.

preposition: A *preposition* shows relationship (*"up," "down," "over," "through," "between"*). As the saying goes, if you can do it to a cloud, it's probably a preposition. The word that follows a preposition in a phrase is in the objective case. Use *"me,"* not *"I,"* as the object of the preposition in the phrase *"just between you and me."*

present, reveal: Not the same: *"present"* (introduce it), *"reveal"* (something was hidden).

principle, principal: Don't confuse *"principle"* (belief) with *"principal"* (school leader or primary concern).

privileged sources: All circumstances of a crime must be attributed to *privileged sources.* Privileged sources include the police, sheriff, FBI; prosecutors; court records and testimony; regulatory agency proceedings; and Congress in session.

process graphics: *Process graphics*, sometimes called "how-to" graphics, use pictures and diagrams to describe a process or show how something works or how something is done. Often these involve "cutaway" drawings to reveal the inner parts of an object.

producer: *A producer's* job description varies depending on the medium. In general, a producer works behind the scenes doing planning, coordinating, management and other tasks. Various levels of decision-making powers are defined by their titles: *executive producer, associate producer, coordinating producer, line producer, producer.*

production assistant: A *production assistant (PA)* is an entry-level position that involves doing various tasks to assist with a television program, a film, a digital media production or some other creative enterprise. A PA may work across multiple departments.

profanity: *Profanity* is language commonly considered to be crude, usually in the form of slang for sexual activity or bodily functions. As such language seeps more and more into routine conversation, profanity becomes more difficult to define. Know your news organization's policy on whether to use it or not.

prominence: Important people such as political, religious, business or cultural leaders have *prominence*, a quality that goes beyond just being well-known. Otherwise insignificant details become newsworthy when a prominent person is involved. That's why prominence is a news value.

pronoun: A *pronoun* takes the place of a noun. Subjects like *"I," "we," "you," "he," "she," "it" and "they"* are pronouns. But so can a word like *"one"* be a pronoun, as in this exchange: A friend says, *"I have chocolate bars,"* and you say, *"I'll take one."* The longstanding policy of using a person's preferred name and title now carries over to pronouns. As the AP Stylebook puts it: "As much as possible, AP now uses *'they/them/their'* as a way of accurately describing and representing a person who uses those pronouns for themself." The Chicago Manual of Style adopts the same policy under *"Pronouns"* with a sub item *"singular they."*

proved, proven: It can be *"proved"* (verb) that you're a *"proven"* (adjective) success. Keep those words to their primary parts of speech.

proximity: Events that occur within a news organization's circulation are important to its audience. Many smaller newspapers and broadcast outlets pursue the "local angle" in almost every story they produce, realizing that community news sells. That's why we consider *proximity* to be a news value.

public opinion poll: A scientific, nonbiased *public opinion poll* is a type of survey or inquiry designed to measure the public's views regarding a particular topic or series of topics. Interviewers question people chosen at random from the population being measured. Responses are interpreted through statistical analysis.

punctuation rules: Yes, there are many *punctuation rules* to know, but don't lose track of their purpose. At its best, punctuation provides clarity, nuance and efficiency.

Q

Q&A: A *Q&A* type of story consists of a short introduction, then questions and answers from an interview. Answers usually must be edited for length. Typically no quotation marks are used for the answers. If you must edit answers for any reason, be sure to make that clear to your readers.

quiet, quite: These get confused with a slip of the tongue or pen. Remember: *"quite"* (just so), *"quiet"* (shh).

quotation: A *quotation* is any part of written text enclosed in quotation marks and attributed to a source. It's often called a direct quote to distinguish it from a *paraphrase*. Three qualities define a good quote: **When someone important says something newsworthy:** The emphasis is on *who* and *what*. **When someone says something new:** Often the quote will be a straightforward, newsworthy statement. The emphasis is on *what* is said. **When someone says something with a flair:** Often such a quote brings out the human dimension of an otherwise complicated or dull story. The emphasis is on *how* it's said.

quotation marks: Words contained within *quotation marks* have special status, so be careful using them and be sure to use correct punctuation. **Never add quote marks to written copy, even if a sentence sounds like a quote and is attributed to someone.** Quotation marks, double and single, are something to watch when using another piece of punctuation: the question mark.

These sentences are correct: *"What should I do?" she asked.* (No comma needed after the question mark.) *"Her question was, 'What should I do?'"* (Note the single quote, then double quote.) Keep commas and periods inside the end quote marks.

R

rack, wrack: Don't confuse *"rack"* (your brain) with *"wrack"* (ruin).

rain, rein, reign: Don't be fooled by words that sound alike but are spelled differently, such as *"rain"* (water), *"rein"* (in) and *"reign"* (over).

raise, raze: Big mistake to confuse them as these are opposites. Remember: *"raise"* (elevate), *"raze"* (destroy).

ran, run: Use *"ran"* only in the past tense (*"I ran a mile yesterday"*). Otherwise, use *"run"* as in *"is run," "has run," "have run," "will have run."* Not "ran" for those participles. So you would say: *"He ran a great business for many years; his brother would have run it into the ground."*

random sample: Respondents to a survey are chosen through a randomized process to ensure that each member of the population has an equal chance of being picked. That's called a *random sample.*

RAW format: The *RAW format* of an image preserves all the information gathered by the camera's photo sensor. RAW images allow the photo editor to get the most out of an image, such as objects in shadows.

readout: A *readout* is a smaller headline that runs under or near a larger main headline and provides a secondary element to the story. It is also called a *subhed,* a *drop head* or a *deck.*

retouching: Many professionals advocate no electronic *retouching* beyond that needed to clarify a picture: removing dust and scratches, correcting color and tone, and restoring sharpness lost in the scanning process.

rewrite train wreck: Every mistake a copy editor fixes in your copy chips away at your credibility as a writer. This reaches a tipping point when the copy editor starts rewriting your story and inadvertently introduces errors. That's when the train wreck occurs. Clean copy gives editors confidence that you have paid attention to detail. Fixing embarrassing and tedious mistakes yourself before you submit your work reduces the chances of a *rewrite train wreck.*

rites, rights: Don't confuse *"rites"* (like last ones for a funeral) with *"rights"* (fight for them!).

rounding errors: In reporting percentages, the numbers are usually rounded to one or two decimal points. For example, 12.54832% would be rounded up to 12.6%, following the rule to round up from five or more. A breakdown of percentages should add up to 100, but sometimes due to rounding you might get something like 100.2%. If the difference from 100% is large, more than 1%, then consider carrying the percentages out to another decimal place. Some publications simply report that the percentages add up to more than 100 "due to *rounding errors.*"

rule of thirds: When cropping, divide the image into nine equal parts by two equally spaced horizontal lines and two equally spaced vertical lines. Place your center of visual interest using the *rule of thirds* so that it lands along these lines or where they cross to create a more dynamic composition.

Ryan-O'Donnell Hierarchy of Editing: This is something like Maslow's hierarchy of needs, only for writers and editors concerned about quality writing. We started with the basic needs of a stylebook (**Chapter 1.5**), then moved to safety from spelling errors (**Chapter 1.6**), then the love and belonging that comes from joining with fellow grammarians (**Chapter 1.7**), and then the esteem that accrues from a perfectly punctuated sentence (**Chapter 1.8**). Then we arrived at the top tier of language skills—standard English usage (**Chapter 1.9**)—also known as the *self-actualization* of a writer or editor.

S

sample size: Survey research relies on sampling to make its methods affordable, so the smaller the *sample size,* the less expensive the survey. But often you get what you pay for. Researchers interview a manageable number of people, then apply the results to the population at large. A sample that is small will have a large margin of error and probably won't represent the actual opinions of the populace.

scanners: What we call *"readers"* are really *scanners*. Research has shown that readers scan a website or newspaper page for bold text, bulleted items and informative subheadings. Often this *big type* is all that they read.

seed approach: The *"seed approach"* to headline or title writing works best for feature stories. It involves using a word or phrase (the seed) to brainstorm clever headlines, titles and chyrons. For a story on Valentine's Day, the "seed" of valentine inspires expressions like "red hot," "sweetheart deal," "run for the roses." The seed approach also works well for creating advertising slogans. Advertising guru Jeff Goodby used a process like the seed approach to come up with the "Got Milk?" campaign after a woman in a focus group remarked, "The only time I notice milk is when I run out of it."

semicolon: A *semicolon* replaces *comma-but*. You could say, *"Congress passed the bill, but the president vetoed it."* Or simply, *"Congress passed the bill; the president vetoed it."* Semicolons are used to separate items punctuated with commas in a complicated list. So you would write, *"He is survived by a wife, June; two sons, Wally and Theodore; and a brother, Charlie."*

SEO: Search engine optimization (*SEO)* is a technique for writing online titles that attract Google and other search engines and increase a news item's visibility. It makes use of keywords that are attractive to searchers.

Seven Flashing Lights: On the first sweep of editing a story, editors should keep their heads up to identify killer mistakes. We created a checklist of things to verify or guard against, something we call Seven Flashing Lights: 1) names and titles, 2) numbers, 3) locations, 4) quotations, 5) bias and stereotypes, 6) getting played by anonymous or untrustworthy sources, 7) getting sued for slander or libel.

should of, should have: We know *"should of"* kinda sounds like *"should have,"* but there's really just one choice: *"should have."*

sidebar headlines: *Sidebar headlines* go with a related story that runs on the same page with a main story and takes a separate headline. Good sidebar heads use elements that echo, but not repeat, points in the headline for the main story.

simile: A *simile* is a comparison of two things using *"as"* or *"like."* It's the first figure of speech listed in The Zinger Factory (**Chapter 1.4**). Good writing, like effective teaching, works best by making associations. Good editors say to writers, "Tell me what it's *'like.'"* In so doing, you compare something new with something familiar to readers, listeners or viewers. For example: *She was as strong as Gorilla Glue. Learning grammar was like getting a root canal—needed but painful.*

simple series: A simple series of words, phrases or clauses is the subject of debate over the need for a serial or Oxford comma before the "and," as in *"yes, no, and maybe"* (Chicago style) or *"yes, no and maybe"* (AP style). The same goes for *"out the window, across the roof and into the backyard"* (AP) and *"He came, he saw, and he conquered"* (Chicago).

skeleton approach: The *skeleton approach* to headline or title writing works best for straight news stories. The key words from a story's lede or nut graph are written out in order in one sentence that becomes the "skeleton" for the final headline. Same words, same order. So if a lede begins, *"The city's school board president was re-elected Tuesday in a close vote. ...,"* then the skeleton headline would read simply, *"School board president re-elected."*

slander: *Slander* is defamation of a person's character or reputation in spoken form. The AP Stylebook notes that even though broadcast reports are spoken, in many states, spoken defamation is still called *libel.*

slash: Sometimes it makes more sense to use the *slash* rather than a *hyphen,* as in *"red state/blue state divide,"* but don't rely on it to say everything you mean. Sometimes the slash forces the reader to do too much work and clarity gets lost in the effort to save a couple of words. Take this sentence: *"We should go to the study session and/or the party."* Better: *"We should go to the study session or the party, or both."*

snippet: A partial quote, sometimes as short as one word, is called a *snippet.* It is different from a *full quote,* which can stand alone as a full sentence.

sound-alikes: Mistakes such as using "it's" for "its" tend to start with the ear as many words sound the same but have different meanings and spellings. These usage errors fly under the radar of spell-checkers, giving editors job security.

spelling: Correct *spelling* is defined by your stylebook, not any dictionary you can find online. If a word is not listed in the stylebook, it will refer you to a particular dictionary for the correct spelling listed first with a definition.

splits: *Splits* occur in a headline or title when writing falls across two or more lines and key words are split from one line to the next. Not all splits are possible to fix, but be careful of ones that create misunderstanding, such as this adjective-noun split: *Girl swallows dog/identification tag.* Other examples of splits are preposition-object *(Pope plans/flight to/Poland)* and helping verb-main verb *(Biden will/find funds/for Ukraine).*

spreads: *Spreads* apply to articles displayed across more than one page. In newspapers and magazines they may be called *"double trucks"* as a pair of facing pages. Photos are run across the fold to establish the look of one big page. Spreads make headline and title writing particularly challenging.

stanch, staunch: These look and sound similar, but one is a verb and the other is an adjective. Best to substitute in your mind the words they mean to keep them straight: *"stanch"* (stop), *"staunch"* (firm).

standard English usage: This deals with word choice. When the issue is whether to say "annoy" or "aggravate," "like" or "as," "between" or "among," or "insure" or "ensure," then we're talking about rules for standard English usage.

statistics: Some words, like *"statistics,"* are tricky. Typically words ending in *"s"* are plural: *"The cats are playing."* But not always: *"Statistics is my favorite subject."*

stereotype: Related to bias, a *stereotype* is a widely held and overly generalized belief about a group of people, often based on race, gender, age, education, sexual orientation, geography or economic status. A stereotype can be positive, negative or harmful. Editors should be on guard to keep writers from being accused of using stereotypes.

stock photo: Commercial photographers sell their work through *stock photo* sites. Stock photos are usually staged to produce ideal images. Stock images can be useful for advertising, or for social media posts, or for creating photo illustrations for news and feature stories if the final product is clearly labeled as an illustration.

style: A writer's *style*, or a unique tone of voice or a clever way with words, is different from the use of the word *"style"* to refer to stylebook rules.

stylebooks: *Stylebooks* are many things: almanacs, grammar books, reference and usage guides, and reflections of changes in our language and culture. Mostly they provide a way to achieve consistency in matters of abbreviation, capitalization, punctuation and spelling. They aren't sacred, however, nor are they values-free. Your organization has control over making exceptions to rules that don't make sense to your readers, listeners or viewers. Those exceptions are captured on *"local style"* sheets.

subject: The *subject* of a sentence is the doer of an action verb (*"She"* ran) or the receiver of the action of a verb in passive voice (*"She"* was interviewed). Sometimes a subject is not stated, or implied, as in *"Celebrate!"* (*"you"* celebrate).

subject-verb agreement: This is a test of your grasp of singular and plural and your ability to link subjects with verbs. If the subject is singular (substitute *"it"*), the verb must be singular. Likewise, if the subject is plural (substitute *"they"*), then the verb must be plural. *Subject-verb agreement* gets tricky when the two get separated in a sentence like this: *"The gravity of the errors—and there are many mistakes—make the boss go bananas."* What's the problem? The subject is *"gravity"* (it) so the verb must be *"makes,"* not *"make."*

subjunctive: *Subjunctive* refers to a verb's mood. A verb's conjugation (*"was"* or *"were,"* for example) changes when the mood shifts from *"indicative"* (she *"was"*) to subjunctive (she *"were"*). So in the indicative mood, you would say, *"She **was** a movie star,"* but in the subjunctive mood, you would say, *"She wishes she **were** a movie star."* In addition to a *wish*, mood changes with expressions of *doubt, prayer* or *necessity, or when making a demand, a resolution or a motion, or making a statement contrary to fact.*

summary graphs: *Summary graphs*, also known as *blurbs*, are short paragraphs that add information to headlines and allow readers to get their news quickly as they scan print and webpages. Summary graphs may serve as *excerpts* online.

survey research methods: *Survey research methods* are based on mathematics for gathering reliable information and opinions on the issues of the day. These methods include sampling strategies and statistical inferences that consider the probability of error. Unfortunately, the reliability of these methods have been questioned as society changes and bias can enter from many different directions.

suspect: A person arrested in connection with a crime is a *suspect*. Some news organizations will not print a suspect's identity until a person has been charged with a crime. Assume a suspect is innocent and avoid convicting the suspect in your reporting.

sweeps: An editing strategy involves working in *sweeps*, so editors can focus on matters large and small, but not at the same time. Ideally, a first sweep should focus on the BIG MISTAKES; a second sweep on transitions and embarrassing errors, such as those dealing with grammar, punctuation and spelling; and a third sweep on errors dealing with the stylebook, standard English usage or tightening writing to eliminate needless words.

syntax: *Syntax* is the system and structure of the language that helps you build strong sentences.

systematic or stratified sample: Researchers divide respondents by gender, marital status, age, income, education and party affiliation, then choose randomly from within those groups in proportion to the population as a whole. This is called a *systematic* or *stratified sample*. The results can be reported by demographic group where comparisons are meaningful.

T

table: A *table*, the simplest information graphic, lists figures by categories in columns and rows, and allows the reader to compare them. Tables can be built using a newspaper or magazine's text editing system without resorting to special graphics software.

tabloid journalism: Traditionally, *tabloid journalism* is a sensational mix of crime, sex and entertainment evolving into a "sophisticated sensationalism" in the words of designer Mario Garcia, a newspaper strategist. Page size for the New York Post, a typical tabloid, is 11 x 12 inches.

takeaway: An advertising term for the message left in a consumer's mind after seeing an advertisement. It's a concept useful for editors trying to assess a story's focus.

tape-recorder journalism: *Tape-recorder journalism* is the practice of letting the audio recorder run and using quotes at length, in essence letting the story write itself. A story filled with quotes requires less thinking on the writer's part but more work for an editor. Quotations are best when they are rare and powerful.

target reader, listener or viewer: The person an editor can picture to make judgments ranging from story topics to word usage. This approach to editing, popular for print, online and broadcast magazines, contrasts with the general audience concept used for newspapers and the Associated Press Stylebook.

tedious mistakes: *Tedious mistakes* deal with the stylebook, or standard English usage, or tightening writing to eliminate needless words. Such "mistakes" may go unnoticed by many readers. They remain important, however, because they may matter greatly to your supervisor.

television news producer: A *television news producer* gathers elements of stories from various sources, adds stories and visuals, then works with a news director to create a rundown for a newscast.

tense: In grammar, *tense* means time. Verbs have different tenses to indicate different points in time. Some languages, such as Mandarin Chinese, have just one tense: *"I go today," "I go yesterday," "I go tomorrow."* English verbs have six tenses: present *(go),* past *(went),* future *(will go),* present perfect *(has or have gone),* past perfect *(had gone),* future perfect *(will have gone).*

than, then: These are often confused, but they can be easily corrected with a little focus. Remember, *"then"* (time), *"than"* (compare). *"I'll see you **then**, though I know you can run faster **than** me."* Remember, *"than"* needs a comparative adjective, so you would say *"different from"* (positive form) but *"more different than"* (comparative form).

there, their, they're: Don't be fooled by words that sound alike but are spelled differently, such as *"there"* (a locale), *"their"* (the owners) or *"they're"* (they are).

they: Anytime you see *"they"* in a sentence, ask, "Who's they?" It should have a clear antecedent, or word that gives it meaning. Too often writers or speakers just wing it, attributing some idea or opinion to a nebulous *"they."* These days *"they"* can be the preferred pronoun of a singular person, so that may need to be explained. Remember our rule above all rules: Avoid possible confusion.

3-shot: A *3-shot* is a *closeup*. On a page it can be the portrait of one person. In a video or film, it's usually accompanied by a sound bite. The 3-shot often needs other photos to make its meaning clear because it lacks context. It typically follows a 1-shot, or establishing shot, and a 2-shot, a medium shot. Clever filmmakers may open a story with a 3-shot.

timeliness: *Timeliness* is a news value. Elements of timeliness that make a story newsworthy start with "hot topics" currently in the news. The "scoop mentality" is another element: Does the news organization have the story first? The difference in social media is measured in seconds. Add to that stories relating to a season, such as the annual "Black Friday" consumer stories.

title: A term used in magazines for headlines. In online news presentations, the *title* works as a headline for a story published on a website. The title can appear in other places, such as the heading for an excerpt on the news organization's home page. Then, of course, there is the title for a book.

to, too, two: *"Nah, it doesn't hurt to much"*—you mean *"too."* Don't be fooled by words that sound alike but are spelled differently, such as *"to"* (somewhere), *"too"* (also or too much) or *"two"* (number).

topics as news: Some news organizations plan coverage around *topics* such as education, crime or public safety, environment, health, careers or finances.

transition: A *transition* is a word, phrase, sentence or paragraph that moves a story from one main point to another.

treatment: A *treatment*, typically a one-page document, is a term used in filmmaking. It helps a writer test out an idea before investing energy in writing a complete screenplay. A treatment includes a draft title, a story synopsis and a description of characters.

tripod headline: A variation of the hammer-main headline combination is the *tripod headline*, which rests on three elements: a main headline, a hammer and a special display treatment of a key word or phrase. Tripod headlines often appear in two-page magazine *spreads*.

truth: This one is tricky, especially for editors working for advocacy associations that raise money for the truth they see. Although it's comforting to believe in *one truth*, several things can be true at the same time. Truth can be found in fiction and non-fiction. Journalists must be loyal to truth, though that's easier said than done. Truth has at least three dimensions: what someone is telling you, what's really going on and what can be seen from a historical perspective.

twist a cliche: *Cliches* are expressions you've heard a million times, so don't make it a million and one. Remember our rule: *If you have heard it before, don't say it again.* Instead, give them a twist and create something fresh. Turn *"the bloom is off the rose"* into *"the bloom is off the robes,"* as Maureen Dowd did in an opinion piece about Supreme Court ethics. Or twist an overused expression like *"shock and awe"* into something like *"shock and aw shucks"* or *"Shaq and awe."* You can bend one end of a cliche or the other, leaving enough of the original to be recognizable. It's the fourth technique listed in The Zinger Factory (**Chapter 1.4**) as a way to create a memorable line.

2-shot: A *2-shot,* also known as a *medium shot,* brings the audience closer to the scene. It follow a 1-shot, or an establishing shot. The medium shots have a strong center of visual interest and include relevant context. They have great storytelling power.

U

UBL: The 9/11 Commission Report, the U.S. government's official document on the terrorist attacks on Sept. 11, 2001, uses the shorthand of *UBL* to refer to Usama Bin Ladin, leader of a terrorist group called al Qaeda ("the base"). According to AP Style, those names are spelled Osama bin Laden and al-Qaida. Whether it's an *"o"* or a *"u,"* an *"e"* or an *"i,"* or a hyphen or not, that's a judgment call by editors who are translating phonetically from Arabic. It's one good reason to have stylebooks.

Ukraine: Writing or saying *"Ukraine,"* and not *"the Ukraine,"* shows favoritism to an independent Ukraine rather than the view that it is a region of Russia.

unconfirmed allegations: Be careful of statements from bystanders, especially when those statements are accusatory or incriminating, and doubly so if the speaker is anonymous. These should *never* make the news.

unconscious biases: The 56th edition of the AP Stylebook added a new chapter on inclusive storytelling that cautions writers to be alert to the possibility of *unconscious biases*, which may lead to writing that turns off readers. The chapter urges writers to be sensitive about using certain words and phrases, and to be aware of how they are choosing sources and story ideas. The AP's 56th edition added more than 25 new or revised stylebook entries, including references to antisemitism, race-related coverage, Muslims, Indigenous Americans, Asians, people with disabilities and guidance on using "transgender," "nonbinary," "gender fluid" and "gender dysphoria." The AP's 57th edition added a "+" in LGBTQ+ references and an entry on obesity.

unique, unusual: If *unique* means one of a kind, don't say *"very unique"* or *"somewhat unique."* Something can be *"very unusual,"* however.

Urban Dictionary: *Urban Dictionary: Define Your World* is a crowdsourced online dictionary of slang words and phrases that was founded in 1999 as a parody. These days it can help old-time editors stay current with ways common expressions, such as *"to hook up,"* have taken on new and possibly embarrassing meanings.

usage: *Usage* means precision in your word choice. It's short for standard English usage, which rises above grammar and punctuation to the *self-actualization* of a writer or editor. The AP Stylebook and the Chicago Manual of Style offer a similar list of usage rules, though as usual there are some disagreements. The CMS packs hundreds of alphabetical usage entries into a section titled "Glossary of Problematic Words and Phrases." The AP instead sprinkles usage entries throughout its Stylebook section.

V

verb: The *verb* is considered the most important part of speech because it can deliver a complete sentence in one word, as in *"Stop!"* It can be an action verb (*"run," "jump," "write"*) or a linking verb (*"to be," "to feel," "to smell"*).

video news release: A *video news release*, or video news story, provides ready-made "interviews," often produced by the public relations arm of a major corporation. Some news producers use these interviews without disclosing the source—a bad practice.

W

weather, whether: Don't confuse *"weather"* (climate) with *"whether"* (or not).

well: *Well* is an adjective meaning not sick (*"I feel well"*) and an adverb meaning skillfully (*"She works well"*). You'll see it hyphenated as a compound modifier either before or after a noun or pronoun to avoid possible confusion. For example: *She is a well-known musician. He is well-known, too.*

were, we're, where: Careful pronunciation helps so you won't confuse *"were"* (past), *"we're"* (we are) and *"where"* (location).

who-did-what?: An editor's technique to shape the most interesting way to express a story is to ask a writer, *"Who did what?"* Then like completing a fill-in-the-blank assignment, they work on the best ways to describe the main actor or actors, to choose a strong action verb that coincides with a time element telling when, and to explain an outcome.

word count: The usual way of measuring length limits for magazine pieces is a *word count*. It's also used by some online news organizations, although online news sites enjoy a "bottomless news hole" and don't face the physical space limitations of the printed page.

worst mistake: The *worst mistake* you can make when editing is a mistake you introduce. Your job is to improve copy. If you do a great job of cleaning up a story but introduce a typo, all that hard work goes for naught.

Writing + Editing: Don't try to write and edit at the same time. It's a two-step process. Remember **Core Principle No. 1: Use the Writing + Editing formula.**

Y

your, you're: Don't confuse *"your"* (not *my* or *ours*) with *"you're"* (you are).

Z

Zelensky: Wait, isn't it *"Zelenskyy"* with two *"y's"*? The official website of the president of Ukraine spells his name *"Volodymyr Zelenskyy."* And so that's the way you'll see the name spelled for the AP, The Guardian, Al Jazeera, the "PBS NewsHour," NBC News and CNBC. But The New York Times, The Washington Post, The Wall Street Journal, Newsweek, CNN, The Hill, C-SPAN, BBC News and Britannica say one *"y"* is enough and write *"Zelensky."* Actually his name is correctly spelled: Зеленський. The difference comes through transliteration to English from the Russian alphabet.

zinger: A *zinger* is a figure of speech or a writing flourish that attempts to create a memorable line. A zinger may be a simile, metaphor or personification, or a twist of cliche, a play on a name or the coining of a word or phrase.

Zip-a-Dee-Doo-Dah: Disney dropped it from park parades in 2023 after the lyrics, which won the 1947 Academy Award for Best Original Song, conjured up racist portrayals of Black people.